D1546404

A WORLD TORN ASUNDER

The Life and Triumph of
Constantin C. Giurescu

To Deborah & her family —

a man's story of remarkable survival
& success, a family's saga &
Romania's rocky passage through the

MARINA GIURESCU, M.D.

20th century

Best

Marina
Giurescu

BETTIE YOUNGS BOOKS

Cover Design by Tatomir Pitariu
Senior Editor John Nelson
Photo of Marina Giurescu by Scott Schauer Photography

BETTIE YOUNGS BOOK PUBLISHERS
www.BettieYoungsBooks.com
info@BettieYoungsBooks.com

Bettie Youngs Books are distributed worldwide. If you are unable to order this book from your local bookseller, Espresso, or online, you may order directly from the publisher.

ISBN: 978-1-936332-76-2
ePub: 978-1-936332-77-9

Library of Congress Control Number: 2012946784

1. Giurescu, Marina. 2. Giurescu, Constantin C. 3. Romania. 4. Soviet Union. 5. Communism. 6. Sighet Penitentiary. 7. Historians. 8. Freedom. 9. Michelson, Paul E. 10. Democracy.

Printed in the United States of America

DEDICATION

To my grandparents and their forgotten generation…

"Are you the author of *The History of the Romanian People*?"

"Yes."

"History is being written differently nowadays," the prison official spit out.

"It's possible, but the facts remain the same," Constantin replied.

CONTENTS

ACKNOWLEDGMENTS

I am most indebted to my father, Professor Dinu C. Giurescu, for all his help and assistance in painstakingly verifying the historic accuracy of the events presented and for encouraging me throughout this endeavor. My mother, Dr. Anca Giurescu, also read parts of this manuscript and provided many insightful suggestions.

This book would not have been possible without the editorial help of Mr. John Nelson of Bookworks Ltd. John believed in this project from the very beginning and encouraged me to expand upon its original format. John spent countless hours editing the manuscript and offering many suggestions and corrections along the way. He elevated a raw concept to the polished form that is put forth today, and I owe him a world of gratitude and many, many thanks. His expertise and time proved invaluable.

Many sincere thanks to Professor Paul Michelson from Huntington University in Indiana. He has been a true friend to our family through three generations, and we owe him a big debt of gratitude for safeguarding my grandfather's prison diary: *Five Years and Two Months in the Sighet Penitentiary*. His foreword to this volume is also much appreciated.

I would like to thank my publisher Bettie Youngs of *Bettie Youngs Books* for her expert advice, for her dedication in pursuing excellence in regard to this book, and, for her belief in me. Many thanks to her excellent cadre of professionals: graphic designer Tatomir Pitariu for his breathtaking cover design, and Randee Feldman for a most creative electronic press kit.

I would also like to thank Cynthia Mitchell and Mark Heinicke for their excellent copyedit of the book.

Finally, a big thank you goes to my fiancé, Ken Vlah, who endured many dinners of store-bought salads and pizza so that I could write in the evening at the end of my workday.

FOREWORD

Constantin C. Giurescu (1901-1977) was one of the most significant Romanian historians of modern times. The son and father of distinguished Romanian historians, he had both the good and the bad fortune to have lived in the tumultuous times of twentieth century Romania. On the one hand, he was fortunate enough to have been part of the generation of scholars and leaders that emerged from a world war that went badly but that saw the creation of a unified Romanian national state in 1918, with all the challenges and opportunities that this great event presented. On the other hand, as the title of the present work indicates, he reached maturity in a Romania that was eventually to be a "world torn asunder" during a second world war and its Communist aftermath.

Along the way, he suffered the premature death of his father, Constantin Giurescu (1875-1918) less than a month before the First World War ended (and then his mother in 1920). The older Giurescu was already a noted and prominent historian and a member of the Romanian Academy. He had spent three years doing research and study in Vienna (1903-1906), which allowed his son to become fluent in German. The younger Giurescu was in his last year of high school in 1918 and with his father's death, elected to switch from an engineering curriculum to the study of history.

In 1919, Constantin C. Giurescu began study in the Faculty of Letters at the University of Bucharest, where he graduated three years later *magna cum laude* in 1922, and then won a scholarship in 1923 to the recently founded (1922) Romanian School in Paris, France. In the fall of 1925, he returned to Bucharest to defend a Ph. D. thesis on 14th-15th century Romania, also *magna cum laude*, and was fortunate enough to occupy a recent vacancy at the university in 1926, an appointment that became permanent in 1927. He was also married in April 1926: he and his wife, Maria, eventually had three children, the first of whom, Dinu, became a historian as well.

The major turning point in C. C. Giurescu's career came between 1929 and 1931, when he was a leader in a kind of generational revolt of younger historians, particularly directed at the Grand Old Man of Romanian historiography, N. Iorga (1871-1940). The so-called "New School" called for a less nationalistic and more objective approach to the Romanian past and published its own journal, the *Romanian Journal Historic*, under Giurescu's editorship. Debate was to rage for over a decade between the two schools.

One of the primary outcomes of the historians' strife was the appearance (beginning in 1935) of Constantin C. Giurescu's monumental synthesis of Romanian history, *History of Romanians,* of which four volumes in multiple editions appeared. With this meticulous and lucid work, his place in Romanian historiography was assured.

At the same time, many of these younger scholars became involved in the politics surrounding the return of Carol II to power in 1930. Giurescu was elected to the Romanian Parliament from 1932-1938. In 1938, when Carol II suspended the constitution and established a Royal dictatorship, Giurescu became a high-ranking political administrator and then a cabinet member. This meant that when Carol was ousted by the radical Legionary movement, the fascist front, not only was his world overturned, his life was in danger.

Constantin C. Giurescu survived the military-Legionary regime and its successor, the military dictatorship of Marshall Antonescu. Improbably, the fall of Antonescu in 1944 and the end of the Second World War brought an even greater disruption of his life. As Romania was taken over by the Communist Party and then progressively Stalinized, his journal was shut down, he was relieved of his university posts, and in 1950—as a prominent figure in the pre-Communist political and cultural regime—he was sent to the People's Republic of Romania's death camp at Sighet. At the same time, all of his books, papers, and manuscripts were confiscated; most were lost forever.

His indomitable will to live saw him through five years at Sighet, methodically and graphically described in his prison journal and re-created here with harrowing accuracy. In 1956, at age 55, he was able to resume his academic work, first as a lowly, hourly worker at the Institute of History, and then eventually being restored to his university post in 1963. Ironically, as Communist Romania sought to separate itself from the domination of the Soviet Union (while emphasizing Marxist orthodoxy), Giurescu and other suppressed pre-Communist scholars were called back into service to their country, replacing incompetents and intellectual parasites.

At an age when most people would have been satisfied to have survived two world wars and worse, he resumed his teaching and prolific publication (including important works on Alexandru Ioan Cuza;

histories of Bucharest, Brăila, and Transylvania; volumes on science in Romania; on medieval Moldova; as well as new editions of his syntheses of Romanian history (in collaboration with his son, Dinu). From 1965 onward he became a kind of cultural ambassador for Romania, taught at Columbia University and lectured at numerous other American universities, and was elected a member of the Romanian Academy.

As a result of an unparalleled combination of depth of historical preparation, superb organizational skills, and highly disciplined work habits, Constantin C. Giurescu was the master synthesizer of Romanian history. The lucidity and useful of his monumental narrative was seldom obscured by his inter-disciplinary approach (which took into account the importance of the geographic, social, and economic factors often neglected in such works). This will remain his greatest achievement.

While I write about my esteemed colleague and friend from my own academic orientation, I must add that Dr. Marina Giurescu's superb account of her grandfather's life and times reads like a gripping historical novel of twentieth-century Romania. It tells the human side of history that is so often lost by more objective renditions, and I found the story moving, absorbing, and highly readable.

Paul E. Michelson, Ph.D.
Huntington University

INTRODUCTION

A World Torn Asunder is a factual account of the life and times of my paternal grandfather, the Romanian historian Constantin C. Giurescu; however, I have used the fictional techniques of creative non-fiction to enhance the storytelling.

Born in 1901 in the town of Focsani in the province of Moldova, he spent most of his childhood and adolescence in the Romanian capital of Bucharest. His father was an historian himself and his mother a homemaker, and they provided a comfortable and carefree life for their three children. This was at a time, the early part of the twentieth century, when Bucharest was considered the Paris of the East. But their lives changed drastically with the onset of World War I and the family events which followed it.

After the war and when it came time to choose a career, Constantin decided to follow in the footsteps of his father and read history at the University of Bucharest. It was during his first year of studies that he met and fell in love with his future wife, Maria, the daughter of one of his professors. The 1920s and the 1930s saw him start a family, build a successful career, and launch into politics. It was also during these years that he wrote his seminal work, *History of the Romanian People*. Between the World Wars, Romania was considered one of the most enlightened and progressive countries in Eastern Europe. The years leading up to 1938 were depicted by Constantin in his memoirs *Amintiri,* and it was these recollections that provided the details for the early part of this work.

In the aftermath of World War II and the Yalta Conference, Eastern Europe and hence Romania was among the countries handed over as a victory trophy to the Soviet Union. The Iron Curtain descended low and deep over Romania and its own Stalinist-type purges were initiated. Former politicians, industrialists, bankers, prominent intellectuals and artists lost their positions overnight without trial and countless of them perished in this communist holocaust.

Constantin was imprisoned at the Sighet jail in the northern part of the country. The chapters covering his time there are heavily based on his subsequent memoir: *Five Years and Two Months in the Sighet Penitentiary.* The manuscript was smuggled out of Romania in the early 1980s by Professor Paul E. Michelson of Huntington University (Huntington, IN) and published in the U.S. and Romania after the fall of the Soviet Union.

The remainder of this account is based on my historical research of the events punctuating my grandfather's life. It has also drawn rich inspiration and many details from my father's, Professor Dinu C. Giurescu, own memoirs. They have helped me fill in some of the blanks providing an account of the family's life mostly after 1940.

To pay homage to the Romanian culture and a long gone way of life, I tell the story of my family and its beloved patriarch—a great man of indomitable will who survived his unjust imprisonment and lived to reclaim his career against all odds.

This book is a tribute to him and his forgotten generation.

PROLOGUE

OCTOBER 30, 1977
BUCHAREST, ROMANIA

The days were getting shorter and the late autumn sun seemed weakened. Perhaps it sensed the upcoming loss of its battle with the harsh winds, gray skies, and the wet snows that would soon herald the arrival of winter. But today the sun still had the upper hand, crisp and bright. Gold and bronze-rusted leaves fluttered about in a light breeze, their numbers dwindling with each passing day.

By midday it was warm enough for a stroll, and grandparents with young children, teachers on lunch break, and a few retirees gradually made their way into Cismigiu Park. Cismigiu had been Bucharest's faithful friend for more than a century while political roulette kept replacing the flags that draped its poles. It remained there, a rare oasis of green foliage and sunlight in the midst of the drab and monotone city that Bucharest had become.

It had not always suffered this sad fate, having once been a vibrant city at the crossroads of Europe, full of music, theatre, and laughter. But that seemed so long ago though only thirty years had passed since the Communist regime had taken over in 1946. The city's soul had been stifled since then but no one, not even the Communists, could take this beloved park away from the people.

Gone were the military music concerts in the park gazebo—the military was now here to police and not entertain. Gone were the summer swimming races and the winter ice skating impromptu contests—both deemed too dangerous. One could, after all, drown or break a leg, and miss one's daily indoctrination. Gone were the fairs organized with proceeds to benefit victims of fires or floods—if anyone needed anything now big government would take care of them, just stand in line.

Not all had changed. The statues of the most celebrated Romanian writers and poets of the past still stood, among them the Eminescu fountain, named after Romania's best-known poet. They remained side by side with the benches, trees, and in spring and summer, the roses, lilac bushes, and tulip beds.

An older gentleman now entered the park. He drew the attention of this lunchtime crowd; it might have been his bearing, which seemed distinguished. Or perhaps it was his light gray, well-cut overcoat and his stylish, bulging briefcase that made him stand apart from the nondescript muddy brown attire of most. He walked leisurely and stopped at times to look at a tree or bust. A smile crept across his lips once in a while. Had he recognized an acquaintance or was he just trying to be friendly? Or could it be that the sites brought back happy memories?

He had spent his childhood and first attended school a stone's throw away from the park. Then as a teenager, he went to the Lazar High School. The park cradled the mischief of his childhood, the longings and grief of his teenage and adolescence years. It had seen the young man taking a brief respite from his study and work-filled days. It had then seen the husband and father on a stroll with his wife and children. Cismigiu Park had been there when moments of doubt had taken over, and he needed a refuge away from a life pressing upon him. And now in his latter days, it had welcomed the elderly gentleman returning home from the university. The park and Constantin, Constantin and the park, they had known each other for nearly seven decades.

Constantin decided to sit down on a bench after a while. He may have been tired or perhaps he had time on his hands. His face gradually lost its serenity. It now seemed tinged with sadness, and a frown crept across his brow as he relived the morning visit to his best friend, Nick, gravely ill in the hospital.

He had taken the tram early on; Colentina Hospital was only a half-hour ride away from his home. He remembered only too well the days spent there nine years earlier when a wicked bout of sciatica forced him to strict bed rest, and doctors had frantically run tests to eliminate "alternatives."

It was sunny now but had been overcast earlier, a fitting backdrop for the pain and suffering glaring from the hospital yard and hallways. The old stone buildings were set far apart from one another, separated by trees, shrubs, and grass lawns. The wards were old too, and not much had been done to modernize them. Narrow, army-style beds with iron headboards were lined up side by side with no curtains or partitions between them. The windows had no curtains, and sunlight would flood the rooms at times during the day. Each room had an old iron cart in a corner, piled high with bottles, needles, and charts.

When he had arrived at Nick's room, a fat, overworked, and visibly unhappy nurse was making her rounds, dispensing pills and checking blood pressures and temperatures. With so many to look after and umpteen duties to perform, she could hardly afford a smile or words of encouragement, even for the desperately ill. She was there to work and deliver a service, another bumblebee spun by the Communists into their "ideal worker"—one devoid of thought and soul.

Nick had looked ashen, the face gaunt, the eyes bloodshot, and his features sunken. He did not have the strength to sit up when Constantin walked into the room, though he was able to muster a weak smile and extend a hand to his old friend.

Nick and Constantin. Constantin and Nick. Together they had been placed in a cell at the Sighet Prison decades earlier and had lingered for five long years. Together they had wondered about the fate of their families, the injustice of their imprisonment, and if they would make it out alive. They had both risen to prominence during the last decade of the royal regime prior to 1947—two men reaching the peak of their craft. Nick had been an engineer and a professor, Constantin an historian and teacher, and both had been politically active. Together they had been swept away by the Communist frenzy to redistribute wealth and punish those who had "oppressed" the people for centuries.

Nick and Constantin had supported one another in times of sickness, famine, and despair—all too common during their incarceration. Their bond was strengthened by what they had endured together, and they had remained lifelong friends. But Constantin knew that this time it was different. The cancer that had plagued Nick for the last year was merciless, and no amount of will power or support was going to chase it away.

"Constantin, my friend, thank you for coming. I so wanted to see you one last time."

"Hush, Nick, there'll be many more. Is your pain any less today?"

"A bit, but not much. I got a shot of morphine a few hours ago. It makes me fall asleep while it dulls the ache, but it's the sleeping that bothers me the most. I have this long, interminable rest just around the corner, and I spend my last days here sleeping?"

"God, Nick, don't talk like that . . . don't you remember how in jail we never gave up?"

Nick nodded slightly and his eyes asked Constantin to track the nurse. Was she still in the room? After three decades of Communism, it had become second nature to always be aware of your surroundings.

Eavesdropping could prove disastrous to oneself and one's family. He had already had occasion to regret "speaking his mind" during this long hospital stay, as did another friend of theirs.

This new society had bred (among many things) the professional "informer." This was a cretin willing to pass on information regarding colleagues, patients, and family even. So you never knew who was listening and how they would use or pass on whatever they heard. The safe practice was to keep your mouth shut unless you were 100 percent certain of your audience.

The nurse had left the room earlier, and two other patients were tucked away in a corner and seemingly sound asleep. Constantin nonetheless whispered to his friend, and Nick, on cue, answered back in a half-voice.

"Some things never change, do they Nick? Here we are still speaking in hushed tones twenty years later. Little did we know when we came out of prison that our whole society would gradually become a jail of sorts."

"Listen, my time is running out." Nick put up his hand to quiet his friend's protest to the contrary. "The doctors don't tell me much, and I think their silence means bad news. Plus, morphine is for the very end, and now I get it every day. I may see you tomorrow—and then again, I may not. But whatever happens, please promise me you'll keep an eye on Claire."

"Nick, the way I feel about your Claire is how you feel about my Maria. We are family and watch out for each other." Nick reached out and clasped his friend's hand. "Now about tomorrow—I'm afraid I won't be here, as I leave for Germany. I'm supposed to deliver a paper at a symposium in Heidelberg and will be back on Friday. I'll see you then. Remember that, Nick. Friday."

Nick had stared at him intently for a few long minutes, both wondering what lay ahead, neither willing to admit to their fears and break away from this silent bond. They continued holding hands, lingering under this spell for a while. Then Nick closed his eyes and released his hand, either falling asleep or merely feigning it to let Constantin go about his business.

The elderly man had left his friend with a heavy heart. Their moments together kept replaying themselves over again as he sat on the park bench; he so wished he didn't have to leave town the following day. Being back at the top of his profession and meeting with his foreign counterparts to present his viewpoint on one of Romania's thorny and complex historical issues would normally have been a thrill. But today he felt differently. Nick was ill; Nick was dying, and he should be there for him.

The year 1977 had not been an easy one. It had started with the March 4 earthquake. Some historical buildings, including old churches, were badly damaged in this quake and their repair was still waiting to clear many bureaucratic hurdles. Some even thought that they might be torn down altogether to make room for modern structures.

There was also the issue of his son Dan, a successful architect in Paris. He had decided to leave his employer and open his own practice, and now seemed to have some sort of financial difficulties. And then there was Maria, his Maria of more than a half century, who was doing less and less these days. She was not ill, just weary. Her bitterness over their losses had only grown over the years despite his exceptionally successful comeback in the last decade.

All in all 1977 had thus been a difficult year.

He woke up from his reverie and glanced at his watch: 12:30 P.M. and time to go home for lunch. It remained one of the few traditions observed in the Giurescu household: lunch together, three generations side by side (well, at least as often as work and school schedules permitted). They lived together in the old family home, Constantin and Maria, their eldest son Dinu, his wife, and their two teenage daughters. It was how Constantin had always dreamt of his old age, surrounded by loved ones and working side by side with his son Dinu, who had followed in his footsteps as an historian.

The rest of the day passed in a blur. The meal was followed by a brief siesta and a review of the paper to be delivered in Heidelberg, while Maria packed his suitcase. At 6:00 P.M. it was time for his customary English lesson and conversation with his friend Adrian, who had mastered the language while taking a PhD in engineering in the U.K. before the Second World War.

They sat and chatted about his upcoming travels but also about Constantin's birthday party held four days earlier on the twenty-sixth. Adrian had been there, together with a handful of friends, and raved about the homemade cake, one of Maria's specialties.

"But where was Maria? We all missed her."

"She was actually here at home, in her bedroom. She worked so hard all day preparing for the party until she finally ran out of steam. I felt guilty about allowing her to work like this. Next year, I'll just go buy a cake and some savories for the party."

Adrian could hear the sadness in Constantin's voice and couldn't think of a thing to say to make it better, so quietly squeezed his friend's hand.

"I'm all right, Adrian, I truly am. It pains me to see her unable to enjoy our good fortune. But I also wonder: should I let this blot out everything else that's good in our lives?" He felt that there was more to say, and suddenly switched to Romanian, eager to properly express the torrent of emotions rushing through him. "I do feel so fortunate, Adrian; and despite all the hardships and vicissitudes, I know I have also been extremely lucky. I'm sad for Maria; she has been my rock for more than fifty years, and I will always love her and be there for her. We have a great family and friends. It was my love of them, and my work and career that have sustained me and kept me going all these years. I have been blessed, truly blessed."

Adrian's eyes widened in wonder and a shy smile crept up; never once in their forty years of friendship had he heard Constantin open up like this. He doubted he would hear it again.

The following day at the airport, there were few flights taking off or landing that day in Bucharest, Romania, a country tucked deeply behind the Iron Curtain. The airport, named after the famed aerodynamics engineer Coanda, was a modern-looking grey monolith with a glass façade. But the effect of its airy facade was quickly dispelled once you ventured inside. Military and police guards were at check-in counters, passport control, and access to gates, with their weapons visible and faces stern. And then there were the "other" ones, members of the secret police: the "Securitatea," milling about with passengers and officials alike. It was almost a sport as to who could spot them first. They were the spindly guys in gray suits, either keeping to themselves in corners and taking it all in, or profusely trying to be of help as they asked their questions.

All this security was in place in a country where its citizens didn't even have passports. Applying for one could take years for a ruling, and once you returned from a trip, you had to hand it in to the authorities. But guard they did!

It was stressful going to the airport. One encountered a first ring of security checks before even stepping inside. Tickets and passports were then closely examined and verified. There were more questions, and more anxiety that they would not let you travel this time. A second round of interrogation came with the actual check-in and the passports were looked at again at "Border Control."

Constantin went through the motions and eventually "made the cut." After saying farewell to his son Dinu, he disappeared through the double doors toward the boarding area. He looked as meticulous as ever in his dark-brown suit, contrasting tie, his overcoat draped over his briefcase, and his shiny shoes. He didn't seem impatient and talked only when asked a question. He sat down slowly, looked around, and then opened a glossy magazine: a man at ease with himself. A man who was also tolerant of the barriers that surrounded him, because any impatience or impertinence would have prevented him from forging his way back to prominence.

He had never flown until age sixty-seven, but had been on many flights in recent years, including five trips to the United States. So he no longer boarded planes with the apprehension that surrounded his first ventures into air travel. He knew the routine by now: sit down, buckle your seatbelt, listen to security procedures, try to read, and wait some more.

The roar of the engines grew louder and then they were airborne. The plane slowly gained altitude; he looked out the window and spotted once again the thick barbed wire fences surrounding the airport, a prison within the socialist prison.

As they soared higher, he felt free like a bird—flying did that to him. But he also knew that this lightness of being had also enveloped him last night, allowing him to open up with Adrian. He still didn't know why and how it happened but felt that he'd understand it in time.

He stared down at the meadows and hills doused in bright sunshine, rivers becoming miniature steel ribbons, red tile roofs dotting the landscape. The beauty of the land and the smooth motion of the plane drifted him slowly off to sleep, to dreams of past places and old faces, oh, so very long ago. . . .

PART I
THE KINGDOM OF ROMANIA

Chapter One
AN IDYLLIC CHILDHOOD

The century turned and Constantin was born a year later in the town of Focsani. It was a city that had once sat on the border between the southern Wallachia and eastern Moldova provinces, which had gone on to unite in 1859 and form the foundation of modern Romania.

The boy was named after his father, Constantin, an historian who had briefly "flirted" with mathematics and medicine at the university. The latter was quickly terminated by the sight and smells of the anatomy dissection hall. His father hailed from a family of "free peasants," men who had owned land and were able to come and go as they pleased. Their village was named Chiojd, nestled in the valley of a river and surrounded by gentle, rolling hills. A century earlier you knew you were almost there upon seeing two large rocks standing guard along the roadway. One was brick red, the other one whitish with a vein of blue and together they gave the village its name, which meant rocky in the local dialect.

His father was one of only four children (out of thirteen) to survive into adulthood. Epidemics of mostly childhood diseases and deaths at or shortly after birth decimated families in those days. There were no antibiotics to fight the infectious scourges, and the nearest physician was often a long carriage ride away.

Not only did his father survive but he thrived and went on to be the first in the family to graduate from a university. He chose history, and had he had a crystal ball, he would have seen a long family line following in his footsteps. Some even called it a "dynasty" later on. But the young teacher had no such inklings, and after graduation he took his first post as a high school teacher in the town of Focsani.

As for Constantin's mother, Elena, she was the daughter of a wealthy local merchant. Her father had built a lucrative trade selling fabric of all kinds—silk, blanched linen, cotton, thick wool, and lace. Years later, with the business firmly established and no lingering financial worries, he traveled to Jerusalem and became an "official" pilgrim. As he aged he felt at peace with himself and the world and after financial success and a beautiful family, the pull of the church felt stronger and stronger. So much so that he eventually retired to the Neamt Monastery, in the northeastern part of the country.

His daughter Elena had also known the heartache of losing young siblings. But like her father she carried on attending, in the custom of the day, a girls' high school. There she read literature, learned to cook and sew, and studied German and French. An introduction to "sciences" was sketchy at best and kept mostly in the background. It wouldn't have been put to good use, as after all, she was preparing to be a lady.

Constantin and Elena had met in early 1900 in Focsani. He was visiting friends, and Elena and her father were there as well. People later said they seemed smitten with one another right away. He was quite taken with the beautiful, soft-spoken woman with wide blue eyes and wavy hair, while she found him handsome and "interesting." Here was a young man willing to talk about what he had just read, not just trade and money, she had told herself. The following day Constantin, normally a shy and introverted young man, mustered enough courage to call on Elena's dad. It went well; well enough to receive an invitation to call again. Other visits followed, and shortly thereafter came short walks together.

This love-at-first-sight quickly developed into a comfortable relationship, and by Christmas Constantin was ready to "speak" to his beloved's father. Steadying his nerves and rapidly beating heart, he was shown into the waiting room first. A few minutes later the maid returned, "Sir, please follow me to the master's study." In sharp contrast to his rush of emotions, he found Elena's dad resting comfortably in an armchair. After instructing the maid to deliver refreshments, he exchanged pleasantries with his guest. But the shrewd businessman had sensed there was more to this visit.

"Sir, there is something I need to ask you."

"Go ahead, Professor."

"Sir, I have been very much taken with your daughter since making her acquaintance. There is nothing that would make me happier than to have her as my wife. It would also be a privilege. Sir, may I dare ask you for Elena's hand?"

The old man smiled warmly and extended his hand. "Professor, the honor would be mine, as well. My daughter's happiness is most important to me. And I have seen her face sing these past months."

He was also awfully pleased that his daughter was going to marry a learned man, but he kept that to himself. He had done well and provided handsomely for the family. But by virtue of this marriage Elena would enter the world of letters and all the refinement it held.

"Mr. Giurescu, you have my approval. And now perhaps I should call my daughter so you can talk to her, too?"

The shy woman joined them a few minutes later, surprised to find Constantin in deep conversation with her father.

"Elena, sit down my dear. This young man would like to ask you something."

Her cheeks blushed and her heart began racing. It went so fast that she touched her chest to steady it.

"Elena, dearest, may I have the honor of asking you to be my wife?"

Pure bliss illuminated her lovely face.

"Father?"

"My answer was yes. And yours?"

"Yes, yes, yes!"

Snow fell heavily in the winter of 1900–1901, blanketing roads and houses. It bent trees and buried shrubs and wreaked havoc with the trains, post, and the wedding plans of the young couple. Marriage still required parental consent in those days, even if the couple was "of age." But the arrival of the approval letter of the groom's father had been delayed by the storms, held up somewhere en route. With the wedding scheduled for January 12, the letter was nowhere in sight. Panic mounting, the groom called the postmaster and asked him to inquire along the way. The letter was eventually found and opened at the request of the newlyweds-to-be; the consent was "called in" and allowed the justice of peace to pronounce them husband and wife.

A ceremony was held later that day at the Romanian Orthodox Cathedral. While it was frigid outside, the interior was warmed by a myriad of candles and the goodwill of family and friends. There they stood, finally side by side. The bride in a thick, white dress covered in lace, and the groom dressed up in a severe, tightly cut suit—who knows what he must have saved to afford it. They held hands and listened to prayers and chants. Then they circled the tall candles flanked by their godparents in the tradition of the Romanian church. When they emerged from church, a beaming Constantin held Elena's hand. As snowflakes swirled around, and wrapped in his happiness, he threw reticence aside. Sweeping his bride into his arms, he delivered her into the waiting carriage. Years later they recall how the whole day had felt like a blur—the wait, wind, dancing snow, and the sweet-heavy incense wafting in the cathedral blended into a dreamlike state, haphazardly enveloping the couple.

They settled in Focsani and bought their first house with money given as a dowry by Elena's father. It was a pretty little house with four columns flanking the entrance and a yard upfront. Though quite small it didn't matter to the happy pair; home it was and they were on their own. A central hall flanked by two bedrooms on one side and a sitting area and dining room on the other. The bathroom, kitchen, and pantry were at the back, in the style of the times.

With her husband teaching, preparing classes, and researching upcoming articles, Elena busied herself with the house. She hung curtains, bought furniture, and chose rugs. She loved to place fresh flowers on the round table in the center of the hall—tulips, roses, and mums—each one heralding the arrival of a different season. Then she would sit down and softly play the piano while waiting for her husband to return home. The house furnished and decorated was more or less ready to welcome their firstborn a little over nine months later on October 26, 1901. The boy was named Constantin after his father.

The infant would be bereft of any memories of his birthplace as the family moved months later to the city of Buzau, in the Romanian province of Walachia. This change was prompted by his father's transfer to teach and also direct the local boy's high school, a step ahead from the post in Focsani. But as luck would have it, this move was also short-lived. Within a year her husband won a one-year study scholarship in Vienna. The trunks were hastily packed once again and crates of household items were sent ahead of the family. The parents and baby embarked upon the train journey which would take them to the famed capital.

VIENNA

Vienna was the capital of the Austro-Hungarian Empire and for many at that time, the center of the world. It was grand and gay there at the turn of the century. Imperial glory lived side by side and collided at times with the new art, music, and thinking. Old Emperor Franz Joseph had ruled forever, and many felt he would always be there. Like a benevolent grandfather, he frowned upon new trends in painting, dance, and the new science of psychoanalysis. Shrugging his shoulders and with a little smile, he assumed *this too shall pass*.

This was the city to which a pregnant Elena, her husband, and toddler, arrived in late 1903. The journey had taken them from a little provincial Romanian town to the glitter and smartness of arguably Europe's premiere city. She had worried incessantly during the two-day travel. What would the house and food be like? Would women frown upon her smock? On their arrival she was able to breathe a sigh of relief. Elena discovered her style of dress was perfectly adequate, though less lavish than some. She then went to the market and saw the same produce. As for the language, there were no barriers as both spoke fluent German. The young woman now knew she could make a home there.

As for her husband, he headed to the historical archives building the first morning. After registering himself, he started perusing the document roster. He also found with equal relief that cataloguing was done the same way, except on a larger and more sophisticated scale. Yes, he too would be at ease in this new city.

They first lived in a house on Alserstrasse, at number 2. Years later the toddler, by then an adult, would attempt to locate this house, but found a park instead. He was told buildings had been torn down to make room for it. But in his childhood it was a busy commercial street, with many shops, passersby, and carriages. The hustle and bustle made Elena nervous every time she took her little boy out for a walk. She voiced her concern to her husband who agreed to find "something more suitable."

They looked around for weeks, and after a couple of months they moved to the suburb of Neuwaldegg, on the outskirts of the city. The house they rented reminded Elena of their first home in Focsani, a pretty and functional little dwelling with a patch of garden surrounded by similar cottages.

This house would survive the passage of the years, a testimony that time can occasionally stand still, oblivious to world wars and the changing of the guard. Its tall, majestic walnut tree withstood the test of time, too. This would later bring back memories of the property owner who would not let little Constantin gather walnuts fallen to the ground. The prohibition upset the child who would shout, "Hey mommy, here comes the old hunchback woman." Years later, he would regret his harsh childish words and unkind treatment of her.

Elena would admonish him in her measured, melodious voice, but loud enough for all to hear. The child would apologize, not because he felt guilty but because he feared his mother's displeasure.

In the nearby park there was a pond which seemed more like a lake to the four year old. It was surrounded by children playing, mothers and nannies pushing prams, and there was always a man reading papers. The sight of this gentleman harked back through time. Dressed in morning coat and top hat, he would throw a stick in the water, which his fox terrier deftly retrieved time and again.

Vienna's green heart and one of its leading attractions for children was the Pratter Park with its big Ferris wheel. Years later Constantin would remember his first toy upon seeing the dilapidated wheel again. It was a green devil going up and down on a stick, depending on how you pulled on the string. Had they bought it at the amusement park when his aunt and uncle visited and treated them to an outing? Had he played with it in the park? Or had the circular motion of the wheel recalled the back and forth cadence of the toy? Memories of the toy and park would always be cherished together.

But what Constantin would recall most vividly about Vienna was his mother, young and beautiful. He remembered Elena going to the market holding her little boy's hand. Years later he would close his eyes and still see her inspecting cheese, meat, fruit, and flowers, smelling them before making her selection.

She used to dress up in the afternoon and take them for a stroll, Constantin and his brother Horia, who was born in Vienna in early 1904. She chose her outfits carefully as "You never know whom you might meet." Elena favored a sky bright blue, a color which she had decided made her eyes sparkle. With a matching hat and often clutching a long umbrella, she proudly walked her children around the neighborhood. And then she would play the piano while waiting for her husband to come home from the dusty archives. Images of the cheerful, content woman and her melodious music would always stay with her older son.

But this happy time passed too quickly and the intended research was completed. By 1906 they were ready to return to Romania and to Constantin's new position.

BUCHAREST

Their next home would be in Bucharest, the Romanian capital. Constantin' assignment was as professor of history there at one of the city's major high schools. His wife—somewhat mechanically—had all their belongings packed and unpacked again, for the fifth time in as many years of marriage. Wishing to be close to the school at first, they rented a house nearby. It was a functional little home for with enough bedrooms, a study and a dining room and it would do for now. "We'll get to know the city first," they decided. "Then we'll look around for something more suitable" which meant they would be moving again and probably soon.

Had Elena come to Bucharest from her hometown of Focsani, she would have marveled at the architectural style and elegance of the central buildings. She would have been taken with the large tree-lined boulevards, the seemingly nonstop hustle and bustle, and the art and culture of the city. But after two years of living in Vienna, she decided her new city felt more like a younger cousin of the grander European capital she had just departed.

A cousin perhaps, but an up-and-coming one as Bucharest had earned the nickname "Paris of the East" (or of the Orient) at the beginning of the twentieth century. That was based in part on its general layout with wide avenues converging in a central plaza, mirrored upon Paris' famed center point, the Place-de-l'Etoile. This moniker was also partly due to the cultural and financial venues and its level of sophistication.

After Carol I first became ruling prince in 1866 and then King of Romania in 1881, Bucharest was gradually modernized and greatly expanded. Gas lines, electric lights, pure water and sewers were installed. The streets were paved, and the central river enclosed between stone embankments. Imposing buildings, such as the Central Post Office and Bank, music halls like the Athenaeum, and hospitals, were erected. Its reputation as a learning and cultural center grew steadily. The University's College of Medicine, Schools of Commerce and Engineering, Art Institutes and ecclesiastical seminaries abounded and expanded. Theaters and music clubs of all sorts proliferated.

The European visitor arriving there around the turn of the century would have encountered a thoroughly modern but also a picturesque city. Churches with domed cupolas and turrets added a touch of whimsy, while the many parks and lakes provided splashes of green and oases of coolness in the summer.

This is where Elena, Constantin, and their family settled little by little into their new life. Little Constantin, now six years old, would spend his days in the yard, unless it rained hard. That's where he would haul out his stored possessions: a ball, a wooden circle he rolled and chased after, many sticks of various sizes and shapes, and a bag full of marbles.

On clear days, his mother would tell him, "Remember now, you stay in the garden. Children can come in and play, but you aren't to go out."

"But mommy, I won't go far, just to the street corner, to see what's around it. How would other kids know I'm here?"

"'In' means in; do I make myself clear? Or would you like me to tell your father tonight?"

"But mommy . . ."

"No but. Remember the gypsies?"

Mention of the gypsies would bring the argument to an abrupt halt. He had been told they took children away, particularly those who disobeyed. And he had seen them before: dark and fierce, their dusty caravans piled high with junk. This bit truly puzzled him. He even spotted one with a three-legged dog tied to its back and barely keeping up. His mom said they stole everything they got their hands on, including children. Then they packed everything in a cart and moved on so they wouldn't be caught. He wouldn't have told anyone, but yes, he was terribly afraid of the gypsies.

But being a six year old, he did open the gate once in a while. He would peek out into the street: with no gypsies in sight, it must've been all right to at least look. He would see horse-drawn carriages and occasional passersby, but no children, only grownups—men in day coats and women in frocks and hats. It was all rather boring until an old man arrived pulling a colorful cart with sweets. He couldn't contain his excitement, and ran back inside asking for a coin. By the time he realized he shouldn't have been able to spot the cart in first place, it was too late to deny it.

"But I was only out by the gate. I just stood out there and didn't go anywhere. Please mommy, please, an ice or at least a hard candy?"

"Boy, I know you aren't stupid . . . so you must be deaf at times. 'In' is still in, back in the house, no sweets and no yard tomorrow."

He ran back to his room as he scrunched his eyes tightly. No, he wouldn't cry in front of his mom. But once by himself, he kicked the wall and smashed a pillow down. Oh, how he wished he had an older brother to play with! When his mother found him moping about the next day, she asked what was bothering him.

"Mom, what I really, really want is an older brother."

"Constantin, it can't be done," his mother said shaking her head. Just like that, with no explanation. So he remained quiet, afraid to ask, careful not to upset her again. The grownups had such firm ideas about what was possible and what wasn't! "But you are my big boy, my helper, my sweetie, and don't forget that."

He gathered that was supposed to make him feel better; and perhaps it did. After a while he busied himself with colors and paper and drew an ice cream cone, dreaming of the one that had slipped by him. And by the time his dad returned home at night, it was all seemingly forgotten and no one said anything.

Constantin would later reminisce about how he wished he had seen more of his dad when growing up. The young history professor (barely thirty years old at the time) would depart for the high school after breakfast. There he taught Romanian history, all grades at first, and also acted as director. The remainder of the day would then be spent at the Academy library or at the Archives studying and researching for his planned books and articles. Hard work eventually yielded a manual of Universal History for the fifth grade among his earliest achievements. He also worked on the documents gathered in Vienna, which would be printed into a one-volume booklet format a decade later. But for now his days were long indeed, and by the time he returned home, the children would often be ready for bed.

And that is why the little Constantin would recall most vividly vacations with his parents rather than the day-to-day life at home. Holidays were when dad was around just like mom, and when he saw his parents holding hands.

Elena's oldest sister, Marie, had recently remarried after her first husband, a military doctor, passed on at a young age. Marie "stayed in the family": her current husband Chiril was a lieutenant-captain whose regiment traveled across the country for "exercises." That early summer of 1907, they had been sent to the southwest, close to the Danube and the Serbian border.

It had been a violent spring in Romania, bringing bloodletting and death upon the country. A peasants' revolt, which began in the northern part of the country, spread quickly like wildfire. The discontent had stemmed from inequalities in land ownership and unfair labor practices. The latter were used by the "intermediaries" who administered the lands, organized their workforce, and also sold crops for landowners who did not care to be bothered with such operational matters.

The spark of discontent traveled fast and as their ranks swelled, the police and army were quick to rally and perhaps as many as two thousand peasants lost their lives. The government was blamed for much of this unrest, and so it fell. And in the aftermath, the party previously in opposition, specifically the liberals, returned to power. It had become a familiar game of political preeminence that shifted periodically back and forth between conservatives and liberals at the helm.

An uneasy calm finally prevailed by the summer of 1907. And so Constantin's parents thought it safe enough to visit Elena's sister and her family. A journey by train was a special and rare treat for the children. The trunks were carefully prepared days in advance. The traveling clothes were washed and ironed. Straw hats where taken out of the hat boxes and clean hankies were at the ready. And on the morning of departure, a basket of sandwiches, fruits, and water bottles was put together by the maid.

Constantin could barely contain his excitement. The cars were big and shiny; the locomotive blew thick smoke and bellows of steam. After a loud whistle the train started moving so fast it almost made you dizzy.

"Sit down boy, no running out of the car."

"But I need to see what is on the other side."

"You'll see it on our return home."

"And if I'm asleep?"

So his parents tried to keep him occupied, telling him the names of towns they passed through and stories of their rulers in centuries past. After a while the rhythmic motion of the train and Mom and Dad's soft voices put him to sleep. When he woke up, startled, it was night. And after they all ate from the basket, he fell asleep again.

It was daytime when they arrived in Turnu Magurele, a little town a few miles from the Danube River. Its main claim to fame was having been used as the southern army base during Romania's War of Independence from the Turks in 1877. Had it not been for this notoriety, it would have probably remained another dusty and monotone burg where the arrival of the train and the post delivery were the two main daily events.

"Aunt Marie," which is what Constantin would call her for the rest of his life, and her husband lived in a comfortable house with a large yard. At least it seemed that way to the children used to their small garden in the city. The little boys had summed it up: "It's so big that you can run through tall grass and bushes and past trees and when you turn around, you still can't see the house."

There was a vineyard there too, and the fruit was already ripe and fragrant at the end of August. Upon their arrival, the maidservant brought out a plate piled up high with juicy, big, sugar-like yellow-green grapes.

They were so good that Constantin decided it would be fun to eat some more directly off the vine. When the sun started going down and the grownups sat down to talk and drink glasses of wine, the youngster headed into the vineyard and ate to his heart's content. He felt sick overnight and couldn't tell his mom as she would have been very upset with him. So she stayed up all night worrying that maybe the travel and all the excitement had been too much for the child, indeed. While he felt guilty and vowed to be good, really good, in the future.

12

Chiril, Aunt Marie's husband, took him to the regimental barracks one day. There he saw soldiers doing training exercises on horseback. They were quite a sight with the brightly covered uniforms and the horses' coats shining in the morning sun. The boy marveled at their ability to move together at the same time—Uncle Chiril said it was called unison ("a grown-up word" thought Constantin).

"Uncle, what are they training for?"

"They're training to be ready, just in case."

"In case of what?"

"They need to be ready if there's war."

"What's war?"

"War is when countries fight each other. Countries sometimes get into arguments just like people, and if they are really mad at each other, they bring out guns and fight with armies."

The six year old didn't quite understand how you could get that mad. He was beginning to understand that so many things were different about grownups.

It was awfully warm the day after his visit, and so they decided to take a boat ride on the Danube to break the stifling heat. It was the boy's first time on the water. They cruised for a while and then crossed over and got to the other side in no time at all, though the river seemed so wide. The water was calm, so Constantin's father taught the boys how to throw a pebble in such a way that it skimmed across the water's surface before dropping in. It was great fun, and they practiced seemingly forever with various sizes and shapes.

On the other side they saw fishermen sitting or standing, while holding long rods and patiently waiting.

"What are they waiting for, Dad?"

"For the fish to catch."

"How long does it take?"

"Could be half an hour, could be hours; you never know."

"Sounds sooo boring. I eat fish whenever I want; Mom just sends Ana to the market."

His Dad laughed heartily, the way he did on vacations and Sundays, with no worries to wear him down. The little boy didn't think it was so funny, but then again, grownups could be strange.

The breeze on the river was so delicious and the light so beautiful that, when the time came to return to Bucharest, they took a bigger boat and cruised the Danube to the city of Giurgiu where they boarded the train. That ship had a sitting area and big paddles that moved the boat along, and watching them churning kept the boys occupied for quite a while.

Constantin loved the cruise so much that he asked his Mom to promise that every visit to Aunt Marie would from now on be by boat! Water had begun to spin its magic on the little boy.

Chapter Two
SCHOOL DAYS AND FUTURE PROMISE

The little boy was growing, and first grade was looming right around the corner in 1908. A spirited parental debate had ensued earlier that year, arguing the merits of top-notch schools versus good location. And in the end, they agreed on both criteria: it had to have an excellent reputation and had to be in a "nice," friendly neighborhood. After a couple of years they felt better acquainted with the city and better informed to hopefully find the ideal school.

They settled on a borough centered along Stirbey Voda Street which led from the Royal Palace, in the center of the city, to the Military High Command. It was mostly a residential area with one or two-story houses, many with gardens. There was also a sprinkling of stores and a pharmacy, and the local produce market wasn't too far. The Cismigiu Park, Bucharest's "oxygen center," lined up a short block down from Stirbey Voda. All in all that's exactly what the young couple had in mind.

The local school offered grades one through four and had great renown and following among the professional class. It was also located next to a church, which appealed to Elena: she could easily attend services and would get the boys in the habit of accompanying her. They rented another house (yet again) almost across the street, and after settling in the boys were taken to church for first confession. The inside felt daunting to the children: dark, with severe faces peering down at you from the smoky frescoes, the air thick of wax and incense. The boys thought the priest was awfully old, and his serious but also sad demeanor sent shivers down their spines. His thick beard and tall ecclesiastical hat were also of concern to the youngsters who decided his appearance was very strange indeed.

"Confession is telling the truth in front of God, boys; better think first before opening your mouths," she admonished them as they walked down the aisle.

A cold unease overtook Constantin: the moment he had dreaded for months had now arrived. His mother had stepped away and the child faced the stern man in dark robes.

"Is there anything you want to tell me, son?"

He knew he had to get on with it.

"Father I have sinned. I ran into the vineyard and ate many, many grapes when mom and dad weren't watching. I was really sick overnight and afraid to tell them what I had done. So I threw up and let them think it was from the trip. I thought if I told mom, she would get really mad at me."

The child's heart raced and his eyes squinted shut while waiting for the priest's verdict.

"Son, you are forgiven, but you must promise to never do this again and to always listen to your mother."

Oh well, this was not nearly as bad as he had feared. So the seven year old figured that he might be able to do something naughty once in a while, as long as he confessed afterward. It would be a while before prayers were added as penance to make confession more burdensome.

The first day of school was September 15, 1908. Constantin would later remember having woken up at the crack of dawn, barely able to conceal his excitement. He had been staring at the school building for a couple of months now, heart yearning to go in and bursting with curiosity. He had carefully studied its wrought-iron guard separating it from the sidewalk and the inner wooden fence dividing the boys' building on the left from the girls' on the right. Thank God they each had their own yard; he couldn't possibly imagine sharing the playground with the girls! He had received a brand new short haircut the day before and was secretly pleased; why, he looked like a big boy now. His mother came in to check on the uniform and after a quick glance decided they were ready to head out.

"Pick up your bag, and let's go."

"Can't I just go and you watch from the gate?"

"Not on your first day; I need to see what's going on."

He would recall his mom crossing the street with him, and how he kept glancing nervously around. He was old enough to cross on his own; what would other children say if they saw him with his mom in tow? But once in the classroom, his fears were allayed at the sight of other doting mothers. Elena talked to the teacher, assessed her son's desk and didn't leave before checking the "safety" of the courtyard. She must have been reassured as she returned smiling, hugged her little boy, and told him she'd pick him up later.

School was easy in the beginning, as Constantin had already learned to spell, count, and even read a bit while at home. But he kept quiet because the teacher, who hardly ever smiled, carried around an "all purpose" stick. It was used to silence the noise in the classroom, point to the map or blackboard, and strike a student's hand in case of mischief. The boy had decided on the spot he didn't care to find out what the stick felt like!

His favorite part of the school day undoubtedly was the big mid-morning 30-minute break. It was when the boys would gather to play "the game" of the moment, just like they did before and after hours. "The nib" was an early favorite: you held one in your hand, fist closed over it. Someone came and held one over your hand: "bang-bang." You opened the fist: if the tips of the nibs pointed toward each other, your partner won, if not they were yours. A silly children's game, but it caught on fast and soon many boasted to having the largest collection. Constantin had about 200 by the second grade and hid them at the bottom of the school bag so his mother wouldn't find them. Then fortune smiled the other way, and they were mostly gone by Easter.

Studying came easily for Constantin, and he did well in school from the beginning. It was good enough to deserve being placed "in charge" of the classroom when the teacher needed to step out for a moment.

"George, you stand by the door and watch through the keyhole," he would advise one of his friends at such a time.

The boys would walk about, "trade" stamps or marbles and chat. Suddenly the alert would sound. "He's coming, he's coming, three doors down, sit, sit down!" And they would scramble to return to their desks, sometimes knocking over the inkpot, or dropping their books.

As the first decade of the century drew closer, Elena found herself unexpectedly and happily pregnant again. Her unspoken wish for a girl might become a reality, and the young parents decided the time had come to own a house.

Constantin Sr. had continued his ascent up the professional ladder. His research in the Viennese archives and subsequent editing of his conclusions, as well as his knowledge of German, French, and Latin, had brought him to the attention of the Ministry of Foreign Affairs.

So when the position of director of archives became vacant, the young history professor seemed a logical choice. He started there in April, 1908 and was first overtaken by despair. Upon taking hold of his department, he discovered an antiquated series of rooms filled with cabinets and shelves bursting with binders, documents, and books. Some were seemingly grouped chronologically, others haphazardly filed together. The dusty rooms were looked over and found to be a real fire hazard.

Not one to give up easily, a list was drawn of what needed to be accomplished. While he worked side by side with his assistants, an inventory took shape and they started cleaning up the mess. Everything went into storage for a while; floors were then polished, new windows installed, fireproof cabinets and new shelving was ordered. When the cabinets arrived, the real work of properly filing and indexing the material started in earnest. Many months later, it was finally done and higher-ups were invited to view their new collection, which drew abundant praise.

He worked and then worked harder, and long hours became even longer. But not once did colleagues or loved ones hear any complaints—such was his work ethic. Working at the ministry was regarded as an honor and no effort would be spared to make his government proud. Constantin's work and initiatives would earn him praise and several medals. They also gradually brought about an improvement in the family finances, ultimately making it possible to receive the credit necessary to purchase a home.

Fortune smiled upon the young family. In the spring of 1910, a pair of houses around the corner from the boys' school (and their own rental) came up for public auction, after their owner defaulted on his monthly dues. They provided the 10% cash down payment, and then held their breaths while listening to the rapid, high-pitch staccato of the public auctioneer. A few hours later, a beaming and very pregnant Elena and her husband would walk away as the proud owners of houses numbered 47 and 49 on Berzei ("Stork") Street. Elena couldn't help but joke that storks normally brought you babies, not houses.

"The stork just delivered us two houses," she joked with her husband. "Hopefully a baby girl is next!"

They decided to rent number 49, the one closer to the street, and live at number 47, tucked away in the back. But this was not going to happen just yet. Both houses first needed many upgrades and repairs. They had running water and sewer but no proper bathrooms or central gas heating, and lighting was done with petrol lamps.

For a while there were workers every day, with noise and dust everywhere. Gas heat was installed, bathroom fixtures put in, the kitchen refurbished, and new fences were erected. Finally, two tall pine trees flanked the entrance and fruit trees were planted in the yard—apple, pear, cherry, walnut, and quince.

In late May their house was finally ready. And after the furniture was hauled over from around the corner, the following morning they woke up for the first time in their own home. The much wished for girl arrived barely a week later and was named Elena after her mother. Everyone would later call her Lelia.

Visitors from any major European city strolling through their neighborhood before World War One would have felt very much at home. Comfortable houses and prosperous small businesses were the hallmark of these upper-middle class boroughs across the continent. And as often was the custom, one particular building stood out among the others, "anchoring" the area. The most elegant and imposing house on Berzei Street was owned by a dentist who had once been Bucharest's mayor. The house was a sight to behold, and for a while the little boy told his parents that he was going to become a dentist so he could afford one, too.

With school out in mid-June, the boys set out in earnest to explore their new surroundings, accompanied by their mother or the maid. The fun started at the front gate watching the tramway pulled by horses: the cars were closed-in during the winter and open-air in summer. The best part of the ride was when it came to the hill and needed two additional horses to pull it up. What a show it was to watch the freshly harnessed horses huffing and puffing up the hill. And if you wanted to get on or off between stops, all you had to do was motion with your hand or shout. Riding the tramway was quite a thrill for the boys, while their mother was less pleased with the wind blowing her hat off and the dust sprinkling her attire.

If you turned left coming out of the house and kept walking, you would arrive at Bucharest's north (main) train station. The street leading there was lined with stores and workshops. There was a tinsmith, locksmith, and an "exotic" food store with rich cheese, olives and salami aromas inviting you inside. But the best treat was the station itself: little Constantin would stop on the bridge overlooking the tracks and stare at the shiny cars and locomotives. The Pacific engine with its many sets of wheels of different sizes emerged as the favorite after a careful survey.

"I might drive a locomotive when I'm a grown up," he announced to his mom. She laughed and advised him to stick to dentistry instead. He couldn't quite understand what was so funny and once more decided that grownup behavior was often puzzling. It was best left alone, as questions were never answered to his satisfaction.

Besides the train station, the other treat was going to the produce market. He liked to accompany either their helper Ana or his mom when she was looking for something special to cook for dinner.

"Remember now, no running, hold my hand at all times, don't pick anything up, and don't eat off the tables," she said, reciting her litany of dos and don'ts. "And if you're good, you get lemonade."

At that he remembered the old man carrying a long flask on his shoulder. He would pour chilled juice into one of the six tin cups attached to his belt and wait for you to finish. Yes, it was definitely worth listening to mom!

It was great fun at the market in those days, crowded with everyone shouting at the same time. Some were praising the fresh fruit, or the plucked chickens, and the air was pungent with juicy peaches, sharp cheeses, flowers, and sour milk. People were happy and satisfied with their lives, and friendly and kind because of it.

But there were also gypsies milling about the market and that worried the child. Mom said they were there to sell their goods and not steal, for the most part anyway, but you still had to watch your pockets. And you always bargained with them as they would first ask for double or triple the price. They added color to the scene with olive-skinned men hauling around carts of metal racks and pots while the women wore brightly colored, long skirts and heavy chain necklaces and sold flowers and boiled corn.

Long summer holidays were taken seriously in Romania and in Europe in general during the first decade of the last century. It was still cold, gray, and frosty when families would gather around fires and start plotting their warm-season travels.

Just like today you could visit grandma and grandpa, often in the country. Or the family might have chosen to go "take the waters," a popular custom a hundred years ago. Romania had her own first-rate spas with mineral water, salty lakes, or mud baths with acclaimed health benefits. Some of them were ranked highly by locals and foreign travelers alike who came from afar. Or, one may have chosen to rent a cottage in a fashionable mountain resort like Sinaia where the Romania royal family spent its summers at the Peles Palace. And for those who couldn't leave town they would have walked to the city park to listen to the military band.

But first and foremost summers were all about fun and holidays, and 1910 was no different for the young Giurescu family. Early on Elena was once again busy changing diapers and feeding a baby. So it fell to her husband to take the boys to the amusement park fair held twice each year on the outskirts of the city. This year the youngsters were especially looking forward to it. With mom at home, they would be able to eat to their heart's content and go on as many rides as desired.

A visit to the park and fair was a special treat to be cherished in those days. Cinemas with their miraculous pictures were scarce; gramophones were expensive and a luxury for most. The radio wasn't yet a part of one's household, and children were too young to go to the theater. For the boys the anticipation had built up for weeks, with dreams of new, thrilling and scary rides, marvelous magic tricks, and sweets so delicious they left one longing for more.

They took the tramway all the way to the end of the line, and to their delight watched horses being changed not once, but twice. This was followed by a short carriage ride and then, all of a sudden and just like a mirage, stood a spectacle of bright colors and loud sounds. There were the vivid fences in garish hues, the giant Ferris wheel looming over the stalls, and the aromas enticing you to hurry in.

Little Horia, six and a half, found the clowns funny but they were already a bit silly for his nearly nine-year-old brother. He preferred such wonders as the "serpent boa," the "spider with a woman's head," "the strongest man in the world," and the unbelievable "man who swallows fire." The boy felt nearly certain that they were all gimmicks but couldn't for his life figure out the tricks, no matter how much he stared and tried.

Though they all had their favorites, they agreed on one thing: the sweets were sensational—fried golden dough balls rolled in powdery sugar, candy of all sorts, and pies and ices.

Dad decided Horia was too young for the scary rides, but Constantin was given the "green light." Up he went: one, two, three times, flying high above it all and dreaming of the flying machine that Dad had recently talked about. Perhaps one day he, too, could climb into the skies and see the whole wide earth beneath him, thought the boy.

The second half of the summer of 1910 was spent at their paternal grandfather's house in the northeastern part of the Walachia province, some 130 km from Bucharest. The boys feared the family would skip the visit that year on account of the baby. But after deliberations mom had decided they were all going: baby, nanny, and Ana the helper, too. Preparations took even longer than usual and the boys felt they'd never be ready. Finally, on July 20, trunks and baskets were loaded into the coach taking them to the train station and they were on their way.

They were seasoned train travelers by now, but the cars still held the same fascination. Once aboard Constantin again imagined himself at the engineer's controls releasing the steam and making the train roar down the tracks. He was now certain: this would be a lot more fun than being a dentist.

They settled in two cars, with Elena wistfully warning the children that the first leg of the journey was to be brief and the easy part. An hour and a half passed in a blur and they disembarked, which seemed to take forever, in Ploesti. There they were welcomed by Francu, the owner of the transport carriage in grandpa's village. They piled everything up high on the carriage and headed out down a long, endless first stretch on a dusty road. The baby cried incessantly; Horia was bored and annoying everyone. Constantin tried to ignore him and read his book and finally they arrived at Valeni, a little town tucked at the foothills of the Carpathian Mountains.

They all needed rest and food: children, parents, and horses alike. In those days travelers stopped at Mrs. Marghioala's, a local restaurant-tavern. It was a special treat for the young family accustomed to eating home-cooked meals every day. What a thrill it was for the children to be able to choose whatever they wanted! There were grilled meats, thickly cut potatoes, and hearty soups, plus ice-cold water from the pump, and wine for the grownups. And then there was desert: apple strudel freshly baked every day.

The horses drank water from a long trough and hay was spread out for them to eat. The boys went outside after lunch and watched how the driver rubbed the horses' long necks and pulled their ears to freshen them up for the next leg of their trip.

The scenery turned prettier as they headed northeast into the hills covered with pastures and orchards. With the climb getting much steeper, the horses started puffing.

"Could they fall and faint, Francu?"

"No, lad. These are the finest horses there are; they aren't mules."

Shortly afterward the road started descending, and they paused to freshen up by the river. Meadows were dusted in flowers everywhere: bright red poppies and fragrant, pink buds as far as the eye could see. Then back on the road, and all of a sudden they came upon two large rocks—one blue, the other one white jutting out of nowhere and heralding the entrance to Grandpa's village. You knew you had arrived and the "real" summer holidays were about to begin.

For the boys days blended into one another with not a care in the world. They were busy with their cousin Victor, with considerable time being spent in and by the water. They had built a rudimentary dam and tried to swim in the basin of sorts it had created. They also competed with each other, diving first from the riverbank and later adding height to their dives from rocks and boulders.

In between running, swimming and growing an inch or so, the growing boys felt hungry all the time. They would look for hazelnuts—though admitting "defeat" to Victor's sisters who knew all the fine spots—and berries and later on, apples and pears. Victor's mom taught them how to dry apples for the winter: you sliced them thin and dried them in the sun on wooden planks. Then you mounted them on thread, and finally put them away in cardboard boxes. They were skeptical at first, but back home the apples turned out to be delicious and were gone before the end of the fall. And finally, just before returning home to Bucharest, the pumpkins became ripe, bursting with flavor. Dad helped bake them on an open fire and then sprinkled a little sugar on top. The taste was so rich that they nearly melted in your mouth!

The entire summer they had been able to roam their kingdom of hills, pastures, and orchards. With fall approaching now—and the end of the holidays in sight—the boys longed to explore the "last frontier," the one off-limit area: the beehives. They had been warned:

"The bees don't like to be bothered; they'll sting; and if it's bad enough, you can die."

They nodded their heads but still tried to at least get closer at times, only to be deterred by the ominous dark cloud swarming about the hives.

One day they spotted Grandpa among the beehives, looking very odd, indeed. His face was covered with a net, a thick low hat and a smoldering smoky rag over his hands. They wondered if he'd gone mad but he explained later, never one to waste words:

"It's all cover for safety, the smoke keeps them away." Then he went about carving the honeycomb. They decided it looked like an awful amount of trouble to go through just to get your honey on bread with butter! Exploring the beehive had suddenly lost its pull on the youngsters.

The only "cloud" on Constantin's sunny holiday horizon was the visits to the local store with mom or his aunt. There were so many other things they could have done, instead of which they had to dress up and go along to town. He thought either mom wanted to show them off, or perhaps she didn't want them rolling around on the grass or in the mud all day long. He tried to behave on such occasions so as not to embarrass her, keeping quiet while the village women oohed and aahed around the children. The storekeeper often saved the day when she offered some candy, making the outing somewhat worthwhile.

It was around this time and in the village that he started learning a bit about money. He had heard mom paying 20 cents for five eggs, which sounded awfully cheap. But then she had explained how their currency, the "leu," was actually gold and the equivalent of one Swiss franc (plus 5 cents). He had heard that the Swiss were good with money so the child decided their money must have been strong, too. And indeed, in those days prior to World War I, the Romanian currency was one of the strongest on the continent. The leu of that era would later be recounted as Romania's most powerful and stable across the years.

The summer holidays were drawing to a close, and the decade would follow suit a few months later. With the country and its society growing in leaps and bounds the next ten years held such promise. Fate had hopefully read the script as there was much to look forward to.

Chapter Three
BROTHERS HEAR THE DISTANT WAR DRUMS

The first decade of the new century had come and gone and Romanian society was flowing along, still fluid but in search of itself. It was a traditional society in many respects, where your vote or lack of one was dictated by income—for instance, fifty peasants counted as one vote. And where the upper class did not even need a passport since their faces and names were recognized by the border patrol. But it was also a world which enabled those gifted but born in less auspicious circumstance to advance in life. Some would have chosen a military career or the law. Others could become administrators or teachers. And little by little they swelled the ranks of the growing middle class.

And as their lives improved, they found themselves seeking out leisurely pursuits. They could have gone to the theater or concerts, or simply out for a beer at a local tavern to listen to some easy music. They might have sent a messenger to bring a carriage and go for a leisurely stroll around the lakes surrounding Bucharest's periphery. Or they may have even found themselves depicted in the pages of the weekly *Claymoor* that took to chronicling the capital's vibrant social life. And a busy life it was! This daily newspaper described in detail the parties of the previous night: guests; fashions of the day; the fine wines, cigars, and champagne. Plays, concerts, and special events on public holidays also received prominent coverage. As for society's wealthiest, they could have decided to travel abroad to "take the waters" at Karlo Vivary or perhaps visit Vienna with all its imperial glory.

The political life of this era enjoyed broad stability previously unbeknownst to Romania. Old King Carol I, a German prince brought to the throne thirty years earlier, was universally liked and respected. A firm believer in the two-party system—conservatives vying with liberals, which he did his best to strengthen—he ruled "by the book," obeying the country's constitution.

All in all life was good in Romania in 1910, mostly flowing at a languid pace punctuated by bursts of exciting new trends and innovations. Elegant buildings were being built in Bucharest and some of the larger cities. Visitors venturing to the Black Sea coast would return raving about the Pavilion in the harbor town of Constanta. It had initially been destined to be a seaboard cottage for Romania's Queen Elizabeth. But the aging royal couple increasingly spent most of their time in Bucharest or at their summer palace in Sinaia. So the magnificent seaside rococo-style building was converted overnight into a luxury restaurant and casino, attracting elegantly attired couples out for an evening of fine dining and those chasing a fast fortune.

On other fronts, the nation was falling in love with a marvelous new invention: flying machines. And hearts beaming with pride were celebrating their own adventurous sons who ventured into the skies. Aurel Vlaicu, born in the then Austro-Hungarian Transylvania, had built his own plane and first flew it in June 1910. He would go on to win several prestigious European prizes over the next few years. As for his weekend gliding shows on the outskirts of the capital, they gathered huge cheering crowds. In the same year another Romanian, Henri Coanda, designed (with French backing and support) the world's first jet-powered aircraft.

As for the Giurescu family, life continued to be centered on the children and the household for Elena while work remained her husband's main focus. His career flourished and his publications had earned him a nomination as a member correspondent of the Romanian Academy in 1909. Three years later in 1912, he realized the first step of his dream to be a full-fledged professor, being nominated as a substitute teacher at the Faculty of History of the University of Bucharest.

Rather shy and not demonstrative, he didn't talk about his feelings on the matter. But deep down in his heart, he knew that reaching out to a student audience filled him with great satisfaction. He marveled at their curiosity and said their astute questions often made him look at historical facts from a different angle. His courses' sound, scientific content and his gifted oratorical delivery made them immediately successful. Attended by a record audience, they would be declared mandatory the following year.

As for Elena, she felt content, having been brought up to believe that a woman's dreams should be centered on marriage, children, and an efficiently run household. And that was precisely where she found her focus as the century and marriage headed into their second decade. She had a loving, handsome, and successful husband at her side and three beautiful children. Living in a comfortable and elegant house, they also boasted of a rental next door. She felt proud to have managed all of this, but was also deeply grateful for her good fortunes. A devout Christian, every evening found her in deep prayer over the religious icons hanging above the bed. She gave thanks, but also asked God watch over them all, and to keep her husband healthy and strong and her children safe. Then on Sundays they all went to church and then took a stroll, weather permitting, through the Cismigiu Park.

As for the young Constantin, the new decade provided him with the biggest challenge of his budding life. He was facing the admission exams to high school, which in that era began with the fifth grade. He studied hard and sat for written and oral tests emerging at the end of the session with the highest score. And so in September 1912 he was headed to the Lazar School, one of Bucharest's two elite learning institutions of the time. It was a time of joyous celebration for child and mother, one that called for a special treat. She decided to take him out, just the two of them, with no baby or annoying brother in tow.

"Mom, you really mean it, just the two of us?" he kept asking over and over again.

"Just us, baby. It's your big day and you're my big boy, always have been, always will be."

"Can we do anything I want?"

"Anything, but remember: just this once."

They put on their finery, the child beaming proud in his sailor's suit—the "dress up" attire of young boys in those days. While his mother chose her good morning silk with elaborate lace collar and cuffs and shiny short ankle boots. Smiling and holding hands, they walked along Stirbey Boulevard to Palace Square and from there on to the famous Capsa pastry shop. It was there that fashionable Bucharest gathered—politicians, writers, industrialists, and beautiful women. People came for coffee, lemonade, fine sweets and gossip or merely to see and be seen. After chocolate eclairs, cream puffs, and lemonade, the boy and his mother went to the movies, a rare treat at the time. They were showing a "long feature" that day, a Romanian rendition of its Independence War of 1877. The pictures were rather rough, with the art form still in its infancy. The film was devoid of sound and color and filled with mechanical, repetitive motions, but nothing seemed amiss to the child, such was the thrill of the novelty.

Later on, with school in session the students studied hard. The curriculum was extensive and well rounded and all classes were mandatory. Besides literature, mathematics, sciences, history, geography, and languages (German, French), they also took music and drawing. Their teachers and masters were fine pedagogues, classically trained and attired in suits or morning coats; discipline and respect were emphasized as much as academic achievements. Lazar High School would provide him over the years with a solid foundation and instill in him a firm discipline and work ethic.

The summer of 1914 found them once again in Chiojd at Grandpa's house. The boys, nearly teenagers now, continued to swim and roam the hills while their mother was happy to spend time alone with her daughter, a beautiful and lively four year old.

A long summer together and on vacation, and not a care in the world, they thought. Until one day in July, Dad sat them down and explained how Archduke Franz Ferdinand, the heir to the Austro-Hungarian Empire, and his wife, Sophie, had been murdered in Sarajevo.

"Where's that, father?"

"Here, look at the map," he said and patiently pointed out Bosnia and Herzegovina and its capital Sarajevo, and explained how those lands were part of the Austrian Empire. "It happened at the end of June; the assassin was a student."

"Why did he do it?" asked one of the boys.

"It was bad timing for the Archduke's visit. It took place during the local national holiday, when people there wished they were free of the Empire." He made sure they understood the implication. "And now the Austrian Emperor Franz Josef has decided to seek revenge and other countries have jumped in, too. Germany is siding with Austria, whereas France, Russia, and Great Britain are backing the Bosnians and Serbs."

The boys listened patiently. "And what does this have to do with us, Dad?"

"Romania may enter the war on one side or the other." Ever the historian, he patiently explained each alternative.

"So why are you so upset if we aren't even at war yet?"

"Boy, haven't you been listening. We will sooner or later be a part of this, and countries are torn apart by such wars."

This sobered the child and ended the conversation and the boys went to bed, thoughts drifting to the soldiers they spotted marching a year earlier. Constantin had seen them during a second visit to his Aunt Marie, who by now had moved to the town of Galati on the Danube. The boys had been waiting at the train station when they had seen the reserves marching down the road. His Uncle Chiril had led an entire battalion of three thousand men. They were headed for the border with Bulgaria where skirmishes had taken place. He now remembered the awesome sight of them in formation: their captain on horseback, troops marching behind at a perfect clip. He had felt reassured by this force of arms; they surely would be able to defend them come what may, and on this note he fell happily asleep.

They returned home at the end of the summer and not much happened at first. War was raging on, and both sides in the conflict wanted Romania's support. In school most of Constantin's classmates were rooting for allegiance to France. Theirs was the unofficial society language at the time, and the country had long had a love affair with all things French—their fashion, architecture, and literary trends. The young students spent time plotting out how the Romanian armies should enter Transylvania and liberate the areas where their brothers formed a majority. This province, now part of the Austro-Hungarian Empire, had been part of Romania hundreds of years earlier and many of her people spoke the same language.

Such might have been the youngsters' wish, but Romania was bound to Germany and Austro-Hungary by a secret military and political treaty signed three decades earlier. This treaty was to be activated only in case of attack by Imperial Russia on any of its members. And despite the lack of confrontation with Russia at the time, the old Romanian king thought it honorable to enter the war on the side of its sworn allies.

King Carol I's conflict was deep, torn between constitutional duties toward his kingdom and his blood ties to Germany. Calling an emergency Crown Council of current and ex-prime ministers and prominent members of the government, he asked for their advice, while also stating his preference. All but two of those present advised against entering the war on the side of the Austrian Empire. More so, it was pointed out that Romania was under no obligation to join: Austro-Hungary had started the war and the aforementioned treaty referred only to an attack by Russia. Stone-faced, the king listened to his country's collective voice: at the request of the gathering, Romania would remain neutral for the time being. If the sovereign felt defeated, he never publicly let on. And some thought that this disappointment might have precipitated his death less than a month later in early October 1914.

The end of an era had come to pass.

A new world was ushered in on the morrow. As the king had passed away without immediate descendants, the title went to his nephew, Ferdinand, who was married to one of Queen Victoria's granddaughters, Princess Marie. And many thought this blood tie to Great Britain was surely bound to muddy the already murky Romanian political waters. It was surely just a matter of time.

Weeks passed and fall became winter. War raged in Europe while life in Bucharest went on punctuated by warfront updates in the various dailies. Young Constantin's parents took to sitting up and discussing the news at night after dinner. The boys found themselves gradually caught up in the various alliances and frontline battles. After a while they realized that provided they kept quiet and mostly didn't ask any seemingly stupid questions, their parents wouldn't hush them to bed. On many a night, you could have found all four in deep thought going over the map of Europe while little Lelia slept blissfully unaware of the impending storm.

On Christmas Day 1914, the family gathered around the decorated fir tree with sweets and gifts like any other year. But as they sat down to lunch, Dad reminded them of those less fortunate. He told of children whose lives had been torn apart by the war, without homes, presents, or a father, and Elena said a prayer for all.

The year 1914 had cast a dark shadow upon the world.

Chapter Four

SIDES ARE DRAWN, AN UNCLE PERISHES

Romania was still a neutral country in 1915, but nobody knew how much longer this would last. People went about their daily lives but a sense of foreboding hung like a dark curtain of clouds. The pros and cons and various scenarios played themselves out in public forums and on the home front. And Constantin, ever the historian, continued his impromptu analyses. He was certain the country would enter the war and win territory either way.

Both alliances wanted them on their side. The Germans had remained hopeful as the new Romanian monarch, King Ferdinand, was German by birth. Their "carrot and stick" was the promise to liberate part of Moldova (a former Romanian province) from the Russians and rightfully return it to its people.

But the king's wife, Marie, was British, a granddaughter of Queen Victoria (and a cousin of Alexandra, wife of the Russian czar). Marie was determined to stir sentiment for the opposite side, that of the "Entente" (Britain, France, and Russia). Most public opinion favored this course, as this camp's victory would have led to the liberation of Transylvania (the western land) from the Austro-Hungarian Empire and its return to Romania.

In the meantime everyone seemed to have an opinion one way or the other and rumors were rampant. Despite their country's persistent neutral stance, war had already taken center stage in their lives.

Constantin's young boys learned to avidly read the dailies and their questions seemed to please their father greatly. He always had an explanation ready, or at least a theory. But to one particular question he held no answer: it had to do with gossip surrounding the secret passage of German troops en route to Turkey.

"Is it true?" Elena had asked. At first he didn't know. But then stories started circulating. Some claimed to have seen the troop trains while others had been told so by insiders. When Constantin learned of grains and other foods being illegally sent to Germany for profit, he became greatly distressed. Why, he was agitated enough to publicly protest:

"Imagine boys sending food to bolster our possible future enemies and getting rich in the process. That is so dishonorable!" Honor being, above all, what governed this man's highly principled and disciplined life.

Toward the end of the spring, he received a letter from his brother Ionica, a colonel in the Romanian army. Ionica was coming to town to fetch some supplies and had been given a brief leave. He wanted to make the most of this respite and wondered if he could take the boys along on a trip. Little Constantin had in the past traveled by himself to see his aunt, but the two brothers had never been away together without their parents. Elena was mostly worried about her young Horia, the eleven year old who was always running around and dreaming up mischief.

"You think we should let them go?" she asked her husband.

"Why shouldn't we? The boys are growing up; it'll do them some good to travel without us. They'll have to make their beds and wash their ears without you reminding them."

"Now, seriously, I am worried about Horia not listening, getting hurt. . . ."

"Well, that happens at home, too . . . Elena, let them go. It'll be their summer adventure, who knows what awaits us in the fall. And you know how much Ionica loves them."

And so it was decided: the boys were to travel with their uncle. Ionica came to Bucharest and picked up his nephews, after fetching the needed supplies. He cut such a dashing figure in his shiny uniform with tall boots and cap! As for the boys, they were excited to go away with their favorite uncle, who was so much fun and seemed so much younger than their dad. He laughed at their jokes and pranks and never seemed to think their questions were strange. Why, he even ate candy and ices at odd times, just like them!

After repeated reminders to wash hands, brush teeth, and talk only when spoken to, the boys were ready. They boarded the train and headed to Urziceni, some 60 km northeast of Bucharest. Ionica's regiment was stationed in that dusty little town in the middle of nowhere amidst the thick wheat and cornfields of southeast Romania. They spent a week at the garrison and despite the summer's stifling heat, the boys stayed busy. They marveled at the guns and horses and went on horseback rides. Constantin was also allowed to fire a rifle for the first time: he needed three tries to hit a pigeon. And once he saw the poor bird spiraling down, ruffled feathers and with a swooshing sound, he vowed to leave pigeons alone in the future. But the rifle intrigued him and he vowed to learn more and see what other use he could put it to. As for Horia, he was sorely disappointed to have been deemed too young to attempt such a thing.

"It's not fair; I never get to do any of the grownup things my brother's allowed to!"

"You, too, will be able to try it out in a few years."

"It won't be the same. What if the war is over and you no longer have a rifle?"

"Horia, I'll hold on to my rifle just for you."

The child beamed and his sorrow was soon forgotten. And on a day when one felt it couldn't possibly get any hotter, they boarded the train again and headed to the harbor of Constanta on the Black Sea. The journey was dull at first, passing through endless fields of wheat parading by the window.

"Uncle, I've been wondering. Why don't you get married so we have another aunt to visit and cousins to play with?" Constantin finally asked.

A shy and wistful smile played upon his uncle's lips. "War is upon us, boys. I'll most certainly be called to duty. And when you fight a war, you may perish. . . ."

"No, no, some do, but you won't; you won't, you know that."

Ionica saw how such talk visibly distressed the boys and decided it was time to bring out the sandwiches, creating a "diversion" as taught in military school.

"Here, boys, I've packed some salami and cheese. And we have juicy peaches for dessert." While they ate, little Constantin reflected upon the grownup habit of avoiding unpleasant topics.

A couple of hours passed and all of a sudden there it was in all its glory. They had seen pictures and drawings and read about it but nothing prepared them for its vastness. One moment they were sitting bored and staring out a window. The next there popped out this steel ribbon which grew wider, bluer, and shinier as the midday sun hit it with a full blast. It was the sea, their Black Sea.

They arrived at Constanta and checked into a hotel. This was a first for the children who had only stayed with relatives during past travel. That first night they ate in the restaurant of the Casino building, the famous pavilion which had been built for the old queen. The boys found it far grander than their only other restaurant experience, the rest stop in Valeni on the way to Grandpa's. Here were waiters in black coats, just waiting for a sign from you, and the menus were written out on ornate thick paper. They sat on red velvet chairs and marveled at the sateen tablecloths and thick embroidered napkins. Glancing around, one was surrounded by a myriad of wall mirrors, their reflections casting an opulent aura about the room.

The following day they took out a small boat. Constantin found the bob-bob, lull-lull sensation heavenly. But he was greatly puzzled when his uncle and Horia were taken ill and threw up. As for the captain of the dinghy, he didn't think anything of it. He said it happened all the time; it was called seasickness, and many suffered from it.

Within minutes Ionica had gone from pale to ashen and eventually was almost green. He finally spoke up, "Captain, I think we should return to shore."

Little Constantin found the courage to speak up, "Uncle, may I please go with the captain after we drop you and Horia off?"

His uncle was uneasy, feeling responsible for the well-being of the children whose parents were some 120 miles away. The captain seemed to sense the man's unease.

"Sir, Colonel Giurescu, the sea is calm and will stay so. I can take the older boy out for a while and still have him back in time for supper."

Ionica could have questioned the captain's savvy. But after studying his weathered, lined face and callused fingers, the Colonel decided the boy was in capable hands.

Constantin and the captain spent the afternoon out to sea, going farther and farther until the boy felt like Gulliver the Giant looking back at a miniature crescent shape—the shore left behind. When they returned with a basket of fresh sardines and sun-burnt cheeks, the child knew he had found his new most favorite hobby: sailing.

The following day Ionica took them to the museum to view Greek artifacts: statues, pottery, and bronzes. The Greeks had colonized the area around the Black Sea in the sixth and seventh centuries BC, and the colony of Histria (on Romanian soil) had been one of their more prominent establishments. To the boys the artifacts were more like a bunch of items haphazardly displayed in a rather dark building which held little interest. They hadn't been enthusiastic about this outing but had gone along nonetheless. Still bored, young Constantin looked for something to do and asked a guard where the objects had been found. They were apparently mostly from Constanta but also from Mangalia, a town some thirty miles to the south. It had been known as Callatis during the Greek times. He was told excavations were still in progress and students working there would bring a vase or plate wrapped in thick cloth, and hand it to the staff to start the cleaning and cataloging process. Despite the initial lack of enthusiasm, it began to sound all rather interesting to the fourteen-year-old boy. Coming up with bits and pieces of your past and trying to put it back together seemed like a grownup puzzle. It was there in Constanta that the boy began to understand his father's passion for history.

But like all good things the trip eventually came to an end. The return to Bucharest was uneventful and the parents were happy to have them back home. Elena was also relieved to hear her boys had behaved themselves and nothing had been disrupted on account of their visit. As for Uncle Ionica, he stayed overnight, eager to spend one more evening with the family. The certainty of the upcoming war and his deployment weighed heavily on his mind. That night he shared with his brother and Elena the details of a will that had been drafted months earlier. His nephews were to inherit the property and land he owned in Chiojd, as well as an additional cornfield in another county.

Elena thought it bad luck to be talking about wills under such circumstance. It was almost like her brother-in-law had a death wish, and she tried to deflect the topic. "Instead of chatting like this, think about getting married. You aren't getting any younger."

"Come on, Elena . . . you, too? The boys pestered me on the trip; they want more cousins to play with."

"I guess we all agree, then. So it's decided?"

"Duty to country comes first. But I promise I'll give it serious thought after the war."

They drank some wine the last night together and had a few hearty laughs over Horia's childish pranks. The following morning they hugged each other, perhaps a little tighter than normal, the unknown future weighing upon them.

Months flew by, and suddenly a new year was ringing in again. The snow melted, winter turned to spring, and Romania was still neutral. The summer of 1916 found Elena and the children once again in Chiojd at Grandfather's house. For two months Elena had known she was once again pregnant. It had happened just as with Lelia, without trying and when she least expected it. Except that now she was thirty-seven years old with a teenage son and two younger children, and her husband was never home, working from sunrise to sunset. And they were almost certainly headed into a seemingly endless war which had already been tearing the continent apart for two years. Adding to her anxiety was that she hadn't dared to tell her husband yet. She had seen him consumed by deep, continuous worry for their well-being, and she feared bringing in another life in these unsettled times.

On August 14 she put the children to bed early and retired herself, grateful for a few extra hours of sleep.

Constantin thought he was in the midst of an awfully noisy dream, pealing bells and a forlorn horn, when he woke up to find his mother standing over him, short of breath and flushed.

"We're at war; they're calling up the troops."

Young Constantin's first thought was about his dad. "Will they send Dad away, too?"

"I don't think so, sweetie; he's too old and his eyesight is poor."

The youngster breathed a little easier, though his thoughts immediately wandered to his uncle. "What about Uncle Ionica?"

"He'll be called to duty. And we must pray for his safe return."

It turns out Queen Marie of Romania had gotten her wish in the end. After complex and lengthy deliberations, a secret agreement was signed between Romania and the Western Powers—France and the United Kingdom (plus Russia) to enter the war on their side. Upon it and in case of victory, Romania would be able to annex any part of the Austro-Hungarian Empire inhabited at the time by a majority of Romanian-speaking people. All eyes were now set on the main objective: regaining Transylvania. Written guarantees were offered to protect territorial gains at the end of the war. Military assistance was promised and Romania was assured of equal status at a future peace conference. Thus the country suddenly found itself facing a formidable enemy: the alliance of Germany with the Austro-Hungarian Empire and Bulgaria. Of immediate concern was the latter as it formed Romania's southern border, the two countries separated only by the Danube River.

Once at war, one would have thought that the country had a new direction and a sense of how to proceed. But on the contrary, Romania found itself again pulled apart by opposing tides. The military high command believed the first attack should strategically take place in the south, while Prime Minister Ionel Bratianu gave priority to the political prize of Transylvania and encouraged an attack to the north. Focusing on the latter would prove to be disastrous for Romania and her citizens.

In the confusion of the first moments, Elena had wanted to return home right away to be with her husband. But a telegram received a day or so later urged them to stay in Chiojd for the time being, until matters became clearer.

"Dearest Elena, I pray you stay with my father for now. I miss you terribly, too, and am worried sick about you and the children. But no one seems to know how long our troops will be able to hold out in the north. I will be at your side as soon as the ministry approves my leave, and together we'll decide what's best for us.

"I love you, dearest, your Constantin."

He also wrote of how the Romanian army had needed only a few days to enter Brasov. It was the most important town in southern Transylvania, a scenic old German outpost nestled at the foot of the Carpathian Mountains. He had read of joyous crowds welcoming their liberating troops. Women in folk garb, colorful long skirts and embroidered linen blouses, and children waving the red-yellow-blue tricolor Romanian flag had come out to greet the tired soldiers.

But this joyous mood turned somber only weeks later. The rapid Romanian advance was soon halted, the initial success having alarmed their opponent who swiftly deployed several divisions. At the same time, an attack was being mounted in the south by the Bulgarians over two disputed counties. Their troops were part of a multinational force led by German military legend General August von Mackensen. The presence of this southern front confirmed, if only weeks too late, the military leaders' savvy. The Romanian army thus needed to rapidly deploy a troop division to this new front. But given its numbers and level of outfitting, it was unable to sustain two concomitant large theaters of operation. In early September, a fierce battle took place in the southeastern part of the country, in the town of Turtucaia. The Romanian forces were defeated there by the Bulgarian army at a steep cost: some 6,000 lives were lost and more than 20,000 of their soldiers were captured.

Constantin joined his family later that month. When he climbed out of the coach, pale, sad and quiet, they could tell immediately something was terribly wrong. Even the normally boisterous boys sensed it and headed to their room without asking any questions. They tried to read while craning their necks to catch the murmuring of their parents' conversation. It mostly escaped them, though they could hear their mother sobbing.

They didn't have to wait long: their father came in, put his arms around them, and barely whispered, "Boys, you won't be seeing your Uncle Ionica again . . . he fell at Turtucaia." Constantin paused to allow them a moment. "He saved some of his men, pushing them back from the enemy line, while continuously firing his own weapon . . . until he was gunned down."

Gasps, disbelief, and then silence followed. Little Constantin wanted to cry but recalled how mom always said: "Big boys don't cry." So he squeezed his eyes shut for a few seconds and slowly re-opened them, with only a single tear rolling down his cheek. He re-called how on their trip they had pestered Uncle Ionica to get married. How they kept asking for cousins to play with and of his response, "Let's wait 'till the war is over, and see what happens."

He now wondered if his uncle had had a premonition. Suddenly he remembered Uncle Ionica staring at the sea standing next to the Constanta Casino on the evening of their fancy dinner there. He was laughing and gazing into the distance and pointing to the stars in the ink-dark sky. That was the lasting image of his uncle who had now become one with the sun, wind, earth, and sea.

Their father then recounted the heavy defeat the army had taken at Turtucaia. Panic was rife in Bucharest, with many thinking it was only a matter of time before foreign artillery would be rolling into the capital. So he thought it best for the family to remain in Chiojd, tucked away in the mountains for a while longer.

The following morning Elena woke up cramping in a pool of blood and by midday she had miscarried. It was to stay with her, this secret. She knew the pain Ionica's death had brought her husband and couldn't bear to have him to mourn this unborn child at the same time. She stayed in bed for a couple of days claiming "women's problems" and stating "she simply needed to rest." A cousin brought her herbs steeped in hot water, which were supposed to help with the "cleans-ing," while another woman lit a candle for the lost "poor little soul."

They remained in Chiojd for a while longer. The house became very crowded as one of Constantin's older cousins arrived with his wife and three grown-up children. One of them was already married with a baby in tow. Though the boys began to grasp the seriousness of the situation, they were still young enough to relish the ongoing adventure. Here were eleven adults, three children, and a screaming infant sharing two adjacent small houses. Everybody tripped over one another, never finding anything where they had left it. As for the boys, they wandered off most of the day, with their parents oscillating be-tween worry over the children's whereabouts and relief to have some peace and quiet in the house.

Mostly, everyone waited for news from the front and a clue as to what they should do next. The wait wouldn't be long.

Chapter Five
WORLD WAR I COMES HOME

By late September 1916, the enemy's progress had momentarily stopped, bringing about a much-desired break. Elena and Constantin often debated late into the night, the merits of staying in the country vis-à-vis a return home. Schools were bound to be in session soon and they wished for the boys to return to Bucharest, harboring significant reservations over the quality of an education in the village. As for the children, they had hoped for an indefinite extension of a stay at Grandpa's—so much more fun than the studies which awaited them at home! In the end, and with no immediate threat to the capital, Constantin decided the time had come to return and await further developments in Bucharest. But hearts were heavy as only God knew what was in store for them. A possible draft loomed large, and not many felt immune regardless of age. An occupation of the capital was also of concern, with all that entailed—food shortages and foreign armies patrolling the streets. And if refugees fled to Bucharest, the overcrowding of the city could bring epidemics and rain more death.

The Romanian army's losses continued to mount on both front lines, despite the soldiers' valiant efforts. The men were mostly on their own, with only rather anemic support from their Russian allies, military promises of assistance already forgotten. The imbalance of forces was accentuated as the Bulgarians—their enemies to the south—were bolstered by repeated fresh supplies of German troops. That fall the weakened Romanian forces faced concomitant attacks. They were hit both from the northwest, through the Carpathian Mountains, and from the southeast, where the Bulgarians continued to be supported by their allies. Casualties were heavy, counting around 250,000—many dead, others prisoners of war.

By early December the south and southeastern parts of the country were lost to the Central Powers. This included the capital Bucharest and the main harbor of Constanta. Two thirds of Romania, as known prior to the fall of 1916, was now under enemy occupation, and the new frontline was established in southern Moldova. Its government, including the Parliament and the king, relocated to Iasi, the Moldovan capital. The country's gold stocks—the entire national reserve of 274 tons—were sent to Tsarist Russia for safekeeping, never to be returned.

As the victorious German army drew near, panic spread across Bucharest. Houses were boarded up, silver household items buried in the ground, and cellars emptied. Bank accounts were cashed in. Jewelry and family papers and clothes for every season were thrown into traveling trunks for fast getaways.

Elena felt panic at first about what to take. They didn't know when they were leaving town, where they were headed, or for how long. Her husband, the one she always turned to for advice, was short on answers this time. "Take whatever you think is absolutely necessary, do your best; as for a place to live in, I don't know dearest, no one is certain. . . ."

So she went about inspecting room after room: armoires, cupboards, and storage trunks. Elena drew lists and set aside piles of clothing, sheets, towels, books, and dry goods. She was ready to pack the trunks, when one day her husband came home early and short of breath, announcing:

"The ministry has assigned me to stay in Bucharest and manage the archives. They feel someone needs to stay behind. The collection is too large and some of the documents are too delicate to travel."

Elena drew in a sharp, deep breath. The sudden relief of knowing they weren't leaving was mixed with fear of what might lie ahead. Occupation by the Germans loomed, together with uncertainty regarding schools and food shortages. But every time panic took over, she reminded herself that things were after all just as expected in wartime. Why, they were among the luckier ones, still together and in their own home. Knowing they would remain in Bucharest, at least for the foreseeable future, they tried to return to a quasi-normal routine. The children were put back in school, and their father headed to the ministry every morning. But daily signs and sights reminded them that life, as known before their summer entrance into the war, was now over.

German Taube planes and the famous Zeppelins periodically dropped bombs. The first raid was the one they would never forget. Humming sounds far away got closer and louder, followed by a sudden deafening roar and clouds of dust. Agonizing wails gradually rose up, accompanied by the piercing siren of the ambulances followed by dead silence. You came out of the shelter and saw ruins and splattered blood everywhere. And you realized what fate really was. Here you were still standing and your neighbor was dead in the house next door. It had all happened because someone had pushed the bomb-release button a second earlier, or later, than they could have.

This game of lightness and darkness, of silence and noise, went on for a while that early winter. Streetlights, of the kind still manually lit in the evening, were shrouded in heavy felt bags at night. It was also forbidden to have indoor lights showing, and this was reinforced with steep fines. Elena pinned the window drapes closed and covered them with dark sheets to blot away any luminous shreds. The children imagined at times that they were watching a movie except they were also living it. First came the searchlights crisscrossing the sky looking for enemy planes, then the whistle of bombs being dropped, and finally there was the rapid staccato of the defense guns firing.

The "home front" mirrored the battlefield for a while. Horia first, then his father, started burning up with the typhoid fever raging through the city. The child got well rather fast, but his dad lingered in bed for many days, his body heaved by deep chills and greatly weakened. Little Constantin escaped the fever but turned a pale golden hue and started throwing up. The family doctor told Elena the boy had contacted hepatitis through something he must have eaten or drunk. He kept to bed for days and sipped broth and tea, his skin eventually cleared and his energy and appetite returned. The girl, Lelia, by some miracle, stayed well throughout, and so did her mother, the latter perhaps too busy to get sick.

On December 6, 1916, the first German battalions marched into Bucharest and immediately set the city's ammunition depot on fire. It burnt up the hill with a deafening roar, a red glow illuminating the cold winter night for the entire city to see. The children were terrified, but as the rumbling noise began to settle down, curiosity took hold of them. They parted the curtains ever so slightly to witness an awesome sight. Row after row of German soldiers passed their house on horseback, while those on foot marched at a precise clip, clad in gray, long coats with shiny weapons perfectly lined up on their left side.

The Germans took up "court" in the center of the city, and in defiance to the country's ruler installed the field kitchen in the courtyard of the Royal Palace. The citizens of Bucharest used to joke, or lament, depending on mood, about gypsies setting up camps and cooking in the city's parks. Now everyone could stare at how soup was being prepared for the German high command!

The German commander was the famous General August von Mackensen. His nickname, "the breaker of front lines," was due to his many frontal assault successes during the first two years of the war. Constantin and his brother, Horia, would occasionally see him on horseback, surrounded by his entourage and heading for a stroll toward the lakes' district. The mere sight of this legendary man, proudly dressed in his hussar uniform with the traditional hat embroidered with skull and crossing bones, was enough to instill fear in the boys' hearts. But there was also a more human side to the general, as recounted by their father. Upon hearing how the Bulgarians had stolen a priceless collection of Slavic documents and art objects and loaded them up to take them "home," Commander Mackensen had called the border post. The truck had been stopped and the valuables returned to the Bucharest museum.

The German's allies, the Bulgarians, took up residence at the famed Capsa Hotel. The establishment was located in the very heart of the city, just two blocks from the Royal Palace and university. It also housed a restaurant and a pastry shop; it was there that Elena had taken little Constantin to celebrate his admission to high school. The store previously enticing passersby with its aromas of freshly baked goods and warm chocolate stood mostly empty as the shortages of sugar, butter, and cocoa began to be felt in the city.

One night Constantin senior came home early, his faced creased with deep concern. Elena could tell right away that something was amiss. "Elena, children, we are being asked to house a German officer."

"Not in my house, dear. The children are young; they could be harmed if the man has a temper and gets angry with them."

"Dearest, it's an army order we must follow. We have no choice. Children: don't talk unless asked a question. Be brief and polite. Don't say a thing about the gun and no bragging about the food supplies."

The issue of the gun was a particularly thorny dilemma. They had been requested to turn over all weapons: rifles, guns, swords. Despite this edict, Constantin had kept a small revolver, feeling the need to defend his family against an intruder outweighed the risk of being discovered and arrested. He hadn't wanted the children to know. But as luck would have it, the boys happened upon their parents looking for the best hiding place. They were sworn to secrecy, and the parents could only hope the children understood the gravity of the situation.

And so their guest arrived, a stocky middle-aged man from Bavaria with a thick, bushy beard. He was a quiet man who went straight to his room that first night and kept to himself afterwards. His silence put Elena somewhat at ease. She was relieved not having to make small talk, and she really didn't care to play hostess to an unwanted guest. So it would have been overall tolerable had it not been for his smoking habit: his thick, sausage-like cigarettes stank to heaven. The odor soon permeated everything, clung to upholstery, kitchen towels—there was no escaping it. Windows had to be opened in the middle of the winter, with wind and snow colliding with swirls of smoke and canceling each other out. Tempers flared with someone complaining about the cold, odor, or both, time and again.

Elena's worst fear, of being harassed when alone in the house with the man and her little girl, fortunately never materialized. Their guest never made any untoward or inappropriate gestures or remarks. But the unease remained, more like a raw fear. In the evenings she let out her frustrations at having to lodge and help feed a foreigner, the enemy at that, while food was scarce at home.

The war was wearing on everybody and across the continent. German factories had trouble keeping up production to outfit their troops. The farmers couldn't grow enough to feed them. Horses died on the battlefield and there weren't enough replacements. All were hungry and tired, troops and animals alike.

Life in occupied Romania continued to get harder as the Germans requisitioned carriages, horses, and bicycles. A request for metal objects of any kind soon followed. Pots and pans and cauldrons, gates and knobs were melted to make new weapons. Lighting gas was next and had to be turned in, too. It was followed by sugar rationing: a family could keep only five kilos. Elena, normally law-abiding, agonized over the chest with twenty-five kilos of sugar that they had painstakingly stashed away for months. Should she comply with the regulations, despite her worry about the family? Then out of the blue a magnificent idea overtook her: she would set out to make sugar syrup and jam. There were no rules against storing sweet pastes and liquid in bottles and jars! She enlisted the help of the children, and for a couple of days they all boiled sugar and peeled and chopped fruit. Having started to bend the rules, if ever so slightly, she decided that saving a few pots and frying pans wouldn't be all that wrong as long as she handed in the big laundry cauldron.

By Easter the German army's need for more metal became so critical that church bells were removed and melted down. Only one was symbolically left behind for each city. For Bucharest it was the gigantic bell at the Archdiocese, a gift from old King Carol I. He had been gone for barely a couple years but so much had already taken place since his death. Would he have recognized his capital city had he walked about it today? Would he have squinted at the sight of the Germans in residence at the Royal Palace, wondering if his eyes were failing him?

As they entered the new year of 1917, the people of Bucharest felt numb. The city was swarming with Germans troops and food was scarce. News from the front was bad, and the winter was harsh with its short, overcast days and long blustery nights. Most went about the motions of daily living mechanically, mind and body disconnected. Romanians were weary and cold; most worried about tomorrow while some felt too tired to even glance into the future.

Others, like Elena and Constantin, carried on and did their best to maintain a semblance of normalcy for the sake of their children as much as their own. The resilience of their children was encouraging and fed their being, serving them well. The lunch menu may have been monotone, but they still sat down together for meals every day. And while churches may have lost their steeple bells, they still attended service on Sundays.

Their eldest son, Constantin, saw his young world turned upside down in the spring, when his high school was requisitioned by the Germans for troop quarters. Students were temporarily moved to a location not too far from the Giurescu's home, a mere ten minute walk. It was across the street from the Cathedral of Saint Joseph, Bucharest's main Catholic establishment. The building was also across from the Lazar students' "archenemy," the other elite capital school—Saint Sava College—bringing the boys' competition so much closer to home. Most of the students attended classes in this new location, while others had fled with their families to Moldova to escape the occupying army.

The first morning after the move, the headmaster walked in with a visibly distressed face. "Boys, I come here with a heavy heart. I want you to stand and say a prayer for the soul of your classmate, Tommy. He was taken by the typhus that raged north of the front line this winter. His parents had left to keep Tommy safe and ended up burying him far away from home. This is one of the many faces of war, boys, and its real tragedy."

The teenagers looked at one another in disbelief. Tommy? One of them was gone so soon? The war once more felt personal to Constantin, reminding him of Uncle Ionica's death at the Battle of Turtucaia. Staring around the room he saw the sad faces and quite a few tears. He was by no means alone, many of the boys having lost fathers and uncles in the preceding months.

The new school was a short walk from the Central Post Office where daily war communiqués (French, English, Russian, and Italian) were pasted. Young Constantin could have read the news in the dailies brought home every night by his father. But it was so much more interesting to mingle with the crowd gathered at the Central Post, striking up a conversation and getting into a debate. He took to swinging by there almost daily after school, though a feeling of guilt plagued him on many a day. The office wasn't exactly on his way home, and his mother did not want him wandering the streets full of foreign soldiers. If only she could understand that he was almost sixteen years old, practically a young man, she would give him more freedom. Why, he had even heard of boys lying about their age to fight in the war.

The spring term passed without any major war developments while the rumor mill continued unabated. People had heard how the Romanian army was reorganizing, and a major attack was planned for the summer, but it was hard to tell the truth of it. For once the rumor turned out to be accurate. Better equipped now and under the guidance of a military mission headed by French General Berthelot, the Romanians scored two major victories during the summer of 1917. The first was at Marasesti in July; the second was a month later in Oituz. The army was thus able to maintain the front line established seven months earlier and ensure that whatever remained of free Romania (Moldova) stayed unoccupied.

Constantin, Elena, and the boys followed the army's progress on a giant map they had pasted to the dining room wall. That summer they had stayed in town, concerned that the troop movement would have made travel to Grandpa's treacherous. But the excitement of the military victories made summer pass by fast. Fall heralded the arrival of a new study year and the location of their school changed yet again. This time the boys headed up on the hill of the Archdiocese, with Constantin delighted to be farther away from home and relishing his independence.

His mother still worried about him being out and about on the city streets. But with each passing year, Elena felt that she could trust him more and more. He was a good boy, her oldest son. He studied hard and tried to listen to her and his pranks were harmless, just a child's game. She so wished his brother could be more like him! But Horia didn't care for studying, fought with her whenever he had a chance, and listened only to his father—and only because he was afraid of him.

The other news troubling her and many in the fall of 1917 were the events unfolding in Russia. People there had taken to the streets and toppled their ruler, the Tsar. She didn't particularly care who led Russia, but her husband, who understood so much and explained things so well to her, was very concerned. So she added prayers to her list for the Tsar, his wife the Tsarina, and their beautiful children, who were now under house arrest. Suffering and misery of any nature saddened her, and she prayed to God for their safety and release.

"I guess I am still trying to understand what this means for us. We are neighbors and allies, but we are also independent, have our own country," Elena had said.

"There's utter chaos in Russia, dearest. Their armies have abandoned the front lines and will be signing an armistice with Germany."

"But the Russians haven't helped us much. Why should it matter to us?"

"If they allow passage for German troops, we'll be left surrounded by the enemy, that's why."

He was so clever, she thought: it was all obvious once he spelled it out for her.

And indeed, torn by internal strife and the fighting in the larger European conflict, Russia chose to exit the war. A peace treaty with the Central Powers—chiefly Germany—was signed in the town of Brest Litovsk. And just like her husband had predicted, Romania was left isolated with enemies all around her. With no other options, the country was forced to follow suit and sign an armistice with Germany, too. It took place in December 1917 and felt so utterly bitter—the Romanian army's victories during the previous summer reversed with a stroke of the pen. The signing of the armistice ironically took place in Focsani, the city were the Giurescus were married and where their first son was born. King Ferdinand, still in residence in Iasi, Moldova, refused to ratify it.

Terror, bloodshed, and poverty tore through Russia in the aftermath of their so-called proletarian revolution. But in the midst of these vicissitudes lay a silver lining. One of the initial proclamations of the new republic was to allow people of their various territories to decide their future. They were to choose if they wished to remain Russian, or return to the land of their ethnic brothers. And this is how the Romanians living in the province of Bessarabia came to vote by referendum in March, 1918. Their decision: leave what had now become Bolshevik Russia and return to Romania.

Other than this bit of good news, it was grim in Bucharest during the spring of 1918. Both the entrenched Eastern and Western Fronts had not changed significantly in the last year and a half. Worn out by the occupation and food shortages, Romania was forced to sign the equivalent of an end-of-war treaty with the "Central Powers" (Germany, Austro-Hungary and their allies) in early May 1918. The terms of this act known as the "Treaty of Bucharest" were heavy indeed for Romania. Her oil fields, envied by nations around, were to be turned over to the victors. The Germans were also to take control over the country's financial system and were given a "lease" to control the Black Sea ports for "ninety-nine years."

And just as its citizens were trying to mentally adjust to the treaty, Romania's fortunes and those of most of Europe took a turn for the better. The Americans had entered the war the prior year. The presence of their large armies on the Western Front was now proving to be the tipping point in the ordeal that had ravaged the continent for over four years.

Constantin was named secretary of education for Bucharest during the spring of 1918 and his work schedule only intensified, with days blending into one another. The children barely saw him, and Elena waited all day for a little time together in the evening. She often watched him fall asleep early, sometimes in mid-sentence of a conversation. How she longed for their early days in Focsani when he taught high school, and she only worried about having dinner and fresh flowers ready for him. Had it been only seventeen years?

In the summer of 1918, she decided to take the children to Chiojd. With the military action virtually stopped on the Eastern Front they thought the passage safe enough. The children were yearning for open vistas, not having left the confines of the city in two years. But her husband stayed behind: many schools were damaged, teachers had died, books and supplies were scarce for the fall semester

A letter to a cousin would later stand testimony to the man's plight:

"My time is consumed by this honor bestowed upon me by the ministry . . . there are so many hardships and so few available to help . . . I fear we may not win. I do what I can: work, work passionately like never before . . . from 5 A.M. to midnight. The task seems overwhelming . . . and the administrative machine unused to rules and regulations. I am holding on . . . for how long, remains to be seen."

When he joined them in the country a few weeks later, everybody was shocked by his gaunt appearance. From the coach stepped down a pale, thin, tired man whom they hardly recognized.

"Mom, is Dad sick again?"

"No dear, just very, very tired."

Elena couldn't stop worrying, remembering how his recovery from typhus had taken twice as long as Horia's. She feared another illness would find him severely weakened by this nonstop work schedule and unable to fight back. The children worried, too.

"Mom, you don't want to tell us, do you? I really think Dad's sick; why is he sleeping all day long?"

"Sweetie, I told you already, he needs to rest. Let him be and you'll see your Dad again."

Their grandfather was worried, too. He had lost two sons during the war: Uncle Ionica in battle and another to hepatitis, and Constantin was his only remaining child.

"Boy, cut back on work. Is it worth killing yourself now that the Germans didn't? God help you if you fall sick again, you're half of what you were."

After a few days of rest, fresh air and wholesome food, he appeared to regain his vigor and all breathed easier. They said it could happen to anyone, to be depleted once in a while: the main thing was to fully recover. Grandpa, the boys, and little Lelia all agreed: their son and father looked like himself again by the time they headed back home to Bucharest. Elena wasn't quite so certain.

Chapter Six
LOSING BOTH PARENTS

As the war was winding down during the summer and fall of 1918, the epidemic known as the Spanish Flu exploded in Romania too. It had already caused millions of deaths across the planet since the spring and claimed more lives than the war itself. Many thought it had started in Spain, judging from its name, but this was not how the moniker had been earned. With news of all kind generally censored on account of the war, neutral Spain was at liberty to report events as they were unfolding, including the spread of this pandemic. The world first learned of the flu's staggering toll from Spain, and many erroneously inferred the disease had originated there.

Elena's husband was among the first to fall ill. It seemed like the usual cold at first, with fever and sore throat, so nothing was made of it. Soon a heart-wrenching, nonstop cough followed and the fever did not relent. The tall, thin man lay in bed heaving and burning day and night and hardly able to eat or drink. Elena, frantic with worry, did not quit his bedside, ready to attend to his every need. She also feared for the children, who had thus far escaped the disease and who were fending for themselves with the help of a maid.

The family doctor came twice a day, checked his temperature and listened to Constantin's chest. He prescribed cough syrup, advised to keep cold compresses on the patient's chest, and encouraged him to try to drink water and sweet tea. But the doctor mostly shook his head and told Elena he had no medicine to offer. "We must wait for nature to run its course," he would mutter over and over. What old Doctor Oprescu did not share with Elena was his deep apprehension. He was seeing patients die all around him, mostly young adults in seemingly good health. Having been in practice for many years, this new pattern puzzled him. In years past the flu had first killed the old and very young, the children. But this new strain was different and also very lethal. Soon a hush took over the city and funeral corteges became an almost daily sight.

Constantin's children had difficulty grasping the severity of his illness. Why, they had all had colds before and had recovered in no time. Equally upsetting was that they weren't allowed to visit their parent's room, with Elena fearing the spread of disease. Young Constantin, a boy of seventeen now, had an inkling of the deeply troubling situation when he shared news of the illness with his schoolmates. They began averting their gaze and some walked away, avoiding the topic altogether. An old wife's tale suggested that such talk could bring bad luck and jinx you. Or perhaps they had heard of the many who had perished in the past weeks.

One morning Elena sent the boys to church. "Go pray, pray hard, pray from the bottom of your heart, and ask God to spare your father."

They entered the cold, smoky, dark church. It was quiet inside, with no wailing women, nothing to distract them. The boys knelt side by side.

"Dear God, please spare our father. Please let him survive. He takes care of mom and us. He teaches and helps a lot of people. He is a good man, dear God. We'll give you everything we have if you make him well again."

The two shaken boys then lit a candle and placed it in the box for the "living" while carefully avoiding the one for the "departed," such being the tradition of the Greek Orthodox Church. Then they went home hoping for a miracle.

That evening their mother said dad was delirious and nothing he said made sense. Then he went on to cough up blood and his shakes worsened. Elena wept quietly, rubbing his hands and praying by his side. The children went to bed with a heavy heart.

When they awoke the following morning, it was the silence that startled them. No voices, coughing, or heavy breathing came from their parents' room. Young Constantin got up and found his mother sitting by the front window, staring despondently at the passing world. She motioned him to the bedroom door. There lay his father, the ashen face finally at peace, almost illuminated by a smile. The agony of the previous days and the thrashing was over. His forty-three-year-old father was no more.

He turned and silently hugged his mother. She held him tightly for a long time, her face swollen, her eyes rimmed in red and dark circles. She suddenly seemed so much older than the night before. Then he noticed little Lelia tugging her mother's long skirt, looking just as forlorn and lost.

"Go pray for your father's soul," she whispered. "There's nothing else left."

They crossed the street, and in front of the church a profound anguish overtook Constantin. He stared at his brother and shouted, "How could God allow this to happen? Has God forgotten us?" Turning his back on the church door, he went home without another word; from now on he was on his own.

At home there were painful and practical matters to tend to. Elena moved mechanically, as if in a daze, and could hardly eat. It fell to her sister Marie to arrive and help prepare for the funeral. Energetic and determined as always, Marie took hold of the situation and addressed every detail including the task of buying a burial plot at the Bellu Cemetery. It had not crossed the minds of the young couple to be preparing for the final journey, despite the war years.

Constantin was laid to rest on a windy, dreary, wet October day. Family, colleagues, and students gathered around the freshly dug grave to pay homage to the father, husband, and professor. The weather mourned with them as yellow-rust leaves blew about festooning the sad cortege with its wind-swept shroud. Young Constantin and his brother flanked and supported their mother, her swollen face hidden by a thick, black veil. And when the religious ceremony and speeches were over, a grief-stricken Elena could not bear to tear herself away from the enormous pile of flowers and wreaths covering the gravesite. Marie let her mourn for a while then she gently took her arm and guided her sister to the waiting carriage. They rode out in silence, Elena and the boys too heartbroken to utter anything, while Marie couldn't help but notice the many freshly dug graves, testimony to the ravages of the flu and long war. A whole generation had been decimated and countless families, like theirs now, had been devastated in the aftermath.

Had Constantin lived a couple of months longer, he would have seen Romania's dream of becoming whole again come true before Christmas. Late in the war, with Bulgaria defeated, Romania tossed the previously signed treaty with Germany and her allies aside. The army was mobilized and the country reentered the conflict in early November. It was but a day before fighting was officially concluded on the Western Front. From then on events unfolded rapidly.

On November 28, 1918, the people of Bukovina—a province to the north of Moldova—voted for union with the Romanian kingdom.

Three days later, on December 1, representatives of Romanians living in Transylvania gathered in the town of Alba Iulia. There they proclaimed their desire to reunite as well, like their ethnic brothers in Bukovina and those in Bessarabia before them. The Germans living in Transylvania, the so-called Saxons, followed suit two weeks later.

These declarations were officially endorsed by the Versailles Treaties at the end of World War I under the right of national self-determination. At the same time, Germany agreed to renounce all the benefits of the Treaty of Bucharest. At Versailles, Romanian Prime Minister Ionel Bratianu eloquently argued about his country's contribution to the war in 1916–1917. He emphasized how her efforts had stalled and eventually dampened the Austro-German eastern exodus. And this is how it came to be that all lands with a majority of Romanian-speaking citizens were reunited for the first time in over three hundred years. The dream had become a reality and the losses—too many to count—had not been in vain. But for Constantin Sr., it had come all too late.

As for his son and namesake, he went to watch the Victory Parade in central Bucharest in December, 1918, which heralded the official end of the war. In the preceding weeks, the Germans had started leaving and dismantling their stores and depots. Many had been afraid of clashes with the local citizens, but that never materialized and the retreat was mostly orderly. On the day of the parade, Constantin and Horia joined delirious, swelling crowds in cheering their war heroes. They watched Romanian, French, and British soldiers being showered with flowers and draped with flags. They saw faces shedding tears of joy but also of despair at the lives lost, and in their midst the boys felt less alone.

Elena was crying when they got back home, having just returned from the cemetery, which she visited almost daily. She tried hard to keep her composure, for the sake of the children. But at times she simply couldn't contain her grief and despair. Money was tight and so the maid was let go. Elena cooked, cleaned, mended clothes, and helped Lelia with her homework. She who used to sing while going about her household chores was silent now. Whereas before she would bounce from room to room and task to task, her motions now acquired a certain mechanical rhythm and little by little she began to wither away. Marie's hopes that her sister would rally for the sake of the children gradually faded as well. Elena was, simply put, devastated by her loss and her depression deepened with each passing month. Doctor Oprescu tried various tonics and visited often to check in on her. But after a while he too had to admit that potions and good intentions were incapable of mending such a broken heart.

There were days when Constantin woke up hoping that his father's death and its aftermath had all been a nightmare. Would he awake to find his father smiling and mother singing? Then he would see Elena standing in the kitchen—a thin, pale, sad woman absentmindedly buttering her toast—and he knew the bad dream was a poignant reality.

The boy had for years wanted to become an engineer, having always enjoyed mathematics. While his dad lay dying, he decided instead to pursue history and follow in his father's footsteps. Could his choice have been driven by grief and desire to honor the man now gone? It could have easily been seen that way, but now, months after his decision, he continued to contemplate his new direction with clarity. Watching momentous historical events unfold had stirred a passion in him. Yes, this was what he desired and had to do. He felt this course would give life a renewed purpose and make it worthwhile again. But the regret of not having shared his intentions with his father lingered. Once he felt certain, he shared the news with his mother. "Mom, I've decided to pursue admission exams to study history. I really feel the pull."

Elena managed a weak smile, her face a little more animated. "The joy it would have brought your father. How you two could have written side by side."

And despite this momentary lift, she continued to fade away.

One day he returned home to find his mother collapsed on the couch, too weak to go about doing her chores. Lelia, who was now nine years old, held Elena's hand and kept begging her, "Get up mommy. I am hungry; please get up."

Elena's eyes were shut, though not asleep. Constantin gently squeezed her hand and whispered, "Let's put you to bed, mom; you need some rest." Then he sent his brother with a word to Aunt Marie. "Say I need her as soon as possible." Hours later she was at her nephew's side. The hope she had harbored for months—that her sister would recover for the sake of the children—was gone. Now she had to concede that something had to be done, and mother and children alike needed to be taken care of. Marie tried, the best she could, to involve Elena in all the decisions. But the more they talked, the more Elena seemed to drift away. This continued until Marie finally uttered the words she had dreaded to voice for a while, "Would you like to go away, dear, and try to rest and regain your energy?"

To her surprise her sister did not put up an argument. "Would be best for everyone, wouldn't it?" she muttered. Her sad, empty smile broke Marie's heart.

Elena was to go to a monastery not too far from Focsani. The nuns there would take care of her and try to get her to eat and rest and perhaps a miracle would take place.

As for the children, Marie sat down with Constantin. "Boy, your mother needs to rest if she is to get well. You are now the head of the family, and you and I need to make some decisions. I always say it's best to sleep it on it, and so we'll talk tomorrow morning."

The young man felt numb, first his father and now his mother going away. Who would take care of Lelia? Should his brother go to military school as was his wish? Would Mom ever be back? He wished he could pray and get some answers or hope. But then he remembered God's deaf ear while his father lay dying. "I'm truly on my own now, aren't I?" he asked, not waiting for an answer.

Constantin went to sleep with a heavy heart. He woke up the following morning and decided that his sister would go to live with Aunt Marie and her husband. They had recently moved to Bucharest, lived nearby, had no children, and were welloff. With Marie's husband retired from the army, both had ample time on their hands. His brother, Horia, should pursue military school as was his wish; he had never liked studying anyway. As for his mother, Constantin knew deep down that she would never recover but kept that to himself. Telling Aunt Marie would only upset her further.

Elena remained at the monastery and passed away less than a year later in 1920 at the age of forty-one. They were told she had died of typhoid fever and its complications, but Constantin knew better: his mother had died of a broken heart.

He was nineteen and alone.

Around him the country was free and whole again and her king returned to Bucharest. The Royal Palace reverted back to being just that, no longer used as the German's field kitchen. Romania's citizens didn't wake up dreading the news of the day. Nor were they compelled to rush to the Central Post Office to view the latest military updates and casualty reports.

Despite the initial political and administrative difficulties of governing the reunited territories, gains were slowly made. Great expectation was kindled in the hearts of the people, especially among the peasants who had been promised a vast land reform by the king. It didn't happen overnight, but little by little Bucharest and its people were regaining the pace of life without war. Food shortages eased up after the first post-war year. Streets and homes were lit again at night, and church bells were gradually being replaced. Cafes, beer gardens, and restaurants with open-air terraces popped up around the city. People were eager to get together over a coffee or drink and hear a little easy music. They wished to chat, share their losses and to move on the best they could.

The Germans were gone and the memories of earth-shattering air raids were fading away. One was no longer afraid to venture outside, and so people took to walking the city's grand boulevards with relish, even if no particular business called them to "the center." Cars started showing up on city streets, though trams were still drawn by horses on their twelve routes and would remain so until the mid-1920s. On many winter days you still saw horse-drawn sleds on the snow-covered streets, particularly in the area bordering on the Lake District.

The city had woken up and it was alive again.

Had it not been for his father's passing, young Constantin would have probably lingered after class with his friends. Or they may have headed to the Cismigiu Park for a lemonade or ice cone or taken in a "picture." But the young man now had more pressing concerns. The nineteen-year-old high school student had previously been preparing for a mathematics and physics major. He could have continued upon this path and become an engineer. A university degree would have been followed perhaps by a doctorate in Germany, which was at the forefront of the mechanical advances in the 1920s. He might have then carried out a lifetime of methodical labor, and his occupation would have stayed in demand despite the turning tide of the country's regime. The nature of his work would have been devoid of any political dimension, its precision not lending itself to controversies. He would have of course married and had children. Many years later, with the century winding down, he would have smiled upon his large family and raised a toast to their good fortunes. And he would have attributed all this to his early love of mathematics.

It could have happened this way, but it wasn't meant to be. Young Constantin had felt the tug of history pulling at his sleeve even before his father's passing. In practical terms it meant he now needed to defend a Bachelor in Arts (rather than the Sciences) prior to reading history at the university. That in turned translated into an additional study load in his last high school year. The task was difficult enough, but unfortunately the boy didn't have only scholastic concerns. Financial pressures were mounting as the Romanian currency was precipitously devalued and inflation skyrocketed after the war. His father's pension, which would have been generous in years past, was barely adequate for the boy's few needs. So he had to learn to budget himself carefully, aided by the "family council" in charge of the estate. He was relieved knowing his sister was well taken care of by Aunt Marie, and his brother, Horia, was away at military school (where tuition covered living expenses as well).

Constantin had decided to stay in their family home. A woman by the name of Sofia was hired to look after him. She came daily to buy and prepare his food and also cleaned, washed, and mended clothes. The boy spent long days in school and at a library, and the thought of a warm meal awaiting him at home was of great comfort. Sofia tidied the kitchen and glanced around the house before leaving around 7:00 P.M. It was after her departure that the dead, surrounding silence hit him hard. There he sat alone, and with the eyes closed he could almost hear his mom's laughter, his father's baritone voice, and even Horia's bickering.

But Constantin was fortunately blessed with a practical spirit quite unusual for his young age. He literally took things a day at a time and gradually steeled himself against remorse. He kept repeating to himself, "A day at a time, a day at a time now," and "worry only about tomorrow." He had no barter with questions no one could answer and instead plunged into work.

One of the requirements needed for the Bachelor in Arts degree was a proficiency in Greek. It not being offered at his school, so he decided to attend a university course offered by Professor Parvan, who was an eminent historian, archeologist, and friend of his father. The boy put on his best suit, mustered all the courage, and went to see the professor, nicknamed "the maestro" by his students.

"Professor Parvan, sir, thank you so much for receiving me. I am here to ask permission to attend your Greek language course in preparation for my exams."

"Mr. Giurescu, indeed. It is a pleasure to meet you. I was a sincere admirer of your father, and his premature passing has been a tragic loss for all of us."

"Professor, I hope to follow in his path and read history this fall. Father died before I could share my decision and I shall always regret it. But I'll try to carry on and make him proud."

"Well, there you have it then. Mr. Giurescu, welcome. The course opens on October 15." And the professor, a man of few words himself, left it at that and took leave of the young man.

Constantin would never forget the professor's inaugural lecture. It was dedicated to the memory of those who perished in the war, heroes who made the ultimate sacrifice so the country could be reunited. The auditorium was packed, including parents who had lost their children. There were women in all black, some still wearing the thick veil of mourning, and men in suits and hats with black ribbons pinned to their left arm. With the faculty, students, and visitors, every seat was filled.

Professor Parvan entered the room—a tall, thin man in a severe coat with high collar. The silence was absolute; you could have heard a pin drop. In his measured baritone, he delivered a moving eulogy: ". . . with their young years, they multiplied the endless years of the country. Sleep in peace, my children, sleep in peace."

Everyone stood up at the end, most brought to tears. The professor himself had profound pain etched on his face, from the memory of the wife and child lost to typhoid fever during the winter of 1916–1917. A room stood united in sorrow, another proof of how raw and deep the wounds of war still festered. To Constantin this was a reminder that he was not alone in his grief.

Aunt Marie also tried to make him feel less lonely. She dropped in on the boy at least once a week, and on Sundays the family took lunch together. This weekly lunch was a rather formal affair. The dining table was dressed with good china and silver, a lace tablecloth, and fresh flowers in the center. Three-course meals were served: soup, meat with potatoes, and a rich homemade dessert such as dumplings filled with jam or fruit tarts. There was lemonade for the children and wine for the grownups. Interesting conversation was expected and table manners were scrutinized.

Little Lelia seemed to be adjusting quite well to her new surroundings. She was a quiet child, rather like her oldest brother. The girl applied herself in school where she did almost as well as him. But she so missed her mother who had always been by her side. Yes, she envied her brothers, who had grown up together and with their parents. But, like Constantin, and despite her young age, she tried to steel herself and not dwell on the past.

Marie ruled the household with a sharp tongue, though it was her husband who had been in the military. One day she decided Constantin was too shy and lonely, and so made it her business to invite a distant niece to Sunday lunch. Amelia was seventeen years old, sweet and beautiful, with wavy black hair and blue eyes. She provided a light note to their somewhat somber gathering, sitting prettily across from Constantin in a cascade of pink ruffles, her hair tied in a ribbon of the same color. She smiled easily, though she clearly seemed to have no idea what her hosts and her young cousin were talking about at times. But on and on the boy talked about his Greek studies, and how he was embarking upon writing his first article. To Amelia it all sounded foreign, rather like Greek itself.

With lunch over, Amelia and her parents took leave after profusely thanking their hostess. Aunt Marie walked them to the door and said her goodbyes. Then she turned around and stormed back in the dining room. "Boy, you sat there going on about your Greek. And you didn't happen to notice how you made Miss Amelia yawn?" She paused to gather herself. "Here I am making an effort to introduce you to a fine young lady, and you waste our time."

"Aunt, I have exams coming up; I've no time for girls right now."

She smirked. "Like father, like son. I never understood what your mother saw in that bookworm."

Hurt by that slight, the young man wisely let it go. He knew that continuing the exchange would only inflame his aunt further. He shortly took leave as well, secretly relieved that his lack of attention had ruled out an invitation to take tea with Amelia's parents.

With nothing further to distract him, reading and studying occupied his final year of high school. The boy's efforts were rewarded when in June he passed the full complement of exams and was awarded a Bachelor in Arts degree. He was headed to the university.

PART II
A YOUNG MAN

Chapter Seven
THE PROFESSOR'S DAUGHTER, MARIA

The University of Bucharest was an imposing, classically built, severe stone building in the very center of the city. It presided there at the intersection of two of the town's main arteries. The Boulevard Queen Elisabeth was named after King Carol's I wife who had been greatly admired by her people, while the Avenue Bratianu took its name from the family at the head of the Liberal Party, a true political "dynasty." The Royal Palace was a mere ten-minute walk away, and the "Military Circle," where the commanders of the armed forces socialized, took meals, and watched shows, was across the street. Many theaters, hotels, and restaurants dotted this fashionable city center.

As for the university, it was spread over the equivalent of a couple of street blocks, housing many departments—Literature, Languages, History, Geography, Philosophy, etc. over several floors. A doorman in uniform, including gloves and cap, stood by the front door, rain or shine. He knew the faculty members by name and greeted them with great respect while the students were whisked away with a cursory hand motion. Back then schools went back in session on September 15, and graduate schools followed two weeks later. October 1, 1919, Constantin's first day at the university, was one of mixed emotions. There was satisfaction at embarking upon his chosen path, but also sadness at not being able to share the moment with his dad. His father's colleagues, friends, and foes treated him with compassion, even pity at first. But, as months went by, he became just another student.

The boy felt he needed to work harder than the others, much harder. The need to prove that he hadn't fallen into this specialty because of his father's prominence was never far from his thoughts. Some critics would years later malign him by claiming he had taken over his father's unpublished manuscripts. But in the beginning, they were willing to postpone judgment. As for his peers, at first some of the other students felt awkward around him. Many had lost fathers in the war, but few if any had gone through the agony of losing both parents. As time passed their attitude didn't seem to affect him and so little was made of it. He became one of them, eating cafeteria meals together, and studying late in the library. Some gradually became friends; friendships with Victor Papacostea and Alex Rosetti were to last a lifetime.

The class embarking upon their studies that fall of 1919 counted among its ranks students from the recently reunited lands of Transylvania and Bessarabia. It was the first time these young men were free to study in their native tongue, alongside their Romanian brothers. On occasions such as an inaugural course day or holidays, some struck a colorful chord in folk garb indicating their county home. Though young men formed the majority of the student body, there were also several women who read History alongside Constantin. They proved to be serious and hardworking, and some teachers thought they applied themselves more than the men. Zoe Bals stood out among them. Not only was she beautiful in the classical style of a Byzantine mosaic but also excelled at her studies. The first year she shared half of the prize instituted by Professor Parvan in memory of his wife and child while the other half was awarded to Constantin.

In the 1920s a university education was a serious business and surrounded itself in decorum. Teachers and students alike wore suits and tie and shoes were carefully polished. The educators often walked through the front gates in hats and gloves, and an umbrella and coat were added depending on the season. A teacher's mere presence demanded respect. Questions required answers. Answers needed to be based on facts, and facts had to be known "cold." Professor Onciu was legendary for his rigorous protocol; when a student enounced a personal opinion, the professor thundered from the podium:

"What is the base of your statement? Where is the document?" His severe and rigid demeanor was also backed by his appearance: a heavyset man with a beard, moustache, and wavy, leonine hair. Many shuddered and Constantin always prepared diligently for Onciu's classes, afraid he would be caught without proper documentation. His father had been in the professor's first class at the university; the son would turn out to be in the last one.

Other teachers also stood out but none was as revered, admired, and beloved as Professor Parvan, "the maestro." To the young men he symbolized all they aspired to be: a scholar, educator, and patriot. To Constantin (and his father before him), he was also a devoted friend. When Elena passed away, he offered Constantin a part-time position of research assistant at the National Museum, knowing the young man was in dire need of a supplemental income. The professor had thus wanted to alleviate his financial worries so time could be devoted to studies. Until the time of his passing in 1927, Professor Parvan was never far away from his star pupil's academic career.

Constantin continued to enjoy learning and opted for a history major and geography minor. Already fluent in German and French, he also elected to take one year of Italian. He had noticed how some of the older documents regarding the Romanian territories were in that language and thought it would come in handy. And rather in a hurry, he decided to graduate in three rather than the customary four years, eager to embark upon professing his craft. The task was possible, providing approval was granted by the Faculty Council and that all requisite courses were passed. His professors looked askance at this overachiever, tacitly rolling their eyes.

"Sure, you could try that. Practically no one has succeeded doing it in years, but why not try," the teachers being certain that the young man's enthusiasm would exceed his stamina.

Having chosen geography as a minor, he could never have guessed the dramatic impact of that decision on the rest of his life. The dean of the geography chair was Professor Simon Mehedinti, who organized the school's year-end field trips. Students and faculty explored together various parts of the country, visiting towns, villages, battlefields, and ruins. There they drafted detailed maps of remote areas, mapped ore mines and salt excavations, and drew the depths and courses of rivers.

Constantin had saved his money throughout that first year. University tuition was free; books were borrowed from the library, and he didn't pay rent. He had put aside whatever he could, dreaming of a summer trip outside the city, the first in over two years. While waiting to find out the destination, he could barely contain his excitement. But when told they would be sailing the Danube, memories of his first ride on the river with his parents brought a passing cloud of sadness.

On the chosen departure day, the professor, students, and other guests gathered at the train station. It was awfully hot and crowded, with everyone pushing and shouting at the same time. Peasants with heavy baskets of fruit and live chickens in cages, pickpockets, and well-dressed couples in day travel suits were crammed on the narrow platforms scurrying to reach their assigned cars. With the chaotic embarkation over, they rode to the town of Giurgiu and boarded the ship. From there they were headed west to retrace in reverse order the journey undertaken by Constantin and his parents some thirteen years earlier. The first day on board was one of mixed emotion, with the happiness of being on the water deeply overshadowed by a stop at Turtucaia where his beloved uncle Ionica had perished in battle four years earlier.

On the second night onboard, the weather was balmy and calm. Constantin went up to the deck and saw a small group of students in the midst of a lively conversation. He approached them and spotted a tall, striking-looking young woman beside the professor. She had dark hair and piercing dark eyes, but the most striking feature was the intensity of her gaze. The yellow hue of her dress and the gentle ruffles around her neckline provided a lively contrast to her hair and eyes. He quietly stepped forward and listened in, and after a while the professor noticed the young man, motioning him closer.

"Mr. Giurescu, I don't believe you've met my daughter Maria."

"Pleasure, Miss Maria," was all he could utter, bowing his head, shyness battling the desire to stare at her lovely features. He felt his reply sounded rather inadequate but left it at that, afraid of making a silly or socially inappropriate reply. "Tongue always tied," he told himself, "why can't I think of something clever?"

"The pleasure is mine, Mr. Giurescu," is what he heard back while a smile illuminated that pretty face, the gaze focused upon her new acquaintance.

As for the professor, with his host duty adequately fulfilled, he was now able to turn his attention to the group. It had been a dry summer, and the animated gathering was deploring the ongoing drought and its effect on the future crop harvest. Constantin could not help but remember his lunch with "Miss Amelia" at Aunt Marie's. His talk about the Greek language course had made the poor girl yawn. What were these men doing here, talking of droughts and poor crops in front of such a lovely young lady? He was desperately searching for a line to direct the conversation to more mundane topics when one of the students posed a question.

"Perhaps we should ask Miss Maria what her opinion is, now that we've talked our heads off. You have been most kind and patient, Miss."

And no one was more surprised than Constantin when the young woman proceeded to share her views.

"Gentlemen, the grain crop is suffering, and so are people and animals. Crops are down, so we'll have less money to buy and plant seeds next year. At our vineyard we are looking at sturdier grape species for the future, those that do well with less water."

With a concise delivery she had showed her clear understanding of the topic; her remarks were in sharp contrast to the loud and haphazard debate of the young men.

Her father somehow sensed the group's surprise. "Now, now gentlemen, I say you don't argue with Maria here. She spends every summer at our country estate riding around the fields and chatting with everyone in her path. She's done her homework!"

He glanced around and sensed the young men's continuing unease. Were they expected to reply and say something clever? Would changing the topic of conversation altogether be a better course? He rescued the group once more. "I think it is time now to head to dinner, wouldn't you agree, gentlemen?"

Professor Mehedinti now led the group to the dining room. Maria was seated at her father's table, where they were joined by two other senior teachers. Constantin was positive she hadn't been there the first night as he couldn't have possibly missed such a lovely sight. He tried to glance once in a while toward the professor's table, but others obstructed his view. As for the young men, they sat together in small groups, had spirited discussions, and enjoyed a fine meal, followed by coffee and cigars.

When Constantin went to bed later that evening, sleep was slow in coming. He kept replaying in his mind the brief and prosaic encounter on the deck. Thoughts of Miss Maria swirled around him, and images of her striking figure flashed in front of his eyes. He had read about moments like this and had thought them an author's fabrication, the stuff of romantic reads. "So it does happen," he told himself: he had suddenly fallen in love.

As days passed he began to think that Maria might have taken a liking to him, too. They sailed and toured together for almost a month and were always surrounded by others, but hardly a day went by without their eyes locking. He would search for her in a gathering only to sense her staring back, to his surprise. They exchanged pleasantries with one another and, always in a group, discussed the merits of the sites visited. And though nothing personal was said, once the trip was over Constantin returned home with his heart feeling the flutter of the happiness to come.

Seeing her back in Bucharest turned out to be easier than one might have thought. Maria's father, Professor Mehedinti, held weekly "salons" at his house after the fashion of the times. He was the editor-in-chief of the *Literary Conversations*, a monthly which set the tone for the Romanian literary movement at the end of the nineteenth and beginning of the twentieth century. The attendance at salons was eclectic: writers, professors, politicians, wealthy industrialists, and actors. Students were also included, particularly the "promising" ones. Constantin was fortunate enough to be asked to attend on a fairly regular basis. All milled around while the hosts provided refreshments such as sandwiches and drinks. The conversation flowed from group to group, covering the events of the days, the exchange of ideas occasionally punctuated by loud disagreements.

"Mr. Lovinescu, it is such a pleasure to see you here. I didn't know you attended these salons!" said an imposing gentleman addressing the budding literary critic.

"I myself am surprised to see you here, too, Professor Iorga . . . but utterly delighted."

"Have you heard that Mr. Marghiloman is back in town?"

"Are you certain? I thought he had taken refuge in Buzau, hiding after the debacle of the Treaty of Bucharest." The gentleman was referring to the part played by former Prime Minister Marghiloman in negotiating the peace treaty with the Central Powers in 1918.

In another corner of the room, the editor of *Literary Conversations* was holding court.

"All of Bucharest is heading to Alba Iulia to the coronation. The special church has been completed and people say it is quite a jewel."

"Have you heard what the expected dress code is?"

"Morning coat and tall hat for the gentlemen and day dress for the ladies, with hats a must, too."

While nearby a more heated discussion could be heard, of a very different kind:

"His latest poems are disturbing . . . there is no rhyme to the verses."

"Yes, there is, but it is inconsistent."

"Precisely. It sounds truncated; it simply doesn't flow."

"Yes, it does, and his poetry is so much more complex for it. Are you stuck in the last century expecting every line to be of the same length and to rhyme?"

Such was the buzz of the room. In the meantime the hostess oversaw the maids passing trays of finger sandwiches, assorted cookies, lemonade, and glasses of wine. The highlight of the evening usually was a writer's reading from their latest novel or collection of poems.

Maria would glide around the room on such occasions: tall, slim, and elegantly dressed. She listened intently to the debates of important guests, never showing boredom, never interrupting. The evenings offered her and Constantin opportunities to talk. And while yet again surrounded by others, they would at times find a quiet corner or take a stroll in the large garden and continue their lively conversation away from the gathering.

It was on a still, warm, fall day she had first suggested, "Why don't we step out for a moment, Mr. Giurescu? I feel I need a bit of fresh air; it's rather stifling inside. . . ."

Grateful, he jumped at the suggestion and followed Maria through the salon's double doors. He had not yet seen the garden and a true paradise awaited him: tall, full oaks and bushes shielded them from the sanatorium located right behind. The roses had long shed their delicate petals, but rust and yellow chrysanthemums were coming into their fall prime. The young man felt suddenly uncertain of himself: it was so much easier to make small talk when surrounded by others. With her uncanny sense of timing, Maria provided him with the perfect opener. "Father's salons are brilliant and stimulating, but I get a bit tired once in a while. That's when I need to come into my garden and stare at the sky. . . ."

"So true, Miss Maria. One needs to take a rest once in a while, just enough time to reflect upon the discussions."

"Are you heading back to the library later this evening? You often tend to leave us rather early."

Good, he told himself; she had taken notice of him. "Not tonight, Miss Maria. Winter will be upon us before too long. I'd be amiss not to enjoy this balmy evening for a while longer."

She flushed slightly, her cheeks the color of a pale pink blush rose while a small smile illuminated his face. And it wasn't so much what was said but more what was implied, and in due time the young man understood his feelings were reciprocated. Luck appeared to have finally smiled upon him, as unbelievable as it was. Maria had seemingly chosen him, a poor student with an unfashionable receding hairline.

Constantin was also introduced to the hostess of these gatherings; Maria had been named after her mother. This formidable lady was the daughter of a very wealthy landowner, Mr. Cicei. He had been born in Transylvania, which was part of the Austro-Hungarian Empire at the time. Then he had moved to Romania and bought a vast estate in the second half of the nineteenth century. Of his several children, only Maria and two sisters survived into adulthood. They had been educated at a "girls' school," just like Elena, after the fashion of the times. When it came time to get married, their unions were arranged, such was often the practice in those days. One married a wealthy landowner and their fortunes doubled overnight. Another one didn't fare as well, her military husband spending all of her money over the years at horse races.

As for Maria, his youngest daughter, her father decided to unite money with the prestige of academia. He settled on Simion Mehedinti, an up-and-coming geography professor at the university, active on the literary front and a member of the Conservative Party. Father and daughter had attended a party given by a prominent author and on the way home Maria had asked: "Which one am I supposed to marry, father?" such being girls' obedience in those days.

Simion, born in 1868, hailed from a village in southern Moldova named Soveja. Simion's exceptional academic abilities and persistent studying (including earning a PhD in geography in Germany) had propelled him early on to the top of his profession. When he married Maria, her substantial dowry enabled them to buy a large house in Bucharest and a vineyard with a country house. Thus they settled into the comfortable lifestyle of the Romanian upper middle class crossing the bridge between the nineteenth and twentieth centuries. The husband was able to focus on his scientific work without financial worries. The wife entertained and oversaw the country estate and their town home. Two children were soon born: Maria was first in 1903, named after both parents—Maria Simona. Her brother, Emil, followed two years later.

Constantin gathered early on that Mrs. Mehedinti was de facto ruler of the house, just like his aunt Marie was in hers. She did that efficiently aided by a sharp tongue, an iron fist, and the help of a cook and two maids. Her house was impeccably decorated in a Romanian traditional style. The visitor coming in through the imposing front door would have been taken with the beautifully carved oak furniture, embroideries, ceramic dishes, and vases full of fresh flowers. The mistress would make her daily rounds, from the kitchen in the basement to the top floor, checking up on supplies and menus. On many a day one would see her storming into her husband's study. There he was, sitting in deep thought, surrounded by books and papers.

"Simion, it's the cook again! I asked her to fetch a leg of lamb from the market, and she brought back the greasiest one I've ever seen. My sister's coming for dinner, and what will they think, that we have no money left for a fine cut of meat?"

The professor, normally a mild-mannered man, hated to have his work routine disrupted by mundane matters. On such an occasion he would launch into a bilingual Romanian-German tirade, venting his own frustrations.

It was Mrs. Mehedinti that Constantin worried about during his courtship. Yes, it was certainly her, as the professor was often too absorbed in his work to notice social subtleties during the salons. But his wife would pop in out of nowhere on such occasions and quickly scan the room, sometimes nodding to herself. Nothing had yet been said, yet he could have sworn she had detected the undercurrent between her daughter and a certain young man.

As weeks and then months went by, Constantin and Maria started going on walks, sometimes taking a cake or ice cream. The first time he came to call on Maria on his own, he found her mother sitting in the salon and busying herself with a lace crochet. Maria was also there, absentmindedly leafing through a magazine. Mrs. Mehedinti's gaze bore sharply on the young man. He mustered all the courage he could and after a few formal pleasantries uttered, "I am here to invite Miss Maria to join me for a walk to the lakes."

"Let me ask her," said the grand lady, as if her daughter wasn't seated next to her.

"I heard him as well as you did, mother," Maria's replied. "It will be my pleasure, Mr. Giurescu," she added.

Maria almost ran out of the room while Constantin took polite leave. "She treats me like a mute child!" Maria almost shouted the moment they were out of the house.

"Now, Miss Maria, she is trying to shelter you. By the way, may I call you Maria?"

"Certainly. So I may call you Constantin then?"

He breathed a bit easier. They had at least crossed this first layer of formality. The itinerary had been carefully planned ahead: a tram ride to the entrance of the park, followed by a leisurely stroll and ice cream by the lake. But after witnessing Maria's anger upon being treated like an absent participant, he decided to consult her. "Would a tram ride to the park suit you? We would be fresh by the time we arrive and able to take a longer walk. It would also save us time."

"That sounds perfect."

It was a glorious spring day with the sun shining brightly in the midst of a clear, blue sky. Lilac was blooming; the daffodil and tulip buds were opening up, and the grass had the fresh green color of renewal. To the young people it felt as if nature celebrated their good fortune and hope hung imperceptibly in the air.

They chatted for a while about the flowers, the grey-blue color of the lake, and the like. Maria felt emboldened enough to tackle a more personal question, "What about your parents? You've never said anything about them."

A deep silence was followed by a brief answer. "They're both gone, I'm afraid."

Maria was at a loss for words; how was it possible that her father had never shared with her the plight of the young man? "Oh, father," she thought, "always absentminded like a mad scientist."

It was as if Constantin understood her unease and added, "I usually don't talk about this. Many, of course, know at the university, and I don't want the others to feel sorry for me. My father died of the Spanish Flu right after the war in 1918. Mother followed him two years later."

She stared at him. He did seem older than his years, and now she understood: he had grown up fast out of necessity.

"You're very courageous. And father says you are also very bright. Be careful, that can be quite a dashing combination!"

In just a stroke of conversation she had managed to soften his sorrow enough to bring about a half smile. He thought to himself, "Me, quite dashing, who would have thought."

Emboldened, he gently touched her elbow and led her to the refreshment stand. It stood next to the pavilion where military-style music was played on Sunday afternoons and on holidays. There were jam-filled pastries, butter cookies, ice cream and lemonade from which to choose. Constantin enjoyed eating, but conscious of his perhaps too healthy appetite, let Maria choose first.

"I'll have a strawberry-filled pocket, some chocolate ice cream ... oh yes, please also add some whipped cream to that, and of course, lemonade."

He was relieved: here was a young woman with a healthy appetite and he needn't be embarrassed by his own choices! They sat convivially on a bench facing the lake, made small talk, and savored their sweets. Then they strolled leisurely to the nearby Minovici Villa, a true architectural jewel. Its graceful lines were in the style of the Romanian eighteenth century and its fame lay in the myriad little bells whistling in the gentle breeze. Under the clear blue sky the bells and the hearts of the young couple sang softly in unison.

By the time Maria was escorted home, their cheeks were flushed and their faces were smiling. Mrs. Mehedinti looked them over and told herself: "It's hopeless; they must have fallen in love . . . how unsophisticated." Then she rolled her eyes, the grand lady having remained a staunch believer in the value of arranged marriages. "Why," she would ponder, "look at how perfectly well my life had turned out for me."

And so it was innocent enough at first, two young people strolling side by side and getting to know one another, until the day when both understood they were to become one in the future. After months of walks, too many cakes to count, and a few silent pictures, Maria felt emboldened enough to ask one day, "I would like to accompany you to the cemetery when you next place flowers at your parents' graves."

They young man nodded silently and gave her hand a gentle squeeze. She would never know his parents, but Maria wanted to acknowledge her respects at their resting place. This thoughtfulness brought her even closer to his heart, "As if that could be possible." A week later, standing together side by side and watching her place a bouquet of white lilies over the marble plaques bearing his parents' names, he felt a strange peace. Past and future stood side by side, separated by the dew-covered, sun-streaked soil.

They were secretly engaged three years later the old-fashioned way, with Constantin on one knee professing his affection, asking her to be his wife and promising to always love and protect her. They vowed to get married as soon as Constantin's financial resources would enable him to officially ask for Maria's hand. In the custom of the day, a young man was expected to be able to support, besides love and cherish, his betrothed. They also decided not to share the news with the family, afraid that Maria's mother might do her utmost to derail their plans. As for the ring he presented her with, it would remain hidden in Maria's jewelry box, away from her mother's prying eyes.

It was shortly before this secret engagement that Constantin graduated from the university in three years (instead of four), just as he had set out to do. He had worked hard, long hours and had enjoyed every minute of it, being truly blessed with a passion for history. The hard part was deciding now which path to embark upon. Teaching, hardcore research in the archives, and fieldwork equally captivated him.

He briefly toyed with the idea of focusing on archeology. It harked from the summer following his second year of studies when he had assisted maestro Parvan at Histria, the remnant of a Greek colony long gone. Excavations had started there a few years earlier. The professor's office, the staff's living quarters, and the space which exhibited the newly found artifacts were all housed in the same modest building. Constantin would always recall the evening of his arrival at Histria:

a deserted land, the fading light shrouding the ruins in mystery. The weeks spent there were among the happiest of his studies.

Back in Bucharest later that fall and in his third and last year of studies, he went into Professor Parvan's office one evening. He found the maestro poring over the pages of his latest textbook, which he had just received back from the editor.

"Oh, young man, so I'll have to labor all alone over the proofs and write up the indices," he jokingly said.

"Professor, it'll be my pleasure to assist you." In the weeks to come Constantin once again felt the pull of methodical research while assisting his teacher. Eventually he decided upon a future course of action as the final year at the university progressed, after much deliberation and discussion with his mentors. Professor Onciu, the one who always asked for documents and historic proof, was instrumental in advising him. When the young man professed his indecision, Onciu thundered, "You sit for a PhD and go on teaching, that's what you are going to do." Later on Constantin heard how the same professor had confided in a colleague. "That boy will one day occupy my chair at the university." It was thus settled: he would pursue a doctoral degree, as early as feasible, and would eventually teach and write.

After graduation and while waiting to embark upon the next step, he started working as a research assistant at the National Museum, finally able to earn some badly needed money. His assignment was to catalogue the many objects, books, and paintings previously stored there and often exhibited haphazardly. In doing so he saw the symmetry to his father's work. But it also reminded him of the day when Uncle Ionica had taken him and his brother to see the historical artifacts at the antiquities museum in Constanta.

The life's circle was coming back around as the hopes and dreams of one generation were carried on by the next. And everything seemed suddenly possible since he had met Maria.

Chapter Eight
STUDIES IN PARIS

Constantin graduated from the university in 1923 with a dual major in history and geography. Five years had already flown by since the passing of his father, and his mother had been gone for three years. Sometimes it felt like a lifetime, but most days he woke up wavering on the edge of a happy dream as if they had just taken leave. He thought of them often, wondering how life would have turned out if the dice had rolled differently. His dad would have had so much advice, and perhaps they would have written or done research together. His mother's laugh would have been there at the end of the day, and he was certain she would have loved Maria. The hurt of their enormous loss never went away. But the same pain gradually, imperceptibly, steeled his resolve. He couldn't change the past but understood it was up to him to shape the future and honor the memory of his parents. So he set about it methodically, the same way he approached any task, big or small.

That is not to say that the enthusiasm and idealism of youth didn't lightly stroke his student years. Patriotic feelings were strongly stirred in the aftermath of the war and the reunion of the lands inhabited by Romanians. Constantin joined some of his colleagues at a few meetings of the National Liberal Youth Club. Each gathering debated a different topic and members often invited guests, such as members of Parliament, academia, or of the business world. One evening the question at hand was: "How greater Romania had been built." Young men were flushed with enthusiasm and loudly began to shout.

"We are all standing together today thanks to our fine military!"

"I've never seen more gallant men than our soldiers!" someone else added.

But an elderly and seasoned politician tried to shift the discussion in a different direction. "Calm down, you firebrands, fighting and gallant our soldiers were indeed. But our goals were attained mostly through diplomacy with the European great powers."

And on they went. Constantin stood there quietly and listened to both sides. "Why, the older gentleman is absolutely right," he thought, recalling talks with his father during the war. The next time he was asked to attend another gathering he politely declined while telling himself, "My friends are too idealistic."

Months passed and other opportunities presented themselves. University students later known as "the generation of 1922," who symbolized the post-war youth, became increasingly active on the country's social scene. They were advocating a more "civilized" political dialogue, with less bickering and more honesty. Various magazines with younger editors at the helm helped articulate these lofty goals. Some of the history students invited Constantin to join in such a discussion promoting an open political dialogue. He listened and asked what practical steps could be undertaken. He heard emotions ramping up but no solutions. "It's all a bit too theoretical for me," he concluded and once more turned down future invitations.

Having concluded he held no taste for politics at this junction, he decided to wholeheartedly concentrate on his career. The first step was passing the exams enabling him to teach high school. Next would be studying for and obtaining a PhD, imperative for gaining the expertise required for a university assignment. The hope was that such a position would prove satisfactory to Maria's parents and enable him to officially ask for her hand. These were the bold strokes of the master plan. But for the most part, he woke up every morning merely facing the new day, the past having taught him to expect the unexpected.

Studying for the teaching exams proved to be arduous after a long workday at the National Museum. The exams called for a primary and secondary specialty, and his dual major in Romanian history and geography certainly helped. But there was new ground to be covered as well. One had to master all topics taught in grades 5 through 12 which included universal history, besides that of Romania. Emphasis was also placed on teaching techniques which had received little attention during the university years. He applied himself as always, and after three months sat for oral and written exams. In addition, there were also two "hands on" teaching sessions for students of different grades. After two days of intense concentration, he emerged slightly dizzy and nauseated, the efforts of the past months finally catching up. Despite feeling he had done well, doubts plagued him while waiting for the results.

"Why do you put so much pressure on yourself?" Maria asked, her heart aching at her fiancé's anguish.

"Everything rests upon this. I need not only to pass, but do well, to be seriously considered when I apply for a PhD."

"You've always excelled; why worry so much?"

He paused for a moment; taking his face into her hands, Maria could see the blue-gray eyes wondering off, far away. His candid answer jolted them both.

"I'm tired, dear, tired of waiting for the day when I can stand tall in front of your parents and ask for your hand. Every time I face your mother she looks down on me, the poor orphan who won't be able to offer her daughter anything but love. Love, which to her is no rationale for a union! More than anything, I want us to be together, but also to do you proud."

And proud she was, her eyes and face lit up by a bright, open smile when the exam results were posted: he had placed first in both specialties.

Then fortune had, amazingly enough, smiled once again upon Constantin. University professors had unanimously nominated him for a scholarship at the Romanian Postgraduate School in Paris. When summoned by Professor Parvan, Constantin's thoughts first raced to some of the archival documents his teacher had requested and he had yet to secure.

The "Maestro" was smiling. "Young man, you're headed to Paris!"

His surprise was such that he just stared back, speechless at first. "Paris, sir?!"

The Maestro nodded his head in disbelief, his piercing eyes staring intently. "Yes, Paris, our postgraduate school there."

"I can't thank you enough, sir. But I am simply stunned; I didn't even know I was among those being considered."

"Why wouldn't you be, after graduating at the top of the class and being fluent in French? Once in Paris take time before settling upon a topic of research. It will likely become the backbone of your doctorate. Choose carefully."

"Sir, I am honored by your trust. I shall consult with you by mail before making my final decision."

After he took leave of the professor, his thoughts flew immediately to Maria. And his bright horizon darkened suddenly, the excitement of the upcoming trip dampened by the separation it implied. Indeed, knowing he wouldn't be able to see her for many months made his happiness less than complete.

He called on Maria immediately, anxious to share the news. She was home, and her mother fortunately was out so he didn't need to waste time on small talk. "I was awarded a scholarship to the Paris school! Me?! Can you believe it?"

She nodded her head, carefully considering its implications. "But it means we won't see each other for maybe a year . . . so my heart cries and laughs at the same time."

One of Maria's many qualities that he admired was her practicality. And even at such an emotionally charged moment, it shone through. "Of course they chose you, you're their rising star! And despite the separation, we can dream of your return and of you soon being in a better position to talk with Father." And with that, she gently took his hand and they went for a stroll in the garden, heads bowed slightly together, voices in a whisper, smiles on their faces.

The following days flew by in a whirlwind. The passport was issued in only one day and travel visas followed promptly. With most of his clothes and books crammed in two suitcases, he was ready to travel abroad for the first time since his childhood visit to Vienna. But he couldn't leave before visiting with his siblings. Horia, a recent graduate from military school, was pursuing a career in the army. His sister, Lelia, continued to thrive under the care of her aunt, growing into a beautiful teenager. With Horia on his own and his sister well situated, Constantin now felt able to contemplate traveling abroad in order to continue his studies.

The big departure day had arrived, and Maria had insisted upon seeing him off. He had tried to discourage her, worried how the young woman would fare in the busy train station after his departure. But he was also secretly pleased by her wish to be by his side for a few more moments.

"You'll write often, won't you?"

"Certainly, dear."

"And don't you let those fancy French girls turn your head around," she said in jest.

"No one is smarter and dearer than you. It's all the young men your mother is going to invite over that I worry about."

A broad smile illuminated her face. "They'll all be wasting their time!"

Suddenly they heard the familiar "All aboard!" followed by a ruffle of embraces and shouts on the surrounding platform. They hugged and kissed tightly and Constantin took leave of her. In his car he lowered the window and waved at Maria, who was blowing him kisses. He stood there until her slim silhouette clad in a smart navy dress and matching coat and hat became progressively smaller, a sharp dot at first, then gradually blurry until it faded away.

He had no money for a sleeping car, and so the two-day journey was made in regular coach. The so-called express "Arlberg" took him through Hungary, Austria and Switzerland before crossing into France. Two days of mountains, cities, and villages glided past his window, punctuated by brief stops, sandwich after sandwich with hot coffee, and a bunch of apples.

The scenery captivated him at first, but after days of being unable to wash properly and sleeping poorly in a coach seat, he was cranky, dirty, and tired by the time the train pulled into Paris's East Train Station. It was dusty and crowded, and the morning was gray and drizzling. The streets seemed frantic, and he was fatigued, seeing or feeling no "light" during the first few hours in the so-called City of Light. In a foul mood, he wondered about the origin of this moniker. But his disposition began to change shortly after arriving at his final destination.

Together with other Romanian students and teachers, he was lodged in a three-story home in Fontenay-aux-Roses, a Parisian suburb. Time had stood still there where gracious buildings intermingled with old chestnut trees on wide streets. Paris might have been shaken by the Great War but here on the edge of the city, its core still breathed with the vibrant life of its turn-of-the-century glory. The short ride to the school took him through several roundabouts with imposing statues—generals and kings of times past followed by a residential area with large homes surrounded by intricately decorated wrought iron fences.

The administrator of the school greeted and showed him to his quarters on the second floor. "You have everything you need here."

He took it all in: a large bedroom with bed, armoire, table and chair, bookshelves, and a sink. The windows faced the street, and if he stretched his arm he could almost touch the chestnut tree. "It will be beautiful in the spring when the white candle-like flowers bloom," he thought. Then, turning to his host, he said, "Yes, Sir. Thank you."

"The housekeeper comes twice a week. You take care of the rest."

"Yes, Sir."

"And remember: no girls are allowed up to your room."

He smiled shyly. "You have nothing to worry about. I have a fiancée back home."

After unpacking and settling in, hunger took hold. Why, it had been over two days since he had last had a hot meal. When asking the administrator, the reply was, "We usually take lunch in our dining room, but on Sundays you are on your own as the cook is off. There are a few restaurants toward the center, and it's only a ten-minute walk or so."

And it was after a lunch of leek soup, grilled beef with potatoes, cheese, and a plum tart, that the first quintessential French moment presented itself on his very first day. The bill had arrived with an unspecified 0.55 francs charge.

"Waiter, if you don't mind, what is the 0.55 for?" he had asked.

"Sir, it is 0.70 for a quarter liter of wine and 0.55 if you don't have any," said the server with a haughty air.

The young man smiled and thought to himself, "Almost like a penalty tax." And so he went ahead and ordered the wine, and embarked upon a lifelong affair with the grape byproduct.

As he settled into classes and research assignments, selecting a topic for his future doctoral thesis became a matter of serious consideration. After countless hours at the National Library, he came upon several documents regarding Romanian officials in the fifteenth and sixteenth centuries. He was certain they hadn't yet been interpreted and they piqued his interest. Once certain, a letter was sent out to "maestro" Parvan.

"Thinking of a study of Romanian officials in the sixteenth century: their ethnicities, the social system, the unique position of the Romanian provinces at the crossroads of Byzantium/ the Ottomans and the rest of Europe and its imprint on the matter . . . Please advise me."

The response arrived a month later. "Hardly any work has been done on the topic to date. I trust you will take detailed care in copying the documents faithfully. One must be able to refer to an accurate source. I approve of your choice."

Besides studying, the young man also took time to explore his temporary home, gradually falling in love with the city, while in his heart yearning for his real love back in Bucharest. His colleague George, who had lived in Paris for a while, took Constantin one day to the "very center." Leading him by the hand, he ordered his friend, "Keep your eyes tightly shut, and open them only when I say so!"

Moments later he received the "green light." The sight he gazed upon would stay with him forever: the vista took your breath away. Standing right under the Arc du Caroussel in the Tuilleries Park and close to the Louvre museum, he could see the famed Champs Elysees Boulevard leading straight to the Arc de Triomphe. This was the stuff of Paris dreams, which songs extolled and paintings portrayed. He blinked once, twice, thinking the vision would dissipate, but no, it was still there. One could feel light and beauty all around, and a sense of endless possibilities, and he dared hope once again.

He often wrote to Maria of the sites he visited: Notre Dame Cathedral and its austere beauty and her glorious, more luminous "cousin" on the same island, the Sainte-Chapelle. Time was also spent at the Pantheon where great scientists, authors, and politicians were buried and, of course, at the incomparable Louvre. But he also wrote of strolls in Bois de Boulogne, where the old trees reminded him of Bucharest's. Oh, there were so many Parisian faces and places he wished to share with her, monuments that they would need to return and to see together. Weeks rolled by and after a while Paris began to feel like home. He woke up to the clanking of glass milk bottles being delivered. The aroma of fresh bread coming out of the oven indicated it was breakfast time. Pungent cheeses heralded the arrival of lunch. He had heard how one became French only when able to tell the time of day by the surrounding scents. Well, he was rapidly becoming an honorary Frenchman indeed!

As summer drew to a close, Constantin dashed back home under the guise of checking up on his sister while his being yearned to see Maria again. Horia, a young dashing officer, joined him on the visit to Aunt Marie. Every time they saw their sister, she so reminded them of their mother: the same blue eyes, gently wavy hair, and a sweet disposition. As for Aunt Marie she hadn't changed one bit. You heard the same litany of complaints: the cost of living, political turmoil, lazy maids, summer heat, his being away. The two young men nodded in agreement, enjoyed their lunch, thanked her profusely, and eventually took their leave.

His correspondence with Maria had continued throughout his stay in Paris. He had thus learned of her family's upcoming summer travels to their country estate, though the dates hadn't been firmed up at the time of their last exchange. Full of anticipation but also apprehension, he went to her home and rang the bell. Silence greeted him. One more ring; he could hear the shrill sound reverberating through the house. Glancing around he saw drapes and shutters drawn everywhere. Eventually there was a soft shuffle, and the door was cracked ajar by an old caretaker. "They're all in the country for the summer."

And with that the door closed and he stood alone again, deep disappointment etched on his face. Though he knew the Mehedinti's vineyard was in the town of Odobesti, undertaking the trip and calling on them uninvited was out of the question. All he could do was turn around and head back to Paris to complete his course of study, and hope that time would fly by until they could be together.

In the meantime, far from Bucharest, about one hundred miles to the northeast, Maria sat on the veranda of her family's cottage. She appeared to be concentrating on knitting and the choice of colors for an intricate pattern, while her mind wandered far away. Her request to remain in Bucharest that summer had fallen on deaf ears.

She had approached her mother before leaving. "I'm thinking of staying behind this summer; I can go to Aunt Margot's house. Georgina and I are thinking of taking a drawing class."

"What on earth are you talking about?" her mother asked in her usual blunt style.

"I'm talking about not going to Odobesti this year. There isn't much for me to do there."

"There's just as much as last year. And I don't remember asking for your opinion."

And with that rejoinder, the conversation and the matter were settled. Mrs. Mehedinti was accustomed to having the last word, indeed and this time would be no different. If she had her doubts regarding Maria's potential summer activities if left behind in Bucharest, she never said anything. As for her husband, the professor carried on writing, oblivious to the tug of war between wife and daughter.

They went about packing their many trunks while the maids prepared the house for the summer. Gauzy covers were placed on the furniture, the curtains were drawn, and the food supplies were moved to the cellar. Away they went for the better part of two months, with Maria seething every day at her inability to communicate with Constantin, as the post from Bucharest was not being forwarded.

The preceding months had been hard enough on her. She had gotten used to seeing him quite often and deeply missed their conversations and walks together. She seemingly carried on without him: tended to her parents' guests, went to "tea" and dance parties, called on relatives, read, or went shopping. She often joined her friends at the Romanian Youth Club where they socialized and danced, sometimes in folk costumes. But deep down she felt empty, and dreamed of his return, her longing confirming the strong feelings they had for one another.

And here she was now, tucked away in the country, with little to do. Long walks around the estate and time in the vineyard filled her days. There were horse rides as well and long luncheons with friends and relatives calling upon them. The days passed somehow but in the evening, loneliness got a hold of her. With only gas lamps to provide light, reading was tiresome and one went to bed early. To bed, with sleep and dreams of her future together with Constantin. But there were nights, too, when sleep was slow in coming and thinking of the future kept her up many a night. She knew that upon marrying she was to receive farmland as her dowry, and an idea began to take hold. She was going to have her own vineyard operation and would start it from scratch. The thought energized her and her days began to fill up. She spent time talking to the manager, learning about varietals, and taking in as many details as she could about the process of turning grapes into wine. Here was finally something worthwhile doing, and not even her mother could find fault with her daughter's new interest.

One morning Maria woke up early and went to the kitchen to have some tea and toast before heading out. She was moving around quietly, feline-like, mindful not to wake up the rest of the household, when she heard her mother talking to Aunt Margot, "Well, I am glad that balding young man went to Paris. I hope this is the last we've seen of him. You know, he fancied himself as Maria's suitor."

"People say he has a bright future."

"Bright? What are you talking about? He's going to teach and write a book or two. The only shine I see is his receding hairline."

Margot bit her tongue; it struck her as rather ironical that her own sister's husband wrote, was a professor too, and didn't exactly boast a head full of hair.

"Maria. Maybe they're in love."

"Margot, are you going along with this modern nonsense that love conquers all?"

Margot paused, choosing her words carefully, always weary of her older sister's viper tongue since childhood. But Margot was also especially fond of her niece and close to her. "All I am trying to say is to perhaps give him a chance. Time will tell."

Maria's world felt suddenly dark and cold, despite the warmth of the early-summer morning and the sun gently climbing over the horizon. She had long sensed her mother's animosity toward the man she was in love with. But to hear it spoken so boldly sent shudders down her lightly clad body. She could have stepped in to the kitchen and confronted her mother, but what would have been the good of that? It would only increase her mother's wrath and confirm her instincts. Instead she walked in lightly and wished the two women a good morning, watching their faces and necks turn deep red. She busied herself with a bowl of milk and some bread and jam, while attempting to make small talk until she took leave.

The mask dropped as soon as she stepped out, and a deep sadness took hold. She felt so lonely all of a sudden. Maria's beloved grandmother, her mainstay, had passed away a decade earlier. Her mother either didn't care about her feelings, or worse, outright disapproved of them. Constantin's parents were gone, too. "We are alone," she thought out loud as she walked the pastures dotted with the fresh morning dew. An overwhelming need to cry welled up until warm tears started flowing down her cheeks. She carried on, for how long she couldn't later recall, until the sun began to burn her face. Wandering the fields had taken her into the hills, and pausing briefly, she gazed upon the bucolic scenery. Fields carpeted with bright flowers led to the formal gardens of the white house with a red-shingle roof. Vineyards laden with pearly yellow or plum grapes surrounded everything, almost as far as the eye could see. The town was barely visible from the top of the hill, a wisp of a white-reddish wave toward the dusty horizon. And taking it all in she began to feel lighter, as if the surrounding beauty had awakened her hopes and dreams again.

It was there, where sky and earth kissed one another that she vowed to always love and support Constantin. Yes, she would do her utmost to have a happy, successful marriage. "Why, success is the best revenge," she reminded herself, and wiping away a few tears she smiled at the beauty and richness of her land. "Besides, we'll be together before long."

Chapter Nine

EARNING A PHD, MARRYING MARIA

Constantin returned to Paris, eager to complete his study and research as quickly as possible. A shining sun and clear blue skies greeted him this time, a bright contrast to the heavy skies encountered a few months earlier. It was as if the city had decided this adoptive son had proven himself worthy of his temporary home. Summer gradually gave way to fall, and its myriad rust and golden tones festooned the city's wide, tree-lined boulevards. Winds swirled the leaves about, turning the sidewalks into a patchwork quilt until winter's steely hues took hold. The young man took in the beauty of the passing seasons while carrying on with his routine, much like he had done in Bucharest. There was study in the archives and classrooms, visits to museums, an occasional concert or weekend trip, followed by more research. And after a while he felt as if he were turning on a merry-go-round, which perhaps Paris had become for him. The thought struck him one day when pausing briefly in the Tuilleries Park, close to the Louvre museum. He had sat down on a bench, glancing around absentmindedly. The analogy had come while focusing on the children's carousel: there it was turning around, over and over, while surrounded by the old elegance of the city and its park.

"Why, it's just like my life here in Paris, going round in circles, sheathed in a world of beauty, until . . . " breaking out of his wistfulness, he realized, "It's time to go home."

But he couldn't leave before buying a small gift for Maria, something she'd hopefully have for years to come. On March 1 of each year, and in a celebration of love and the upcoming spring, sweethearts, mothers, and sisters were presented with miniature flowers or tiny ornaments to wear on their lapels or collars. He couldn't be with Maria this year but would present her with his token of his affection upon return. After much deliberation he settled on a small ivory statuette pendant, a graceful figure, because "she can also wear it later on a chain."

"Please make sure you wrap it carefully," he told the salesgirl, "and would you please weave a red and white ribbon together and tie them around?"

"Why so, Monsieur?" asked the girl in her thick Brittany accent.

"It's our spring tradition in Romania, Mademoiselle. We offer these small gifts on red-white strings, to pin on your attire."

"Oh, that's so romantic, Monsieur. Red for love and white for purity, isn't that so?"

He smiled, having never reflected upon the symbolism; the girl's theory seemed plausible enough. "I believe so, Mademoiselle."

The girl blushed and smiled, secretly pleased with her intuition.

Constantin smiled, too, as if he could picture the delight in his fiancée's eyes.

And when the study year drew to a close, he returned to Bucharest. The journey home was considerably more comfortable than his previous rides. An exhibit of rare and old Romanian art objects had just concluded in Paris and valuable centuries-old embroideries and silver were going back to their homes in museums and churches. Given their value, transport had to be by a special train car with enhanced security. One of the organizers knew Constantin and arranged for him to travel aboard this car. "Yours will be another set of eyes guarding our priceless treasures."

Thus he headed home, bringing back not only plenty of material for his doctoral thesis but also postcards and memories of the sites visited, while the aromas of warm bread, chocolate, and cheese were woven into the threads of his coats.

He returned home in the spring, around the feast day of St. George in late April. He disembarked at the North Train Station, loaded with suitcases so heavy with papers that he could barely make his way through the station. The train had pulled in early and had found the city preparing for another busy day. There were peasants on the way to the markets, carrying baskets overflowing with produce and buckets full of bright fresh flowers. A stand was selling freshly baked pretzels rolled in salt or sesame seeds, the air full of their tempting smell. Only then did he realize how much he had missed Bucharest, all of it: the hustle, bustle, colors, and flavors.

Constantin had sent advance word of his arrival to Maria and had arranged to meet her at the Capsa pastry shop, far from the prying eyes of the servants and her parents. The Capsa, which had seen the little boy celebrate his first scholastic success, had later embraced the young man and his fiancée. Not one normally given to frivolous gestures, the young woman had decided on a new dress in her favorite blue hue with a matching ribbon, which beautifully offset her dark hair and eyes. Their reunion was joyous, and from the first, it felt as if they had never been apart.

He had arrived early and asked the server to bring his small gift box along with Maria's order. The formally dressed waiter obliged and fell into the act, setting the stage for a memory to be cherished by all. How could one forget Maria's delight when she spotted the charming package alongside the crème-filled eclairs—elaborately presented on a small silver tray with a red rose in the center?

In the coming weeks they started plotting their future together, as neither was prone to waste time. Heads bowed together, a fairy tale was spun, the dream of youth, albeit filled with the prosaic details of the day-to-day life. He would set forth to write his PhD, without which he could not aspire to a university position. He'd get it done in record time, defend it (of course successfully), after which a teaching post would miraculously open up. A magical clock would then chime on the hour when he could officially ask for Maria's hand, and his Cinderella would no longer have to return home to the wicked mother. The enthusiasm of their young age and love for each other assured the script would unfold as conceived.

Constantin threw himself into writing his doctoral thesis, the very foundation of their plan. The topic had, of course, been chosen while in Paris, where some of the preliminary research had been done. Parvan had encouraged him to uncover facts and cast them in a new, fresh light:

"Bring forth the data and dress it up attractively," the maestro had advised.

Many a day had been spent in the French National Library in Paris, a true treasure trove. Many an evening now found Constantin still at work, analyzing copies of texts long forgotten. It was neither a small, nor an easy task, considering the precise and somewhat dry nature of the topic. Despite this handicap, the young man felt hopeful as he advanced. He intertwined the ethnicities of the officials harking back to Byzantine days with the unique stamp cast by life in the Romanian territories. He presented parallels and analogies to counterparts of neighboring countries. Thus he hoped the study would be of interest not only at home but also to scholars from the surrounding Balkan lands.

He carried on until the writing was finally done and the big day had arrived. He was calm in the knowledge that he had delivered his best, and the hard work was behind him. Defending the thesis was more of a formality than anything else, and so he headed into it confidently. The candidate in his best suit sat across from the doctoral commission—two of his history teachers, including Maestro Parvan, the dean, and a well-known researcher. The latter seemed determined to find fault with something—anything, or so it appeared. At one point he indicated disapproval to a stated fact and referred all to a certain page. Constantin, diplomatically, pointed out the page number was incorrect. The researcher, visibly uncomfortable, fretted, coughed, and apologized. The candidate smiled calmly and replied, "It's quite all right." Professor Parvan later joked how he had difficulty in assessing who was the candidate and who the interviewer.

By the end of the morning, Constantin Giurescu was declared "Doctor in history, philosophy, and letters . . . magna cum laude."

He was barely twenty-five years old.

Following his and Maria's master plan, a university position opened up shortly thereafter. Professor Parvan invited his star pupil to dinner one evening and delivered the much hoped for news.

"A new assistant professorship is being created at the history desk, at the university. We need more help as student enrollment is growing. You must submit an application immediately."

"That would be a list of my degrees, articles to date, and the like, Sir?"

"That, as well as a formally printed copy of your doctoral thesis."

"But Sir, I don't have one; there are only the typed pages submitted to you and the commission."

"Those won't do. Go talk to Nicholas Avram, at the Horizon Publishing House. Tell him I sent you and see if he can be of help."

The following morning, bright-eyed and hopeful with the utter innocence and ignorance of his twenty-five years, he walked into the editor's office. He was greeted there by a middle-aged gentleman in starched collar and dark suit. He sat down and quickly explained his predicament. "There's one more thing, Sir. I forgot to mention I need it in six days."

"No problem. I think we can get it done. You just need to move in here to make all corrections on site." A friend of his father lent him the money to pay for its printing.

That evening Constantin was headed to the publishing house with his pajamas, toothbrush, and a stack of notes. He would later hardly remember anything, but for the fact that six days later he proudly clutched the printed book and went home for a long hot bath!

Back on track, his application for the university teaching position was formally accepted. Within days he was headed to the Ministry of Education to take the traditional oath of faith toward his academic specialty, country, and laws. With a hand on the cross and deeply moved, his thoughts wondered back to the father whose very desk he would occupy shortly. That evening he invited Maestro Parvan to dinner to thank him and celebrate the joyous news.

But the best part of his small triumph was he could finally approach Professor Mehedinti and ask for his daughter's hand in marriage. Dressed up in his finest suit and taking along two large bouquets, he ran up the stairs and rang the doorbell. White roses were for Maria while her mother was presented with pink ones. The professor received him in the study in his customary dark suit with its mandarin like high collar, "Mr. Giurescu, congratulations on your nomination. The dean has informed me we'll be colleagues."

"Thank you, Professor. It is a great privilege."

"I presume the reason you came was to share this good news with me?"

"Well, of course, but Professor, there is something else I came to talk to you about."

Then there was silence, the young man visibly nervous and searching for the right words, leery of rejection. "Professor, I have come to ask for Maria's hand. I would be honored if you were to consent to our marriage."

If the professor was surprised, he never showed it. He arched his eyebrows ever so slightly, and in his measured timber replied, "Mr. Giurescu, I am in favor of this alliance." The young man could only smile in response. "And may I ask, is Maria aware of your intentions?"

Constantin once again felt uncertain; would a "yes" answer imply the young people had been plotting this course of action for quite a while? A "no" would have seemed odd, too; the professor must have, after all, seen the two of them together many times?

He decided on the best approach: honesty kept brief. "Yes, sir, she is."

"And she is in favor of it, too?"

"I do believe."

"Well, then, we must call in Mrs. Mehedinti, she'll want to start planning the wedding right away."

As for his future mother-in-law, her reaction was equally brief. "Well, if that's what you gentlemen have decided." For once she kept her misgivings and whatever else she may have felt to herself, but not before adding, "It's about time, Mr. Giurescu," and that settled it.

"And now, gentlemen, perhaps we should ask Maria to join us."

She stepped lightly into the room and scanned their faces quickly. Her mother had a haughty grin while her father smiled quietly. Seeing Constantin nod slightly, she breathed a sigh of relief. "It must have gone well," she thought to herself.

"Maria, dear," said her father. "I was delighted to hear of Mr. Giurescu's proposal and I am in favor of it." Without wasting a moment and in front of her parents, Constantin went down on a knee:

"Maria, dearest, would you please be my wife?" he asked and slipped the light purple sapphire on her ring finger, having borrowed it back from Maria. The ring hidden at the bottom of the jewelry box could now see the light of day!

Tears of joy flowed while Mrs. Mehedinti asked the maid to fetch a bottle of vintage champagne from the cellar.

From the start it became apparent that Maria's mother would "direct" the wedding according to her own script. This was one of those rare occasions when the society hostess could shine in all her glory and be talked about for years to come. Her daughter was more often than not informed rather than consulted about the arrangements. Maria didn't care for lavish and expensive flourishes and had wished for a smaller, more intimate gathering. Hers and her mother's strong personalities often collided, creating sparks. But after consulting with Constantin, they decided to let Mrs. Mehedinti organize her dream reception, both eager to peacefully embark on their life together.

The gifts started arriving at Maria's house a couple of weeks prior to the wedding, as was the custom of the day. They were displayed in the large salon, with the most impressive ones upfront. An expensive Rosenthal china dining set, silver cutlery, and fine crystal goblets were there for all to see and admire. As for the bride's parents, they settled on a large plot of land as a dowry.

On April 15, 1926, an extremely anxious Constantin greeted Maria in front of the altar in the Domnita Balasa church, an architectural Greek-Orthodox jewel of the eighteenth century. The ceremony was to resonate with them over the decades. Being the first wedding officiated by the young priest, he put his soul into it, the chanting and prayers adding to the solemnity of the moment. They couldn't have asked for a prettier day: the sun shining brightly after a long winter, with an explosion of lilac, tulips, and daffodils showing that nature, too, had woken up. Once the young man saw his bride walk down the aisle in a simple elegant gown and string of pearls, with a head veil dressed in innocent, fragrant lemon flowers, his nervousness melted away. From that moment on, it was just the two of them, the rest a mere backdrop to their day.

The reception was held at Maria's parents and billed as one of the society weddings of the year. The house had been polished from top to bottom and gleaming chandeliers shone above it all. Large bouquets of flowers adorned every table and shelf and rich lace overlays had been placed over satin tablecloths. There was meat and fish and assorted appetizers and several cakes covered in white icing and garnished with candied fruits. The wine came from their vineyard and the best French champagne was served. Mrs. Mehedinti presided over it with a proud smile of self-satisfaction. And not even her friend's Lizette's comment, "Look what our daughters are putting us through," (a not-so-veiled rebuff over Maria not choosing her own son) could cloud her day. As for her new son-in-law, the grand lady had sharp advice:

"Men must be led and trained."

"I thought only animals were treated as such," he rejoined.

"Boy, you keep quiet. I know what I'm talking about."

He swallowed his response, unwilling to argue with new his mother-in-law, letting the grand lady revel in her importance of the moment. Maria kept her gaze down and her mouth shut, too, eager not to let her mother's viper tongue ruin the magic of the day.

And so Maria and Constantin's life together began once the last champagne cork was popped and the last piece of cake eaten. The offer of a lavish honeymoon abroad from her parents had been turned down by the young couple.

"I'll let her have the wedding, but I want to decide on my honeymoon," Maria had said. Constantin had said his preference was to take his bride on a trip of his choosing, one he could afford and plan for himself. And so they headed to a northeast country lodge, the first night spent in a peasant's cottage along the way.

The caretaker had shown them around and had warned, "Be careful, there are ghosts here."

They had laughed heartily; then exhausted by the long train journey and the excitement of the prior day, sleep came readily. Pitch dark and in the middle of the night, three knocks were heard.

"Who is it?" Silence. Constantin pulled a gun out. He waited then shouted, louder still, "Who is it? Answer or I'll shoot." More silence.

Three more knocks. And so it went on for a while. Constantin finally pulled the trigger, and to his amazement nothing happened. The gun, previously in good working order and properly loaded, would not fire. "Nonsense, of course; I don't believe in ghosts," would have been his answer when earlier asked. But from that day forward, he acknowledged there were phenomena beyond his comprehension, best left at that. Neither he nor Maria was prone to superstitions, but when recounting the night's events to the caretaker's wife, they watched an equally mysterious ritual. The old woman crossed herself deeply three times in a row. Then she turned sharply and spat as hard she could and said, "To keep the devil away from you two lovebirds." Her husband shrugged his shoulders and uttered, "Welcome to married life."

They were finally together.

Chapter Ten
POLITICS BECKONS

As the 1920s progressed, the background to this story began to change, ushering in modern times. Horse-drawn trams on the city's eighteen routes were gradually replaced by electric cars. The horse-drawn sleds fared better and remained in high demand throughout most of the decade, fueled by record snowfalls several years in a row. Construction boomed and the city gained blocks of flats, office buildings and hospitals. Theater flourished as new companies were created and the Romanian Opera came into being in 1921. But personal touches reminiscent of life in a smaller town still survived in the metropolis. Dairy, poultry, and produce orders were delivered by vendors to a customer's doorstep, and personalized orders were always honored on time. The music man still walked the streets pulling his dusty music box around, and once in a while gypsies brought a "dancing bear" to fairs held in the suburbs.

Old and new still very much lived side by side in the city Maria and Constantin returned to after their honeymoon. Once back they lived at first with Maria's parents, while taking out a loan to expand Constantin's house. A second floor was built; the basement was expanded and central heating was added. Maria consulted with the builder, electricians, and plumbers and supervised every step of the work. The renovations took the better part of two years, during which time the young couple started a family. Their sons Dinu and Dan were born in rapid succession in February 1927 and November 1928. And with three generations living under the same roof, tensions built between Maria and her mother, who perpetually disagreed over household arrangements and child rearing.

"You spend too much time with the babies. What is the nanny for?" Mrs. Mehedinti would complain.

"She's here to help out, Mother. I'm their mother and I'll spend as much time with them as I please."

The older lady would leave it at that, only to resume the bickering hours later, "Why do you mash and dice spinach, potatoes and carrots? One vegetable is enough."

"I'd rather prepare all three; this way they are bound to eat at least one if the others are not to their liking."

Playtime in the yard brought more dialogue. "Dinu is rolling in the grass and you just sit there staring at him."

"What would you like me to do, Mother?"

"Well, make him stop it. His clothes are filthy. Why, I even saw him chewing on grass."

"Let him run, he'll sleep better. As for the grass, it's good for the immunity."

While this went on, the men wisely stayed out of it all, teaching classes and writing papers. And all breathed a sigh of relief when the young family was able to move out and into their own home.

It was a sight to behold, and the proud father and husband could hardly believe his eyes. The house now had graceful arched-stone carvings around the windows, and the front door and a second floor balcony was surrounded by slender columns. There were gleaming hardwood floors and heavy crystal doors separating the rooms on the first floor. He had a new study, and there were many bedrooms and everything else they could possibly need. In the newly redone basement, there were a laundry and ironing room and rooms for any household help. The cellar had been greatly expanded and its many shelves awaited jars of pickles and marmalade and bottles of wine. New flowers had been planted in the yard and the old fruit trees had been pruned and trimmed.

Soon after they moved into the house, their third child was born: a girl they named Simona, who would later be called Mona by family and friends alike. Her father couldn't help but reflect on the parallel to his own childhood. Here were once again young parents with two sons and a daughter, the girl born soon after moving into the newly redone house. With apprehension he hoped the similarities would end there, while wondering what might be in store for them. But with work taking up most of the day, there was little opportunity for reflection. It was around the same time—and before he turned thirty—that he became an associate professor at the university. He had succeeded once again in shortening the normally lengthier academic path. The occasion was greeted with a reception-celebration held in his honor at the university. A barrage of questions awaited his arrival:

"Do you believe because of your youth that students will respect you any less?"

"I hope they'll respect me more because of what I have accomplished. Plus, being closer in age, we can better understand one another," he had replied.

Each university educator chose a main research topic in those days.

"Professor, have you selected an area of interest yet?"

"I think we lack a comprehensive history of the Romanian people."

The answer was greeted with silence, unease, a little nervous laughter and mostly disbelief.

"Isn't that a little ambitious?"

"Perhaps it is, and that is why I am starting early."

The audience eventually gave up on their line of questioning. As for the young man, he continued to dream bold and big, hoping to be able one day to deliver the books his dad would have written had he been given the time. "This one's going to be for you, Dad," he had muttered softly while standing in the very rotunda which had heard his father's lectures and from which he had watched his parent's eulogy.

The decade of the 1920s was slowly coming to an end, enjoying the most prosperity the country had known since the end of the Great War. But the ripple effect of "Black Friday," which had taken place a continent and an ocean away, soon erased those gains. Within months the prices of agricultural produce, gas, coal, wood, and all staples of the country's exports plummeted. Grains lost two-thirds of their value and even the price of wine went down by 50 percent.

In this economic meltdown remained a relative "silver lining": real estate. Maria, Constantin, and the family spent their first summer holidays at her parents' country estate with resumption of the same family dynamics. They had hoped the pastoral setting would melt the tension experienced while living under the same roof in Bucharest, but that was not to be. The only one able to occasionally break the strain was Maria's brother, Emil, quite the court jester and very gifted at imitating people. He was credited as being the only one to make his mother smile just as she was vowing to disinherit her daughter and leave her husband!

Because of the strained family relationships, Maria did not look forward to returning to her parents' estate the following year. She yearned for a summer place of her own and was also eager to capitalize on the relative value of the land received as dowry. She also wished to take advantage of real estate prices having held their own. Long discussions took place on many a night:

"We could keep the land as is and try to develop it," was Constantin's opinion. A budding scholar he might have been, but his business sense was virtually nonexistent.

Maria saw the difficulty of doing that but, ever tactful, had added, "We could, but it's going to be challenging. The terrain is varied, and we'd have to work in different directions at the same time."

"I see."

"What do you think about dividing the land in small parcels and selling it to the locals? We could use the proceeds to buy and start a vineyard."

She was cleverly drawing her husband in, handing him the lead and asking him to sanction it. Delighted, he approved of her logic, cherishing once again her practicality. He felt so fortunate—here was his beautiful but also smart, sensible wife.

Maria's dream of years past was becoming a reality, and she threw herself wholeheartedly into the process. At first she supervised the breakdown of the lots, aided by her mother's property manager. Day after day she drove around the countryside, sought and listened to the advice of winemakers. She visited sites and discussed their merits. Eventually they settled on the Odobesti Vineyard, not too far from her parents' land. Once again she made sure to consult her husband and let him make the final decision. Maria interviewed the staff on the premises, liked and kept the administrator, but also made it clear she was to be involved in all major decisions. Not only did she eagerly learn about every facet of winemaking, but also in time she would develop a terrific business sense.

For a while it all seemed to fall into place. The family had managed to remain relatively prosperous despite the general economic deterioration, not in small part due to Maria's dowry but also her keen practical side. Constantin's academic career was blossoming, and not one to rest on his laurels for long he began to yearn for new horizons to explore. They soon presented themselves in 1930, when he too was swept in the swirl of controversy and action surrounding the country's monarchy. The political "bug," which he had shrugged off only a few years earlier, was now catching up to him.

The last years of the 1920s had brought about a shaky political situation in Romania. King Ferdinand, who had seen the country united in 1918, had passed away of colon cancer in 1927. His eldest son and heir, Prince Carol II, a notorious playboy, had been forced, only months earlier, to renounce his succession right. This had happened in the aftermath of a scandal, which had erupted when the dalliance of the very much-married Prince with a certain Ms. Elena Lupescu was leaked to the press. The reporters had run wild with the story peppering the dailies with details true or fabricated. Upon Ferdinand's passing, the throne went on to Carol's son, the five-year-old Michael. And while the little boy king continued to play with toy soldiers, the country was run by three regents. These three pulled and tugged against each other and occasionally fought with the Dowager Queen Marie, to the great delight of the press. Cartoons were passed around right and left as the country slowly slid into confusion.

It was in 1930, in the midst of this chaos, that an eclectic assortment of business and political interests decided the time was ripe to return the playboy Carol II to the throne. What might have been their motivation? Could it have been wishful thinking on the part of some that with a sole figure in charge, one knew whom to blame when things went wrong? Did the tacit understanding that "in politics you sometimes are forced to swallow a croc and not only a lizard" underlie the belief of others?

This movement to restore Carol II to his birthright was by no means embraced by all and, in turn, led to more bickering. It took quite a bit of persuasion until the leaders of the main parties were eventually brought on board. A large group of politically nonaffiliated intellectuals also jumped in the fray. Constantin was among them, affixing his signature to many others on the petition, hoping for a new start. It was a seemingly innocuous act at the time whose implications no one could have guessed. As for Maria, normally ready to support her husband's decisions, she had mixed feelings. It might have had to do with her father's views, less than enthusiastic vis-à-vis Prince Carol's return. Or perhaps she thought that academic work already filled up Constantin's busy life. To cousin Georgiana she summarized it, "Politics always end up messy or outright dirty."

Her husband quickly felt the same drive in his budding political life as in his professional pursuits. After joining a faction of the National Liberal Party, he then entered a race for parliamentary deputy. The thirty year old thought his recipe of hard work, plus some campaigning, would suffice. But for once it didn't quite work out that way for him. He lost this first race—with not enough money, savvy, and perhaps not enough luck to blame. Maria had said, "Well, perhaps it all worked out for the best this way; you are busy enough."

"Dear, there were lessons to be learned. But I see no reason not to try again. You know I don't easily give up."

She laughed, "No, that wouldn't be you!"

Two years later he started organizing early by rallying friends, professors, and industrialists to his side. He cleverly chose a county in an area where he had personal ties. His parents had been married there, and he had been born in the county's capital of Focsani. Their vine-yard at Odobesti wasn't too far off, either. This second time around he threw himself into the new campaign, crisscrossing the county several times. He met with people from all walks of life, sat down with the peasants and heard their grievances. He told them who he was and how he would try to remedy their complaints. They must have heard him, as victory was declared in his favor at the end of voting day in 1932.

That fall he was seated on his party's side of the aisle in Parlia-ment. On inaugural morning he left the house in ceremonial dress, wearing tails and a tall hat. The first session was a rather solemn affair, with men seriously attired in suits trying to run their country. But once the shouting and arguing began in earnest, it struck him how human it all was, despite the pretension, razor-sharp snide remarks, and bom-bastic comments—or perhaps because of them.

As politics and teaching filled his days, Maria oversaw the chil-dren, household, and finances. She was reminded of her father's words to her mother upon their marriage, "You, my dear, will be our interior minister, while I'll be in charge of foreign affairs." Maria was a hands-on mother, despite the nanny's help: she played with the chil-dren, chose their clothes, knitted for them. Later on she would be the one supervising their homework, choice of schools and activities. She took pride in making her home an efficient and modern household and enjoyed entertaining, both their friends and her husband's varied guests. And while in Bucharest, she continued to monitor the activity at the vineyard from afar. With production firmly established and after a couple of good crop years, she began to entertain ways to increase her profits.

She approached her husband one day. "I'm thinking of selling the wine here, rather than go through the distributor, and have to pay him a commission."

"Sounds like a good idea. And where would you sell it?"

"Why, I said right here, in the yard. Put up a sign by the gate and let everyone know what's afoot."

"It makes good sense. We are close to the market; many people are passing by and are going to see the sign."

But Maria's mother was less than pleased with the plan. "You'll be like a fishwife peddling her stuff. What is everyone going to say, with your husband a professor and parliamentary?"

"It frankly doesn't matter to us, mother. I want to make some money. You see, we'd like to build a vacation cottage somewhere, perhaps in the mountains."

By mid-fall Maria had received the first barrels, put up a sign, and started selling wine by the bottle. She had set up a table at the front gate; there were bottles for sale, but the customers could also choose a small barrel if they wished. The wine was available for tasting, which she encouraged people to do before making a purchase. Every week she took the money to the bank and deposited it in a special account. The wine was of good quality, word eventually got around, and in time her little business became quite successful. It, of course, also depended on the vintage, some years better than others, but despite these natural oscillations, the balance of the account grew steadily.

The year 1932 also brought one more event into their already busy lives. Maria was called to help plan and host her sister-in-law's wedding. It was to be the first large reception in their house since it had been rebuilt.

Lelia had graduated from the university (French language and literature) and had become engaged. Her fiancé was her senior by fourteen years and a prominent engineer. People frowned upon the age difference, and some looked "knowingly" at one another, assuming "the worst." Aunt Marie fretted about these rumors and counseled her adoptive daughter about giving the engagement more time. But Lelia was in love, of age, and had come into the small inheritance left by her parents. Her decision was firm and thus the wedding was settled. It took place on a beautiful spring day, reminding Maria and Constantin of their special day a few years earlier. Large bouquets of lilac had been set around the house; champagne was chilled in an ice tub in the kitchen, while handmade tortes covered in white frosting patiently waited in the cellar. Brother and sister had argued the day before the ceremony, Lelia wanting Constantin to give her away.

"Lelia, it should be Aunt Marie's husband, not me. You've lived with them for twelve years, and he's been like a father to you."

"Yes, he has and I am awfully fond of him. But it's Dad who should be at my side and he's not here. You are my link to him, please do understand."

So it was her oldest brother who marched Lelia down the aisle with her nephew Dinu the ring bearer. There he was this little boy, in his best suit with shorts and matching shirt, absorbed in the moment and terrified of dropping the rings. All the while his brother Dan ran around and created havoc, reminding the guests of his Uncle Horia.

But, as always, center stage was reserved for the bride, who took their breath away, a young beautiful woman in a cascade of lace. Prayers were uttered by all for the newlyweds, and they must have been heard as their marriage turned out to be a long and happy one. As for the gossip surrounding the rather rushed engagement, it was curbed when Lelia did not have a baby nine months later. Their two girls were born after a couple of years.

So Maria and her husband had packed a lot into their lives in just a few years. With the household in good order, the boys in school, and Mona playing with her dolls under the watchful eye of the nanny, the young parents felt the time had come for a trip away, just the two of them. It was to be the exotic honeymoon they'd never had as well as Maria's first trip abroad. Having earlier joined the "Romania Tourist Society," they took advantage of a special packaged deal on the famed Orient Express train. It would become the lasting memory that would sustain them both during turbulent times ahead.

This was a happy time of their lives, and they looked forward to days alone together. There had been so little of it since their marriage in 1926, having been always surrounded by someone: Maria's parents at first, then the children. Maria threw herself wholeheartedly in planning the trip and chose her outfits carefully for her first foray into a few European cities.

But the trip did not begin under good auspices—with the departure doubtful until the last minute as Mona, the youngest, had come down with a sore throat. "Shall we leave?" a worried Maria kept asking herself and the pediatrician. It went back and forth until they established the child was well enough after all. By then they had missed their connection and spent the first leg of the trip to Ljubljana on a different train. They were rushed onto a ferry to Trieste where they finally caught the Orient Express train and proceeded through Venice on their way to Paris. It was early winter, dreary and cold; the rail car rattled and dead leaves were swirled around the windows by the erratic winds sweeping through Northern Italy.

Constantin wondered aloud, "I guess our timing might be a bit off."

"Come on, we knew this ahead of time . . . It isn't for nothing that it's called the 'off-season.'"

"I know, but still, it would be nice to see a bit of sun."

"We will, dear, once we cross into southern France. And don't forget: this off time came at 'off' prices," reminded the ever-practical Maria.

And once again she was right: within hours they were traveling along the Mediterranean coast and a balmy breeze replaced the icy winds. The weather roller coaster continued on their way to Paris, with grey skies taking hold once again.

It was winter in Paris, but it didn't matter—such was the joy Constantin took in showing Maria his "home" of years past. Here they were finally together taking in his favorite view of the Arc de Triomphe, and staring all the way down the Champs Elysees Boulevard. Hand in hand and in hushed voices, they marveled at the gothic magnificence of the Notre Dame Cathedral. Minutes later, they were mesmerized by the gorgeous stained-glass window of her "cousin" Sainte Chapelle, just a stone's throw away on the same Ile-de-la-Cite in the middle of Paris. And when they felt chilled to the bone, they stopped for soup, crusty bread, and a glass of wine. It wasn't long before Maria understood how the charm of the city had taken such a hold on her husband.

When it was time to leave, they looked at one another and agreed, "We *must* return."

The next leg of their journey wound down the wine region of Rhone River Valley, meandered through lemon groves, on to Avignon with its old papal seat, and finally took them to Nice. The air was warm and there were flowers all around when they disembarked. Suddenly they felt *happy*—a tranquil, content happiness. Lazy days followed with trips punctuated by the ritual of the meals and their protocol, as only the French knew how to take an aperitif, wine, cheese, and desserts seriously.

They would later recall the south of France as that one quintessential moment of beauty and light on their trip. And their hearts felt heavy when the train pulled out of Nice on its way to Milan. Traveling fatigue gradually started to set in, with the mind overwhelmed by the kaleidoscope of sights. Tired they might have been but they wouldn't have missed Da Vinci's famous *The Last Supper* for anything in the world.

One more rite of passage needed to be observed before they left Milan. "We must go to the Opera; they say it's one of the best in Europe," Maria had told him.

"As you wish, my dear. It's not quite my cup of tea, but I'll go along," her husband replied.

It's not that he didn't like the music. He truly enjoyed the theater, but there was something "off" about the two rolled into one. It was quite a puzzle listening to a dying character sing for another ten minutes, or witnessing a beggar sing when asking for bread and sausage! The lack of logic put him off, but for Maria's sake he refrained from any critical comments and kept his yawning to a minimum. More than anything he wished to see his wife enjoy herself and bask in the grandeur of the moment, an evening at the lavish La Scala Opera in Milan.

From there it was back to Venice, the city they had passed through at the beginning of the trip. A whirlwind tour of the Grand Canal on a gondola and a visit to San Marco's Square took place under a light mist. The grey of the skies blended in with the water, palazzi, and bridges, making it hard to tell where the sky ended and the water began.

When the time came to return, hearts were full of wonder and light, and souls had been touched by the beauty of the lands visited. But by the end of the trip, both had agreed, "We can't wait to see the children and be home again." Besides, Maria had some ideas of her own, and time was becoming ripe. As for Constantin, "The" book was waiting to be written.

Chapter Eleven
HISTORY OF THE ROMANIANS

In the early to mid-1930s, Bucharest had started to rival the grand European cities, some visited on their recent trip. Its reawakening in the aftermath of World War One was somewhat tempered by the Great Depression. But once the dark economic clouds cleared, the city re-emerged even more vibrant and cosmopolitan than it had been at the onset of the Great War.

The arts continued to flourish, the Romanians being huge fans of both the theater and music. International repertoire plays gradually replaced the sugarcoated concoctions favored in the early part of the century. Opera, initially played in local theaters, got its own grand home and attracted important European vocalists. American jazz was introduced in the 1930s and people took to it immediately. When Josephine Baker visited the city, tickets sold out within hours. It was the smart thing to do in those days: dress up, go out at night, and sip cocktails in a cabaret while listening to the latest jazz tunes. Many new museums and art galleries opened, and private collections such as Zambaccian, Storck, and Avachian added to the options available to art lovers.

The city continued to grow, and at an even faster pace than in the 1920s. Smart apartment buildings were added on the grand boulevards, many under the signature of the architect Emil Prager. As more and more cars showed up in the city's center and electric trams became ubiquitous, the very wealthy decided to "retreat" to the Herastrau Lake District. It was the residential neighborhood where many foreign embassies were also located. While strolling on those streets, one could occasionally see white-gloved, black-vested butlers answering the door, picking up mail, or taking the dog out for a walk. Chauffeurs wore uniforms including the ubiquitous cap and gloves.

And then there was the fashion of the day, as Romanian women were very keen on their attire, indeed. A Galleries Lafayette department store opened in the center, mirroring its Parisian sibling and embracing all things French. The new, shorter dress styles took off immediately, like everywhere else in the world, and silk stockings became a must. Ladies put a lot of thought into matching their accessories—hats, shoes, gloves, and jewelry alike—and after 1934 furs became all the rage, often worn just like a caplet or scarf.

The city was vibrant again and alive with energy. People milled around, and took in the pastry shops, beer gardens, and restaurants. Life was good in Bucharest, and upon returning from their trip abroad, Maria was pleased to discover her city really measured up to its European cousins. It was much the way Elena, the mother-in-law she'd never met, had felt upon her return from Vienna some thirty years earlier.

Maria sometimes wished she could partake in all the city had to offer, but her mind was often occupied with more practical concerns. With the vineyard well established and the proceeds from the wine sales growing, she wished to build a vacation home where they could all relax during the summer. The children had fun at the vineyard, but her days there were filled with work and started early, even before the sun was up. So she dreamed of a cottage where she, too, could feel on vacation.

She and Constantin had talked about it, Maria admitting, "I'm torn between the mountains and seashore. I love the mountains but never spent time near the sea. They say sea air and sun are good for children. But I'm also worried about the wind, mist, and heat wearing down any house there."

Constantin offered, "You know I fell in love with the sea the moment my uncle took me there more than twenty years ago. Nothing would make me happier. The way I look at it, that's the fate of houses. If the paint peels or the shingles fall off, we'll just fix them, won't we?"

"Let's see then what land's available; perhaps we could take a train ride along the Black Sea coast?"

"Dear, I've got my hands full with the new semester and the Parliamentary session. Why don't you go by yourself? You know land much better than I do anyway."

And so it was settled, with Maria embarking upon a train journey taking her to the coast. One thing they had agreed upon: they wished to vacation in a town where shops and services were readily available, rather than in a small resort. Constanta, the main port on the Black Sea ("too big, too busy, and no charm") was quickly ruled out.

Maria turned toward the city of Mangalia, also a harbor and some twenty miles north of the border with Bulgaria. It had its own rich history, having started as a Greek colony in the sixth century BC (as established by a rare papyrus discovered there). Then during the first and second centuries AD, it had flourished under Roman rule.

But in the mid-1930s it was a sleepy little town. Turks, a prominent part of the local population, sold watermelons, lemonade, and sweets from carts pulled by donkeys. The aroma of warm bread gently wafted in the morning breeze, and they kept their ice cream surrounded by blocks of ice in deep cellars. Fishermen's small boats bobbed in the harbor and a horse-drawn carriage was still a common site in those days.

Land was plentiful and cheap, and after looking at several lots Maria settled on a beachfront property. It was at the northern end of town, where people mostly from Bucharest had started building vacation homes in the last few years. Unknown to her at the time, they would later discover how many of the "new" neighbors they were already acquainted with in Bucharest.

She called her husband before making an offer. "I have chosen a property; it's about an acre and leads directly to the beach. The view of the sea is glorious and unobstructed. I wish you could be here to see: it's awfully pretty, in a rather wild way. There's a little grass and small bushes and a few scrawny trees and hardly anything else. "

"Can you see any houses around? I wouldn't want to be too isolated, particularly if you ever find yourself there without me."

"There are a few sprinkled about. Manoilescu's house is straight behind, about two lots away. Are you all right with the offer amount?"

"Dear, I trust your judgment."

"I'm thinking of looking at builders, providing the offer is accepted."

"So you should, and take your time. The children seem well looked after."

She sighed and smiled at the same time; how would her husband know any details of the children's lives when he was busy all day? She assumed that meant all were healthy; otherwise, he would have been informed!

"That's good to hear, dear. I won't make it a day longer than I have to," and took leave at that, awfully pleased at the trust shown by her husband. Why, she was so fortunate; her friends always complained how their husbands held the purses and how their own opinions never accounted for much.

The sale was completed within days, and Maria didn't waste any time. She asked around, interviewed and hired a German contractor who lived in a small colony north of the city. They drew up the house plans together: there would be plenty of bedrooms, a study for Constantin, and a big dining room with a porch facing the beach. She also asked for a tiled-floor entry hall and small room just to the right of it, as you stepped into the house.

While the house was being built, a carpenter was brought in to craft custom-made furniture. Construction was completed in record time, and the following summer of 1934, the family was able to enjoy their first vacation at the seaside.

The children spent the whole day on the beach, running, swimming, collecting shells, and fishing for crab under the watchful eye of their mother. The house had two floors, and Constantin's study was upstairs. He left the window open all day long, letting the salty sea air drift in. And every time he lifted his eyes they met the sparkle of the sea. Lunch was early afternoon on the patio covered in ivy, and games and walks were organized in the afternoon. Such was the wonder of summer holidays by the sea, memories to be cherished by all.

And if the dilemma of a sea versus a mountain retreat still plagued Maria's mind, it was settled for good the following year. With enough money left over for a down payment and after a terrific wine season, they were able to purchase a small lot in the town of Predeal. It was nestled in the Carpathian Mountains, only a two-hour train ride or fast drive north of Bucharest. Though she still supervised the design, an architect was hired this time. She had spotted the pretty villas surrounding their property and had sensed the need for an expert sensibility. Her future house had to "fit in"; she wouldn't have had it any other way. The "cottage" took shape the following year amidst thick fir trees and near the top of a hill, which was high enough for the boys to learn skiing.

The sight of this house filled Maria with joy. Built like a classic mountain chalet, it sported thick beams, dark green window shutters ("to blend in with the firs") and a red shingle roof ("to match the fall rusty leaves"). To have been able to contribute to the financing and to have supervised the construction filled her with deep satisfaction. Yes, here was another proof that her marriage was turning into a success, just like she had vowed.

While Maria busied herself with the vacation homes, winery, and the children, Constantin spent the middle part of the decade working on "The" book. It was to become, for many generations to come, the definitive history of the Romanian people. His friend Alex Rosetti—a buddy from his university days—was the head of the Royal Foundation, a body overseeing various cultural activities. Alex had researched many topics and thought the time had come for "someone" to write a "monumental" synthesis of the country's history. He had envisioned a book written in a clear prose style, with extensive photographs and maps so it could appeal to many people, not only to scholars.

"I've thought of you, Constantin" Alex had said. "You're young and full of energy. And after years of studying and teaching history, you should know the subject inside out."

Constantin needn't much convincing. After all, had this not been the dream he had announced to the faculty at his welcoming reception, a few years earlier?

"And if I were to agree, when would you expect the first volume?"

"How about one year?"

He could hardly believe his affirmative reply, wondering if perhaps he had lost his sanity. But Alex, a shrewd businessman, had known his friend's answer even before the fateful conversation took place. The young man's ambition to write such a comprehensive work had been shared with many. Besides, there was that family "pedigree" in history, was there not? Being turned down was not something Alex worried about. But not having the first volume completed within a year was a distinct possibility.

After a handshake, the contract was drafted within a half hour and the budding author was promised a first run of 2,500 copies. A somewhat dazed Constantin left the editorial offices with 20,000 lei, a small fortune at the time. He now threw himself into work and wrote in the evenings, on Sundays, and holidays. Wrote at the seaside, from the study overlooking the beach, and later wrote at the vineyard and in Bucharest. He kept writing with eyes affixed on the deadline.

A year later the first volume, all of 586 pages with 135 photos and maps, was ready to go to print. Alex thought, "It'll sell like hot bread."

But Constantin still had doubts, Russo's words still ringing in his ears. "I'm worried Alex; it's quite large, and it might seem daunting to many."

"Nonsense. It's just like I wished: imposing and comprehensive. I didn't commission it for cooks and bellboys."

"Still, I say we need to make it look more attractive. It needs to stand out so it will appeal to many people."

Alex caved in and together they chose an elegant style of print with a catchy cover design. The paper quality was glossy, the photos sharp, and the maps were clearly annotated.

The wait to the official launch wasn't long, taking place at the largest annual spring book fair. Lavishly displayed at the Royal Foundation booth, one hundred copies sold the first afternoon.

"We're going for a second printing in the fall, mind my words," Alex said.

It wasn't that the book was devoid of critics. Professor Iorga, a prominent and controversial historian of the last three decades, led the pack. His irksome appraisal was rooted in the fact that his own complex work had rarely met with such success. A multi-pronged attack was employed in various dailies, questioning unequivocal historical facts and attributing to the author statements he had never made. Some of the articles carried no signature while others came from the professor's cronies. Constantin replied to and disputed some of the accusations, but for the most part preferred to bask in the public's favorable response and carry on with Volume II.

Stopping one day in the Alcaly Bookstore in central Bucharest, he engaged in a brief conversation with a clerk he had known for years. The elderly Jewish gentleman pointed out, "Professor, all these polemics bring you more publicity than any money spent to advertise the volume. People wonder what the fuss is about and come in asking for the book."

And just as Alex had predicted, the second printing came out in the fall and was feted with a dinner at the famed Athenee Palace Hotel and Restaurant. One hundred friends and colleagues sat down to caviar and tenderloin and toasted a flute of champagne to the young author and his publisher. The second volume of the series followed a year later and Constantin knew he had delivered as promised.

Now it was time to keep his promise to Maria.

Every bit as busy, albeit with help, she took care of the children and ran what had become three separate houses and a vineyard. Her days were just as filled as her husband's: she woke up early, before the others, and often before daylight broke out. This quiet time was devoted to her books: accounts of the households and of their savings. She paid the bills and drew up lists of items and supplies needed. She'd then meet with the cook and decide on the daily menus; when they entertained at home, the preparations would be elaborate. Next, she made sure the children were ready for school and they had breakfast together. With the children in school, she went about her daily routine and met with friends. But Maria always made it a point to be home when the children returned from school. Lunch was the family's main meal and Constantin often joined them. A bit of rest was followed by homework, which she helped with.

Of the parents, Maria was the "disciplinarian," the one who followed the children around. She'd ask them to sit straight, keep elbows at their side, and not to speak without being asked. You were supposed to put clothes and toys away at night and shine your shoes for the following day. The light had to be turned off when leaving a room and water faucets had to be checked when leaving the house.

But she was also the one who surprised them at times with the gifts they most wanted. Dinu, their oldest, would reminisce years later about a visit they had taken to the "arts and crafts school." Twice a year the school organized a fair, the proceeds going toward the students' training. He had seen there the most amazing train with several cars, tracks, and traffic lights. He had played with it a bit but when noticing the price tag, which seemed much too expensive, he didn't say anything. His mother must have noticed how his gaze lingered over the toy, as two months later the train found its way under the Christmas tree!

It was Maria who decorated the Christmas tree when the children were young; she wrapped the gifts and also supervised the feast. Every detail was thought of ahead of time, and no one was allowed to peek before the "official" arrival of Old St. Nick.

"He must've been through, children. Come quickly, he just dropped a pile of presents!"

"Oh, Mom, we missed him again, just like last year," Dinu would complain.

"We told you to let us sit by the tree to wait for him."

Dan would chip in, "We couldn't sit there all day, silly, we would have been hungry."

Their eyes would widen every year at the sight of the ornate tree, as if it were the first time. The candles were lit, and then each child was asked to help light the "sparkles," little sticks hanging from the branches. Shiny gifts were stacked under the tree, and the table nearby was piled up high with traditional sweets, including the "Christmas log." Even after they discovered "the origins" of St. Nick, they continued to relish the Christmas holiday together. It was just like they did with Easter and how they looked forward to seaside and mountain vacations. Tradition played an important part in their lives, enjoying these comfortable rituals side by side, unaware of the dark clouds looming ahead.

Constantin felt it was Maria's turn to be surprised now. His promise had been to take her on another trip once the first volume of his *History of the Romanians* was completed. Last time they had traveled, she had chosen the itinerary and taken care of the details. This time he planned everything and one day he came home and said, "Pack your bags, my dear. We're leaving a month from now."

Her eyes widened and a large smile lit up her face. He hadn't forgotten his promise!

"And where are we going?"

"I wish I could keep it a surprise . . . but you need to pack accordingly . . . for a cruise on the Black Sea."

"A cruise . . . why, that's absolutely wonderful! I must buy a few new dresses, a couple of hats. Oh goodness, there's so much to do!" At that she planted a long kiss on her husband's lips.

Romanian cruise liners had quite a following in the Eastern Mediterranean and the Black Sea at the time, based on their excellent service, speed, and reliability. The whole fleet had been painted in white, hence its moniker "the swans of the Orient," well known to the passengers of the day.

And so it was that a month later they embarked on the train that would take them to the harbor of Constanta. Maria had chosen a navy dress with polka dots and a straw hat with navy ribbon, while her husband wore cool cream-colored linen. The children saw them to the train station with mixed emotions. While excited to be without their parents for ten days or so, the boys wished they could have traveled, too, while Mona was certain she would miss her mother.

"Next time you'll come with us, boys; in the meantime, listen to your grandparents and behave. Mona, Mommy will think of you every day and send you good-night kisses." And at that they took leave of the family, trusting the children would be in good hands.

They embarked later that afternoon, and sailed before sunset on the *Transylvania*. She was a sight to behold, all gleaming in white with the Romanian flag flying high on her mast. They settled in quickly and enjoyed a lavish dinner the first night. Then after coffee they walked on deck and took in the dark-ink sky dotted with bright stars. The gentle bobbing of the boat lured them to rest, and Maria, normally a light sleeper, was astonished when she woke up nine hours later!

It was the following day that they met Adrian, who would become a lifelong dedicated friend, lawyer, hunting and fishing buddy, and English tutor. He had first approached Constantin on the voyage. "I read your book, and I am one of your admirers."

"Are you an historian?"

"No, I'm an attorney and found your history book easy to read, despite not being a specialist. But I must be honest and admit to skipping over some details."

"What appealed to you the most?"

"Its clean style and impartiality. You present the facts and the background in logical sequence, without the embellishments found in so many other books."

"Well, thank you, it's very kind of you. I try to stick to the facts and let my readers supply the emotion as they see fit. Are you traveling by yourself?"

"Yes, Professor."

"Would you like to join my wife and me for afternoon tea?"

"It would be my pleasure."

They learned more of one another over tea served in delicate porcelain cups and accompanied by the traditional trimmings of English "high tea": scones, thick cream, and miniature sandwiches. Adrian had done part of his legal training in London and delighted in all things British, sharing with his new acquaintances anecdotes of the time spent abroad. Constantin had believed for quite a while how English was becoming increasingly necessary; it was to "gradually replace French as an international communication language."

"You must speak English fluently, don't you?"

"Of course, it's quite an easy language, compared to German or French; the grammar is a lot less complex."

"That's good to hear; I'm planning to improve on the bits I was taught in high school."

"You really should; I can recommend someone."

Little did they know at the time how years later Adrian would be tutoring his friend. Maria had also thought English would be a good language for the children to learn early on and wanted to know more. And so conversation flowed easily, and by the time they took leave of one another, promises were made to resume their discussion over the next days.

That evening the captain had warned of storms heading their way, after they had watched the skies darken progressively throughout the afternoon. Thunder began to pound, punctuated by bolts of lightning while the angry sea foamed up. The boat started rocking sideways and vertically and china elaborately set on dining tables slid every which way. Maria begged to be excused, her face white as a sheet. Her husband tried to accompany her to the cabin but she had insisted,

"There's no point in coming along. I need to throw cold water on my face, lie down, and turn the lights off. You stay if you feel up to it."

Mostly everyone had cleared the dining room but Constantin, his new friend, and a few others who felt no seasickness whatsoever. Adrian glanced around, "Shall we stay?"

"Why not? I am hungry," replied Constantin.

Dinner was excellent as always and the service superb, the staff glad to have some customers. As for Adrian and his new friend, shared common passions were soon discovered.

"This fish tastes so fresh it's as if it had just been caught."

"Do you enjoy fishing, Adrian?"

"Enjoy?! I absolutely love it! I'd go every Sunday, if I could. It is my favorite hobby, that, and hunting, too."

As these happened to be Constantin's favorite recreational pursuits as well, the two men proceeded to recount tale after tale of special fortunes and mishaps, like only true huntsmen would, until the time came to retire for the evening.

The night cleared the storm away, and passengers awoke to sunshine and calm seas the following morning. They stopped in Istanbul and rushed on to Aya Sophia, the Byzantine Cathedral turned mosque and then museum. There they took in its precious mosaics of the Virgin with child—a rhapsody of blue and gold albeit chipped by the passage of time. The "Blue Mosque"—a symphony of blue, green, aqua and white tiles—the Byzantine basilica of Kahrie Djami, with its priceless byzantine mosaics; and the Sultan's Palace at Topkapi, filled a couple of days. From the grand terrace of the palace, they took in the sight of the Bosporus Strait, the channel of water dividing the two continents of Asia and Europe. It seemed quite tranquil despite the coming and going of the boats and the bustle on some of the quays. Many fishermen were bobbing about in small dinghies, and along the shore a few stray cats lingered around awaiting their lunch.

Next stop was Greece, preceded by a delightful day at sea, where life revolved around meals. A hearty breakfast was followed by the midmorning "snack" of a sandwich and a cup of broth. A multi-course lunch, five o'clock tea with cookies, and finally a sumptuous dinner filled up the remainder of the day. Everything was included, other than alcohol, and passengers outdid one another enjoying the many culinary delicacies.

In Athens they checked into a hotel before rushing to the Acropolis to view the Parthenon Temple, followed by the National History Museum and Art Gallery. They had some time on their own that first afternoon in Greece, and so Maria suggested a visit to a rug store. Constantin acquiesced, regarding it as an inevitable consequence of traveling together, and eager to please his wife. Pottery, silver, and carpet stores abounded on every corner, and the owners practically begged them:

"Come in, come in lovely lady and her gentleman; this is where you find the world's most beautiful rugs."

"Well, we're just looking for now. . . ."

"Look, please look to your heart's content . . . such exquisite quality . . . such rare good value. . . ."

But Maria knew exactly what she was in the market for. "Could you please measure the deep red and gold one in the corner?" she asked.

"Now that one is really special, Madame . . . you'll always regret if you didn't buy it."

Constantin silently watched Maria bargain with the merchant, a knot tightening in his chest each time such a transaction took place, the whole process unnerving. He had to admit, though, there was little to worry about. His wife seemed totally in her element and standing her ground at each turn!

Needless to say, the purchase was made without anyone "advertising" the customs tax waiting upon their return—which pretty much eliminated the "rare" deal. "Oh well," Maria thought, as they placed the rug in the home entry hall and enjoyed it every day after, and pretty soon the tax sting was forgotten.

There followed trips meandering between the islands and hugging the coastline. A breathtaking scene awaited them the night of their return to Athens, the whole town twinkling with brightly lit wax candles. Thousands of Christians walked along holding them and greeting one another with "Christ has risen," as Easter midnight mass was being celebrated in the tradition of the Greek Orthodox faith.

A trip to Corinth, Delphi, and the famed temple of Apollo preceded their return home. The temple was where people had once come to "consult" the oracle before embarking on a military campaign or settling in a new town. The inscription on the frontispiece: "Know thyself," seemed a rather good starting point and had become an oft-copied phrase.

As they started to leave, a dark-skinned woman, more like a gypsy, tugged at Maria's skirt. "Miss, Miss, you must let me read your palm."

"Oh, nonsense, I believe in no such thing." Maria firmly stood her ground as the woman kept insisting. Constantin became quite impatient and handed the gypsy a few coins. "Here, take these and leave us alone."

"Thank you, mister, thank you. But I don't take money for nothing. So, I stare at your face, I read it, and say: you'll go up, come down and rise again."

Both he and Maria shrugged and dismissed the woman's silly words: it was time to return to the boat.

And so, after visiting wondrous sites and with happy memories, they embarked upon the journey home. Constantin, ever the professor, reflected on how useful such a trip could be to students of history, and thought of the next chapter of his book. In the meantime, his wife tried to imagine the problems the children and homes may have encountered during their absence.

What neither could have anticipated was the storm brewing.

Chapter Twelve
POLITICAL UNREST UNDER STORMY SKIES

In 1938 dark, ominous clouds began to blow across Europe, and Romania was cast under their shadow. King Carol II and his many governments had kept the country running between 1930 and 1937, and the economy had grown steadily, to peak in 1938. But the time of relative political stability was running out. Elections held in December 1937 were indecisive, with no party achieving a ruling majority, despite active campaigning on all sides and a flurry of satirical newspaper cartoons. It was with concern that Constantin and his father-in-law read the returns together. The poor showing of their Liberal Party and the rise of the right-wing faction worried them. As for Constantin himself, he had fared better than many of his colleagues, being re-elected county deputy for a third consecutive term.

A transitional government followed, and a certain sense of panic swept through the population. Large bank withdrawals took place within weeks, and transfers of capital abroad became common. Political antennas were attuned, and with no firm announcements or facts to back it up, the rumor mill kept churning.

Alex Rosetti, the publisher, called his friend Constantin one morning in February, 1938 saying, "I've heard they're gathering tonight at the 'Millionaires' Club.'"

Constantin had a vague idea but wanted Alex to clarify. "Who's gathering, Alex?"

"Well, all that matter, everyone with real money: the industrialists, big bankers, landowners."

"What do you think is going on?"

Alex had no idea, but knew it was unprecedented. "No word has leaked out, but I bet it's going to be big. They hardly ever get together like this, unless there's a death, and I haven't heard of anyone important being at their deathbed."

The Millionaire's Club was housed in a lovely, turn-of-the-century building next to Alex's offices. It was a social club of sorts in the British tradition. The wealthy usually gathered there to take lunch, read newspapers, smoke cigars, or merely chat. Later that evening Alex watched the congregation arrive, many by chauffeured cars, others by foot despite the cold, gray night. They stayed on for hours, and from his window Alex could see how the large chandeliers next door were lit well into the evening. He paced and paced and remained in the office past nine o'clock, hoping to "hear" something, anything, and run a "special" edition! But the lights next door shone on, and fatigue eventually caught the better of him. Once he arrived home, he fell into a restless sleep, and upon awakening dressed quickly and ran out to buy the dailies. This is how he came to hear the following morning that a new government was announced. It seemed the millionaires sent word of their concern to the king about the state of the economy, warning of the grave consequences that awaited the country if the banks and monetary system collapsed. The sovereign had listened and responded.

Within two weeks a new Constitution was created, giving extended powers to the king but also signaling the beginning of a more authoritarian rule with a mock parliament. Then the king went one step further and abolished all political parties in March 1938. This decision was partially motivated by his concern over the rise of the ultra-nationalistic right-wing party, which had carried 15 percent of the vote in the failed December elections. Unwilling to single out a specific entity, he settled for dissolving all parties.

If these changes had a positive outcome, it was the arrival of an energetic minister of the interior, Armand Calinescu, who would become prime minister a year later. His main goals were outlined quickly: to stabilize the economy and to align the country's foreign policy with that of Britain and France. This positioning alongside Romania's "traditional" allies was viewed by many as critical to its sovereignty. It was also crucial as Hitler, the German Chancellor, securely ensconced at the head of the Third Reich, was pursuing the abolition of some territorial treaties concluded at the end of World War I. This German revisionist policy could have posed a grave threat to Romania's acquisition of Transylvania.

Constantin had watched the Nazi rise in Germany. A centrist at heart, a member of the Liberal Party, and a scholar of history, he was alarmed by any form of political extremism. That was why the emergence of the right-wing nationalistic party in Romania concerned him deeply. He followed uneasily how this party changed its name several times until it decided upon "All for the country"—catchy enough to attract the gullible. He watched, with apprehension, their clipped marches in green shirts and with belts across the chest reminiscent of military attire. The magnetic personality and histrionic speeches of the party's leader, a former law student named Corneliu Codreanu, only increased its appeal. As for his followers, they were a mixed group. Some were young idealists in search of a cause, others individuals disgruntled with the traditional parties. There were even some clergy attracted by the party's religious zeal. Symbolic monetary contributions were offered by a few industrialists, not unlike their German peers in the 1930s, a "just in case" handout for whatever may come. And so the party swelled its ranks.

The more steam they gathered, the more vocal they became. Emboldened by their growing popularity, they proclaimed disdain for the League of Nations as an Allied sham. As Constantin read their foreign policy manifesto: to "align Romania to Germany and Italy once we ascend to power," he felt the skies were turning very dark indeed.

The family went about their daily lives with a growing sense of unease and concern. The year 1938 was to be remembered as tense, one in which many countries felt on the brink of war. And the historian in Constantin couldn't tell yet if it was just another phase of their ever-changing political kaleidoscope, or the forbearer of a dramatically different era for their country and all of Europe.

As for Calinescu, the recently elected interior minister, he decided the threat of the nationalistic "All for the Country" party was too grave not to be addressed. He pondered and waited for the right opportunity, which soon presented itself. A life-threatening letter sent by the party's leader to a prominent politician was the spark that brought the hammer down.

"We, as elected officials, cannot tolerate any such threats against our citizens," Calinescu had stated. And so he ordered the arrest of the party leaders including Mr. Codreanu. A rapid conviction followed and brought a sentence of ten years of forced labor.

While this tempest burst in Romania, a much larger storm was gathering over Central and Eastern Europe. The annexation of Austria, the so-called "Anschluss," had taken place in March 1938, having sent seismic waves across the continent. A part of Czechoslovakia known as the Sudetenland—lands inhabited for centuries by ethnic Germans—had met with the same fate. Constantin read about these events and would later remember trying to grasp their import for his country, having gathered early on that Hitler wouldn't stop at Austria and would carry on this expansionist policy. Only God knew how far he'd go and for how long, until he changed the course of history.

He and Maria worried what the future might bring but tried to maintain their normal summer routine for the sake of the children. Before leaving for the seaside, they went to lunch at Maria's parents on a warm June day, when all doors and windows had been opened to let in the breeze. The table was festively set up as always, and in its center sat a large bowl of cherries freshly picked from their garden. The children and their twin cousins, Emil's children, were grown enough to play without creating the havoc of years past. It all seemed so peaceful in the old house, until Professor Mehedinti came out with a German edition of a map atlas of Europe. He handed it to his oldest grandson, Dinu, who had turned eleven.

Professor Mehedinti went and sat next to his oldest grandson, Dinu. Despite his young age the boy already had a keen interest in geography and history.

"Do you know what happened this spring?"

"Father said Austria was taken over by the Germans."

"And do you know why it should matter to us?"

The boy blushed; was he supposed to be aware of it? "No, grandfather."

The older gentleman smiled and opened up his atlas. "Here, let me show you where all these countries are. He patiently pointed out how the atlas depicted both the current borders as well as those in 1914, prior to World War One. Having his grandfather explain the issues on the map began to help the youngster understand how neighboring countries could stake claims on his.

"So what do we do, Grandpa?"

"We get ready, boy. We prepare our strategy. But I'm sorry to say we're late already."

As if on cue clouds rolled over their picture-perfect day, reminding them of their vulnerability. And their tranquil moment was no more.

The family left by train a few days later. Until this summer they had traveled by train to Constanta followed by a cab ride to Mangalia. But the train line had been extended now all the way south, offering a quicker and more comfortable journey, without direct exposure to the scorching heat and dust.

Once at their vacation house, they settled in quickly and the children enthusiastically embarked upon a month of swimming and playing on the beach. These were happy times: the weather was wonderful and food was cheap and plentiful. They held impromptu lunches and parties with their neighbors and everyone's mood improved. At the end of the stay, they took a special trip, a friend driving them all the way south to Caliacra, almost to the Bulgarian border, where the children saw dolphins for the first time. The high boardwalk made for impressive vistas while the clear, sunny day and the blue sea provided the perfect backdrop. The trip made such a lasting impression upon Dinu, that in the fall it became the topic for "your favorite summer activity" essay. The carefree day and its fleeting image would be carried in his heart for years to come.

Tension continued to rise that fall. The day the university year resumed on October 1, Constantin returned home early, quite agitated. "Our party leader was informed by cable of events which allegedly took place in Munich yesterday."

Maria steadied herself. "Has another country fallen?"

"No, or at least not yet. But France and England have ratified the takeover of the Czech Sudetenland by Germany. It's as good as giving the whole of Czechoslovakia away."

"How could that be? And what about the League of Nations, didn't they take a stand?"

"Not a sound from them either. It seems that everyone is ready to appease Hitler, desperately trying to avoid a larger conflict."

"You think they have succeeded?"

"Only time will tell. The British Prime Minister Chamberlain headed home and declared 'Peace in our time.' I wish I could be as hopeful as he is."

They didn't have to wait long. By November the southern part of Czechoslovakia was next, ceded to Hungary in one of the many ramifications of the Munich accord. Poland jumped into the fray, too, annexing one Czech county for herself. The steamroller was moving fast, seemingly unstoppable.

As for the Romanian king, he traveled to Paris and London to gauge what economic and military help Romania might secure at this time of crisis. On the return trip, he made an unofficial stop in Germany, meeting there with Hitler and Goering, the commander of the German Air Force (Luftwaffe). Goering was already eyeing Romania's rich oilfields and vast gas supplies, both critical to the German war effort. In exchange the Sovereign was offered a wide encompassing German-Romanian alliance.

It was also during these talks that the Germans asked the king to reconsider an earlier decision. They were keen to see a return of the extreme right-wing party (the Romanian equivalent of the Nationalist German movement) as part of the government.

It would have seemed a secondary issue (given the magnitude of the mounting world tension), but it turned out to be the spurt that set a bloody stream in motion. The king understood that reversing his earlier position would have come at great personal peril, in light of his previous stance. He was not going to have the Germans dictate to him who should and shouldn't be in his own government. So he decided to disregard altogether the Germans' offer and suggestions. In a dramatic departure from his entire tentative past stance, he set out to curb, once and for all, the far-right threat in his country. Picking up the phone, he gave the order to dispose of the heads of the party, starting with their leader. Codreanu and thirteen others, already prisoners, were strangled and then shot in the back while seemingly "trying to escape" in late November 1938. The matter had been settled swiftly, at least for the time being.

Dinu and some of his school friends had gone to "greet" the king upon his return. It had become a familiar sight, with people lining the boulevards along the royal route upon such important occasions. They waited, joked, drank lemonades, and waited some more. But to their great disappointment, the official cars never showed up. One of Dinu's mates picked up the evening edition of a newspaper and, being bored, the boys scanned the notices for something of interest. Sandwiched between various headlines, they read a small notice announcing Codreanu's execution, without providing details.

Later that evening his father explained the magnitude of the bloody events of the day. "The leaders of the All for the Country Party were executed today."

"Weren't they in prison?"

"Yes, Dinu they were. The king felt that despite being jailed they could have triggered street violence; their following is still impressive."

Dan chimed in, as only he could, "So they are all dead now. Why do you worry?"

"Boy, the leaders are dead but there are plenty of party members out there. I fear revenge. You must be very careful when you walk to school. If you ever see a crowd gathering or hear shouts, just pick up the pace. Move fast and don't talk to anyone. If boys talk about it in school, just say you don't know anything about it and walk away."

Dan nodded, eager to go back to his cartoon books. Dinu said, "Yes, Father," and thought the matter must have been serious indeed, as his father appeared truly concerned.

A few months later, in February, 1939, Constantin was called by the prime minister to the Royal Palace. With the relatively new government attempting to bring in new young faces, he was offered the position of "Royal Resident." It was the equivalent of governor of some ten counties with full administrative powers. His assignment: the recently organized Lower Danube administrative province with the seat in the Danube harbor of Galati.

Maria supported him, albeit less enthusiastically than in the past. His position in Parliament required him to attend three or four sessions per week for a couple of months in the fall and spring. But this new post in a different town meant he would temporarily have to give up teaching at the university. The household would have to move, and children would have to be enrolled in new schools. All this weighed heavily on her mind.

"It'd be easier if you went now, and I stay behind with the children to let them finish the school year," Maria had said and he had agreed with her logic. She had also shared her concerns with her father. "Father, I don't want to worry Constantin, but I fear this deepening political involvement of his. What if the All for the Country party is resuscitated, and the current officials become targets? We could all be in danger then."

"Maria, dear, let's break this apart. The party may or may not re-emerge. Your husband is now a governor and not a minister in a high post. You're moving to a provincial town where it is easier to offer adequate security to the governor. I say: don't worry too much for now."

She embraced him and left feeling better. Her father had such a way to alleviate most concerns. If only her mother could have been more like him.

But barely a month or so into Constantin's new position, ominous news once again sent shivers across the European continent.

"Remember what I had told you about handing over Czechoslovakia in Munich last fall?" he reminded Maria.

"Well, it's happened." And as he was about to tell her, his sons boisterously walked in.

"What's happening, Father? Is it something bad again?" Dinu asked, as even the youngsters had recently learned to anticipate misfortune over good news.

"Czechoslovakia has fallen to Germany. It surrendered under the threat of an air strike."

Young Dan couldn't hide his disappointment. "You mean they didn't fight at all?"

"Would you want your people to be wiped out by bombs falling out of the sky if you were in charge of a country?"

"I guess not."

"You guessed correctly. There was nothing anyone could have done once their heavy border fortifications were overrun."

Maria wanted to know. "What about Britain and France? What was their reaction?"

"Strong condemnation . . . firm verbal sanctions . . . this and that . . . all rhetoric. The stage was set last fall, that's where the ball started rolling. The cooperation in Munich showed the Germans they could continue to dream big."

"Will there be others, Father?"

He pondered for a moment; the boys were still so young, only eleven and twelve years old. The father wished to shield them as long as possible while the realist knew honesty should prevail.

"I don't know. No one knows. But I fear turbulent times ahead."

Silence set in until Maria reminded her sons there was still homework to be dealt with, sending the youngsters to their rooms.

The spring passed without further developments. Constantin spent the week at the new headquarters in Galati and returned home Saturday afternoon. With the end of the school year in sight, Maria started planning the move and by the summer she was ready. The furniture was covered, the cellar was checked, and finally the gas and water were shut off just before leaving. The children were mostly excited by the adventure ahead and its new sources of fun while Maria was mostly apprehensive.

In the late 1930s Galati was an active, noisy harbor town on the Danube. It was hot and sticky when they arrived, and the lazy river breeze did nothing to dispel the thick July heat. When the wind blew, one felt no relief. It only brought swirls of dust; whiffs of boiled corn and fried dough rolled all in one insinuated itself into every crevice.

Maria busied herself at first with setting up the house. It was a grand, spacious mansion centrally located, making it easy for the children to get to their schools. It was also close to the gubernatorial headquarters, allowing Constantin to join them for lunch on most days. The children spent the first few weeks making friends and swimming in the river. Maria seemed less taken with her new "entourage," but graciously tried to visit with "the wives" to blend into her new surroundings.

School was just around the corner, set to start on September 15. Maria enquired after the various requirements (uniforms, manuals, desk items) and was told the boys had to get a military haircut style nicknamed "number 3." Dinu and Dan were less than thrilled but complied knowing it would have been pointless to argue with their mother.

With the boys set to go to high school, the question remained where to enroll Mona. After careful pondering Maria decided on the public grammar school close by. This raised quite a few eyebrows with the local elite, accustomed to sending their daughters to the Catholic school of Notre Dame de Sion.

"Let them gossip," Maria had said. "The boys went to public school and have done just fine. I want her to grow up just like the other children, be one of them."

As for her husband he threw himself into work, as he always did. Together with his team, they drew up a work plan and a budget, both for the near and the distant future. Ushering in a new style of accountability, he had his program printed in a brochure, for all to see.

After months of research, he concluded that the planting of new forests was a priority. Many trees had been indiscriminately chopped off the surrounding hills that would lead to water erosion. They tried to pick species best matched to the soil and to create arboretums in larger villages for future sources. He then drew a plan for comprehensive irrigation in the county, one badly needed after years of drought. This was followed by a plan for a new road to Focsani, his birthplace. A "highway" of sorts across the mountains was also being considered. As for matters closer to his heart, Constantin allocated money for new architectural diggings in north Dobrogea, the south province.

Constantin was told that he made a good manager, and this pleased but also surprised him, given his lack (to date) of administrative skills. But being a quick study, he "learned on the job" and adapted himself quickly. Yet he was so wrapped up in the frantic pace of his new position that the traumatic events of early fall literally stopped him dead in the tracks. Lately he had barely taken notice of the dark, ominous clouds gathered in the sky above.

PART III
THE SECOND WORLD WAR

Chapter Thirteen
MAINTAINING NEUTRALITY

The political game of cat and mouse had continued earlier that year, culminating with the fall of Czechoslovakia. The Western powers' hope remained that with every concession offered the likelihood of war would be removed. However, Germany felt that each aggression tolerated by England and France brought them one stroke closer to the ultimate goal. Their dream was to erase the map drawn at the conclusion of WWI, with the Versailles Treaty, and reestablish Germany as the preeminent European power. A crucial building block toward this goal was ensuring that the Soviet Union—a force to be reckoned with and harboring her own expansionist agenda—would not be drawn into a larger European conflict. This was achieved with the crafting of the German-Soviet Nonaggression Pact. Also known as Molotov-Ribbentrop, it was named after the Soviet politician and German foreign minister, respectively. The pact seemingly assured that the Soviets wouldn't muddy the German waters, and when signed in August 1939, the treaty practically divided Europe into "spheres of interest." As for the Romanians, they felt left on uncertain footing, despite earlier promises of assistance by England and France if their independence were to be threatened.

On September 1, 1939, Constantin woke up early on a crisp late-summer day. As dawn turned to light, he was already on the road to one of his customary inspections. He exchanged a few pleasantries with the chauffer and then asked to have the radio turned on. With some kind of static in the background, the distant voice was crackling and making it difficult to understand.

"Could I have heard right?" wondered Constantin, and then he asked the driver. "Would you be so kind to turn up the volume?"

"—The German army, under the orders of the Fuhrer . . . has advanced. . . ."

Within minutes they understood that Hitler's troops had invaded Poland. Silence settled in the car, while the radio announcer carried on, in a rushed voice, details pouring out.

"Do you wish to return home, Sir?" the driver had asked.

"No, thank you, Cristea. I will call my wife and the office from our next stop for any updates."

"Very well, Sir."

At his destination it seemed business as usual, with the sleepy small town heedless to the forces unleashed in the greater world around them. Constantin visited city hall and the police station, where town officials wanted to know if "the news" were true. "I only know what I heard on the radio," he replied. The mayor didn't press him; he had his own issues at home and Poland felt far enough. After the inspection was carried out, the two men headed home to Galati, eager to hear and read details of the Polish invasion.

Later that evening Maria had asked, "Any word from England and France yet?"

"No."

"Do you think they'll close their eyes once more?"

"Hard to tell, but I don't think so," Constantin replied.

"Why?"

"Britain can't renege on the defense pact signed with Poland less than a week ago. It's a formal agreement, unlike the verbal embroidery spun around the Czech story."

"Has there been a Romanian official reaction?"

"Not yet."

"Really, nothing from the king?" Marie asked, concerned about any government response and its consequences for them.

"As I said, not yet; besides, he's in a challenging spot. The decision to side with one camp or another ultimately rests with him."

"We'll probably be drawn in sooner or later."

"We might. It might well happen sooner than most anticipate."

Maria's heart felt heavy.

Two days later, on September 3, Britain and France declared war on Germany. As for Poland, it collapsed in seventeen days, its demise hastened by the Soviet Red Army's invasion from the east. The Molotov-Ribbentrop nonaggression pact had curbed the ability of Germany and the Soviet Union to engage in direct conflict. But it had not specified that the two countries couldn't both attack—at the same time—another nation.

By the middle of the month, the first carloads of Polish refugees pulled into Galati. The locals silently watched the parade of dusty cars with torn mattresses, pillows, and suitcases piled high. They saw women crying, men with bleary eyes, and blond children, their eyes widened by fear. They came, rested a bit, refueled, and kept going— God only knew to where.

The remnants of the Polish army briefly reassembled in southeast Romania, and then quickly decamped and headed for England. The Polish National Treasury made an equally brief stop at the National Bank in Bucharest and then continued on, probably toward Switzerland. As for Romania's aid to the Polish refugees, it was decried by Germany, which issued an official protest.

Constantin and Maria wondered if this uprooting of people and cultures would sweep across the continent. Men and women were fleeing the madness unleashed and abandoning their homes and country. Judging by Hitler's professed ambitions, they feared this would continue unabated for quite a while, and adding to their surprise was how fast the military operations had unfolded. On September 1, Poland was a free country, just like Romania. Less than three weeks later, the nation had been occupied.

The family went about its daily business as best they could. But somehow they felt suspended in time, the movie of their lives stopped at September 1. General unease grew with each passing day. With no word forthcoming from the King, the political gossip was rampant with scenarios of war and alliances.

The wait wouldn't be long. On September 11, the king called in the general council and Prime Minister Calinescu, the latter recently appointed minister of defense as well. The sovereign went around the table and asked his main advisors to present their viewpoints. The prime minister went first, stating his position in favor of the "traditional" alliance with France and England. If disregarded, he was prepared to hand in his resignation. But others were not as convinced, leaning toward negotiations with Germany. The sovereign listened to all without interrupting. Then, after hours of debate, King Carol II first thanked the council, stated his appreciation for the positions presented, and concluded the meeting by announcing the country's strict neutrality. Some cheered while others shook their heads in disbelief, muttering under their breaths.

The evening dailies ran a double edition announcing the news to the nation. And that evening the diplomats breathed easier at the French and British embassies in Bucharest, as an official alignment with Germany had been feared. In Allied circles, in Paris and London alike, Prime Minister Calinescu was viewed as the person best suited to pull Romania their way. Away from the general council and as a private citizen, the king had agreed with the prime minister's position as well. But as a sovereign he felt neutrality would serve the country better.

And just when Romania thought it had found its direction, tragedy struck, and this time much closer to home. Constantin, Maria, and the children were taking lunch when the phone rang. Maria got up to answer, eager to protect her husband's brief lunch break.

"Oh, good day to you, Mr. Miloteanu."

Constantin arched his eyebrows; his secretary hardly ever called if it weren't for pressing news. He got up while his wife was replying, "Yes, I'll put him on right away."

"Mr. Miloteanu?"

He listened for a couple of minutes, without interrupting. "Thank you for calling so promptly. I shall stay in until I hear back from you." He returned to the table, his color ashen.

"The prime minister was shot to death."

Some members of the far right-wing party (out of favor and without their fallen leader) had returned from Germany illegally and had organized a plot. Then they had carried out their task boldly by shooting and killing the prime minster in broad daylight.

The assassins then pressed on and stormed the central radio station, near the scene of the carnage. There the criminals managed to announce their bloody feat to the nation before being apprehended. The prime minister's wife was arranging flowers in a vase, waiting for her husband's return when the radio delivered the bloody news.

Constantin's secretary immediately came to the house. Panic had set in, and many feared other dignitaries could be targeted as well. Protection needed to be instituted, and a military guard was posted at the front door. Maria, never one to take kindly to authority, felt the measure was "useless."

"They could easily kidnap the children from school if they want to hurt us."

Her protests fell on deaf ears, her husband arguing the necessity of enhanced security at such an uncertain time. "Besides, the children aren't going anywhere until I feel it is safe," he announced.

"Well, I can't be locked in; I have errands to run, food to buy."

"Dear, please, you can't possibly leave the house right now. There's nothing that can't wait."

Maria recalled her apprehension when her husband had been appointed governor. She, who had never been superstitious, had felt a chill when learning of his new position. Her father had been able to calm her for a while, but her worst fears were being confirmed now.

The guards stood by for a week until the unrest settled down. Their house was never directly targeted, and neither were the gubernatorial headquarters. The children stayed home for a few days, and the delight at not having to attend school was tinged with the disappointment of having to miss an invitation to one of their new friends' homes. The oldest boy, Dinu, at age twelve, understood that something "really important" had taken place. Because of that he saved the front page of the dailies with some photos. He was going to share these with his grandfather once back in Bucharest, and he was certain his granddad would shed some light on this matter.

The king's answer to the assassinations was decisive. The killers were executed at the murder site, with the bodies left out for all to see. "This is the fate of the country's traitors," stated an accompanying banner.

More bloodshed followed, as the new prime minister decided to "settle the score." Three members of the nationalistic right-wing party for each county, 251 in all, were sentenced to death. Their bodies were once again displayed in public places.

News was called in to Constantin's office as it developed. Swift punishment of the killers had been a foregone conclusion. But the bloodbath that followed raised unease among many. On September 22 the boys returned from school to find their mother in tears. She hardly ever cried, so something awful must have taken place, they thought. Why, they were certain someone must have died. Sure enough, she confirmed their suspicions right away. "Alex Cantacuzino was among those killed."

They hadn't heard the name before. "Who was he, mother?"

"A friend from my early twenties, we often went out together in those days."

When her husband came home late that evening, she told him, "I can't possibly comprehend why these executions were necessary."

"They weren't. The new government overreacted, believing its actions would deter future criminal acts."

"Do you think they will?"

"I'm skeptical. Violence usually incites more violence. But whatever the future holds, what pains me is the loss of lives. These were men who, despite their political affiliation, had no direct connection with the prime minister's assassination."

"Like Alex Cantacuzino."

"Yes, just like him. You know, Maria, nothing good shall come out of this."

And nothing did.

Within days Constantin was recalled to Bucharest when the king created a new "Front of National Renaissance." Its first order of business: keep the country out of armed conflict (and the military intact) and postpone litigious conflict over borders for as long as possible. Constantin was asked to join the new "Front" as secretary general.

He left Galati with a heavy heart, disappointed by not being able to continue the work he had initiated there. He was returning to be a small spoke in a large wheel, with layers of bureaucracy and egos to be mollified. He answered the king's calling with unease and concern, but answer he did, believing in his foremost duty as citizen of the kingdom.

As for Maria, she would have normally celebrated a return to Bucharest. But knowing that her husband was being pulled deeper and deeper into a political quagmire tempered the happiness of being home. If only he could toss aside politics and go on teaching, she told herself. If only.

The fall flew by in a blur, and Christmas break gave the family a chance to regroup at the mountain villa in Predeal. It had snowed heavily and the bright white coat shimmered under the sun. It was hard to imagine the German armies getting ready to crisscross the continent when all was so peaceful there in the mountains. The children skied and their parents took long walks, but they also stayed in touch with the world, listening to the radio in the evening and reading the dailies.

The Christmas tree was still ornate, with gifts piled underneath. Their dinner was still rich and plentiful. But one couldn't help but think of what next year might bring.

Days later, 1939, the most tumultuous of years, had come to an end. But the storm unleashed would continue to roar.

Chapter Fourteen
ROMANIA DWINDLES

At the beginning of 1940, Romania was still neutral and at a cross-roads in its fragile balancing act, and the main policy goals outlined at the creation of the Front of National Renaissance still prevailed. The need to remain outside the European conflict, postpone territorial disputes with the neighbors (Soviet Union, Hungary, Bulgaria), and maintain the military intact as long as feasible, were repeatedly emphasized. But with each passing month these tasks became increasingly difficult.

The country had watched uneasily as the Soviets had contributed to the invasion of Poland. Then less than two months later, in November 1939, they had invaded Finland under the pretext of a centuries' old territorial claim. The world had expected a speedy conclusion to the conflict, much like that witnessed with the fall of Poland. But this new campaign dragged on for nearly four months as a harsh winter and the country's rugged terrain played to the advantage of the Finns, who were accustomed to both. It was only when the Finnish Army had exhausted its war supplies that an interim peace was declared in March 1940.

This new aggression emphasized to the Romanian government the critical danger represented by the Soviet Union. With the European conflict gaining momentum, the country would eventually be faced with choosing between the lesser of two evils, and a Crown Council was called once again. Gathered at the end of May, it changed the direction outlined less than a year earlier. It now concluded that a Soviet threat against the country, its society, and way of life, exceeded the direct peril posed by Nazi Germany. At the imperative request of Berlin, oil and gas supplies were now promised in exchange for military equipment. The country was not to directly enter the conflict—with neutrality still maintained—but her position had palpably shifted. Some accused the government of "selling out," but to many it seemed merely an attempt to maintain for a while longer its state, army, and institutions.

A moral fiber was struck with Constantin. A deeply loyal man, he had sworn allegiance to the country and king. But as an individual he had favored the earlier position of neutrality. Why, he had even hoped for an alliance with Britain and France, which would have been in keeping with the nation's historical trend, most recently in WWI. Torn and conflicted, and after much reflection in those rapidly changing times, he placed his fate in the hands of his sovereign. "We must all stand united," he uneasily concluded.

A few days after toasting in 1940, the family returned to Bucharest from the Christmas holidays. They were coming home to work, school, and an uncertain future. Now with the war underway elsewhere on the continent, their growing apprehension mirrored that of the entire country.

"I so wish we could stay here and watch the snow melt and the spring flowers sprout everywhere," Maria had whispered to her husband on the porch in Predeal on their last night there.

"Don't worry, dear, we'll be back soon, perhaps for Easter."

"Don't worry? What, with the Russians practically breathing down our necks and the Germans tearing through Europe?"

"Maria, hush, we're not in yet, and there's no way of telling how all of this will turn out for us."

"Despite what Ica told you yesterday?"

Ica was the nickname for Mihai Antonescu, a lawyer and prominent magistrate. He had been a guest of General Ion Antonescu, who was to become the country's future leader (and no relation of his); the general's villa neighbored Maria's in the hamlet of Predeal. Ica had dropped in to see Constantin, whom he'd known for many years, and talk had inevitably focused on the war. Ica had forecast, "It's going to be long and tough, but the West will prevail in the end."

"Oh, Maria, come on. No one, not even Ica, has a crystal ball. He merely stated his opinion."

"Mind my words: nothing good will come out of this war. I feel it in my bones."

He gazed at her questioningly. Why, she'd never been one to rely on premonitions during all these years together. "We're all tense," he told himself, while adding, "Hush, don't raise your voice, you'll wake up the children. As for Ica, everyone is full of ideas these days."

She dropped the matter; indeed afraid the children would hear her and start to worry. Mona, at age ten, was too young to follow the events. But the boys were showing a keen interest, mapping out military campaigns, much as their father had done in the First "Great War." The atlas given by their grandfather—shared, despite Dinu's protests ("He gave it to me")—was providing the canvas for the events. That was how they charted later that spring the German push into Norway and Denmark. Then followed Oslo, the Norwegian capital, taken after several ports had fallen and naval vessels were sunk.

Constantin came home tired one evening, looking forward to a quiet evening at home. But it wasn't to be; once inside he heard the radio, its volume turned up, unusually loud. Dinu jumped up to greet him, "There's news, father. The British destroyers have attacked the German's navy at Narvick, in Norway. Quick, you must show us on the map where that is."

His brother Dan added, "You haven't even told father the most important part. They say the Germans were hard hit."

"May be the Allies will start beating them," chimed in Dinu.

Their optimism was short-lived. Despite initial successes and hard fighting, the British and their allies were forced to pull out of Norway by the beginning of the summer. Denmark herself had fallen and surrendered earlier in April. Though Romania was still neutral, and with the press trying to objectively cover both sides of the conflict, Constantin noted the interest his sons took in the Allied offensive. Despite his country's show of neutrality, many felt a natural affinity with France and Great Britain, and strong cultural ties bound them to the French. And many remembered they had been allies only a quarter of a century earlier in WWI. But Romanians also felt intensely patriotic, and were keenly aware of the territorial threats looming on the horizon.

It was in this frame of mind that the country celebrated its National Day on May 10, 1940. Constantin was invited to watch the parade from an official stand erected in Palace Square. His secretary had suggested, "You could take the boys along, Sir. There are some seats reserved for children of dignitaries."

At home he had consulted with Maria, "I'd like to bring Dinu to the festivities."

"The boy should be in school, not dillydallying with dignitaries on some stand. He has no business being there," she told her husband.

"Maria, the boy wants to see it, be part of what's going on. Please let him."

Reluctantly she agreed. So father and son went and sat side by side. Romanian blue, yellow, and red flags plastered the square, and a large crowd, some wearing folk costumes, filled the street, as far as the eye could see. The orderly parade of troops outfitted in their new uniforms, including helmets, impressed the thirteen year old, giving him a sense of reassurance.

"There are so many of them! They'll be able to defend us, won't they, father?"

"They'll certainly try their best," was the tentative reply as his dad couldn't help but recall a propaganda reel he had recently watched at the German Embassy. A deep sense of foreboding had overtaken him at the sight of troops marching in goosestep with the arm shot up in the Nazi salute. The screen had been filled by seemingly endless hordes marching in unison while the sky above was covered with perfectly aligned plane squadrons. A shower of bombs was then unleashed, with their screeching, deafening noise.

"As close to hell as you'd imagine it," he had later told Maria. The audience had been in awe of this spectacle and many had wondered, like him, who would be able to stand up to this onslaught.

They soon learned how crushingly fast the German wave nicknamed "Blitzkrieg" could sweep through Western Europe. Each morning Constantin received daily communiqués at the ministry, and in the evening he read local and foreign dailies. Belgium, Luxembourg, and the Netherlands met the same fate as Norway and Denmark before them, and all had fallen by the end of May.

France was now all that stood between Germany and the English Channel, and it relied heavily on the so-called Maginot line. This a military fortification had been built after WWI along its border with Germany in order to defend a direct assault. But the German strategy had been well thought out, and was cognizant of the terrain. Their armies had moved on to Belgium first, according to the Fall Gelb ("Case Yellow") plan. In this manner they were able to circumvent the Maginot line, attacking France through Belgium and her heavily wooded Ardennes mountain region. The Allied armies, which had pushed into Belgium, were cut off, and as a consequence, the British expeditionary force and some French soldiers had to evacuate the continent from Dunkirk. The toll was steep, with countless casualties and abandoned military equipment.

With Allied morale at an all-time low, events unfolded rapidly after this.

Italy soon joined Germany in declaring war on France and England as well.

The French collapse appeared near.

In mid-June Constantin and his family took a few days off and traveled to northern Transylvania, staying at one of the royal lodges. On June 22, while taking lunch with one of the administrators and making small talk, they heard on the radio: "France has capitulated; France has fallen," shouted the announcer.

Together they tried to digest the unfathomable. Speechless they stared at one another. France was defeated and the German gray uniforms were parading on the famed central Parisian artery—the Champs Elysees. Maria broke the silence first mumbling, "We're running out of time." No one replied. Nor could they have guessed how little time was indeed left.

Constantin eventually said, "We must head home. I will be needed in Bucharest. Besides, we'll have better news there and more details."

They drove back to Bucharest the same day, the atmosphere in the car thick with worry. How starkly it contrasted with the lush orchards and fields of gleaming wheat flying past their windows, while peasants went about their daily business, unaware of the turning tides that would soon engulf all of them.

With Germany unleashed on the Western Front, it was now the turn of the Soviet Union to launch its own campaign of territorial expansion. On the morning of June 27, 1940, Constantin's secretary called to inform him of an emergent crown meeting. He raced out of the house, to join a room full of ministers and officials. Rumors flew around as they awaited the king's arrival:

"We've been declared war on?" "Are we declaring war?" "Are we joining the Germans?"

When the king arrived, all were struck by his appearance. Gone were the self-assured strut and cocky grin, replaced by a near-shuffle and a drawn-in, worried face. "News can't be good," they whispered to one another.

They soon learned that the Soviets had laid claim, in the form of an ultimatum, to the Eastern Romanian lands known as Bessarabia and part of Northern Bukovina.

The dignitaries were contemplating two stark options that morning. Accept and give up century-old lands and their citizens. Or, turn the ultimatum down and have the Soviets march in and the country ravaged by war.

"Have you made contact with the German chancellery?" a minister asked.

"Yes. Their advice: avoid conflict at any cost."

A heated debate ensued, weighing the pros and cons. The king consulted with the head of the armed forces. "How many troops? How well equipped? Are they ready?"

They had seen soldiers parade barely a month earlier and hearts had swelled with pride. But thinking of the vastness of the Soviet Union and the millions ready to bear arms, Constantin saw the futility of it all. The king promised to make further contacts abroad and adjourned the meeting. With no further business to detain him at the Palace, Constantin headed home to share the shocking news and the country's desperate situation with his family.

Hearing the update, Maria added, "The Russians weren't going to sit and watch the Germans gobble up the continent."

"What's going to happen, father?"

Constantin shook his head. "I honestly don't know. We'll find out soon enough."

It wasn't like his father not to have answers, thought the boy; why, the war was getting to everyone.

A Romanian attempt at negotiations fell on deaf ears, and the course of action was decided. Soviet tanks would be rolling into the Romanian territories of Bessarabia and Bukovina at 2:00 P.M. on June 28. The government was forced to accept the conditions as no viable alternative existed. This course of events underscored the widely held belief that the Soviet Union held the most danger to them, present and future. The decision also carried the hope that by accepting the current terms, the rest of the state would remain intact and would not be ravaged by war.

The nation suddenly plunged into fear, confusion, and mistrust. Old solemn and recent promises to maintain the country's borders had been broken, and many held the king personally responsible for this "national tragedy." "A weakling, a coward, a man without a backbone!" shouted the dailies. Some claimed warning signs of the Soviets' proclaimed thirst for power and that the vulnerability of the disputed lands had been ignored until too late. Others wished for military action, as defeat on the battlefield was preferable to this "national shame."

Refugees from the provinces trickled into Romania in the coming days, bringing stories of despair, cruelty, and destruction. They told of bells tolling precisely at 2:00 P.M. on June 28, acknowledging the transition of power, of tears and silent prayer. They told of Soviet activists throwing stones and spitting on the locals. They recounted how the Romanian flag had been cut down and replaced with the "red menace" of the star and sickle. While some of the refugees were angered and ready to fight, most seemed exhausted and resigned to the inexorable advance of the Soviet power and its future menace to Romania.

Constantin met with several history teachers who had taken refuge in Bucharest and attempted to find them positions. He was told, "You'd better run, Professor, fast and far away. *They* are coming this way, too."

He had wanted to hope that the Soviet's claim to the northern Romanian lands would stem the tide. But as a historian and politician, he knew better: the door had merely been opened to other regional disputes. On many hot July nights Constantin tossed and turned, as sleep was hard to come by. In silence he questioned himself, over and over:

"Was it wise to accept the Soviet's territorial claims? Should we have fought to defend our lands?"

And then he remembered the fate of Poland, the pictures of devastation, her army drifting through the continent. Balancing the two, in the end he sadly concluded that acceptance of the Soviet ultimatum had been preferable to the destruction of the entire country. War had been averted, or at least for now.

A new government, this one more pro-German, did little to alleviate the national anxiety. On a personal note, this change meant that Constantin was released from his ministerial post, returning to his Chair at the university and to his parliamentary seat. Maria breathed a deep sigh of relief but wisely kept it to herself, sensing her husband's turmoil.

July flew by in a blur, hot, dry and dusty, with the country taut and ready to snap like a pulled-apart rubber band. More aggression was certainly to come. But no one knew from where and when to expect it. In the meantime more bad news came from the Western Front. The Germans had launched the Battle of Britain with heavy aerial bombing of coastal shipping centers. London was bound to follow, everyone said.

By the end of July, Maria had made her case for a much-needed vacation. "The children are restless, and I need to get them out of town. Their friends are away, and it is too hot to play outside all day. I'm tired. You're exhausted."

"But dear, I'm needed here; there are still meetings, negotiations. Our fate can change in a flash."

"You should come with us and catch your breath."

Deep down he knew she was right; yes, he felt awfully tired and truly needed a break, too. "Dear, you were right: it will do us all good to get out of town."

She smiled widely and her eyes lit up, the way only Maria's could. "I'll start packing your trunk, dear."

The train journey took them across fields of grains and on the steel bridge across the Danube before winding down across dusty Dobrogea in the southeast. Suddenly they couldn't wait, craning their necks to catch a glimpse of the sea at Constanta. They briefly spotted some of the country's large ships kept in the harbor there. All that remained was a straight dash south to Mangalia, less than an hour-long journey.

As soon as they settled in, the sea started working its miracle again. The children spent the days on the beach. Afternoons brought bike rides, volleyball games, and tennis matches. Constantin resumed his morning writing routine. Closing his eyes and listening to the gentle splashing of the waves and smelling the damp sand and salt air, he could pretend at times that all was well.

Unfortunately it wasn't. Newspapers and radio reports kept them abreast of how the German war machine continued to churn across the continent. Closer to home they heard of Hungary clamoring for most of Transylvania. The province represented most of the central and western part of Romania. As for the dispute between the two countries, it had been a recurrent conflict for ages.

One late morning the boys charged in the house shouting, "Dad, our friend Michael ran over, his dad heard we just shot down two Hungarian planes over Transylvania! They were flying across our land."

The older boy, Dinu, was particularly excited. "Once we enter the war, we'll certainly win, I'm telling you, Dad."

"Boys, I've been telling you things are not always what they seem. I really don't know what would become of us. . . ." he said, his voice trailing off. Getting hold of his emotions, he added, "Go back on the beach, I need to work on a few more pages and I'll join you after that."

The boys were disappointed. They simply couldn't understand their dad's unease and lack of enthusiasm towards war. Just like their father in his childhood, they marveled at how different grownups really were. Why, wars seemed so heroic, the military leaders even glamorous. Could there be anything braver than fighting for your country, side by side with your brothers?

Hundreds of miles away and behind closed doors, arduous negotiations of the Hungarian claim over Transylvania were taking place. Romania considered the province an integral part of the country. A majority of her citizens spoke the same language and many shared the same faith. The Hungarians looked upon it as part of their kingdom before WWI and aspired to restore pre-war borders. The tone of the outcome had actually been set a month earlier, in July, when Hitler had written bluntly to Romania's King Carol II:

"If Romania does not settle the Hungarian claims . . . the destruction of the state will follow sooner rather than later."

If some thought the threat to be merely theoretical, they only had to look at the bombs pounding Britain, or remember Poland's fate. Berlin's demand on behalf of their allies the Hungarians had sealed Romania's fate.

On August 30, 1940, lunch was taken under grape vines while listening to the radio, as they did each day. That was how they learned the king had once again acquiesced to foreign claims, this time in the form of the ultimatum received from Berlin: almost half of Transylvania had been handed over to the Hungarians. The decision was once more justified as a necessary step to pacify the country's enemies and avoid entry in the war. Days later a sliver of Dobrogea in southeastern Romania went to the Bulgarians (also allied with the German-led Axis) in yet another territorial dispute.

The summer's grim toll of the ill-fated year 1940: a third of the country's territory and population had been lost in a little over two months. A united Romania, the long sought-after dream accomplished in 1919 in the aftermath of the Great War, was once again no more.

The family went back to Bucharest a couple of days later, the return journey unfolding in a mostly somber mood. Constantin was of the opinion, "The king's days are numbered. All are holding him responsible for the losses of lands."

Dinu chimed in, "If he abdicates, will we enter the war?" At which his brother, unwilling to be left out, had added, "Father always says King Carol is the one who wants to stay out. Of course we'll enter the war once he's gone."

"Boys, wars are much more complicated and dangerous than you can imagine."

Maria said in a foreboding tone, "Wars bring nothing but death and destruction. You shouldn't wish it upon us."

"Everyone is fighting but us," chimed the boys.

"We will fight to defend ourselves. And the next few days will be critical," their father added.

The boys grinned: perhaps they would see their army fight after all.

Indeed, two days later the king entrusted General Ion Antonescu, a prominent military leader, to put together a new government. The general intended to bring about a coalition of the various parties, but the opposition refused to participate. There would be no talks or compromise before the King's abdication, they had said.

Blamed by all and isolated, with no public or political support, King Carol II stepped down on September 6, 1940. Prince Michael, his eighteen-year-old and only son, became the new king and went on to confirm the general's investiture. More so, Antonescu was declared "Leader of the State" with expanded legislative and executive powers. Truth be told, the general attempted to compromise, despite being close to the far-right party, the Iron Guard, and with a strong pro-German allegiance. While bringing the Iron Guard to the forefront of the government, he also included some members of the traditional parties—the Peasants and Liberals. These had remained committed to a parliamentary democracy and maintained their historical orientation toward Britain and France. But Britain, with bombs falling on London raining down death and destruction, was in no position to offer an alliance. Nor was fallen France, with one puppet government in Vichy, France and another one exiled in England.

Romania had dwindled and stood isolated facing a bleak future alone.

Chapter Fifteen
Internal Strife and Bloodshed

It wasn't like Maria to dwell on premonitions or the "feelings" associated with them. But now she couldn't shake off the deep apprehension felt since the beginning of the war, a war Romania had not entered yet, but which had already recast its borders and reshaped its political arena. Like she had done since childhood at such times, she once again turned to her father. Worries and questions without answers kept him up at night, too, and Maria learned how her parents were contemplating spending time abroad if things on the home front took a turn for the worse.

"Your mother and I have been quietly transferring some of our savings to Switzerland. You should talk to your husband about it."

"I will. But father, I still worry about Constantin and possible political repercussions. Even more so today, since the prime minister's assassination and the killings ordered by King Carol."

"Well, my dear, and you have a reason to worry now, unlike last time we talked about it. I too want to see you all out of harm's way. You need to have a serious conversation with your husband."

Emboldened by her father's support, she approached Constantin that evening. "We ought to think about leaving for a while until matters are sorted out. I am truly worried."

"Where would we go, Maria?"

"Mother has put a large part of her savings in a Swiss bank. We could do the same and live in Switzerland."

"And how would we support ourselves? Do you think they're desperate for a Romanian history professor at one of their universities?"

"You could find a teaching post somewhere and I could bake or sew. We all speak French and German and could get by. . . ."

"Maria, we can't abandon our country at one of her darkest hours. I am needed here."

"Doesn't your family need you, too? What if they come after us because you've opposed the Iron Guard party in your political activity? Have you thought of that?"

"Whom have you been talking to? Who has planted these ideas in your mind?"

"I read and listen. And yes, I did talk to my father who fears their reprisal. Don't forget how the Iron Guard prisoners were killed a year ago by order of the king. You worked for the king, too. With the tide turning, you and others alike could be targeted next."

"Maria, dear, your father worries too much. It's still an orderly country; we have laws. They may take legal recourse, but no, there won't be any violence."

"What makes you so sure?"

"Dear, please, I am still well connected. I promise to let you know if I hear of any such threat. Until then, please try not to brood on the Iron Guard and worry yourself. And remember, your safety and that of the children is of the utmost importance to me."

"Say what you may. I feel it in my bones. There is this steamroller coming at high speed, while we stand still and wait for it to flatten us."

Maria's feelings of approaching disaster were almost prescient as pain, tears, and suffering soon gripped the city. A strong earthquake, 7.7 on the Richter scale, flattened buildings on November 10, not long after midnight. The waves felt in Bucharest were strong enough to travel south across the Danube, all the way to Bulgaria.

Maria and Constantin were in their first-floor bedroom, with the children asleep in their rooms upstairs. Once the ground started moving, Maria rushed to the stairs, but the violent shaking knocked her down, preventing her from reaching the children. For close to a minute she stood frozen in a doorway waiting it out. The house squeaked and swayed and the rumbles of the earth muffled the children's cries. Dinu later remembered waking up and watching in disbelief as books flew off the shelves. Mona, not even ten, was terrified and called out for her mother.

The moment the quake stopped everyone ran toward one another and met half way down the staircase.

"Was it a big bomb, Mommy?" Mona cried.

"No, Mona dear, an earthquake," Maria said, hugging her daughter.

The child remembered vaguely studying that in geography class. "What's that, Mommy?"

"Every once in a while the earth moves deep down inside and starts shaking."

The child nodded quietly, too tired to reply, or perhaps satisfied with her mother's explanation. As electricity was out, Maria grabbed a candle and walked around the house to assess the damage. A few vases and plates had fallen and were broken.

"Well, maybe it just felt worse than it was . . . let's try to get some sleep now," Constantin said.

In the morning they woke up to alarming news. Buildings had crumbled, mostly in the center of the city; many were still trapped underneath and feared dead. Fearing aftershocks, the government cancelled school for the day, to the delight of the children. Worried about her parents, Maria headed to their house taking Mona along. The boys were told to stay home, but of course they headed out as soon as the coast was clear.

A spectacle of desolation greeted them. Piles of rubble stood surrounded by dust. A chaotic rescue effort was mounted while a crowd desperate for news of their loved ones waited. Nowhere was the scene more vivid and raw than at the site of the collapsed Carlton building. Once the tallest building in the city, it had housed a famed movie theater and many people had lived on its upper floors. It was a new construction, barely a decade old, but down it had crumbled like a deck of cards.

The black mood that gripped the city was darkened further as "coverage" was ordered at night, with all lights blocked out in anticipation of possible bombing attacks. Thus the day gained a new ritual: put the paper up late afternoon, take it down in the morning. War was getting ever closer.

Shortly after the earthquake, tears and blood flowed once again, just as Maria had feared. And like the earthquake, there was no warning sign. A murderous rampage tore through the city on November 26–28 with seventy-two people dead at the end of this carnage. Members of the Iron Guard, "the Legion" (previously known as "All for the Country"), newly risen to governmental prominence, had avenged their comrades fallen a year earlier. A swift punishment was delivered to those they deemed responsible, just as Maria and her father had warned.

First, a score of political detainees held in the Jilava Penitentiary were killed on orders of the new leader of the Iron Guard, Horia Sima. But the murderers didn't stop there. Professor Iorga, famed historian and member of the Romanian Academy, was picked up in the middle of the day from his mountain villa. He was thrown in the back of a van, driven away, tossed out and assassinated at roadside. The Iron Guard held Iorga responsible in part for the fall of Codreanu, their former beloved leader, and they had not forgotten.

Professor Madgearu, a well-known economist and secretary general of the Peasant Party, was removed from his Bucharest residence. He was dragged to the nearby Snagov Lake and woods and left for dead. Scores of others met the same fate, including some members of the city police force. Two former prime ministers—Tatarascu and Argentoianu—were saved only owing to the rapid intervention of one of the military leaders.

Maria became frantic when the first casualties became known on the twenty-seventh, urging her husband to go into hiding until the killing spree ended. Their trusted friend Marin Popescu-Spineni, secretary of the Faculty of Letters and Philosophy, called immediately and offered safe harbor.

Constantin tried resisting at first. "I'll go, but only if you and the children come along."

"They're after you, not us," Maria said.

"They might kill you if they don't find me home."

"No, they won't. They haven't touched any of the wives or children."

"I can't leave you alone," Constantin insisted.

"We won't be alone; we'll go to my parents."

He saw the logic in her position and finally agreed, quickly leaving for his colleague's house but not before making sure she and the children had left for the grandparents'.

Days later the head of the state, General Antonescu, condemned the killings and promised to punish those responsible, thus opening a rift within his own government. And while this tear was gradually developing on the home front, the country's position in the frame of the larger European conflict shifted as well. Within a month Romania officially entered the "Tri-Partite Pact" of Germany, Japan, and Italy, and her position as an avowed enemy of neighboring Russia was thus sealed.

The year 1940 was ending on a somber note, with the country one step closer to actively entering the war.

Despite the morose, dark general mood, the family still put up a big Christmas tree that year. Maria continued to believe in providing the children with as normal a life as was feasible under the circumstances. She still trimmed the tree herself, as she had done since her marriage, and took pride in the growing collection of antique ornaments. She so cherished the tradition of decorating on Christmas Eve morning, and as always, allowed her family to come into the room only when the tree was adorned, with gifts piled underneath.

But the spirit of the Christmas and New Year's Eve celebrations were short-lived as bad news continued to mount. In January 1941, Constantin was informed that he was to be suspended from the university. Those academics that had collaborated with King Carol's regime were being targeted now. Constantin and his good friend Alex Rosetti were told of an upcoming transfer to a state research institute while others, like Mihai Ralea, another colleague, were going to be dismissed altogether.

Worry about Constantin's academic future had begun to set in when the suspensions were fortunately reversed later that month. General Antonescu had acted swiftly and had finally eliminated the Legion from all official functions of the government. Their voice no longer held a say on who would be dismissed and who would be allowed to stay.

On January 21, Dinu was in a geography class at his Saint Sava High School, when the teacher called out, "Mr. Giurescu, the headmaster requires your presence."

He was stunned to see his mother standing by the headmaster. "Mr. Giurescu, you are excused. Please accompany your mother home."

"Why, mother, what's going on?" he asked, worried that something had happened to his father.

"I'll tell you on the way home. Keep quiet and let's wait for your brother." Once Dan showed up, they stepped outside. The streets were quiet, with few passersby. Outside the army's general headquarters on Stirbey-Voda Boulevard, they noticed a tank by the front gate.

Another odd sight awaited them at home: their father was back before lunch. "Boys, there's unrest in the city."

"Unrest, father? We didn't see anything on the way home."

"The general is firing all the ministers and prefects connected to the Iron Guard Legion. A large disturbance is feared." Their father added, "I want you to stay home for a couple of days. Things could become violent."

The events of the following days would come to be known as the "Rebellion," and the news became public early on January 21. Nick Caracaleanu, a good friend (who had headed Constantin's cabinet while as Royal Governor and minister in 1939–1940) and his brother rushed to his house. Constantin was a potential target, based on his past political stance and activities and his friends worried for his safety, fearing the wrath of those now deposed from power.

The men had rifles, and Constantin, Nick, and his brother posi-

tioned themselves by the first floor windows with plenty of ammunition by their side. The drapes were lowered, leaving a razor thin
"window" of observation. Then they waited while the dog was let
loose in the yard, counting on his reputation for attacking and often
biting strangers.

In the meantime Maria took the children to the back entrance of
the house. There she had positioned a ladder against the wall separating it from their neighbor.

"If we come under attack, you climb over the wall, jump into the
next yard, and go to your grandparents," she told her children.

Dinu wondered how a woman and three children were going to
make it through the streets to their grandparents' house, at least a for-
ty-five-minute walk. The journey would have taken them through the
center of the city and past the Palace where there would surely be
unrest. But he decided to keep quiet, sensing his mother's desperation.

She fortunately didn't have to resort to it. A brief moment of panic
arose when members of the Iron Guard showed up on their street,
marching in formation and chanting. However, they passed the house
without any untoward disturbance and proceeded to a nearby club of
theirs.

Constantin and his family stayed bunkered in for two days. Listening to the radio proved confusing, as reports were conflicting at first.
Finally, on the twenty-third, some good news: those fighting had been
ordered by their leader to lay down their arms. As if on cue, the radio
started broadcasting patriotic Romanian songs and a few phone calls
confirmed what had just been heard. The standoff was over, and those
responsible had been apprehended.

When the dead were counted, those spared shivered and thanked
God for having been allowed to live; 353 civilians and 21 army members had been lost.

"We've made it once again," said Maria, and then to herself, "but
who knows for how much longer?"

She knew deep down that the darkness sweeping their world was
unstoppable, and was bound to touch them. The preamble had been
the blood, fear, and tears of the year past.

Chapter Sixteen

ALIGNING WITH GERMANY, FORSAKING THE PAST

During the spring of 1941, German tanks and troops moved through the outskirts of Bucharest on their way to the Southern Front, and on to Greece. Around the same time, German officers started showing up in the streets and cafes of the city, their presence bringing apprehension to those old enough to remember the Great War. But this time the Germans weren't arriving as a conquering army occupying the city but as a presumptive future ally. The officers were courteous toward their Romanian counterparts and were impressed with their standard of living relative to Germany. Stores were still full of goods in Bucharest, including plentiful amounts of food, even delicacies such as caviar, fine meats, and cakes, in stark contrast to the shortages that had been felt in Germany since the late 1930s. And just like their fathers had done twenty-five years earlier, the soldiers bought cheese, sausages, and chocolates, sending care packages back home to their wives and children.

War was getting close to home that spring. Yugoslavia surrendered to Germany and most of Greece fell in April. The Greek government in exile was relocated to the island of Crete, which Winston Churchill had vowed to defend. But the bombing of the island had continued unabated, and once the German paratroopers landed on Crete, the battled lasted only seven days. By the end of May, the Greeks and British were forced to evacuate, too.

On June 12, 1941, the Romanian de facto leader, General Antonescu, traveled to Germany and met with Chancellor Hitler. He was informed there of an imminent German attack against the Soviet Union, and Hitler wanted to know Romania's position. Assurances were given by the general: yes, Romania would be fighting alongside them. It was a momentous decision, and one which belonged to Antonescu alone. From a juridical standpoint the country's leader held the right to decide matters of war and peace. Besides, a strong current of public opinion was also on his side, with many favoring an alliance that could lead to the liberation of Bessarabia and Bukovina, the territories taken by the Soviets a year earlier. In response to the question: "which is the lesser of two evils," many if not most Romanians continued to view the Soviet/Bolshevik threat as the gravest of dangers. Stories of deportations, executions, and cruelty, and pictures of mass graves and torched churches had reinforced the belief that any alternative would be preferable to a fall under the Soviets' grip.

Days later Hitler did indeed carry out the plan discussed with General Antonescu. In a stunning breach of the Nonaggression Pact of Molotov-Ribbentrop, the German army and its allies (the Axis) invaded the Soviet Union on June 21, 1941. The same day Romanians and Finns began military campaigns as well, in order to regain their territories annexed by the Soviets in 1940.

Romania had officially entered the war.

Constantin and his family once again heard the news on the wireless, like most critical war developments. They had been at their Predeal mountain villa for only a few days as schools, normally over by June 15, had been let out early that summer. Rumors abounded regarding the troop build-up which continued along the eastern border. Something big was going to happen—and once again, no one knew for sure when, what, and where.

Dinu had taken and passed exams to be admitted to the ninth grade—high school proper—earlier in the month. The boy was exhausted and so was Maria, who had continued to monitor and help with the children's academic progress, so all had decided to take a break from the city. It was easier on the family, as Constantin was also off on his customary long summer vacation from the university's teaching post. His courses might have been over, but he continued to work as an advisor to the Royal Cultural Foundation during the break. As this only required a few hours a week, he opted to travel back and forth between the mountains and Bucharest, being able to carry on his assignments and rest as well.

On June 22, the boys were out roaming the woods, and Constantin had just returned from a leisurely walk. It had seemed another fresh, lovely early summer day. A bright blue sky, with not a cloud in sight, and crisp air provided a perfect backdrop for the majestic mountain clad in the deep fir forest. A few minutes later, this haven was shattered by the calmly enunciated news over on the radio:

"To inform you that the Romanian army . . . has joined the German troops . . . to liberate our brothers in Bessarabia. . . ."

The brief news was followed by the broadcast of General Antonescu's proclamation:

"Soldiers, I order you to cross the river Prut. . . . Crush the Eastern enemy. Free your brothers from the Bolshevik yoke. Make your country whole again. . . ."

"The wheels have been set in motion," Constantin had wistfully said.

"We just don't know where they're going to take us," Maria replied, and added, "I hope they'll turn long enough to free the provinces. Then we'll hopefully just help the Germans with oil and food."

"I wish you were right, but I think we're in with them for the long haul."

"We either win or go down together?" Maria asked, and Constantin nodded his head at this risky prospect.

"And then what?"

"Dear, there is much we don't know . . ." and his voice trailed, uncertain. "But what I do know it's that I'm famished. What's for lunch?"

She smiled; food was often on her husband's mind, particularly when he wasn't working.

"You'll be pleased: I baked a puff pastry with cheese and spinach." At that she went to the kitchen, leaving the matter of settling the world's affairs to later on.

The boys had been quite excited upon hearing the news, with war undoubtedly carrying a certain glamorous aura for the teenagers. They had followed with interest the growing conflict for almost two years, and had decided it was definitely a "gentleman's thing" to enter the war, too. It didn't matter how often their parents warned them, or how many accounts of death and destruction they read about in the press. Everyone was fighting and Romania should, too.

"Oh, Dad, this is the news we've been waiting for!"

"Boys, we've been telling you: be careful what you wish for. Wars start out with men in glossy uniforms and end up with dead bodies in ditches."

General Antonescu had a villa almost across the street from the Giurescu's. They had an open view toward his terrace, and had more than once spotted the country's leader resting or talking to his aides. Dinu and Dan had hoped the entry in the war would bring about a flurry of activity at the General's villa. But they were to be disappointed that the pace of life remained complacent in Predeal that summer.

The radio announced military updates, which were supplemented by the dailies. The army had been amassed earlier that month to the north and east, and so there weren't any troop movements to be seen in the mountains surrounding the cottage. The mountain hamlet remained an idyllic haven, oblivious to the momentous events unfolding a few hundred miles away.

The family remained in Predeal for nearly three months, until early September, when it was time to go back to school.

News from the Eastern Front was good that summer. A swift and successful advance had led to the return of the northern territories to Romania barely a month later, at the end of July.

Many thought the troops would return home after accomplishing their goal, but Romanian units kept advancing alongside the German army toward Odessa. Romanian Army Groups Three and Four were eventually deployed along the Southern Flank, including Crimea. With no written agreement specifying terms of engagement at the onset of the campaign, the Romanians were left with no choice but to press on at the side of their allies.

Dinu started keeping a diary at his grandfather's urging. "You'll see later on how helpful it will be to remind you of events. . . ."

"But I tend to remember well, Grandfather," the youngster had said, somewhat confused.

"Just wait until you're seventy years old. Memories of years past will swirl around in your head. We are living in troubled times. One day you'll want to be able to tell your children."

Professor Mehedinti had earlier taken his oldest grandson to a bookstore in the center of the city, across the street from the University. Dinu, quite shy by nature, felt even more uncomfortable when the salesmen swarmed around his grandfather, well known to many of them. After much ado they settled on a calfskin leather-bound lined notebook. The grandfather wrote down on the first page:

"To Dinu—may you keep track of our times."

And so the boy jotted down his impressions and pasted in photos, articles, and maps. His diary gradually followed the path of the military success that fall: the siege of Odessa on the Black Sea turned into a victory for the Romanian Army in the middle of October. But success came at a steep price: Romanian losses were heavy in this campaign. Nearly ninety thousand men were counted dead and wounded at the end of the offensive, three times as many as during the liberation of Bessarabia and Bukovina.

Romanians once again thought that perhaps their involvement in the military campaign would be over now. Hopes were rekindled by a parade of victorious troops. Constantin took Maria for a walk along

Boulevard Kisselef, the large avenue that led to the lakes district. It was a festive day and both dressed up to mark the occasion, Maria adding a smart hat to her dress and jacket. She even brought a small bunch of flowers, and, together, they took a place alongside the crowds lining the boulevard.

The soldiers marched down the central artery connected, in turn and in a straight line, to the Victory Boulevard and ultimately to the Palace. Many had come out on this beautiful October day, the temperature more reminiscent of late summer despite the surrounding yellow-rust leaves. They watched the orderly military formations pass by while noticing the tired and drawn faces, the dusty and heavily creased uniforms. Many of the men had been away for five long months.

"We should have brought the boys along," said Maria. "They would have seen the less glamorous side of war."

The hope that the Romanians' active participation in the war would cease after Odessa proved unfounded. The army's presence was continued along the Southern Front, with a small number of units advancing into Crimea. Then they appeared to stall, without much action taking place during November 1941. Public opinion became restless and worried, and hypothetical scenarios played out in the dailies.

In the meantime and behind closed doors, Romania's de facto leader, Marshal General Antonescu, was just as concerned. A letter sent by Mott Gunther, U.S. envoy to Bucharest, to the State Department, summed up the General's growing unease.

"He (Antonescu) is in excellent physical shape but extremely preoccupied by the future. He knows Germany will ultimately lose the war . . . but feels obligated to continue their collaboration and hopes for the best . . . as he sees no other avenue open. . . ."

The general had understood the misfortune of the Romanian soldiers fighting side by side with the Germans, stuck together at times "in half a meter of mud." While complimenting the Russian soldiers for their bravery, he wistfully concluded that, "If Russia wins the war she would soon be in position to dominate the world." But the military man saw no option to compromise at such a junction, continuing upon the chosen path.

Winter came early that year, one of the harshest on record. Snow fell and fell until it reached the second floor of buildings in Bucharest and trees threatened to break under the weight of their carpeted branches. Despite the daily cleaning of the streets, traffic became treacherous and many trams were suspended.

Heating and lighting gas was pricey and hard to come by, and people queued in the snow to stock up on it. Compounding everyone's misery was the summer's poor grain crop, leading to rationing of bread, flour, and oil. The "ersatz" (substitutes) showed up for the first time in Romania such as a blend of chicory—roasted, ground, and flavored—replacing coffee. "Essence" of rum and lemon were used instead of their counterparts, while other food choices, including cheese and cold cuts, were still plentiful. And because of the heavy snow and frozen roads, it was almost impossible for peasants to come to market for weeks and sell their meager produce, which had been stored since summer and early fall.

Bucharest was bitterly cold and very white during the winter of 1941–1942. People stayed inside as much as they could and listened to the wireless, and life went on enveloped in perpetual gloom. The reality of being at war had finally arrived home. A sobering reminder was the lists of those who had perished on the front, published in the daily *The Universe*. The tension was also augmented by the ubiquitous military updates broadcasted on the radio, punctuating the days with mechanical precision.

Constantin, Maria, and the boys went to the cemetery the weekend before they became snowed-in for the winter. Constantin's parents had passed away in the late fall, and each year he visited their graves to honor them. Parents and boys put on their heavy coats, gloves, and hats and headed out. By the gate of the cemetery, they bought large bouquets of yellow and rust mum flowers from the gypsy women who held a monopoly of sorts on the flower commerce. Each season they brought out various brightly colored bunches. For spring they had daffodils, tulips, and lilac branches, and in summer there were roses. They sold mums in the fall whereas carnations were the flower of winter.

Despite the bustle outside, it was peaceful beyond the cemetery gates. Tombs, monuments, and trees were covered in light dusty snow and it was eerily quiet, befitting a final resting place. They walked in silence to the family graves where plaques and crosses were partially hidden by heavy ice and snow.

"I so wished I could have known them," Maria mused every time.

The children had never before accompanied them to the cemetery. Maria remembered her own fears as a child and didn't want to expose them to the same. But the boys were thirteen and fourteen now and deemed to be old enough. Mona, only eleven, was left at home, despite her protests. "It's not fair; I'm always left behind."

At first the boys gazed quietly at the tombs; here rested the grandparents they had never met.

"What ages would they have been now?" asked Dinu.

"Well, let's see . . . father would have been sixty-six years old, and mother a few years younger."

"Wow, Grandpa is older than that," said the child referring to Maria's father.

"That was their fate, Dinu."

"Was your father very strict?" Dan asked.

"Yes, he was, but also very loving."

"And your mother?"

"She was the gentlest woman I've ever known," Constantin said.

Dan, looking to stir up trouble, asked, "More gentle than mother?"

His brother kicked him in the shin, concerned by his mother's response and trying to avoid further damage.

Maria's response was surprising to all. "That wouldn't be so difficult, would it boys?"

They all kept a straight face, trying not to laugh. Silence then fell, each lost in thought. Heads were bowed, and the men took off their hats in a sign of respect. Constantin saw happy faces from many years past while the others wondered about the family they never knew.

Slowly they walked back toward the gate where the car waited, and passed the chapel on the way out. It was surrounded by a large crowd, and loud crying and moaning could be heard from inside. Maria stepped in to see the open coffin of a youth in military uniform. A woman knelt at his side, her face wracked by grief and surrounded by relatives crying loudly. The poor woman held the dead young man's hand, unable to let go. This scene would haunt Maria for a long time to come, just as the rows of freshly dug graves with crosses covered in the national flag would, too.

"Take a good look, for this is the real face of war, boys," she told her sons. "This is what you need to remember when the talk of fighting gets you carried away." They nodded quietly.

A few days later they learned how one of Constantin's distant cousins, the aviator Romulus Giurescu, had fallen. War had come home, becoming personal, just as in 1916 when Uncle Ionica had perished at Turtucaia.

Constantin felt as always that staying busy was the best antidote to worries taking over him. Later that fall he had excitedly told his wife, "I've been asked by the War Ministry to coordinate a volume on Transylvania."

"You mean its history?"

"Well, sort of. My task it to show the progress made under our rule since 1918, when it was united with the country."

"What does that have to do with the war now?"

"Well, the ministry wants it translated into German, aimed at the political and scientific circles in Berlin." Constantin paused for a moment. "It is to be hopefully used as an argument as to why the Germans should help us to get Transylvania back."

Maria thought for a few minutes. "And if we and the Germans lose, it will become something else you'd be held accountable for."

"Maria, dear, how many times have we gone over this? Isn't it time you shake off your gloomy feelings? Don't you see life goes on?"

"For now" was her response.

He shrugged his shoulders and carried on. "What else can I do, anyway?" he wondered. Besides teaching, his days were taken up with work on this volume, aided by several colleagues. He had also started writing the third volume of his *History of the Romanians (1601–1821)*, with a focus on the political events. With the story of his people becoming more complex as it advanced into the modern era, he had planned to cover the economical and cultural progress separately. His hands were full, indeed.

He wasn't the only one staying busy. Constantin's brother, Horia, who had formal military training, was immediately mobilized. Deemed too old for active duty at the age of thirty-eight, he was assigned to the Intelligence Department. Maria's father also kept busy, setting down to organize, write, and hopefully later publish his complete works on the science of geography. As for her mother, she continued to oversee the running of the vineyard and country estate. Maria's brother, Emil, a lawyer and factory owner, participated indirectly in the war effort, with his factory manufacturing the thick rope used for yokes by a cavalry that was still represented in the Romanian Army.

Everyone went through the motions of living a normal life during the white, short days and long nights of the winter of 1941–1942. The country waited for the snow to thaw and the cold to break. They also waited for something to happen on the Southern Flank where the Romanian Army was still deployed while an uneasy quiet prevailed for months in that theater of operations.

Events had taken place elsewhere on the Eastern Front late that fall as the German armies had continued their advance on Moscow. Within striking shot, the city was declared "under siege" by October.

As the temperatures dipped below zero in November and the heavy snow fell, the Soviets deployed troops on skis against the enemy freezing just outside the city. The Germans hung on, and by the end of the month their famed Panzer tanks were at the gates of Moscow. With the goal so near and only twenty miles to reach the city, the German advance was suddenly stopped by the harsh winter and relentless Soviet counter-offensives.

And then, two days later on December 7, 1941, the tide of war was turned by a momentous event. The Japanese bombed the American fleet at Pearl Harbor in the Hawaiian Islands, and the U.S. officially entered the war against Japan. Three days later, on December 10, in a fateful decision for Germany and for the world, Hitler declared war on the United States.

The year 1941 was coming to a close and would be remembered as the year when Romania "officially went in."

Chapter Seventeen
THE GERMAN JUGGERNAUT IS TURNED BACK

In 1942 news from the front was regarded as either good or bad depending whose side you championed. Though officially aligned with Germany, many Romanians still felt an affinity for France and her allies. Without much to cheer about on the Western Front, some secretly relished the German stalling on the Eastern Front. As for Constantin, he remained uneasy at times about his country's alliance. A loyal individual, he stayed devoted to the king and determined to support any and all efforts to maintain territorial integrity. But at the same time, the Nazi Party's platform and war of aggression rang far from his own credo—those of a patriotic man and a pacifist at heart. He supported fighting if attacked, but condemned the territorial rapacity of the Germans. Fond memories of his time in Paris as a young man gave him, like many Romanians, a strong sense of a second identity with the French. It pained him to think that his beloved landmarks, like the Champs Elysees, were now occupied by those Nazi uniforms.

Unable to be actively involved in the war effort, he carried on with work, while the dichotomy of his feelings weighed in heavily at times. News and talk of war permeated life from morning to night. He might have taken refuge from it in the evening, had it not been for the boys wishing to review the daily events together. His sons maintained a keen interest, monitoring the action on a map affixed in Dinu's room, and improving their knowledge of geography in the process. Their grandfather had aided along the way. Thus they learned of Northern Africa, of Libya and Egypt, while tracking General Rommel's campaigns. Later on they were to explore the Pacific Ocean, Japan, and the Philippines, and out-of-the-way places like the Solomon Islands.

Air action especially captivated the imagination of the youngsters. They traced the targets of the British RAF bombings on the map— German cities such as Lubbeck and Hamburg. They also learned of the German response with air raids on historic cities such as Bath and York. There was something so incredibly heroic about those men flying at night and taking off in silence and darkness. They had seen pictures of the planes: close up they seemed impressive and solid, as if they had a hundred lives. But up in the air, they appeared small and almost fragile. The youngsters wondered about the pilots' thoughts as they trailed one another, with nothing to guide them but the moon and stars. "What could be on their minds? Are they so very excited? Could they be scared?"

"Boys, you regard this as a show. But these are the same planes that get shot down in the dead of the night. You've seen pictures of the wreckage," their father cautioned.

"Oh father, we know. But they are the truly brave ones, the ones who take the greatest risk."

"Fighting a war is not glamorous, Dan. You fight to defend your land. You fight because it is the honorable thing to do when your country needs you."

"I wish we were old enough to enlist."

The father shook his head. "Don't. Do you remember our visit to the cemetery? Do you recall the woman crying by the coffin of her fallen son? Did you boys see the rows of new graves covered in flags and flowers?"

The youngsters nodded quietly.

"That is the other face of war. And so are the many starving and cold, and those left homeless by its onslaught."

Their mother peeked into the room. "Speaking of starving, is anybody hungry around here?" This was met with nods as they followed her to the dining room.

Having overheard some of the comments, she wished to lighten the conversation. Just like her husband, the boys' talk of war and heroism mostly filled her with apprehension. But she also understood the idealism of their teenage years. It was a fragile balancing act: allowing the children to dream while gently pointing out to them the realities of life. In the same way, she needed skill and patience to balance the expectation for academic excellence while letting them enjoy their childhood, as much as possible in wartime. She had been saving some money toward this latter goal. With spring in the air, she approached her husband days later.

"Dinu and Dan need new bikes; they've grown quite a bit. I've put some money aside."

"Of course, dear," was her husband's absentminded reply. She smiled quietly.

"Very well, then, I'll buy them and have them delivered," she told him.

On Easter morning the children received chocolate eggs with little surprises in the center. When the day warmed up enough, she summoned the boys and asked, "I need help bringing up some pickle jars from the shed cellar; would you give me a hand?" They readily agreed, and followed their mother down the stairs.

Their looks of utter delight and excited shouts were Maria's Easter present, but not before facing Mona's disappointment of not having a new bike herself. But the girl was soon mollified by the knowledge she'd get a new one, too. "You first have to grow up a bit more," her mother had said.

As for the boys, they proceeded to put the new bicycles to good use. On many a Sunday they would head off to the lakes and their surrounding parks. The route would have normally taken them along busy streets. But with many cars commissioned by the army and off the streets, it was less perilous now and so their mother had consented to such outings. And in another sign that the boys were becoming teenagers, they began attending dance parties on weekends. Mona, only twelve, was once again told she would have to wait a couple of years. It led to more protests and tears, and these didn't go away as easily, as the girl craved more independence. But Maria held her ground, believing that firm discipline and rules would only benefit the children later in their lives.

And so, family life as one knew it went on, but with the unusual mixture of being at war without yet fighting on home soil. The surrounding world of Bucharest mirrored the same dichotomy, with the Romanian capital remaining a vibrant city even in 1942. People still went to the theater, listened to music, and occasionally dined out. And after the severe shortages of the winter of 1941–1942, the food supply improved during the spring and the shelves were well stocked again.

With summer approaching and life quiet on the home front, one could entertain travel to the seaside once again. The children in particular were eager to resume their vacation fun on the beach. But Maria wanted assurances that a trip to the southeast posed no safety concerns to the family.

"It's safe to go there this year," her husband said. She was content with the answer, trusting him implicitly without questioning his convictions. After all, he had been the one warning of Soviet planes' incursions over Romanian coastal cities the previous summer.

"There is no immediate threat of bombing of our seaports according to our intelligence," he added.

"And how would you know that?" Dan questioned him.

His parents exchanged glances, uncertain. Was the boy impertinent again, or merely curious about wartime circumstances? "Your Uncle Horia has access to confidential information at the ministry." That seemed to satisfy the perpetually inquisitive boy, who was so very fond of his uncle and in awe of his military attire and the seeming importance of his position.

The decision to travel to the seaside again was greeted enthusiastically by the children. And with a long summer break ahead, the parents decided there was some time for the mountains, too. The stay in Predeal provided them with a unique moment that summer: a special guest at General Antonescu's villa. It was Field Marshal Eric Von Manstein, a prominent German commander on the Eastern Front and veteran of the first Great War. Earlier in the war he had been one of the planners of the invasion of France through the Ardennes region. And now in early August 1942, he had been invited by the Romanian leader to spend a short holiday in the mountains.

Dinu was reading in the yard when he saw a group approaching: Von Manstein and his entourage were taking a walk. The youngster stood up and waved and the General responded, waving back and smiling. An enthusiastic entry was jotted down in Dinu's diary that night: "Saw Von Manstein outside our fence. He even waved back!" A little later he found a photo of the military leader in a newspaper, cut it and pasted it next to his entry, proud to have thus celebrated a special moment of his young life.

The following weeks at the seashore brought an added attraction for the children. That summer they were joined at Mangalia by their cousins: Emil's thirteen-year-old twins. The girl (also named Simona after her grandfather) led dance practices on the patio while her brother was an avid sportsman, always eager to jump into a volleyball match or lead a swimming race.

The one bit of fun that remained off-limits was the motorcycle "races" taking place at their neighbor Mihai Manoilescu's house. They were two lots behind, and little separated the dwellings but for a few scrawny trees and bushes. Manoilescu's son Alexander, then twenty years old, proudly paraded around on his shiny yellow motorcycle, whipping up dust with an incredible roar.

"But mother, we could just sit behind him and spin around the house! Please mother, we just want to find out what it feels like!" the boys would argue with Maria. "The answer is no, still no; you are much too young," she would firmly reply.

But one activity at the Manoilescu's house was not off-limits to the youngsters: the fireworks heralding the end of summer. In awe they watched the magnificent displays, their lives and childhood still shielded and seemingly so very far away from the raging war.

Germany (and the Romanian army fighting alongside) had much to celebrate during the summer of 1942. Operation "Blue"—the plan to capture the Soviet city of Stalingrad and gain control to the oil fields of the Caucasus—was well underway. The city of Rostov-on-Don, a strategic point along the Don River, had been conquered. The road had been opened and Stalingrad was next.

Romanian Army Corps Three and Four continued to participate in the action. As the final push for Stalingrad began, the Romanian commanders warned their allies about the fragility of the front. Their study of the terrain, positions, and strategy had uncovered seemingly large gaps along the lines. These led them to believe that their Russian enemy could easily penetrate their positions. But their warnings were ignored, later leading to disastrous consequences.

Summer gave way to fall.

Constantin began to be increasingly worried about the outcome of upcoming major battles and of the war effort in general. Official news was "filtered" in the press through the lens of the pro-German propaganda machine. But the other side of the story was heard on the BBC, which many a times painted a different story. As an avid student of history, he doubted anyone's ability to conquer the vast Soviet land. "Hitler and his generals should have studied Napoleon's Russian campaign and defeat," he repeatedly told the boys. "At the very least they shouldn't head into another winter with unfinished business." Visions of Napoleon's soldiers freezing to death, with thousands buried in ice and snow, and recent memories of last winter's bitter cold, sprang to mind.

What would a German defeat mean to them? It would imply a gradual Soviet push to the West. What would be their first obstacle? Romania allied with Germany and therefore considered an enemy of the Soviet people.

Both by virtue of its geographical position, as well as by that of its current alliance, Romania was bound to fall first.

So, as 1942 progressed, Constantin felt the need to devise a plan to protect the family if the Soviet threat became imminent. Maria's earlier concerns were now materializing. Protection would also be needed if the Allies commenced bombing Romania. Was he perhaps overly pessimistic? Was his knowledge of history muddling his perspective of the current events? He hesitated about talking to Maria at first, not wanting to compound her apprehensions. So he turned for advice to Maria's father. One day after classes he headed to his in-laws' house, choosing a day when Maria's mother would be away at a bridge game. This way the men could talk without interruptions and without prying ears.

"Professor," he started, "I need your advice."

Constantin then proceeded to share his concerns, and was soon surprised to hear Professor Mehedinti voicing similar ideas. More so, it appeared that his brother-in-law Emil was also thinking along the same lines. While needing to be in Romania to supervise his factory, Emil was eager to see his wife and twins out of harm's way.

"Mrs. Mehedinti and I . . ." (Constantin was relieved to know his mother-in-law had been consulted about these prospects) "have been discussing options. There is Switzerland, where we have part of our savings in an account."

"And Switzerland is neutral."

"So I favored it until I thought of the implications," the Professor added.

"If the Germans start losing and we need to return home, we would have to travel through embattled territory."

"What is the alternative?"

"Turkey. It is still neutral and a boat passage away. We can return home immediately if needed. And it already has a sizable Romanian colony."

As the two men conversed, a plan began to gradually take shape. The extended family would retreat to Istanbul if danger became imminent. Mrs. Mehedinti would inquire through acquaintances about possible accommodations. She would also move part of her savings into a bank represented in Istanbul. The issue of Constantin's employment weighed heavily on his mind. He considered teaching, but where and in what language? Then another idea began to take hold. For weeks he contemplated opening a Romanian historical institute in Istanbul, and started making preliminary inquiries among colleagues. It appeared a viable possibility, one worth exploring further. His father-in-law also offered an alternative.

"You could also teach history at the French high school. Your command of the language and of the subject makes you a good fit."

After taking leave of the professor, he suddenly began worrying how to approach Maria. Would she resent him talking to her father first? The damage was done, and so he opted for the truth. But he needn't worry; such was her relief at knowing a plan was crafted to keep the children out of harm's way. The knowledge that her parents and brother's family would be joining them was also of comfort. For Maria, who had worried incessantly since the beginning of the war, the prospect of going to Istanbul seemed an answer to her prayers.

The military outcome of the fall campaign led them to believe their plan might be called upon sooner than expected. News from the front line became sketchy once the battle for Stalingrad began in earnest in September. Many of the German troops were engaged there during the winter of 1942-1943, while their remainder was mostly tied up in the battle for El Alamein, in Egypt.

By December 1942, the German Sixth Army was surrounded and cut off inside Stalingrad, and had suffered heavy losses. The Romanian corps fighting alongside had met with the same fate, severely diminished by the "Operation Uranus" launched by the Soviet Red Army in November. The bitter cold, hunger, and repeated Soviet attacks gradually weakened the German ranks and their allies. A last attempt to counterattack led by Marshal Von Manstein failed within days, lacking manpower and support. And so by the end of the year the German (and Romanian) units were forced to retreat from the Caucasus. Details were scarce in the Romanian press, but the defeat was grimly depicted on the BBC once reports gradually trickled in from the broken Eastern Front.

The knowledge of so many dying, with countless bodies buried deep under feet of snow, cast a pall of anguish and sadness over the holidays. In December he told Maria:

"I'd much rather stay in Bucharest this year than head to the mountains. We shouldn't be celebrating at such a time."

She understood her husband's feelings, but her pragmatism once again rose to the front. "It might be the last time we go there, who knows where we'll be next year."

"Maria, it doesn't feel right to me. There's too much pain around us."

"Dear, there is sorrow everywhere and we hold no joy in our hearts. But I try to maintain a sense of normalcy in our lives for the sake of the children."

"They're growing up, Maria. They read and listen to the news. They're watching the world change."

"You're right, but we won't gain anything by staying here. I'll still put up a little tree, be it here or in Predeal. It won't be anything lavish and there won't be a party. But it is still Christmas, and the children cherish the tradition."

He took a few minutes to respond, knowing deep down she was right. Not traveling would not help the war effort, and might prevent the children from spending a last holiday in the snow.

"Very well, we'll be going then. But please, no large celebration, no other guests—just the five of us. Give each child one small gift, and if there is money left, please buy something for the war orphans."

As hard as it was to believe, Predeal appeared, at least superficially, to still be the same peaceful winter retreat. A new ski slope had recently opened. Food stores were reasonably well stocked and fire logs were plentiful. But Christmas 1942 was without the joy and light of holidays past. The mountains covered in fir were as majestic as ever, and snowflakes glistened under the light of the moon and stars. But a circle of darkness, its edges still muted and shaded, was closing in around their world.

The year 1943 began with further German losses around Stalingrad. By the end of January, the remains of the Sixth Army under the command of Field Marshal Paulus had to surrender—starving, freezing, and poorly equipped. On January 31, a radio broadcast in Germany was interrupted by the somber Adagio movement of Bruckner's Seventh Symphony, followed by the official announcement of the defeat at Stalingrad. The last remnants of the Axis forces finally surrendered on February 2, with three thousand Romanians among them.

The Germans also met, albeit more slowly, a similar fate in North Africa, where General Rommel was forced to mount a gradual retreat. Bad news mounted for the "Axis" side, as their allies the Italians didn't fare any better that spring. The Western allied powers had begun to pave the way for possible landing sites on the continent as the islands of Sicily and Sardinia and the mainland later came under heavy attack.

As for the Romanians, their fate remained intertwined with that of the Germans that spring of 1943. After all the back and forth fighting and countless lives lost, the position of the Eastern Front was exactly where it had been a year and a half earlier, in November 1941: the Germans' gains of 1942 had been completely erased. And though heavy losses had been endured by both sides, the Soviets seemed to respond with endless supplies and reinforcements. Their enemy told a different story, the winter campaign having left their ranks severely depleted, exhausted, cold, and hungry.

All the while, people in Bucharest carried on and tried to put on a good front, despite the mounting fear. They attempted to go about the usual business and celebrated the religious holidays of the Epiphany in early January and then Easter as in years past. They gathered once again on May 10 for the customary Independence Day parade and the king's greeting. A milestone was reached that year, with the twenty-fifth anniversary of their beloved Bessarabia reuniting with Romania at the end of World War I upon them. Who could have guessed in 1918 that a quarter century later Bessarabia would again be at the central part of a territorial dispute?

More than ever, one was living in the day with a sense of deep uncertainty for tomorrow. As for the war, it went on and on.

Chapter Eighteen
THE FIRST BOMBS FALL

In the summer of 1943, Constantin was asked to participate in a seminar organized by the university in the village of Breaza. This invitation had asked him to focus on seminar techniques. It had to do with preparation of the students, the dialogue he favored in class, and so on. Symposia such as these were periodically organized by the university, particularly during the summer's long vacation, and were meant to help educators at different levels.

A car came to fetch him on July 31. For an hour or so, he enjoyed the leisurely ride to Breaza with the road winding through mountains and low-lying hills. It passed orchards laden with apples, green pastures dotted with lazy cows, and fields of bright summer flowers. The sky was blue with the sun shining high above, and it all seemed so peaceful.

Twenty-four hours later the peace was shattered in Breaza by a strong vibration and a loud booming noise. The seminar's participants had just sat down to lunch, when the entire building violently shook. All scrambled and ran outside, not knowing what to expect. There they spotted the aircraft; Constantin would later tell his family how the passing squad was flying so low that he could make out the pilots' faces. Some were able to spot the American flag on the side of the planes. "Oh, my God," shouted someone. "We're all going to die!" The words were drowned by a series of explosions that followed seconds later.

When the noise stopped, the men looked at one another in disbelief, very much still alive. Some trembled, a few whimpered while others dabbed their faces with napkins and handkerchiefs. Someone finally broke the silence. "They must be heading to Campina." This was a small town nearby, the site of an oil refinery, and close to the Ploesti oil fields. The latter had already been the target of an earlier bombing in June 1942, with minimal damage at that time.

They later heard how the Romanian anti-air defense had reacted quickly and effectively. The U.S. led attack had originated in Libya (Operation Tidal Wave), and the Romanian oil fields had indeed been their target. Nearly a third of the American planes were shot down and 147 pilots were lost. Casualties on the ground were also heavy, with

120 dead and many civilians wounded. But the damage to the refinery, train station, and electrical plant were minimal, and were quickly repaired in the coming month.

The incident showed Constantin how close the war had come to their doorstep. Later that August he once again met with Mihai "Ica" Antonescu, who by this time was vice prime minister. He was taking a few days of respite while visiting the general in Predeal. He called on Constantin, as he always did on such occasions, and the two men had a long talk behind closed doors. Ica advised his friend, in all confidentiality, to make "alternative" plans for the future.

"I can't share intelligence with you, but we fear what lies ahead."

He laid down his case that Germany's losses would continue to mount. The Romanians were anticipated to face severe reprisals from the Soviets in particular and the Western Allies in general.

"You and your family can still travel," Ica told his friend. "You may want to think of a safer place for now, particularly if the bombing of Bucharest starts. Go somewhere while the rest of the war unfolds, and we find out what's in store for us."

"What do you think of Istanbul, Ica?" Constantin asked.

"It's a good choice. Many Romanians are there, and Turkey is neutral. Nick Malaxa's family is already renting a house there." Malaxa was one of Romania's leading industrialists, an engineer by training, who had created the largest steel/metallurgical consortium in the country.

Ica's report and his own information about the steady Soviet advances in the Ukraine reinforced Constantin's fears for his family's safety. In the upcoming months, he and Maria started planning in earnest for an indefinite stay in Istanbul. Through acquaintances they learned that housing was plentiful and cheap. They decided to live in a hotel at first while looking for something suitable to rent. Some money was transferred into a savings account there. Constantin continued to inquire about the possibility of opening a Romanian cultural center in Istanbul, aided in this endeavor by his friendship with the Turkish ambassador in Bucharest, Suphy Tanriover. They also decided not to tell the children about their plans until close to departure time, so as not to alarm them. Maria also worried the children might prematurely share the news with their friends, and wished to avoided spreading panic and rumors.

The wheels were set in motion. Toward the end of September, with school barely two weeks into its session, Maria and her husband gathered the children one evening. "There's something we want to talk to you about."

The boys immediately looked worried. Had the parents heard of the window broken during the morning recess? "They wouldn't summon Mona, though," thought Dan, somewhat reassured.

Their mother continued, "We'll be leaving Bucharest soon. We are going to Istanbul where your father hopes to open a Romanian cultural center."

"All of us? What about school?" Dan asked. Could they possibly take a prolonged vacation again?

"You'll be attending the French high school there." This brought disappointment to the children.

"My French is not that good . . . I can't spell well enough to keep up," Mona complained.

"They'll understand. Because of the war, there are plenty of foreign students there. And you'll improve immediately once you use it every day."

"Are they going to give us school books?" asked Dinu, airing his main concern. A studious boy, he was keen not to leave behind his brand-new manuals.

"Yes, they will, I'm sure, but you should all take a few along with you—mathematics, biology, history. We'll need to make sure they cover what you would've done here. There'll be exams to pass when we return."

"So we're coming back?" Dinu asked.

"Yes. I'm sure, but we don't know when," Maria told her children.

"Are Florica, Maria, and her husband coming with us?" asked Mona, referring to the house help.

"No, they're not," she said, and then quickly added, "but your grandparents will be joining us soon." The children looked relieved. "And your cousins, too."

This last bit of news brought an enthusiastic response from Mona and the boys. Close in age, they often played at their grandfather's house and estate, and the bond had been strengthened in Mangalia the previous summer. This was definitely beginning to sound more like a foreign holiday to them, despite the bit of news about the French school.

It took a couple of weeks to sort out what needed to be taken along and what could be left behind for now. It also took a while to get various papers in order, including school equivalency certificates. Maria and Constantin were anxious and uncertain about the timing of their relocation; life in Bucharest still flowed at the usual pace while war raged in lands near and far. There seemed no immediate threat to the city, nor were Soviet troops poised across the border as of yet.

"Should we wait a while longer?" they kept asking themselves.

Then Maria would remind her husband, "And then what? Try to leave when everybody is fleeing in a mad scramble to book trains and find cars, with other countries closing their borders . . . you remember what happened in Bessarabia when it was occupied by the Soviets?"

Accounts of the Romanians fleeing from the occupied lands still fresh on their minds, and tales of the Soviet cruel and harsh behavior cemented their opinion that an early departure was preferable. By mid-October they declared themselves ready to depart. They were to leave first and settle in; Maria's parents and her brother's family would then join them. Constantin's siblings and their families decided against leaving, seeing no immediate threat to their well-being.

The family left by train and the first night's journey took them across Bulgaria. There were few stops along the way, and one could hardly decipher the outline of the poorly lit cities. The night cloaked trees and fields as they passed by until daylight broke at the border. With Bulgaria at war only with the U.K. (and neutral in the German-Soviet conflict), and Turkey neutral altogether, the visa formalities did not take very long.

They rode on to Istanbul through the mostly flat dusty low-lying land between the Black and Marmara Seas. Pulling into Istanbul, the train slowed down enough for all to see the ancient, crumbling buildings on the outskirts. These gave way to solid, grander structures closer to the center until the train arrived at their final destination. While they were used to the hustle and bustle of the central Bucharest train station, an unusually boisterous and colorful spectacle awaited them in Istanbul. It was here that Europe and Asia and their cultures collided, with a range of garb on display. The station swarmed with locals and foreign visitors. There were men in well-cut suits and women in floral frocks and fashionable hats, but also Greeks and Armenians in their traditional attire. Sugary pastries, roasted pistachio nuts, fried sardines, citrus-flavored paste, and little birds and flowers, were sold side by side. Loud shouts were heard, and children tugged at your sleeves trying to catch your attention and loose coins.

Mona was bewildered. "Is the whole city like this?"

"No, dear. But there are lots of busy streets and, of course, the bazaar where they sell everything," replied her mother, recalling her early visit to Istanbul while on the cruise.

"You all stay close to us until we get out of here," she then added, keeping an eye on her children.

A representative of the Romanian consulate was waiting for them with a couple of cars. It took a while to make sure all the luggage was accounted for, until finally they were ready to head to a hotel. It would be their temporary home while looking for a rental.

Streets were considerably busier and more chaotic than in Bucharest, where most cars had been commissioned by the army and used elsewhere. Besides cars, bicycles, and carriages, the streets were filled with people walking every which way. Their hotel was located near the Taksim Square in the commercial center of the city. The square was named for the building at its center, which had been used for the city's water distribution; the impressive stone structure dated from the early eighteenth century.

After unpacking and dinner in the hotel's restaurant, it was time to put the children to bed and plan the next few days.

"This is the list of rentals recommended by our consul, Maria. He's had his secretary compile it for us." Constantin handed his wife the list. "Adrian Nocea, one of the officials, will accompany you tomorrow."

"I don't need him by my side; I can handle all this by myself," his wife insisted.

"Maria dear, lone women are often harassed in the streets. Worse still, they'll probably charge you more than the place is worth. Neither of us would know the going rate here."

And so the following morning she went along with Mr. Nocea and immediately started looking at properties. She found plenty of opportunities with many good choices within their budget range, and one she liked in particular. Within days they had moved into the spacious furnished three-bedroom apartment a couple of tramway stops away from Taksim Square. The children were delighted, viewing all this as something of a grand adventure, having never before lived in an apartment building. Riding an elevator to their floor made them feel rather sophisticated, like people in a movie. Dinu was already sixteen, and Maria thought he was responsible enough to take his brother and sister along with him to discover their surrounding neighborhood.

After they settled in, the family also started exploring their new home city, taking advantage of the mild late-fall temperatures. On one such occasion they visited Bursa, the first Ottoman capital, and its famed Green Mosque with the tomb of Sultan Mehmet the First dating from the fourteenth century. Another trip took them to Edicule, the famous and much-feared jail where several Romanian princes had met a tragic fate. The cells with low ceilings and a lack of light made one shudder while trying to imagine a prisoner's life in such confines. A group of elderly men overheard Constantin offering explanations to his sons in the Edicule garden. One approached the young family. "What is happening in our country, sir?"

Constantin could hardly believe his eyes. "Why, are you Romanian, too?" he inquired.

"Yes, sir, I left many years ago. My wife and I are of Turkish descent and were born in Romania. When our children grew up, they wanted to resettle in Turkey. But for me, Romania is still my country."

Constantin learned how the man had come from Dobrogea, the southeast Romanian province bordering Bulgaria and the Black Sea. It touched him to hear how after all these years of living on foreign soil that the man still considered Romania "his" country and wanted to have news of her.

Constantin, too, felt nostalgic. His negotiations to open a Romanian cultural center were not progressing as desired. Turkey, being neutral, did not want to condone any activity organized by a combatant in the war. Sure, there were English and French schools in Turkey, but the precedent was not comparable, as these had opened before the war had started. Constantin inquired briefly about teaching and was politely turned away as no history teachers were needed at the French School. Uncertain about their future in Istanbul, Maria and her husband sent word back to Bucharest. The rest of her family was to wait a while longer.

So with the situation in Romania much the same, and little to deter him from returning to Bucharest, Constantin and Maria decided, with a heavy heart, to go back home. While the parents were torn over the decision, the children were immediately happy. After the initial enthusiasm over the new surroundings wore out, they had become bored with studying at home, having arrived too late to enroll for the French school's fall semester. They missed their friends and classmates and their cousins, too, whose arrival had been postponed. Maria was particularly uneasy, and continued to worry about what lay in store for them in their homeland. But she felt a measure of relief knowing her parents had not yet made the journey: travel at their age wasn't quite as easy as it was for the younger generation.

And so, barely a month and a half after their arrival, they once again boarded the train returning home. The return journey went through Sofia, the Bulgarian capital, this time. The train pulled into the station and was held there on account of warnings of Allied bombing. A couple of hours passed, and passengers were asked to disembark. From the train station they were taken to a hotel with a shelter. They waited for a while, but once again nothing happened. Finally, the hotel manager advised his guests to retire for the evening. Back in their rooms, they had barely changed into pajamas when the alarm's shrill warning preceded the impossibly loud noise of bombs exploding. Exhausted and bleary-eyed, all headed to the bomb shelter in the cellar. Some prayed; others cried softly. Mostly they waited. "Thank God they sound distant," Maria murmured, hugging her daughter, as none of the bombs fell near the hotel that night. After the noise died down and the all-clear was sounded, guests were able to return to their rooms.

They were taken to the station in the morning and continued the journey without further interruptions. They got back on a cold dreary December day, with a thin mist that chilled one's bones. Yes, they were home, but it was gray, dark, and wet. Christmas was once again right around the corner. The year 1943 was coming to an end, and had seen bombs fall on Romania's soil. For once no one looked forward to what the New Year might bring.

Chapter Nineteen

THE FAMILY FLEES TO ISTANBUL

The year 1943 had brought a substantial shift in the balance of power between the battling forces. First, in the spring the Eastern Front had reverted back to its position of November 1941. From there it then continued to move westward, due to consistent gains made by the Soviet "Red" army. And it had then culminated in the liberation of the city of Kiev, capital of the Ukraine province.

Compounding these losses in the East was the German defeat in North Africa, where its armies surrendered to the Allies in May. On yet another front, the Allies first bombed and then landed on the islands of Sicily and Sardinia and then at the bottom of the Italian peninsula. By September 1943, Italy had signed an armistice with the Allies.

As for the U.S., its naval forces also scored victories in the Pacific theater, recapturing some Japanese strongholds.

By the end of the year, it was clear that the Allies (led by the U.S., Britain, France, and the Soviet Union) were gaining on multiple fronts. The next defining moment of the war came in November 1943 at the Tehran Conference. It was there that northern France was chosen as the site for the Allied invasion which would commence with a massive landing. It was also there that Stalin, the Soviet leader, rejected Churchill's plan for a landing in Trieste, Italy. This would have led the Allied armies into Slovenia, northern Yugoslavia, and Hungary, and would have created a shield against Soviet aggression after the war. Behind Churchill's plan lay the fear that Stalin had eyed the Balkans for himself. And indeed this was the Soviet leader's strategy, already thinking ahead at hopefully extending Russia's growing sphere of influence. In planning the Allies' future campaign he was ironically supported by the U.S. Commander General Marshall, who favored northern France but for different reasons. The General had felt that a Trieste landing and subsequent advance would have taken his men along difficult roads and led to heavy losses.

Romania's fate, as an integral part of the Balkans, was implicitly sealed at the Tehran Conference.

While its future was being decided 1,500 miles away, the country went about in its dreamy life-as-usual state, and ushered in once more

Christmas and the New Year. A sense of prosperity still prevailed, due to good crops in 1943. A plentiful supply of wheat and other grains meant the stores were still full of bread and pastry products. The grape season had been good, too, and so Maria continued selling her wine out of the front-yard stand.

After two years of war, they were yet to see fighting on home soil. As for the bombing, only a significant one had taken place, that of the Ploesti oil fields. The casualties on the front and the announcements for burials and masses still represented for many the only reality of war in December 1943.

Constantin, Maria, and the children spent a couple of weeks in Predeal. It had been a busy month since their return from Istanbul. The children had to take exams in order reenter their high school classes. Maria had to get the household up in "running order." Constantin had gone back to teaching and also spent time editing a volume containing a series of his father's studies. October 1943 had marked twenty-five years since his passing.

"A quarter century, it's amazing, Maria. I still see him at his desk, just like yesterday," Constantin told his wife.

"So you don't just recall the pain and suffering of his last days."

"God no, though they are vivid, too. But he was such a vibrant, healthy man before that. I so wish you could have known him, and Mother, too. She would have adored you."

"She would have loved anyone who made her son happy," Marie said, touching his hand.

"You're right." Constantin squeezed hers in return. "Maria, I heard a bit of news and I am really pleased today. The Historical Institute is planning a volume honoring my father. It should be ready by the spring. There will also be a tribute at the university. It had all been planned for the fall, but was postponed because of my absence."

"Do you think it will still be quiet by the spring? What if the Allies start bombing? Or, there's fighting on our side of the border?"

"It seems likely at some point, but no one can predict when. We are going ahead with the planning for now. No use in sitting idle waiting for something to happen."

And then on March 10, 1944 fighting finally came to Romanian soil. The Soviet army crossed over and occupied the northern towns of Cernauti and Botosani, among others. There had been enough warnings so the authorities had time to organize an orderly evacuation, unlike Bukovina and Bessarabia in June 1940. Many institutions reacted accordingly, anticipating a rapid advance in the rest of the country.

176

The Ministry of Education followed suit and decided to end the school year early on March 31 instead of June 15.

A day before that, on March 30, Constantin felt deep gratitude while attending with Dinu the university ceremony honoring his father. It was held in the very hall where the professor had taught, and was attended by former colleagues, students, and friends. A large photo portrait of the man being celebrated had been placed above the stage, reminding the audience of his gentle smile. Constantin recalled happier days while hearing so many recollections and glowing tributes, while Dinu learned about the grandfather he had never met. Constantin's father had passed on a quarter century earlier, just when the country was emerging victorious from the First "Great" World War. How stark was the contrast to the sense of defeat and foreboding permeating the country in those early spring days of 1944. Romania, which in 1918 was poised to be whole again, now lay truncated and awaited to find out her fate.

On April 4 Bucharest heard an anti-air attack alarm drill; it had been posted in the morning papers and followed in an orderly fashion by citizens and authorities. Around one o'clock Maria, Constantin, and the children settled down to lunch when the phone rang. Dan answered, "Uncle Horia, how are you?" followed by a few seconds of silence.

"Sure, right away," he said and handed the receiver to his father.

Horia, as a major, had continued his active duty and was now assigned to a building of the Council of Ministries. "There's been a pre-alarm," he told his brother. "A squadron of American planes is approaching the city. Take everyone and run to the cellar!"

Constantin shouted immediately, "Planes approaching, to the cellar right away!"

The cellar was accessed from the house but also from the yard, via a detachable stair ladder. With a ceiling reinforced by a thick cement plank, it also functioned as a credible bomb shelter.

Four adults, three children, and a dog huddled close together and waited. An eerie silence was followed by the noise of the Romanian air-defense guns rolling along. With the house only 800 feet from the Military General Headquarters, they could distinguish the sounds of the various anti-aircraft guns. They were soon dwarfed within seconds by a deafening noise.

"It's getting close . . ." wailed Marioara, the woman who had been the family's cook for many years and lived with them.

Mona held on tight to her mother, but her parents' concerned faces offered no reassurances to the child. Maria grabbed Constantin's hand and said, "We'd give everything up to be alive and not maimed?"

"Everything," said her husband. These words would turn out to be prescient, but that forecast was to come a few years later.

The minutes in the cellar seemed like an eternity, and the noise covered up everything. When the roar became more distant, they became aware of the dog's whimpering, saw Marioara's tears, and could hear Marin's wailing. He was a courier who had happened to have delivered some correspondence to Constantin just before the alarm was sounded. He had rushed to the cellar with everyone else. Once inside he began to shiver uncontrollably and kept repeating, "I'm scared, oh, I'm so scared. It's getting close again; oh, I'm scared!"

With everyone on the edge, the dog continued digging in the ground, probably terrified of the noise and unable to stop.

Marioara's wails became louder. "Oh, no, Miss Maria, the dog is digging a grave; it's a really bad sign." Dinu kicked the dog in response, attempting to make him stop.

Maria admonished him, "Leave the dog alone, boy. Marioara, he's scared just like the rest of us."

And so it went until the horrendous noise returned with the next wave of bombers; it roared above them, and the house shook, as a clutter of broken glass rained in the yard.

"We've been hit!" yelled someone.

They waited as the humming of the planes became more distant and eventually vanished. The all-clear alarm followed, and only then did they prop up the step ladder and climbed into the yard. Stepping on broken tiles and shattered glass, they took in the dust-covered rose bushes and trees before lifting their eyes to look around. Their house was standing, but the one across the street lay in a heap of bricks. A bomb had fallen through a small window into the cellar, killing all who had taken refuge there. Maria kept shaking her head in disbelief, with deep nausea overtaking her, realizing how their own fate had been decided by a fraction of a second.

The toll of the April 4 raid on Bucharest: nearly 3,000 dead, over 2,000 wounded, and 900 houses leveled. The war had arrived home, and some of Bucharest's citizens still could hardly believe it:

"I didn't think they were going to hit us," some had said.

"Surely they should have guessed our feelings," added others.

"The Allies know our hearts are with them; we have always been pro-France and Britain; we simply had no choice this time."

The Allies had evidently not known or cared about the "feelings" of the Romanian public. Bombs poured down from the sky for the next four months, killing more than seven thousand people, while large cities and the oil fields remained the primary targets.

"Now you see what war really is, boys," Constantin told them. "You kept dreaming of the fighting before it even started and wanted us in. Wars turn the world upside down and bring nothing but death and destruction."

While Allied bombs rained on cities, the Soviet advance on Romanian soil continued until April, when inexplicably it stopped for a while. The front line thus stabilized to the north of the city of Iasi, the capital of Moldova, where it remained until August 20, 1944.

In the meantime the bombing of Bucharest continued and fear mounted. Those who could leave their homes, taking shelter in the countryside or mountains, fled. Constantin and Maria weighed their options. The seaside home was deemed too dangerous due to the naval port, a potential bombing target. The mountain villa had been requisitioned by the military. Maria's parents' estate was in Moldova, and too close to the ever-approaching front line.

They settled upon Maria's sister-in-law's country estate, about two hours southwest of Bucharest. It had a big house, large enough to accommodate the extended family. There were many rooms and a large cellar which could be used as a bomb cellar if planes came their way. Going there took them out of immediate harm's way and allowed Constantin, his father-in-law, and brother-in-law to ponder their next move.

It was still quiet in the countryside, where one could stroll through the park and surrounding woods without fear of bombs coming down. Spotting Allied planes in formation headed toward Bucharest felt almost surreal. Here the peasants went about feeding their chickens and taking cows to pasture, a world away from the destruction taking place elsewhere in the country. With all vehicles commissioned by the army, a horse-drawn carriage took them to the neighboring village for supplies. The news of the Soviet advance and movement of troops were followed closely on the wireless. The stark contrast of these tranquil days at the estate with what might lie ahead weighed heavily on their minds.

"The time to act is now," Maria told her husband early one morning. "We can't wait here until the Reds arrive to rape and kill us all." The Reds was the nickname many used for the Soviet Army.

They all knew of the atrocities committed by the Soviet army in the occupied Romanian territories in 1940. Details had also emerged about communal graves in places such as Katyn, Poland, where thousands of Polish officers were buried after being shot to death by the Soviets. Escaping from this occupying army became their preoccupation, and a plan began to take shape. Neutral Switzerland was briefly floated as a possibility, but deemed too risky, as the train journey would have taken them across embattled lands.

Istanbul emerged once again as the most viable choice. Maria, the children, her sister-in-law Wanda and her twins, and the grandparents would leave first. Constantin and Wanda's husband, Emil, would follow when the situation in Romania became critical. The children's safety was first and foremost on Maria's mind. The timing of the Allied offensive worked somewhat to their advantage. Having just completed a school year, the children had an extended spring and summer holiday before resuming classes in September.

"You'll need to take books along and prepare assignments during the break; otherwise you'll forget everything by September," their mother warned Dinu, Dan, and Mona.

The children had been unsettled, even fearful, before their first trip to Istanbul. But this time around they welcome it, eager to cut short the stay in the countryside, where nothing much happened and one couldn't go to the movies or dancing.

Thus, they returned to Bucharest, packed once again, and were back in Istanbul by early May. They rented hotel rooms and within days Maria had found three apartments for herself, her parents, and her sister-in-law, close to where they had lived the previous year. They were also near the French high school, which Maria hoped her children would attend in the fall. So they settled in the best they could and awaited new developments back home and elsewhere on the Eastern and Western Fronts.

It was pretty quiet at first. The women busied themselves with their households; Swiss currency (their savings held in Swiss banks) scored well against the local one so they had no pressing financial worries. Maria also reached out to other Romanian women living abroad, and a social "calendar" began to take shape. The children once again quickly got over the initial excitement of living in a new place and started complaining of "boredom." Even their mother had to admit that it must have felt confining for the active teenagers. They hadn't yet found any new friends to play with and were on school vacation. It took some convincing, but eventually Maria acquiesced and let the boys go by themselves to the beachside resort of Floria. It was on the Sea of Marmara, a short train-ride away, and popular with the young. They could swim, run, improvise volley ball games, and meet other young people there. Dinu was now seventeen, and his mother thought he was responsible enough to undertake the journey and accompany his younger brother and cousin.

News from Constantin, back in Bucharest, was rather sporadic. Letters sent through the mail or via a courier told of a lull in the Soviets' advance, punctuated by periodic bombings of the city. They also told of divided political factions, with one side demanding a change in the country's position and alliances in the war. Much of this wrangling went on behind the scenes and was not published in the state-controlled media, so people relied again on the flying rumors. Like so many times in the past, Romania waited for her fate to be decided by others. Little did anyone know how her future had already been mapped out at the Tehran Conference a year earlier.

As they sat waiting in the Balkans, the outcome of the war was being decided on the beaches of Normandy. Maria and the family had access, for the first time in years, to news accounts from the perspective of the Allies. British and French newspapers were available in neutral Turkey, and the landings in France were widely cheered by the political and intellectual local circles. Dinu bought a new map, having left his in Bucharest, and resumed following the military action and changing front lines. As the Allies gained a strong foothold in Normandy, colored pins representing their armies began to amass on the map, eventually making their way toward Paris. The magnitude of the Allies' invasion and success became such that other news faded. Even the liberation of Rome went by with little fanfare. With one exception: the German V rocket retaliatory attacks on London were covered in great detail by the press. Perhaps they had been unexpected, or perhaps the sheer spectacle of it deserved extended coverage.

Eyes stayed glued on newspaper reports about the Western Front for weeks until action on the Eastern Front, much closer to home, began to heat up again. The Soviet Armies pushed toward Warsaw, the capital of Poland. By the end of July the German-Soviet front thus found itself exactly where it had been three years earlier at the onset of the German offensive.

Maria read and listened to accounts of the Soviet advance, growing increasingly worried for Constantin's safety and the future prospects of the entire family. A telegram heralding her husband's arrival in early August overjoyed her. She kept the news to herself so the children would be surprised. They had just sat down to a light supper of toast, cheese, sardines and fruit one steamy summer evening when the doorbell rang.

"Are we expecting Grandma or Aunt Wanda?" Mona asked.

"No, dear, not that I'm aware of."

"Boys, go see who it is," Marie told them.

Dan, always restless, got up first and went to the door. Maria sat quietly, relishing every second, hearing the key turn until a loud shriek erupted.

"It's Dad; Dad is here!"

Dinu and Mona immediately jumped to their feet and ran to embrace their father, while Maria's face shone with a wide smile. Her husband was here, out of harm's way, and they would face together whatever lay ahead.

"Do I smell freshly fried sardines?" he asked. "Are you having a feast without me?"

Constantin took off his linen jacket and sat down, now realizing how ravenously hungry the long journey had made him. He helped himself to the spread, while the boys told him of their days at the beach.

"Father, we take the train all by ourselves. It's less than an hour to Floria. We walk from the station to the beach; it's not even a quarter hour."

"Have you run into anyone you know there?"

"Well, dad, we met mechanics and sailors from the *Transylvania* on the beach. You remember the ship you sailed on in the 30s." His father nodded cautiously. "They swim there on their days off. They're great fun, full of stories, and like to party."

"Now don't tell me you're partying with the sailors at your age," he said and then, turning toward Maria. "Did you know this?"

"Of course I did; they're just having fun, to help summer go by."

"Well, if it is all right with your mother . . ." Constantin said, and left it at that.

It was now his turn to fill them in on what life had been like in wartime Bucharest in the preceding two months. "The bombings have continued: The Americans hit during the day and the British at night."

"How do they manage in the dark, without seeing the targets?"

"It's awfully clever, they first drop parachutes with flares, and everything is awash in light . . . then come the bombs."

Later on, after the children went to bed, he shared with Maria the other purpose of his visit. His old friend Ica Antonescu, vice president of the government and Foreign Affair Minister, had sent Constantin with a secret message for the Allied ambassadors in the Turkish capital of Ankara. It was part of a multi-pronged effort of reaching out to the emissaries of the Allies in places as Bern, Switzerland; Madrid, Spain; and Lisbon, Portugal, all neutral countries.

"Maria dear, everyone says now we can't save ourselves unless we start talking to the Allies."

Days later he was to travel to Ankara, where, with the local Romanian military attaché, he paid a visit to the U.S. representatives. There he passed on the message from the Romanian government of Marshal Antonescu. Constantin detailed his country's intention to send a high-level emissary to Cairo, Egypt, a city which had become a hotbed of diplomacy and negotiations. The emissary was to carry a letter for the British and American envoys. Its purpose: to state his government's desire to offer any and all concessions in return for having the U.K. and U.S. participate in a takeover of Romania, in order to preempt a sole Soviet occupation of the country.

The message was forwarded to the U.S. State Department and from there promptly on to Moscow, their war ally. The Soviets expressed doubts regarding Romania's true willingness to disengage from the Germans. But the other Allies stated an interest in meeting them in Cairo and seeing what the Romanians had to say.

Even now in the twelfth hour of the war, Romania's main objective remained to avoid by any and all means a Soviet takeover. Unrealistic hopes lingered on that perhaps a second Allied landing might still take place in the Balkans, with memories of the First World War action in that theater remaining fresh in the memory of some.

History did not repeat itself, but the events of August 23, 1944 were next.

Chapter Twenty
THE SOVIET OCCUPATION BEGINS

Marshal Antonescu, a seasoned military man and the country's de facto leader, had admitted in private in 1942: "Germany has lost the war. Now we must concentrate our efforts not to lose ours." But neither his good intentions nor the bravery of the troops could stop the country's slide toward inexorable defeat. The marshal had known deep down that his country had to disengage from its alliance with Germany, and back and forth communications between the two intensified. But Romania ultimately stayed the course—the fear of Soviet occupation driving and dominating all decisions.

Antonescu's representatives and those of the opposing political parties (the traditional National Liberal and Peasant) reached out to the U.S. and Britain and refused to quench their hopes for an intervention. Seeing upcoming defeat, they unsuccessfully attempted to secure promises of an Anglo-American presence on Romanian soil as a buffer to the Soviets.

Some of the Romanian political leaders continued to believe in the "traditional" diplomatic unspoken "rules" of the nineteenth and early twentieth centuries. According to these, the Balkan countries were considered part of the larger European theater, and were not to fall under the domination of a single superpower. What the same leaders did not know at the time was that Romania's fate had already been sealed. The British Foreign Affairs Minister, Anthony Eden, had contacted the U.S. State Department in May, 1944. Eyeing the post-war world, he had stated his preference for Romania's affairs to be managed by the Soviets, while the U.K. would "take care" of those of Greece. If his plan was to succeed, only part of the Balkan region would fall into the Soviet grip. Thus the traditional diplomatic "dictum" of avoiding a single superpower's supremacy in a given region would remain intact.

Where did Romanian King Michael stand? Only eighteen years old when ascending to the throne, he held little formal powers. The dialogue between Antonescu, the official "head of state," and the Palace was limited throughout the war. And though designated as official "Head of the Armed Forces," the king was not even offered the courtesy of advance notice on upcoming offensives.

Despite his young age, and with the help of trusted aides and his mother's savvy, the king gradually understood how a change of his country's direction rested with him. He visited troops, initiated a dialogue with their generals, and strengthened his bond with the military. He reached out to the leaders of the parties in opposition and other political figures. He explored scenarios for extricating his country from the war and studied varied terms of an armistice coming his way from London, Washington, and Moscow. And he waited for the proper conjunction.

On August 20, 1944, just before dawn, a discrete door knock awakened the king. "Your majesty, a major Soviet offensive has begun, troops are rapidly advancing." Indeed, the following days would see rapid inroads made by the Red Army and a progressive retreat of the Romanian troops. The king now knew the time to take charge was drawing near.

Early on the day of the twenty-third, a laconic phone message was sent to the Palace from the general in charge of Romanian Army Group Four. "Everything is ready. You can count upon our faith and we await an answer."

With no reply forthcoming just yet, the same general contacted the country's leader, Marshal Antonescu, hours later. "It is imperative that you order an immediate retreat of our troops. Spare the lives of innocent victims and put an end to a cause we no longer believe in. We are awaiting an immediate answer before taking action. . . ."

But unwilling or unable to change his country's course, the marshal did not answer the call, the military man continuing to believe in fighting to the death.

And then, suddenly, an order did arrive from the Palace. In a radio broadcast to the nation and her army, King Michael declared a ceasefire. He accepted, on behalf of his nation, terms of a unilateral—and not yet signed—armistice including cooperation with the Allied Soviet forces on the territory. The sovereign had understood that his country had run out of alternatives. A continuing offensive would have brought sustained fighting and would have ravaged the entire territory, much like had happened in Italy.

Marshal Antonescu's regime thus fell, brought down by the momentous decision of the King Michael. The twenty-three-year-old monarch had heard his country's call and had answered.

As for the broader implications of the king's decision, it hastened the collapse of the Germans on the Eastern Front. It also opened up the roads for a Soviet advance into the Balkan Peninsula and toward central Europe. The duration of the war was shortened, as the Germans could no longer rely upon the Romanian oil supplies. And the door was also opened for other countries to soon follow suit, Finland and Bulgaria reaching similar political resolutions.

For those living abroad there were chopped-up bits of news filtering in the following days as carried by the French and British press and heard on the radio. Constantin's thoughts immediately focused on a return home, whereas Maria felt her worst nightmare—a Soviet occupation—was virtually underway. She couldn't tell when and how her fear had begun, for it had been tugging at her sleeve since the war had started. But she was certain of one thing: whenever the dark thoughts returned, they chilled her to the bone. A sense of deep foreboding permeated her vision of life in Romania.

"We can start thinking now about going back home," Constantin said to his wife.

"No, we can't, not just yet. We haven't seen a signed armistice; we have no idea what the terms are or how this will turn out."

"Well, of course we won't travel right away. But I feel we are on the right track now, with the king in command and the old parties back in power."

"I'm not sure at all. This is how it seems. But you know the Soviets will want revenge. You know I've always had a bad feeling about this war."

"Maria dear, let the facts override your feelings," her husband said.

"Facts! Which facts? Antonescu is out, the king is back at the helm, and we are no longer allied with Germany. These are the facts. But for now we have no idea what it all means, and what will happen once Germany surrenders."

The bickering continued until Constantin caved in. "All right, we'll wait see what the terms of armistice are and what the next few months may bring."

"Very good, but you'll see, no piece of paper is going to stave off the Soviet retaliation," his wife warned.

A determined and cold edge had developed in his beloved Maria, her husband thought. "It's probably the stress she's been under, coming and going, worrying about the children, her parents," he told himself. The calm and rational man could not fathom his clever wife being overtaken by hunches and premonitions.

As for their children, they followed the developing events back home with interest. But unlike the first time in Turkey, they were now ambivalent about a return home. A long summer in Istanbul and recent enrollment in the French high school had brought new friends and acquaintances, and a new rhythm to their lives. Invitations to dances had started arriving; records of Benny Goodman, Duke Ellington, and Glenn Miller were played at parties and were the latest rage. Another attraction was car rides with Costache, son of the big industrialist Malaxa, whose family had taken refuge in Istanbul as well. What a thrill it was to race along the shores of the Bosphorus Straits! Once in a while the evening would continue with a meal in a restaurant, a special treat for teenage boys.

So they went on studying, enjoying themselves, and exploring the city, while waiting for the parents to make a decision. Of the three children, Mona, though the youngest, felt the most apprehensive about a return. It might have been because she was closest to her mother. But she had also overheard the comment of an American diplomat, a guest of her father's, at lunch one day. "Don't go back, Professor. Romania has fallen into the Soviet lot and it's going to be terrible," she heard him say, and had felt very, very scared. She had wanted to ask her parents about it, but knew that eavesdropping was not allowed. Asking the question would be admitting her guilt so she, too, waited.

To fill in the time Constantin occupied himself writing articles and doing bits of research for future projects. A perpetually active individual, he missed life back home, teaching, and his presence in the country's politics. Besides, a man's duty was to earn a living and support his family. Thoughts and scenarios swept through his mind and kept him awake at night. Suppose they wouldn't be able to return? Could he secure a teaching post in Istanbul, or another country? He wasn't old at forty-three, but didn't feel young either, his life and that of his family's at a crossroads. It had been a straight path until now, ever upward, and now suddenly at a halt. The maddening feeling that hard work and determination for once weren't enough tugged at his sleeve. The knowledge that external forces, completely outside his control, were weaving a web around them grew stronger with each passing day.

He woke up early one morning in November telling his wife, "Maria, I have a terrible pain on my right side."

She laid her hand on his forehead. "Why, you're burning with fever!"

"Yes, I'm hot, very hot."

Normally a calm, reserved man he was now writhing in pain, unable to assume any position for more than a few minutes.

"I'm calling the doctor," Maria said and ran to the phone.

Dr. Georgescu was the physician in charge of the liner *Transylvania*, and many of the Romanians living in Istanbul used him as their family doctor. He quickly came over and examined his patient. Lungs sounded clear, with no cough or hoarseness; he ruled out pneumonia.

"Any diarrhea?"

"No," said his patient, so the gut was eliminated as a cause.

"Show me where the pain is, and describe it to me."

"Along my right side, it shoots from the waist down to my groin . . . sharp, awful."

"Do you still have your appendix?"

"No."

"Have you used the bathroom this morning? Did you notice anything unusual?"

"Yes, I felt a burning sensation."

"Any blood in the urine?"

"No."

Within minutes of consultation Dr. Georgescu had guessed the diagnosis: blockage due to a kidney stone, which had triggered an infection—a textbook classic presentation.

Maria hated hospitals; she could never explain her apprehension, and when asked she'd brush it off and say, "You go in sick and come out sicker, catching germs from everyone else who's in there."

"Would you need to take him to the hospital, doctor?" she whispered.

"Not yet, as long as he can drink fluids on his own. But he if can't, or when, he'll need an intravenous drip in the hospital."

The doctor left prescriptions and the promise to return the following day, unless earlier services were needed. The children were dispatched to school and told not to disturb their father while Maria ran to the pharmacy. Constantin seemed to get worse before he got better, terrified by the timing of his illness. "Mind over matter," his favorite motto, was often repeated to students and his sons. It was ironic how his mind swirled around this time. He looked into the past and saw a frightening symmetry to his father's illness and death. His dad had fallen ill as the First World War was coming to a close; the current war appeared to have entered its final stage. He was now the same age his father had been at the time of his passing—forty-three years old. His dad had three young children and a beautiful wife, as he did. What would happen to his family if he, too, died?

These agonizing thoughts swarmed around and weakened the body further, until one morning he woke up and decided that he simply couldn't allow all of that to happen again. A different mindset took over now, one telling him to fight for his life. The stone was eventually passed, the fever went down, and a couple of weeks later he was well again and once more ready to contemplate a return home. Maria breathed easier, too; her husband was well again and he hadn't required the dreaded hospital stay.

News from Romania remained confusing. Following the August 23 change of course decided and articulated by the king, there was a rapid attempt by a marginal Communist Party to claim credit for the turn of events. As early as August 29, one of their leaders claimed that "The party of the working class . . . inspired and organized the fight to free the Romanian people."

Was it fact or fiction? The answer is the latter, as this party counted only about one thousand registered members at the time, a negligible fraction of the country's work force. Its leader had indeed visited the Palace in the weeks preceding the declaration, when the king had tried to reach out to all opposition parties. But he had been only one of many invited to come and consult with the sovereign prior to the critical decision-making.

The final initiative had been the king's alone with none of the party leaders present at the Palace in the momentous hours of August 23, 1944. The sovereign had assumed responsibility for the decision, while the army supplied the execution, and credit was due to King Michael and the brave armed forces alone.

But the Soviet Union believed otherwise. The armistice Maria awaited was signed on September 12, 1944. It placed Romania under the occupation of the Allies, with the Soviets as representative. Just two months later a deeply concerned Iuliu Maniu, the leader of the Peasant Party, sent a message to the British envoy Stevenson:

"Is the U.K. handing Romania to the Soviets?"

"No," came a laconic reply, despite British Premier Churchill having already had formally agreed to a 90 percent Soviet domination in Romania!

History was being rapidly rewritten at home, with a Communist Party trying to emulate their Russian comrades by taking the lead. In the meantime the occupation Soviet forces proceeded to rapidly dismantle numerous units of the Romanian army. In doing so they were attempting to minimize future internal opposition and diminish the army's role in the country's future.

With the country plundered by the occupying forces, the economic situation deteriorated, rapidly bringing about further unrest. A single ray of light shone amidst that cloudy fall: Transylvania was liberated on October 25 and returned to her rightful Romanian brothers.

Constantin anxiously followed the events back home. The king's announcement on August 23 revived his hopes. Then the mixed, murky news that emerged during the fall planted some doubt. His enthusiasm was rekindled in March, 1945 when George Tatarascu was elected minister of foreign affairs. The politician had been prime minister in 1940 when Constantin had briefly served as his minister of propaganda. "Things must be moving in the right direction," he tried to convince himself while raising the spirits of those around him.

Elsewhere in Europe an Allied ultimate victory was felt to be a certainty. It was no longer a matter of if, but instead people wondered when it would occur. France, Belgium, the Netherlands, Finland were all liberated one by one.

It was in this climate that Constantin tried to press his case for a return to Bucharest while Maria repeatedly tried to delay the trip. "Things are changing too fast and too often; papers back home are full of rumors."

"When haven't they been? The press is truly free again; anybody can write whatever crosses their mind."

"We should wait and see if the current government survives the winter at least," she insisted.

"Or wait for the final peace conference?"

"Precisely."

"And then you'd say we have to see if the peace treaty is respected," countered her husband.

Maria felt the discussion wasn't heading anywhere, so she changed her tactics. "Well, we should wait at least until the end of the school year in May. The children have had enough disruptions in their studies. Not to mention the boys are preparing for the bachelor's exam."

Dinu and Dan were one year apart in age but had been enrolled in the same final year of high school. The excellent secondary education in Romania had enabled Dan, the younger of the two, to "jump" one level. Constantin's brief silence acknowledged her position as they decided to stay in Istanbul at least until early summer. Maria knew she had won a temporary victory as the children's education was of utmost importance to her husband, too.

The spring of 1945 brought fierce fighting, as the Allied armies pressed on to Berlin while their leaders met at Yalta in February to debate post-war "spheres of influence." Losses mounted for the Germans in the following months. Endless bombs rained down on their cities while the circle of the Soviet army gradually tightened its noose around Berlin. On the last day of April, Chancellor Hitler took his life, and two of his generals and his minister of propaganda, Goebbels, the latter with his wife and children, soon followed suit. A week later the German unconditional surrender to the Allies took place on May 7 at the Western Allied headquarters in Rheims, France.

The long war in Europe had come to an end.

For those who'd taken refuge abroad, it was time to go home. Doubts still made many hesitant, despite assurances given by U.S. President Harry Truman at the final Potsdam peace conference. Romania, Bulgaria, and Hungary, he emphasized, were not to become part of a "sphere of interest." What the Romanians didn't know then was the Soviet leader's intention as shared with a Yugoslav counterpart in April 1945. He had stated: "This war is not like the past one; those who occupy a territory will also impose their social system . . . as far as the advance of their army."

But the desire to return to Bucharest was no longer automatically guaranteed by the mere purchase of a train ticket. The Romanian government, under the supervision of the Allied Soviet Commission, now required citizens living abroad to first submit a request to return.

"I have to ask for permission to go home?!" Maria mumbled and shivered. "I need to file a request to go sleep in my own bed? To go back to the houses I have built through the sale of my wine?" This only strengthened her opposition. And she was not alone as some of their friends had serious doubts, too. Even her brother and parents were not overly enthusiastic, and heated discussions continued late into many an evening.

"Governments change every few months; we need more time to understand what's going on . . . the Soviets' presence is becoming pervasive," she would tell everyone.

"No, we are calling for free elections, Maria. It's our country where our homes are. . . ."

"We can always start anew," she would reply.

"Where? At our age? How would we support the children? How would we pay for their university studies?" was her husband's opinion.

"We would work. You can tutor in history and geography. I can sew and bake or help run a household. We could learn Spanish or English and go to South America or the United States," she would reply in kind.

The couple's discussions were held in parallel with Constantin's talks with the Romanian intelligence service in Istanbul. Most advised him not to return, and shared their own plans to relocate to South America, Portugal, Kenya, and the like.

"Don't go back, Professor," he was told.

"The news is bad and getting worse. You might as well get a ticket for Moscow instead."

Then Constantin turned toward the immediate family. His brother-in-law Emil, still in Romania, had recalled his family home, seemingly hoping to continue the work at his factory. As for Maria's parents, they were for once reluctant to voice an opinion. They perhaps wished to refrain from influencing their children, or maybe a new life beckoned less at their advancing age?

Constantin's love for country and profession prevailed in the end. He genuinely believed the tense and tentative political situation on the home front to be improving, despite the official warnings received in Istanbul. Acquaintances and political colleagues from Bucharest wrote of free elections being promised. His friends continued to teach at the university. Alex went on heading his publishing house. Well, all right, perhaps the future was not entirely reassuring. But then again peace needed time to settle in, he told himself. And so it went, back and forth in his mind, all along thinking how Romanian history was his life and Romania his country. Where else could he possibly go and still reach his audience?

The formalities progressed in the meantime and the family received "permission" to return home at the end of October 1945. A defeated Maria packed the trunks with a heavy heart and said good-bye to friends staying behind in Istanbul. The finality of the act had struck her while handing in the apartment keys the night before departure. This brief phase of their lives had come to an end, and going home offered for once no sense of reassurance. She had put up the best argument she could, but in the end had bowed to her husband's decision.

They were to travel by boat, the *Transylvania,* which had been sent by the Romanian government to bring back those who had lived abroad during the war. There had been light rain early on the day of departure, but it had stopped by the time the passengers gathered to take leave and hug friends and family. The sky remained gray and heavy all along and a light fog added to the melancholy of the moment. Could the day be a harbinger of what lay ahead, wondered Maria?

The journey across choppy waters with cold, steady rain lasted a day and a night. One could sense the tension and unease onboard the ship. The staff was somewhat cold and remote where in years past they treated their guests deferentially, ready to jump at the slightest whim. Dinu ran into one of the sailors he had met the previous summer on the beach at Floria. He was delighted to see a familiar face, but was taken aback when the sailor barely acknowledged him. Later in the day the sailor showed up at Dinu's side in a narrow passage. "Things have changed, you will see. But I want you to know I didn't mean any disrespect."

The boat docked at Constanta, on the Romanian shore of the Black Sea. Gone was the frenzy and shouting of years past: a strange silence reigned over the harbor. Dockers moved around mechanically, in no apparent hurry. Maria was the first to notice their new uniforms, adorned by a Soviet-style star, hammer and sickle. The symbol of the Communist Party had been already adopted by the newly created trade union.

She leaned toward her husband and whispered, "Can you feel the tug toward Siberia?"

Their papers and passports were carefully scrutinized; there were no welcome greetings, pleasant conversation, or jokes. Some passengers had their luggage opened up and checked; rumors abounded as no one knew what was being targeted.

"Mind your jewelry and money," said someone.

"Make sure you watch them rummage through your belongings; I hear they steal items if you don't pay attention."

Constantin and Maria's family made it through without having to open their bags and packages. Then they took a cab to the station and continued the journey by train.

"There are no more first class cars." Constantin was told when he inquired about the fare. A fat, loudly dressed middle-aged woman selling tickets delighted in adding, "Everyone travels the same."

The once comfortable "first class" cars were unrecognizable: the plush, burgundy, velvet covered seats had been replaced by wooden benches. Passengers sat side by side with their luggage, live animals in cages, and bottles of wine and packages of food piled around them.

Maria's heart sank once more. "A promising new beginning," she mumbled, sarcasm lacing her voice. Her husband lips tightened, with no reply forthcoming.

Having seen the door close behind them on the docks at Constanta, Maria was pretty sure it would never open again.

PART IV
1946–1950
"THE COLLAPSE"

Chapter Twenty-One
RETURNING HOME WITH FALSE HOPES

War was raging in and around Romania, and bombs were falling on her cities when Constantin's family had left for Istanbul in the early summer of 1944. By the end of that summer, their country's war alliance had changed as they joined the Allies. And when the war was concluded the following spring, Romanians stood among the victors. Could there be better proof of that than having the "Victoria" Order awarded to King Michael by the Soviet State? It had previously been bestowed on only four other foreign dignitaries: General Dwight Eisenhower, the Supreme Allied Commander; and Marshall Sir Bernard Montgomery, ground troop commander during the Normandy Invasion, among them.

But the euphoria of that moment was short-lived.

When returning home in November 1945, Maria and Constantin discovered that their beloved country wasn't quite theirs any longer.

The first presage of Romania's fate had occurred three years earlier in 1943 in Tehran, where the "Big Three" (Roosevelt, Churchill, and Stalin) had met to plan the war's strategy. The main focus had been then on the European theater—the timing and location of a decisive invasion. Had the Allies decided on a landing in Italy, their troops would have fought and beat the Germans in the Balkans. A Soviet invasion and annexation of the region might have been held back. But U.S. General Marshall feared the difficulties that the terrain of the area would have posed to his troops. In picking the beaches of Normandy instead of Italy, the fate of the Balkans was sealed at Tehran.

The next step came in October 1944 in Moscow in the form of an agreement concluded between Churchill and Stalin. It was to establish a Soviet preeminence in Romania at the conclusion of the war, while the U.K. would, in exchange, get the same position in Greece. The Balkan countries would be carved up cleanly, after all.

With the end of the war in sight, the following high-profile meeting took place at Yalta in the Crimea in February 1945. The "Declaration on Liberated Europe" was crafted there; its wording was loose enough to be interpreted according to each side's wishes. The Soviet leader Stalin was eyeing a "sphere of influence" over Eastern Europe, while British Prime Minister Churchill wanted assurances that countries like Poland, Romania, and Hungary wouldn't be "sovietized." Soviet Foreign Minister Molotov worried that such guarantees would encroach on their future plans, but Stalin had famously replied, "Never mind. We'll do it our own way later."

And that was how the post-war shape of the European continent, and the future of her nations were decided at Yalta after having been first outlined at Tehran.

All that remained was the final imprint, which was sealed at the post-war conference at Potsdam in July 1945: now the world had a plan that needed to be implemented.

But few knew at that time of the momentous decisions reached at these conferences, and how the countries of Eastern Europe were bargained like *Monopoly* chips. Not even the countries' leaders were privy to the "arrangements" being negotiated at the time. While the war was winding down, although Romania had finished alongside the Allies, her fate had already been sealed. She would find that out in due time. In the meantime there was persistent hope in the country's political, social, and literary circles that the Allies must have "known" of the true Romanian feelings about the war. At cafes and salons across the country, one could hear these constant refrains:

"We wanted to fight with the British and French from the beginning."

"Most of us didn't favor an alliance with Germany."

"We were praying for a second Allied landing in the Balkans."

Even if those sentiments could have somehow been conveyed to the Allies, they would have been obliterated by the country's juxtaposition to the Soviet Union. It wasn't only one's prior allegiance but also geography that dictated one's fate in the aftermath of the Second World War.

The stakes were stacked against Romania and her misfortune was compounded. Not only was she located on the western border of the Soviet Union, but also they had been wartime enemies until August 1944. Her people might have not known this stark reality at the time, but avoiding a Soviet post-war domination of their country would have been impossible.

The collapse was gradual, with its bold strokes directed by the Soviet victors. First Romania's internal army and border patrols were dismantled, and local police forces downsized. Military training schools were closed or their class ranks shrank. Members of the Communist Party started instigating rallies and protests, whose loud crowds couldn't be controlled by a diminished police force. At such a rally in late February 1945, shots were fired into the crowd by unidentified snipers, creating widespread panic. The army and the government it represented were held responsible. The press publicized the incident and complained of the growing disorder, which underscored the inefficiency of the Romanian government.

This was the country discovered by Constantin and the family upon their return. Their difficulties started immediately, as something was seriously amiss. Their house had been occupied, and inquiries to the local housing authority established that the family had been listed as "missing." In fact nothing could have been further from the truth: both the university and the Liberal Party headquarters had known of their stay in Istanbul.

Maria was fuming, "I can't walk to my own front door, unlock it, and start dusting the place up! I told you I had a bad feeling all along. We should have never come back."

"Maria dear, please be patient. It's a misunderstanding and it will soon be resolved. You know how hectic everything was last year, with so much confusion reigning."

"What confusion? Everyone knew we were temporarily away."

And so the bickering went on, while days were spent submitting the required "proper documentation." They had to show that they were the lawful owners of the house, as well as show the intent to reestablish domicile. Once approval was granted, they could finally reclaim their house. A discouraging sight awaited them: trash piled up, papers everywhere, old food left on tables. The wine left in the cellar was long gone, and so were the many jars of pickles and preserves. The trees and flowers looked withered.

"My God," Maria almost shouted, "my house was turned into a pigsty!" before bursting into tears. Once she got hold of herself, she took stock of the situation. The house needed a thorough cleaning, and the pantry and cellar had to be restocked. Gas, water, electricity accounts were reviewed; they made sure the telephone worked. During this dislocation, they stayed with Wanda, Maria's sister-in-law, who together with her children had returned from Istanbul a couple of months earlier. Maria's parents were soon to follow them, too. While Maria worked around the clock to make the house functional again, Dinu, Dan, and Mona were thrilled to spend time with their cousins, who had also become close friends while in Istanbul.

As for their father, eager to plunge back into work, Constantin wasted no time. His request to return to the history department of the University of Bucharest was soon granted. Hoping to also reestablish ties with his parliamentary colleagues, he contacted George Tatarascu, the leader of one wing of the National Liberal Party. Public opinion was divided in those "stormy" days of late 1945. Some strongly opposed any political compromise and advocated active opposition to the Communist-backed regime. Others, like Tatarascu, felt that a lack of dialogue would eliminate any chance of remaining a viable political alternative:

"We must keep the lines of communication open. We won't compromise and join ranks with the Communists. But we'll try to explore how we can work side by side."

He encouraged Constantin to run for a parliamentary seat in the 1946 elections.

While he was busy piecing together his professional and political career, the burden of reorganizing the household fell once again on Maria. For days she shuffled back and forth between Wanda's house and her own. Marioara, her trusted maid, had returned to Bucharest after having spent the last year in the countryside. And so, side by side, they dusted, scrubbed, and washed the house. The glass doors sparkled again. The curtains looked fresh. The wood floors gleamed and the stove was clean. The house was ready to welcome its family back home.

And it wasn't only housework keeping Maria busy. Mona was enrolled into Queen Marie High School and reentered the ninth grade after Christmas. The boys had both passed the bachelor's exam and were ready for the next step: university or a graduate school. Dinu and Dan had the spring of 1946 to decide which admission exams they would sit for come June. All in all everyone was settling back in the routine of life at home and 1945 soon open the door to the New Year.

In the early weeks of 1946 Constantin's outlook oscillated between hope and apprehension. Shortly after the New Year he told Maria, "Tatarascu told me the British, Soviet, and American foreign ministers met with the king."

"What do you think is going on?"

"It seems the three met in Moscow in December and talked about post-war elections and then traveled here."

"How do you see this?"

"It sounds positive; the three powers are making sure the king is consulted and being informed."

This development buoyed his spirits for a while. But shortly afterwards, his sister Lelia called with news of her own. Her house was in the Lake District on the main boulevard that led through a large square to the center of the city.

"Construction has started in the square. I saw large scaffolding being erected."

"Any idea of what's being built?"

"You won't believe it. There's going to be a statue unveiled to honor the Soviet soldier."

"My goodness, is this how low we are willing to stoop? Honor those who are now trying to take over the country? And what about our troops?! Who's paying tribute to them?"

And his spirits sank. The rollercoaster continued, as soon after hopes were raised again when it was announced that the Soviet Union would leave northern Iraq. Together with Britain they had occupied that country during the war and were now withdrawing.

"See, Maria, perhaps things could change here, too."

"I am less hopeful. Iraq was never included in the Soviet's postwar map."

"Still, you never know. The United Nations may intervene on our behalf, too."

And so it went for a while, with emotions racing up and down the scale. No one was quite certain where the country was headed.

In the midst of this, Dinu surprised his father shortly after their return from Istanbul. He had decided to read history at the university. His eldest son had so far indicated an interest in medicine, a fine choice. History? That would make Dinu the family's third-generation historian. His father's heart swelled with pride.

His other son, Dan, was extremely gifted at drawing and had a knack for mathematics. So his parents weren't surprised when he announced his intent to study architecture. With admission exams scheduled for June, Dan used the spring session to brush up on various requirements. In April Constantin heard how the School of Architecture in Paris, France was offering a few scholarships to foreign nationals, providing several requirements were met. With his parents' encouragement, Dan applied for the scholarship that would change the course of his life.

So a few months after the return from Istanbul, the house was in good order and the children's studies were once again progressing.

Maria felt she could sit down and breathe a sigh of relief. Perhaps Constantin had been right after all; life appeared to be moving on without a hitch. If only it weren't for her nagging doubts and the feeling that a storm was still brewing, she might have even felt some contentment.

And while their daily lives resumed a quasi-normalcy, the surrounding world was anything but normal. King Michael, still the official head of state, had been forced a year earlier, in March 1945, to nominate a new prime minister and a government dictated by the Allied (Soviet) Control Commission. This had come in the aftermath of the unrest that took place in February 1945, when Soviet Deputy Foreign Minister Andrei Vishinky had paid an unexpected visit to Bucharest. In his audience with King Michael, he had blamed the then Radescu government for the country's inability to maintain internal order. Its "reactionary measures against the people" were faulted, too. Vishinky had then demanded a "trustworthy" replacement and advanced a name handpicked by Moscow: Dr. Petru Groza. It was the first time in Romania's history that the dismissal of a prime minister and his cabinet had been ordered by a foreign power.

This new government brought to power a disproportional representation of Communist Party members whose ranks had numbered a mere one thousand before the war. But that was then, and now no time was wasted, nor did they soften the blow on their agenda. A platform was immediately announced, with goals to "democratize" public life and eliminate "enemies of the people" from various institutions. No one was immune, not even the king, who was warned against isolation "from the people," and faulted for being wrapped in a cocoon by his court.

Leading the charge was Gheorghiu-Dej, the leader of the Communist Party. Near-daily speeches condemned the heads of the "traditional" parties: the National Liberals and Peasants. These leaders, he claimed, had sat idle while the country had been dragged into the war by the far right wing party. The rewriting of history had begun, and a communist solution was put forth. The recipe was simple: cleanse the country of the enemy from within and of course, "long live the people and our friendship with the Soviet Union."

The plan to "communize" Romania had been set in motion, but her citizens were still in the dark about their victors' ultimate intentions. Some, like Maria, became more and more apprehensive of the strident rhetoric in the press and unruly street crowds. Others, like Constantin, took a more philosophical approach:

"The Soviet Commission oversees us; they wanted to establish their influence. But we still have other parties represented in the government and the king is still in charge." He was referring to the inclusion of members of one of the liberal parties in the government giving the semblance of a pluralistic political life. News that George Tatarascu, the National Liberal Party leader, was now vice president of the Council of Ministries comforted Constantin. He had served in Tatarascu's government before the war, and knew of the man's views.

"Our man is in, Maria," Constantin said reassuringly.

"You just can't stay away from this merry-go-round, can you?" Marie asked, shaking her head.

"Maria, we can't live in a vacuum. Doing nothing won't advance our cause. Besides, I'm not seeking higher office. I'm merely staying involved. You know I need to focus on my fourth volume of the *History of the Romanians*. Students also need more attention; their studies were turned upside down by the war."

He, like many Romanians, continued to believe in preserving democracy with the king at the helm. Little did they know how the king was becoming progressively isolated by the new government, with his public appearances increasingly sporadic. Unable to rely upon the new internal army, his voice was weakened by the state media increasingly controlled by the Soviet machine. The king was virtually alone and so was his country. But perhaps not all was lost yet. Elections would be held soon, wouldn't they?

Chapter Twenty-Two
RIGGED ELECTIONS

The country was indeed changing course, and ominous signs abounded. Constantin needn't look any further than his own family. His brother, Horia, had been decommissioned and moved to a purely administrative desk at the Army Headquarters. He wasn't alone, as "old school" career military personnel were being marginalized to make room for the "new wave."

"What exactly do you do there, Horia?"

"I mostly push papers around, that's what I do," he said wearily. "I track the number of military forces around the country."

"And that takes the whole day?"

"Of course it doesn't, but I stretch it out; they've threatened to fire people if they see us sitting idle." He paused, It's not so bad though; at least I'm working and I'm not targeted."

Horia was referring to the intense scrutiny some higher-ranking army personnel had fallen under after the war. The country's former leader, Marshall Antonescu, and those closest to him had been arrested and charged with war crimes. The trial took place in the spring of 1946, orchestrated by "The People's Tribunal," and the dailies covered it extensively. Antonescu's fall from power had been initially celebrated in August 1944. But many now realized the scripted nature of the trial, and saw how the accused stood no chance for a genuine defense. The Marshall and his Vice Prime Minister "Ica" Antonescu (no relation), the latter Constantin's friend, were both executed in early June 1946.

Constantin also heard growing concern in his brother-in-law's voice. The orders at Emil's factory had sharply dropped, more than expected at the conclusion of the war. It had become increasingly harder to pay the workers and their discontent grew.

"It's the same everywhere," Emil said.

"Pipes, rope, quarries . . . everyone has seen business shrink. And there's growing unrest among the workers."

"Do you think it's just a phase as the new economy tries to find its footing?" Constantin inquired.

Emil was pessimistic. "I think they're trying to stir up the workers and other employees until they're ready to demand the dismissal of the owners."

The same story greeted him whenever visiting his sister Lelia and her husband Luca, a prominent engineer. Luca was still in charge of his office but was increasingly challenged and questioned by the new recruits.

"They've been sent to stir things up. They're dilettantes, don't know a thing about engineering, but are very outspoken."

"Do they deliver on their work?"

"Hardly."

"So don't you penalize them?"

"I point things out, but I'm told times are changing. I'm more or less warned to keep quiet if I want to keep my job."

Constantin hadn't yet felt any changes at the university, where the faculty body and curriculum were still intact. Teaching history was a fortunate choice, he thought: its course was known, facts couldn't be altered. Or could they?

The spring of 1946 came and went and turned to summer, and the country slid further into discontent. Salaries were often paid late. The cost of living and taxes went up while supplies of food, toiletries, and medicines came down. This worsened the general morale, leading to more protests. Not having adequate food was simply unprecedented in the country previously known as "the bread basket of Eastern Europe." Romania had indeed been blessed with fertile soil, endless grain fields, orchards, and vineyards. But no natural riches could compensate for the terrible drought of 1945–1946. And compounding the food shortages was the "land reform" passed the prior spring. Lots greater than one hundred acres had then been appropriated by the state, with a few exceptions: those owned by the church, hospitals and the royal estates. So peasants put in now the minimal required work, no longer motivated by a personal incentive to make a profit.

Marioara was going to the market one morning when Maria decided to accompany her; she hadn't been to one recently. She dressed modestly, heeding her husband's advice: "Whatever you do make sure you don't stand out."

"Where's everybody?" she wanted to know.

"Well, Miss Maria, it hasn't been very crowded lately."

"Very crowded? It's almost empty."

"Miss, don't get upset; let's just buy what we need and leave."

Maria remembered Constantin advising her to keep her voice down in public places. With protests ranging widely, particularly in the cities, the police were on alert for troublemakers. The two women walked around inspecting the stalls. Certain staples like potatoes, beans, cabbage, apples were still abundant, while fish and fowl were scarce; delicacies like asparagus or endives had disappeared altogether. Not only was the market poorly attended, but it also appeared unusually quiet, voices all somewhat hushed. What had happened to the peasants shouting their wares and following you around, trying to lure you with their fresh produce?

Marioara was examining some carrots when Maria joined her, ready to bargain—since she often said "only fools pay the asking price." It was almost like flirting with the merchant: you approached, showed an interest, asked for the price, were shocked, feigned departing, when a new price was shouted out and so on.

"How much?"

"Two lei for the kilo."

"Two lei for these little, wrinkled, dusty carrots?"

"Miss, please . . ." said the elderly looking, poorly dressed woman selling the carrots.

Maria turned and looked her straight in the eyes. She had developed a keen sense for impostors and was used to gypsies begging for handouts and lying about prices. But this peasant was fair-skinned, and she didn't look like a gypsy.

"Miss, we barely have enough to put on the table. If I sell them for less, I won't make anything on them."

Maria looked at her again and somewhere, deep down, saw the woman's desperation.

"Here's two lei and a half."

"God bless you Miss, you and your family, God bless you," mumbled the woman.

Maria went home with a heavy heart and told her husband, "People are hungry. You should have seen the desperation in this woman's eyes. It wasn't what she said but mostly what she didn't. Her face summed it up. How much longer will people like her be able to survive?"

"These are troubling times dear, much is still unsettled . . . the war is barely over." Constantin tried to encourage her but to no avail.

Maria was still edgy and distraught. "I've tried to warn you before and you didn't believe me. I told you something terrible was coming our way. Well, it's happening now, and it's only the beginning."

He now remained quiet; perhaps deep down sensing that she was right. What choice did they have? They could only hope time would right this turmoil, and life would gradually assume a more normal rhythm.

Much of the year passed in anticipation of the November general elections, the ones many hoped would right the country again. Two divergent strategies coexisted side by side in total dichotomy. Members of the "historic" parties (National Liberal and Peasant), and much of the general public and students, believed in free elections, looking forward to a continuing multiparty democracy. Whereas workers' rallies, press censorship, and an increasing monopoly of radio newscasts pressed for the Communist Party's complete victory in order to promote the newly coined "popular democracy."

Tension between the warring sides persisted in the months leading to the "free elections" guaranteed by the "Big Three" (Soviet Union, U.S., and England), with this insistence being a comfort to many.

Students took an active interest in the electoral process. Many opposed the current Groza regime with its large number of Communist Party members, but not everyone felt this way. Dinu came home one night, heart heavy from the debate he'd been embroiled in with other students. He sought out his father. "We were discussing candidates again. I mentioned Lothar (leader of the Social-Democrat pro-Communist Party), and told the others of his visits to Germany during the war."

"That's correct, Dinu. That's a fact."

"And not only that, father, but I also told them how another one of the upcoming Communists, Macovescu, had worked at the Ministry of Propaganda for Marshal Antonescu."

"And what happened?"

"Most agreed and wanted to know the details. But this guy Daniel, I hardly know him at all, asked me, 'and where was your father in 1938?'"

"I asked how that had anything to do with our discussion."

"And?"

"He told me, 'If I were you, I'd be more cautious.' The implication was: if the Communists were to consolidate power, those who had served in prominent positions under the king would be targeted."

"Did you say anything?"

"No. I suddenly feared for your safety," Dinu replied.

"You did well not to continue this dispute. Daniel's obviously trying to intimidate those who oppose his views. Rest assured: I was only a small fish in a large pond. We'll be fine."

But after the young man left his study, Constantin felt uneasy, wondering where this line of inquiry might lead. Maria's foreboding had now crept up on him. It gripped him further when he later passed through one of the town's main squares. A seemingly impromptu mob had gathered around the central statue there. This was during the trial of Marshal Antonescu, when strong emotions and animosities were running high. People were pushing and shoving one another and shouting, "Death to the marshal! And to those who supported him, too!" He tried to stay at the periphery of the square, avoiding the crowd and careful not to attract attention to himself. "Thank God I'm wearing this old gray suit, I'm blending in with the buildings . . . Is this how we'll be living from now on?" Constantin wondered while hurrying away from the protest.

Days passed while temperatures mounted. The mountain Predeal villa had been appropriated by the army during the last war year and had not been returned. The seaside house had been vandalized, doors and windows dismantled, and it was now boarded up. Money was scarce, so they decided to stay mostly in Bucharest. The university organized a summer trip for students to historical sites in Transylvania. Dinu immediately signed up, and his father offered to be one of the guides, combining an impromptu teaching forum with the summer break.

In the meantime Maria and her mother headed to the vineyards to check on their properties. Though it had been only two years or so since their previous visit, to Maria it felt like another lifetime. Despite Maria's absence during their Istanbul stay, the vineyards had continued operating while overseen by capable managers. The wine had continued to sell well into 1945, but demand had recently diminished, due to the financial difficulties felt by many.

Her mother's estate near Odobesti felt like an oasis in the desert. Life seemed to have stood still there, war and recent unrests passing by it. They were greeted by their loyal staff with bowing heads and clutching hands, while the local women quickly whipped a summer country supper of polenta, sour cream, fresh soft cheese, and soft-boiled eggs. It felt like heaven.

Maria visited her own property the following day with the same enthusiastic greetings:

"We were afraid we'd never see you again, Miss Maria."

"We heard bombs had fallen on Bucharest and we feared the worse."

"And then we heard you'd gone abroad."

"We wondered if you'd ever return and what would become of the vineyard."

She took pleasure in having the manager show her around the vineyard. He had done a great job in her absence: the vines looked healthy, the soil rich, bottles and barrels of wine in the cellar ready to head to the market.

"Would you be taking wine back to sell from your yard like before Miss Maria?"

"I don't think so, Anton. There is much unrest in Bucharest. It is best if you go through your distributors, just like the last couple of years."

"Don't you worry, Miss. I'll take care of it. And remember: we are always here for you."

Their kindness and honesty touched Maria deeply. And her heart was weary, heavy, and tinged by the uncertainty of their future when the time came to return home.

As people's lives steadily worsened, discontent continued to mount. A significant contribution to the dismal economic state was the obligation to hand over 5 percent of the country's economic output to the Soviets, as part of the war settlement. It was amplified by the drought, leading to poor crops, and the subsequent scarcity of staples such as flour, corn maze, and hay for the animals. Humans were hungry, too, and some were pushed in desperation to eat fried acorns or gruel. Others took matters into their own hands and attacked trains transporting grains, stealing as much as they could carry. Inflation skyrocketed and taxes shot up while pensions went down. Peasants suffered greatly and their difficulties soon spread to the cities, including Bucharest.

This was the background against which the preelection frenzy took hold. And hopes that the Communist-backed regime would fall were strengthened by the widespread discontent at every level of society.

The leaders of the traditional parties continued to believe in the power of the electorate, and were boosted by positive early opinion polls. One such survey indicated that only 4 percent of villages supported the current government, while its support among factory workers was placed at 30 percent. These numbers pointed toward a political power shift, boding well for the National Peasant and National Liberal parties positioned at the forefront of the opposition to the current regime.

They wouldn't have dreamt of it a year earlier. But the Communists and other parties forming the "Democratic Block" as well as Moscow began to fear the worst: an electoral defeat. This called for new tactics, and their opponents were suddenly up against a ruthless adversary.

The Communist-controlled press began to describe regime opponents as "fascist" and "anti-Soviet," two of the most derogatory adjectives in those days. Local leaders of the opposing parties were attacked and beaten, at times savagely, and some even died ("one or two per county will suffice" an official had articulated). Several county headquarters of the National Peasants were vandalized or searched by the police. A minister traveling with his wife before the Easter weekend saw his car hit by a truck, the tires cut, and all their belongings stolen. When complaining to the prime minister, he was told these were "the usual risks of an election campaign."

Voting cards were denied to those opposing the "democratic" regime, as people would later find out, and government employees were mandated to vote for the governing Communist-dominated coalition. In another move, gasoline suddenly became scarce to nonexistent, limiting traffic around the country. Thus politicians needing to campaign outside the major cities had to rely upon the railways, which did not reach remote villages.

Election day finally arrived. The date had been carefully chosen, laced with symbolism as Constantin, ever the historian, explained to his family:

"November 19 is the day when in 1942 the Soviet Red Army started a massive offensive on the Don River against the Germans and their allies. Romanian casualties were heavy and the victors want to make sure we remember the slap received."

Also, the vote would take place on a Tuesday instead of the traditional Sunday, the organizers hoping some would be reluctant to leave work.

On November 19, 1946, the citizens of Romania headed to the voting booths. The choice: endorse the "Bloc of Democratic Parties" (a Communist vehicle campaigning under the catchy phrase "sun for our nation"), or revert back to the traditional parties now in opposition.

The circumstances of the rigged election: ballot boxes stuffed full of "pro sun" ballots before the opening of the polls, and stations in "opposition" districts closing before the posted hours. Policemen clutching rifles interrogated citizens on their affiliations before entering the booths. Ballots were handed out with names of the opposition candidates deleted. Foreign observers were not allowed to participate in the counting of the vote, and some citizens were denied voting cards and went to the U.S. mission in order to ask for assistance.

Burton Berry, U.S. Representative to Romania would later sum up the election as a "masquerade."

The "official" results were delivered days later: a stunning 83.8 percent of the vote had been cast for the "Pro Democratic" forces! In the wake of preliminary polls showing an overwhelming—at least 70 percent support—for the National Peasant Party, Moscow had sent urgent instructions. Romania's Groza regime was called upon to rig the elections at "any and all costs." And like a good pupil, it had delivered to the master. As for the actual results, they would remain unknown for decades.

Romania's slide down the road to perdition had begun.

Chapter Twenty-Three
THE KING IS GONE

On the night the election results were announced, Maria and Constantin were home by themselves. Dinu and Mona were dancing at a friend's house, and Dan had left for Paris a few months earlier, having won one of the scholarships to the School of Architecture there.

They had waited on edge for several days for numbers to be posted. It had been agonizing: friends and acquaintances called with conflicting reports while radio announcers and papers speculated endlessly. Constantin himself had reached out to a few people around the country, trying to feel the pulse of the electorate outside Bucharest. Almost everyone anticipated a victory of the National Peasant party, but no one could agree upon the margin. As for his own seat, its fate was in God's hands. Unable to campaign like in the 1930s, he knew he had reached only a minority of constituents.

On the evening of November 22, Maria set down toast, cheese, and fruit on the table. Water was boiling in the kettle, preparing for tea. They sat down to eat and discuss the day when the radio announcer broke in an agitated, high-pitched voice:

"Standby, ladies and gentlemen, election results just in . . . standby."

A moment of silence was broken by Maria. "It all comes down to this; you understand?" He nodded quietly while the wringing of his hands betrayed his anxiety.

Then the voice proclaimed, "Ladies and gentlemen, a resounding victory for the Bloc of Democratic Parties: they have carried nearly 84 percent! Only 8 percent for the National Peasant Party!" The voice carried on with other numbers, the details of which were lost on most of the listeners.

Constantin's face grimaced in apprehension while Maria covered her mouth, and her eyes widened before bursting into tears. She cried and cried for what seemed like an eternity, until her husband took her hand, trying to comfort. "Dear, dear, it's only an election. We're healthy, we're together, and I have a job."

She looked at him in disbelief, pulled her hand away, dried her eyes and slowly uttered, "You don't get it, do you?"

It was his turn now; in a broken voice, he whispered, "I do, dear, I do. But what gives me strength is . . . us, you at my side. We'll make it through whatever lies ahead." He then tried to lighten the moment. "And don't you tell me I talk like a historian—sometimes things turn out differently in the long run!"

She often admonished him for talking like a politician or professor of history, and this last bit almost brought a smile to her face. She stared and then remembered falling in love with him, how his optimism and faith in his work had wowed her. She suddenly felt ashamed: why would she take it out on him? They were on the same side. Besides, she also saw how much more difficult it must have been on him to bear the news. He was the one who had been, for years, in the midst of the country's political turmoil. She pulled his hand into hers and leaned into him. "Yes, together."

A day or so later he found out he had won the seat for the county Mehedinti. Each minority party held seventy seats or so and one of them was his. But the victory was bittersweet. The following day they heard how some representatives of the National Peasant and Liberal Parties pulled out of the government. They cited abuses before and during the elections, with limited ability to campaign in the country, names crossed off ballots, voter intimidation at the polling booths, and obviously rigged results. Preelection polls had, after all, shown quite the opposite outcome.

A bitter Iuliu Maniu, the leader of the Peasant Party, confided to those close to him: "I had been right all along. In 1944 I asked the Brits if they were handing us to the Soviets. They said no. Then earlier this year they sent their foreign minister to convince me to run when I wanted no part of this masquerade. I should have trusted my instincts and not humiliated myself at the end of my career!"

As for the victors, they wasted no time. The Communist Party, led by secretary Gheorghiu-Dej, sat down to name the government, organize the Parliament, and "take advantage of our success in the elections." Days later they demanded that the king sanction the new government. The sovereign was also asked to open the Parliament on December 1. King Michael was torn. Opening the session would amount to a personal endorsement of the results, whereas not doing so would widen the rift already present between himself and the Communist Party.

The king turned to Burton Berry, the U.S. Representative. He had said, "If your government is prepared to offer me more than just moral support, I could proceed differently." At this junction he still held a lingering hope that the U.S. and U.K. would reject the fraudulent election results. But the only assurance he received was a State Department proposal to "consult" with London and Moscow and suggest new elections. The king was on his own, and in the end he decided to open the Parliament, hoping his presence would rally the citizens and show them he remained at the helm.

Days before Christmas Maria received a note from her vineyard's manager. He sent best wishes and assured her "things were under control." He didn't want her to worry, but perhaps she had heard that the town's mayor had been arrested.

"He had campaigned for the Peasant Party," Anton wrote. Days after the campaign was over, he was detained on charges of "election fraud."

The letter went on, as Maria summarized it to her husband. The mayor had apparently won. The local Communist representative, however, claimed success instead, and accused the mayor of cheating tactics.

"Miss Maria, the new mayor came over to the estate today. He wanted to know who owned it. I told him; he answered he'd make sure the peasants here would have a fair share of it in the future. I didn't understand what he was talking about, Miss Maria; but it sounded serious enough that you should know."

A stone-faced Maria asked her husband, "Did you hear anything about a land 'reform'?"

"Nothing definite, dear. There's talk they may want to appropriate large estates, but only rumors for now."

More arrests were made in the upcoming weeks, including factory workers who had campaigned for parties other than the "democratic bloc." Then a brief respite followed, as if the political wave had been frozen by the arctic air sweeping through Romania in January, 1947. Or perhaps the Communists were content with their "weeding," and wished to start rebuilding the country?

One morning Maria was in the kitchen making tea when she heard her mother enter the house. Her parents' house had been "appropriated" by an individual during their stay in Istanbul. Upon their return they found strangers living in the house, the professor's library and manuscripts gone, furniture replaced. Inquiries at the local police precinct led nowhere. They were told that when the professor and his wife left for Istanbul, no one knew if they would ever return. "Citizens" had decided to take over the house and couldn't be asked to leave now, could they? They were hard-working citizens and members of the Communist Party, one of them a manager in a factory, the other one an "organizer."

So Maria's parents were left with no alternative but to go live with their daughter, and a couple of rooms were hastily set up for them on the second floor of the house. There the professor, nearly eighty years old, continued to write, and looked forward to occasional invitations to speak to students and colleagues at the academy.

Mrs. Mehedinti, his wife, continued to complain and bicker about everything and everybody, which made life even more difficult around her. But the day she came down early to the kitchen, she was focused on a more practical matter: that of their gold coins.

"Maria, your father and I need to talk to you. Could you come upstairs?"

"Sure, let me pour the tea and I'll be right up."

She joined them in the little living room off the landing, and her mother wasted no time. "We need to talk about the money."

"Which money, mother? The accounts in Switzerland?"

"No, it's about the gold coins."

"I don't understand."

"I sold part of my land holdings at the onset of the war and rolled them into gold coins."

"And where are they?"

"They were buried in Odobesti, but I dug them out when we visited last summer."

Maria now remembered how her mother had clung on to a heavy leather case during the return trip. "And now?"

"They're under the floor. But I want to move them somewhere safer. So we settled on your cellar."

"My cellar, mother?"

"Yes. It is the safest spot in the house."

Later that evening Mrs. Mehedinti, Maria, and Constantin went down to the cellar. Maria had wanted Dinu to help, but her husband had drawn the line. "The fewer people know, the better it is. And if God forbid something happens and we're questioned, he won't know anything."

They dug late at night, hid the coins, and covered the hole. Then they smothered it with sand, trampled it, and set heavy bottles over afterward, memorizing the landmarks.

Relative quiet lasted into February. Just when Maria thought they may have overreacted in regard to hiding the gold, the Paris Peace Treaties were signed on February 10. They represented the conclusion of the post-war conference held in Paris the previous fall. Romania, Bulgaria, Hungary, and Finland were among the countries whose fate was decided there. "War reparations" were settled, and Romania was ordered to pay the equivalent of three hundred million 1938 USD to the Soviet Union. Borders were discussed, and nations were also assured of their right to "freedom of expression, press, religious worship, public meeting. . . ." Representatives of the Romanian government elected in the aftermath of the rigged elections sat at the table with their U.S., U.K., and French counterparts. The signatures they affixed side by side on the final documents implied an international public recognition of the November 1946 elections. The roll of the dice cast in Tehran and Yalta had continued in Paris.

Once the treaty papers were signed, unrest started again. The quiet proved in hindsight to have been a Communist ruse, designed to show to the world gathered in Paris how Romania moved peacefully and in unity towards rebuilding itself. But with the treaty concluded, the gloves could come off, bringing a wave of political arrests, National Peasant Party activists and local leaders chief among them. The men were accused of plotting to disrupt the country's democracy and "progress" and were swiftly imprisoned. Protest notes sent by their party's leader to the Interior Ministry and to the U.S. Mission fell on deaf ears with no reply forthcoming.

About a month later Constantin came across news of Nick Malaxa, the leading industrialist who had lived in Istanbul during 1944–45. Dinu and Dan had spent many fun days with his son while Maria has socialized with his wife. Constantin was walking home from the University when he bumped into his friend Alex and listened to his story. He later told Maria, "Nick never came back from Turkey."

"I knew they were still there when we left. I could have sworn they returned last summer."

"Well, here's Alex's story. He met Nick's private secretary today on Victory Street. He confirmed Nick waited in Turkey to see how the elections and treaty turned out. And now he has applied for a visa to the United States."

"Was there anything else Alex read between the lines?"

"Yes, and most of it is quite factual. There was much unrest at Nick's Malaxa steel plants in February 1945. One of the leading politicians spoke there; shots were fired and people died."

"What had brought that about?"

"Workers were unhappy with the Communist-backed manager and tried to oust him. Trucks brought in men who stormed the place and bullets hit the crowd. The official blame was laid on the government who couldn't control unrest in factories. Fringe "right-wingers" were singled out, too, to further spread panic among the public."

"What happened next?"

"Communist Party leadership dispatched representatives to the factory. Over forty workers were illegally arrested."

"A warning to workers elsewhere."

"Precisely, and if you ask me, Maria, Nick must know, guess, or fear that the government will take control of the large enterprises."

And indeed the end of April 1947 brought a new law, that of the "Industrial Offices." Under its auspices all privately held industries were strictly controlled by the state. It read like this: though the owner was still an individual, the entire industrial process was "controlled by the state." The stage was set so the "people" could equally benefit in the future. Panic set in rapidly. People tried to withdraw savings and encountered another obstruction at the Central Savings Bank. Another law passed with no fanfare stipulated that only a certain amount of money could be removed per day and per month. Peasants had their own bit of bad news in the form of legislation mandating them to hand in a set percentage of their crops. Control over people's life was mounting swiftly.

Constantin wondered how educators would be targeted. He anticipated curriculum changes with the "new guard" likely wishing to place a personal imprint on molding the next generation. The students themselves had already been corralled into a newly created body. Named the University Democratic Front in 1946, it became the National Union of Romanian Students the following year. Dinu's grades had put him at the top of his class, and as the newly created union wished to enroll the very best, he found himself sitting in on various administrative meetings.

The young man felt uneasy. "I wonder, father, why they elected me. They know of your political past; I thought they were looking for people without obvious ties to the king."

"They want to attract the best and brightest students," Constantin said.

"I feel uneasy, father, almost like I am decamping to the other side."

"This is the new reality, Dinu. Just sit there and nod and act interested; you don't have to churn out ideas. But it's better than being rejected and marginalized by these new fellows. And it may turn out better than we expect."

The unrealistic hope that the Soviet troops would retreat from their territory continued to linger. And despite clear signs that the noose was tightening, some still believed that a complete political turnaround was still possible, Constantin among them.

As for the Union of the Romanian Students, Constantin had been right. They indeed needed to attract top individuals with the hope of converting their allegiances to the new order. All those with ties to the prior regime were simply too numerous and ubiquitous, and couldn't yet be rejected by the country's leaders!

During the spring of 1947 Constantin received a surprising invitation: a Romanian parliamentary group was traveling to Cairo to the first international postwar meeting of its kind.

"Why me?" Constantin asked of his friend Alex Rosetti, who was to join the group as well.

"I am a mere deputy. I don't hold any high rank any longer."

"Neither do I," answered Alex. "I'm told the officials wanted a few old timers on board, some who are fluent in foreign languages."

Constantin fulfilled both requirements; at forty-six, he was ironically considered a political old-timer. As for languages, he easily conversed in, and read, French and German and bits of English and Greek. Maria viewed the invitation as an important and positive step. Perhaps they would after all be tolerated by the new political establishment and maybe Constantin could go on teaching. And she was awfully pleased when she found out the wives had been invited. It was going to be their first vacation abroad since 1938. Sure, they had traveled together to Istanbul but that had been their day-to-day life.

Formal approvals and visas were needed now, unlike prior travels abroad. Their passports had been surrendered upon their return in late 1945, and each application was now reviewed before approval was granted.

The group was led by V. Luca, a prominent Communist leader. They gathered in Constanta to sail on the *Transylvania*. Constantin was overjoyed: his love affair with the sea, which had commenced in his teen years, was still a strong pull.

"The sea offers a sense of calm, of endless possibilities," he would often say.

It was their third trip aboard the *Transylvania*, and she felt like an old friend. Though still comfortable, even luxurious by the day's standards, a certain pecking order became apparent to the travelers. Those in charge of the parliamentary group were treated with special deference whereas the others received polite service.

The passage took a couple of days. It was already hot and steamy in Alexandria in April, the lazy breeze too weak to spell out any relief on the docks. Special buses waited there to transfer them to Cairo where the meetings took place. After hugging the coastline, they descended along the course of the Nile, the drivers eager to benefit from the bit of coolness provided by the river. Cairo was still reveling in its position as a hotbed of diplomacy in the last years of the war. Constantin wistfully recalled his unsuccessful attempt in Ankara, Turkey. He had then brought word of his country's intention to send a high-level emissary to contact Allied Command representatives in Cairo. Romania had been ready to put oil, military bases, and food at the disposal of the Allies, but unfortunately it was already too late. Who knows, he might have even traveled to Cairo himself had the project met another fate.

The conference turned out to be quite conventional, a modest attempt at postwar communication and exchange. The various group leaders presented their new approach to governing, followed by discussions. It was during this more informal part of the conference that old timers like Constantin excelled. Personally knowing some of the participants, and having heard of others, he glided about from one debate to another, switching easily between languages. French was in great demand and his bits of English came in handy, too. But he couldn't help but notice a general reticence over the use of German: the wounds of the war were too raw and deep.

The wives were entertained during the day, visiting the bazaar and mosques, and taking meals together. It seemed somewhat surreal to Maria to be surrounded by women in classic Arabic attire serving them sweet and savory rice bowls, grilled lamb, and pastries dripping with honey. It was during a tea break on one such outing that Mitzi Rosetti approached Maria. Her husband, Alex, was Constantin's great friend who had helped him publish the *History of the Romanians*.

Alex had quietly begun "positioning" himself favorably vis-à-vis the new regime. He had not joined the Communist Party ranks, but in several articles and university speeches he endorsed the "new order" and touted its future benefits. His wife had joined the "Union of Democratic Women."

"Maria," said Mitzi, "you may have heard of my recent involvement with the women's union."

"I have indeed."

"I was wondering if you would like to join us."

Maria was incredulous; Mitzi knew of Constantin's royalist views, of his senatorial and ministerial careers. But Maria, normally quick with the tongue, answered in the calmest possible voice. "Mitzi dear, I am flattered you would think of me. But you must certainly know I'd be of no help in such matters."

"Maria, everyone knows of how you run your household, and how organized you are . . . not to mention the wine business. You built that into quite a success."

"Mitzi, this is precisely the problem: I am a wife and a mother. I take care of my family and home. Time at the Union would be time away from home and I couldn't do both well. It wouldn't be fair to you and the other ladies who work so hard on its behalf."

Mitzi was taken aback and disappointed, but she knew better than argue with her. As for Maria, she was relieved Mitzi did not insist and appeared to accept her argument.

"The union is nothing but an instrument to mold women according to the new political script," she thought to herself.

Once the meeting adjourned, they had a couple of days for sight-seeing. An organized bus tour took them to the Giza pyramid complex, where they marveled at the size of the Great Pyramid of Cheops that practically dwarfed her smaller cousins, the Kephren and Mykerinos. They walked in the dust, sand, and high heat, with heads covered in straw hats, eyes protected from the blinding sun by large, dark glasses.

He had read about the magnificence of the structures and had seen pictures. But nothing had quite prepared him for the sheer impact of the size of the stones and the perfect symmetry of their placement, a true architectural wonder. He took Maria's hand and wandered over toward the enigmatic Sphinx. They stared in quiet at the implacable chipped face resting on a lion's body, a mysterious creature holding the key of its creation. Who might have built it? When? Their reverie was suddenly interrupted by piercing shouts:

"Mister! Madam!" They turned around to see the tour guide running, pointing at them and gesticulating in every direction at the same time. He reached them breathless. "You can't leave the group. It is dangerous. Desert bandits could take you prisoners."

Maria's smile was suddenly replaced by sadness. "We're practically prisoners in our own country, and even here," she replied, turning her back to the Sphinx and walking slowly towards the group. The magic of the day was broken and nothing, not even the festive setting of the farewell reception, could restore it.

Once they were home, the political situation took a turn for the worse. A failed flight escape by a few prominent members of the Peasant Party was the spark that set in motion a cascade of events. The leaders of their party were publicly denounced and its president, Iuliu Maniu, was arrested on July 24, 1947. His party was then dissolved five days later by governmental decree. The explanation put forth was that Maniu had attempted "terrorist" activities abroad meant to destabilize the situation at home. In reality the Peasant Party was being individually targeted because of the strength shown in the prior elections. Fearing their opponents' popularity and their possible resurgence, the Communist leaders elected to have them eliminated from the political arena.

A couple of months later 250 university teachers were laid off. Constantin's old friend Victor Papacostea—they had been part of the same class—was among those dismissed. The measure was veiled under the cover of budgetary cuts, though obviously targeting those who held anti-government views or had been active participants in the prewar political life. Constantin braced himself but miraculously escaped this first wave of university ranks "cleansing."

"You heard what happened today to some of your colleagues and friends. You're hanging by a thread, mind my words," Maria said at the end of the day.

He kept quiet. She was probably right. The cleanup of faculty ranks was likely organized in a step-by-step manner, the most "dangerous" ones eliminated first. But then again, it needn't happen in this manner. Perhaps the frenzied wave would stop there and the madness would die down. Time would tell. So he went on about his business as fall led to winter. Skies became gray and heavy once again, and snow fell early that year.

November brought more bad news. The trial of Maniu and some of the other Peasant Party leaders concluded and heavy punishments were handed out—Maniu receiving life in prison. Then the National-Liberal Party leader G. Tatarascu—Constantin's friend and "boss"— was removed from the government. His party, the last link to a true multiparty democracy, was subsequently dismantled.

November was also ripe with rumors, generated by the king and queen mother's travel to London. They were to attend the wedding of his third cousin Princess Elizabeth. The future sovereign was marrying

Philip Mountbatten, who would be named Duke of Edinburgh. King Michael was deeply torn between the oath of standing by his people and the reality of having become a mere figurehead, without constitutional powers. More so, he feared the Communist backlash would continue and soon target the royal family. The British ambassador to Bucharest had suggested considering asylum abroad. But while he was in London, diplomats and politicians advised the king differently: he must return, as "above all things, a king must be courageous."

Maria and Constantin left the day after Christmas; his elderly Aunt Marie now lived in Focsani, the city of his birth, and they had decided on paying her a visit. At seventy-three she was getting on in years though her tongue was still as sharp as ever. Constantin couldn't help but think of his mother, who had been the younger of the sisters. His childhood with his parents seemed like such a long time ago, and visits to Aunt Marie always affected him. He was unusually pensive on the return trip until workers boarded the train shouting, "The king is gone!" Maria and her husband looked at one another in disbelief, but kept quiet, afraid of unveiling their feelings.

Dinu had been that evening to a tea dance at his friend Odette's house. They were on winter break, with parties in full swing on that December 30 when all looked forward to the following night, New Year's Eve. Young men and women in their best attire milled around, sipping wine and lemonade, flirting and chatting and waiting for the dance to start. Someone turned on the radio and heard that an important announcement would be forthcoming at 6:00 P.M.

"The monarchy is no longer a good fit for the Romanian state . . . it prevents the development of the country . . ." on and on went the announcer, until he concluded: "the people have thus gained the freedom to build a new state, that of the Popular Republic. . . ." Patriotic music was then promptly piped in.

The young people looked in horror at one another: their world, or what was left of it and its past, had just collapsed. The party broke at once. Dinu headed to the train station, anxious to greet his parents and break the news to them.

The train pulled in; Dinu had waited at the end of the platform. His parents approached, worry etched on their faces: "They must have heard," he told himself.

"Is it true?" his father asked.

"Yes. That's the report."

"How is it possible? How could it have happened?" Constantin kept repeating the question over and over.

Later that evening they heard how the abolition of the monarchy was permanent, with "The People's Republic" promptly declared. December 30 was to become the country's new national day.

Years, many years later, people would learn how the king's abdication had been extracted under blackmail. The king had been urgently recalled to Bucharest from his palace in Sinaia where he had just celebrated Christmas. He was told his presence was needed to discuss "urgent family matters." Back in the capital, he received a visit from the Prime Minister, Dr. Groza, who apparently had a gun in his pocket. He had pointed the gun at the sovereign when he attempted to resist. The Communist Party's general secretary, Gheorghiu-Dej, was also in attendance, and threatened to execute a large number of jailed students. Army troops were allegedly amassed around the Royal Palace ready to storm it if necessary, while the streets surrounding the Palace had been closed to public access. All the telephone lines had gone dead.

The year 1947 and Romania's monarchy ended within a day of one another.

Following the abdication, the king and his mother returned to the Peles Palace in Sinaia, followed by two cars transporting selected personal belongings. The minister of justice paid a visit to the former sovereign three days later, bringing along a judge and a public notary. Their mission: to establish a comprehensive list of the royal estates and holdings bearing the signatures of their previous owners.

King Michael, his mother, and a small entourage departed Sinaia on January 3, but not before having their luggage thoroughly inspected: "You can't rob the country and take jewelry, gold coins, paintings, etc. along." They were escorted by military guard and members of the secret police—the latter eager to ensure that the royals remained completely isolated until the crossing of the border.

At the customs post the luggage was inspected one more time, and passports were finally handed to the travelers. The king's read: "Michael, Prince of Hohenzollern," without a mention of his rightful title.

The train reached its destination of Laussane, Switzerland on the fifth of January and was greeted there by over a thousand people, chanting and clapping and bringing tears to the sovereign's eyes.

Six months later he married Princess Anne of Bourbon-Parma.

Almost a half century would pass before he could set foot again on Romanian soil again.

Chapter Twenty-Four
DISMISSED FROM THE UNIVERSITY

The hope of the country miraculously righting itself with the king at the helm was now gone, as was the pretense that the political situation could get better. For a while some refused to believe that the Americans, French, and British had forgotten Romania. But eventually they learned to accept this reality, as the West's only reaction remained verbal. The fate of Romania and of the other Eastern European countries had been sealed, with Moscow having won the upper hand. As for the Allies, they had no means to change the course of Soviet domination.

Constantin was often stopped by students and other acquaintances and asked:

"Professor, how is possible for the civilized world to watch Romania be destroyed by the Soviets without doing anything?"

Always eager to share his knowledge, he would explain how American and British diplomatic inquiries and statements were limited by the peace agreements signed jointly with the Soviets at the end of the war. "They must abide by what they signed," he would conclude. "It's a gentleman's agreement."

Not that there weren't a few attempts to let the world know what was happening in Romania. For instance, a certain Colonel E. E. Parnsworth wrote to the vice president of the Allied Commission on behalf of the U.S. military mission in Bucharest. His letter decried the treatment of the Romanian political prisoners as early as May 1947. He told of the sick and poorly fed men and described the unsanitary conditions and the beatings. He wrote of how the prisoners were denied correspondence and visits. Colonel Parnsworth went as far as describing the conditions as "Hitler-like," a reference to the Nazi concentration camps. To conclude, he had requested the Allied Commission to intervene. But his demands remained unanswered and he hadn't pursued the matter any further.

The Western media's announcement of King Michael's "abdication" triggered little reaction. More so, once the king arrived in Switzerland, he was advised by various diplomats to avoid political declarations.

As for a military intervention to rescue Romania, it was out of the question. Too many countries were still clearing the rubble of the last war, with their ranks of possible young recruits decimated.

So Romania gradually accepted the inevitable conclusion that there would be no one to rescue her. With the lights dimmed, sheer survival became the new goal.

Maria and Constantin, like most of the countrymen, faced the coming year with dread. New Year's Eve, normally celebrated with music, dance, food, and drink, was quiet and somber. Parties planned for weeks or months in advance were cancelled, with most people concerned that the music and noise would attract unwanted attention. Many were also afraid to be out in the streets. Communist Party supporters and agitators unleashed a wave of antiroyal propaganda the day after the king's abdication. Posters carrying a copy of his statement were affixed everywhere: on buildings, lampposts, on tramcars and buses and drew cheers for a new republic.

"It's better to stay in for a couple of days," Constantin had advised his family. "We must wait until this street hysteria dies down."

Even Mona, who at seventeen years of age craved the excitement of the "dancing" tea parties, did not argue with her parents for once, and saw their logic. As for Dinu, he had grasped the concern and even fear in his father's eyes and had understood that a new era had dawned upon them.

But staying in didn't automatically mean one could avoid the Communist-drawn frenzy. Turning on the radio one would have heard "patriotic" revolutionary music streamed over it. Picking up the newspapers provided ample coverage of the abdication. One also saw the lavish praise heaped upon the leaders who had "courageously" gone up to the Palace. The upcoming weeks brought a stepped-up campaign maligning the monarchy, depicted now as root of the country's ills.

Fear and general panic began to set in. People were first afraid of new proclamations and laws, and then they started fearing one another. Rumors abounded of acquaintances, even friends, "switching sides" in order to align with the new rulers. Perhaps they, too, were afraid of counter measures. Others sought political or material gain. Suspicion grew by leaps and bounds. How did you know who could be trusted? If you didn't, it became prudent to remain silent. Thus, streets and markets, once boisterous and full of life, now turned quiet.

Maria and Constantin clung, like many of their countrymen, to family and old, trusted friends. The doctors Titel and Nelu, hunting and fishing companions, were among the tightly knit circle that met periodically for a meal and a chat. Titel's house was right around the corner from Constantin's, and his wife, Suzana, was a close friend and distant cousin of Maria's. They started a neighborhood routine, alternating between houses with home-cooked meals by each host, where conversations and their topics flowed freely. On occasion they would splurge with a dinner out, when a conventional dialogue centered on family updates, work and weather—all "safe" topics for prying ears. As much as they enjoyed going to a restaurant, dining out became a sad reminder of the deteriorating economic situation. Among the "austerity" measures, restaurants were mandated to adopt fixed menus and post them for the upcoming week; meat was to be offered no more than three times per week.

The precarious balance of their daily lives was once more shattered on June 11, 1948, when the "People's Great National Assembly" passed a law nationalizing all major industries. It thus completed the task set by the Law of Industrial Offices the prior year. Factories, banks, mines, insurance, and transportation were taken over by the state.

Maria's brother Emil came to visit the following day. Perpetually sunny and always kidding people, his face was for once somber and the voice tired. "I'll get a tin cup and join the gypsies outside the train station," he said, trying to lighten the mood.

"Now, seriously . . . several 'comrades' showed up yesterday afternoon and asked me to sign a paper stating I was handing over the plant to them."

His mother appeared to hyperventilate and started fanning herself in a state of advanced agitation. "Did they offer any compensation?"

"Are you joking? They barely spoke to me and were marginally civil."

"Were you asked for proof of past ownership?" his father wanted to know.

"Father, I'm lucky I wasn't arrested like some of the big bankers. I was told, 'sign here and get out' . . . no please, no options. They added, 'Oh, and by the way, leave everything behind. Anything removed would be theft and punished according to the law.'"

Had he resisted or protested, he would have met the fate of many. Those accused of plotting against the regime were tried in a mock court and sent to prison. There were also rumors that those arrested were tortured in order to obtain confessions. Later on their families were threatened, some beaten and evicted from their homes.

So his factory, his life's work, was gone. It was just like what had happened to Maria's parents, whose house had been taken over before their return from Istanbul. Their savings' accounts were held by the state and worth hardly anything since the devaluation of the currency. Maria's mountain and seaside houses were also occupied by others, though a change of ownership had not been officially issued yet. On paper they still owned the vineyards and the country estate, but it was only a matter of time before they too would be gone.

Financial strain grew on the family as income from various properties and Emil's stipend to his parents ceased to arrive. Constantin was now the sole breadwinner for his wife, children and in-laws.

And just when they thought it couldn't get much worse, another blow was dealt.

Constantin left the house early one day in July, scheduled to attend the admission exams at the university. A couple of hours later Maria heard the front door being unlocked. She panicked; Mona and Dinu were out of town, although her parents were home. She went into the entrance hallway only to stare at her husband.

"What happened? Are you ill?"

"I'm well enough," he said, though she could see his creased face and hollow, distant look.

"What is the matter then?"

"I was dismissed from the university."

Maria grabbed the back of a chair to steady herself. "Fired?"

"Yes and no. Dismissed from the university but transferred to the History Research Institute of the Academy."

She felt a sort of relief. He would be working after all; there would be an income. Then guilt set in: how could she be thinking of money when his world was unraveling? Education was the core of his career and now that was taken away, too.

Constantin seemed remarkably calm despite his worried face and ashen color. "On the way home, I reminded myself I still have a job and I'm free. Look at Ion Hudita and Gheorghe Bratianu . . . both of them dismissed and arrested. So many others fired, and left alone to come up with something to feed the families."

Thus, Constantin Giurescu's prodigious twenty-two-year teaching career had come to an end.

"What comforted me on the way back home," he told Maria, "was being able to teach Dinu." He had studied history for the past three years, and his father had been among the faculty. "I was so happy that he was following in my footsteps. I thought of my father, how I had been deprived of his knowledge, expertise."

"Our son was fortunate, indeed," Maria said.

"Wouldn't it have been ironic if Dinu had missed my tutorship on account of all this political turmoil?"

Dinu's university class had indeed been the last to enjoy a stellar professorial body, some renowned at a European level in history. The previous year's first wave of faculty attrition was now followed by a massive purge. They were replaced by new faces, many who had fine-tuned their skills at Communist Party meetings instead of the classroom. These teachers with a "healthy" political outlook were needed to mold the new generation. As for the "old timers," they were headed for the dusty library of the research institute, were arrested, or retired—no longer able to "pollute" their pupils' minds.

Most of the students (law, history, literature, etc.) had supported the political opposition. But after the 1946 elections, the political climate changed radically and the students had to adapt, too. Those who tried to resist and advocate the right to decide the course of their future were arrested. Two of Dinu's colleagues met that fate within months. One would later die in jail; while the other, after his release, was not allowed pursue a PhD until forty years later! Those who questioned how history was being rewritten—such as the prompt elimination of the monarchy's contributions—were suspended and their families harassed. The new harsh reality of their lives made the young men and women realize that this was no time for soul-searching or depression. One had to reach deep down, dig in, adapt the best one could, and first and foremost, survive.

A month later, in August, a sweeping educational reform bill passed. Tinkering with individuals at the highest echelon of learning had become insufficient for the new political aims. The very young needed to be molded, too. So the entire system was turned upside down, trying to adopt the Soviet educational style. High school manuals were translated from Russian to Romanian, as the political message had to be cohesive. As for the Russian language, history, and literature, they all became mandatory subjects.

The pace of change seemed dizzying to many. After only one year in power, the new regime had already nationalized all major industries and the banking system, and it had reorganized the educational system to channel its political agenda. People became increasingly apprehensive and braced for whatever measures the New Year of 1949 would bring.

They didn't have to wait long. Talk of arrests started once the cold weather settled in. It was nothing official, word-of-mouth claims only.

The stories seemed so incomprehensible one wondered if it wasn't merely a rumor, but they were enough to set off a new wave of panic:

"So and so was seen departing his house in a long, dark car. . . ."

"Several men in suits went to X's house; he followed them out after an hour. . . ."

"No one has seen Y in weeks. . . ."

This kind of talk alone was grounds for arrest, and making negative comments about the government and its programs became subject to punishment. Most avoided such conversation altogether, except in the privacy of their homes or with trusted friends.

Constantin told Maria how he had heard about the plight of Mihai Manoilescu, who had been Minister of Foreign Affairs in 1940 when Romania was forced to cede part of Transylvania.

"Do you think it's another rumor?" she asked, wanting to know.

"No, this one is certain. It comes from Viorica (one of Constantin's cousins) who is friends with Manoilescu's wife. He was taken away on December 19 and has not been heard from since."

"Taken away? You mean from his home?"

"Yes, they were getting ready to sit down to lunch. A rather large group of men came and asked him to go along with them. He was allowed to take a small suitcase with some personal items. His wife asked if she'd be able to visit. They laughed at her and didn't answer."

"Why Manoilescu?"

"Because he signed off on Transylvania. He never had a choice, but nonetheless his signature sealed the act. He's a symbol to these new leaders of having 'sold' part of the country. Hence he needs to be punished."

Could others be next? How would they be chosen? Maddening thoughts kept Maria up at night. She feared for her husband, worried about Dinu's prospects after graduation, and agonized about the little money they had and how to best stretch it. If Constantin shared her anxieties, he didn't show it. He, like many, preferred to think of these arrests as individual cases or "situations" and not as harbingers of a general trend. Or perhaps he once again believed that work would help heal the inner wounds, just as it always had. Or maybe he sensed that if he wavered, her burden would become unbearable. That one had to remain strong for the other was like an unspoken pact with him.

So they carried on without complaining despite the mounting difficulties, having been raised to keep "a stiff upper lip." Constantin headed to the institute each morning with a sandwich in his briefcase, ready to face another monotonous day. Various topics were assigned to groups of researchers who then divided the tasks. He had always enjoyed working in the archives. So he signed on to go to the archives whenever possible. You never knew what rare document you may fall upon and most often you worked alone, with no one disrupting your concentration. Working on your own also meant not having to listen to the incessant office chatter of daily news and politics.

"Be very careful," Alex Rosetti had warned Constantin. "Some are trained to listen in. They'll run and report you to the authorities the moment you criticize the regime."

That winter of 1948–1949 they muddled along the best they could. The cold weather gave way, and sun came out in early March; snow-bell flowers broke through the cold ground, and spring felt just around the corner. But smiles of relief brought about by the renewal of the earth were fast effaced by the latest political news.

The plenary of the Communist Party, held March 3–5, decided to tackle land reform next. Once again relying upon the Soviet model, peasants were encouraged to join and create "collectives" mirroring the "kolkhoz" across the border. Intimidation, beatings and arrests awaited those unwilling to join. A full-throttle propaganda effort was launched; the advantages of the new system were lauded, and the out-liers were denounced. Class warfare had arrived in the villages where wealthy peasants were targeted on account of their "oppression" of the poorer ones. At least two thousand families of landowners saw their land confiscated, were evacuated from their homes, and sent to live in other villages.

Maria's vineyard was officially gone, and so was her mother's es-tate. Despite not receiving income, grapes, or wine the past year, they had clung to the hope of retaining the properties. That hope and their land were now gone. Maria's mother said after hearing the news, "It's like a nightmare, only worse. Every time you try to wake up to end it, you fall asleep again and the bad dream takes another turn."

As the new "Popular Democratic" regime consolidated its grip upon the country, the general mood turned from apprehension to fear. A new wave of nationalization came in 1949, with hospitals and phar-macies joining the ranks of state-owned institutions. Some stores met the same fate, though small shoe repairs, tailors, and barbershops sur-vived for a while longer.

Dinu graduated from the university with a degree in history in mid-June 1949, and he attended, like most of his colleagues, a rather formal graduation dinner party. Bland speeches, with people afraid to articulate controversial opinions, were followed by a seated dinner and dance which lasted into the morning hours. When Dinu got home, he was surprised to find his parents up already, with Maria crying and his father hugging her. He stepped inside and looked at his father, who pointed to a piece of paper lying on the desk: a letter.

He picked it up and learned how his brother Dan had been severely injured in a car accident in Paris. One of Dan's close friends had enclosed a photo of him lying in a hospital bed, with his leg in traction and large bandages around his head and one arm.

Maria was shaking. "How can I go? I have no passport. They won't let me travel. Dan's going to die, I'm certain," she wailed and a new cascade of tears erupted. Truth be told, though she loved all her children, Dan had always been her favorite, the one most like her.

With pain etched on his face and his heart torn at knowing his son was injured and hundreds of miles away, Constantin tried to think about what to do. Whom could he turn to? He picked up the phone and called Alex.

"I'd turn to Luca," said Alex. "I'll contact him and let him know you'll be calling later today." Luca was the prominent Communist Party leader who had led the parliamentary team to Cairo in 1947. Constantin had met him on the trip and they'd had a few cordial conversations. He wasted no time getting ready, and was soon heading to the Central Committee building, arriving just as it opened for business.

Most of the morning was spent going from floor to floor, repeating his story to yet another bureaucrat, showing the photo and being asked to wait. Luca finally received him around noon, and after a brief discussion agreed to intervene. He picked up the phone and requested a passport on Maria's behalf. A question was posed from the other end; Luca answered, "I know she'll return."

Facing Constantin, he asked, "She will come back, won't she?"

"Yes, she will," he replied.

"You understand I'm giving my personal guarantee? My word is at stake here," he emphasized.

"Yes, I do. And I appreciate it, but Maria will return to her family."

They picked up her passport the following day. What was left of their meager savings was used to buy a plane ticket. Maria had never flown before, but any apprehension was erased by the urge she felt to be at her son's side as soon as possible.

The flight went by in a blur with heavy turbulence rocking the plane up, down, and sideways. Dinu Misirliu, one of Dan's friends, awaited her at the Paris Orly airport. On the way to the Pitie-Salpetri-ere Hospital, he updated her on Dan's condition.

"He's now listed as serious, downgraded from critical."

"Does he have any head injuries?" Maria asked.

"They seem to be superficial; he has no trouble with memory or understanding."

"Does he know I'm coming?"

"No. At first we didn't want to get his hopes up, in case you couldn't get a passport. After you sent the telegram with the flight number, I was afraid he'd get too excited and relapse."

"Will I be able to stay with him?"

"No, they're very strict at the hospital. You'll stay in Dan's studio. I put a few things in the refrigerator. There's also some fresh soap and clean linen."

"Is it far from the hospital?"

"No. Only a few stops by metro. Do you know Paris at all?"

"Hardly. My husband and I visited once for a few days. Constantin had lived here as a student."

Dinu entered the hospital room first to prepare Dan, the nurses having said that a positive emotional shock could be as traumatic as a negative one. Maria stepped in after a few minutes. A description of her son's injuries hadn't quite prepared her for the sight: swollen face, wrapped like a mummy, leg up in traction, arm in splints, a tube in his right chest. She braced herself so Dan wouldn't see her reaction. Seconds later there was not a dry eye in the room.

Dan remained in the hospital for over a month, while Maria cooked daily in his little studio and brought over rich soups and stews. He was discharged in late September, and advised to enroll in physical therapy to strengthen his muscles. They spent a couple of weeks in Paris together, and Dan's friends took turns in driving him to the medical gymnasium. But the weather was turning cooler and wet, and Maria decided her son needed sun. Together they traveled to the south, to the resort of Juan-les-Pins on the Mediterranean. Long walks on the beach, daily stretches, swimming, and home cooked food helped heal him little by little. By late November Maria knew her son was ready to go back to school, and she was ready to return to Bucharest.

Dinu waited for her at the airport.

"Where's your father?" Maria asked him.

"He couldn't leave the institute in the middle of the day."

"Is he all right?"

"As well as can be expected." He then brought her up to date on the political situation and their friends. The fall had been relatively quiet with no new major initiatives. People's councils started showing up mostly in the countryside. Mirrored after the Stalinist model, they were de facto police terror squads, which were meant to maintain the population in constant state of fear. The economy continued to be in dire condition. The produce markets had been mandated to post daily "price controls," and rations for bread and cornmeal had been introduced. To make matters worse, there was now talk about moving peasants to cities to swell the workers' ranks. The concept of them acquiring the necessary skills first seemed to elude the politicians.

The end of December between Christmas and New Year day was rather quiet. The only news was how the Grand National Assembly (official name of the Chamber of Deputies) voted Romania's first five-year plan following the Soviet model. Almost nobody was aware what that meant in real terms for the citizens of Romania, though it was heralded as an improvement in everyone's life. "We'll find out soon, won't we?" was the general opinion. "Can't be good," most added.

The last day of December 1949 Maria's daughter, Mona, went to a gypsy who read tarot cards. She had told her mother, "I want to hear what the New Year holds."

"Nonsense," her mother replied. "You're wasting your pocket money."

"Well, it's mine and I'll spend it as I please," her daughter said, and stormed out of the house.

The gypsy woman lit a candle, shuffled the deck, intoned a chant of sorts, and then asked Mona to pull four cards. The gypsy flipped them face up and immediately started crossing herself, breathing hard.

"What do you see?" asked Mona.

The woman spat hard and crossed herself again; then, in a half whisper she uttered, "I saw the devil. Go pray, Miss, for you and yours."

Chapter Twenty-Five
THE ARREST

After his graduation during the summer of 1949, Dinu had sought a teaching position. He couldn't hope to join the university ranks, now closed to the children of the "bourgeoisie," and those who had had "undemocratic beginnings." But a high school post was still a possibility. In order to be considered, Dinu cleared the next prerequisite—a course in "pedagogical ideology." Party documents were studied and debated there, helping future educators acquire a mindset politically appropriate for guiding the next generation. After its completion he applied for a teaching post, and a couple of months later he was still waiting.

His mother suggested, "You may need to change course for a while." Willing to do anything and start earning some money, he followed the example of his close friend Bebe. Enrolling in a short technical course they studied budgets, work quotas, and workflow on construction sites. Upon completion came his first assignment: new roads were being built southeast of Bucharest. Thus Dinu left home in the middle of April, hugging his parents and promising to visit the first weekend in May.

Friday, May 5, 1950, was an ordinary day. Maria went to the market in the morning, once more noticing how drab and sad the city and its people looked. They had dined the night before with their great friends Titel and Suzana. The café had been almost empty; the music was gone and the food was mediocre. Besides, few ventured out of their houses now, particularly at night. As for attire, it had become nondescript, as if one avoided attracting attention.

Constantin had worked that Friday like any other, and had come home tired but looking forward to the weekend. Maria's brother, Emil, had come by in the evening and brought along a bottle of wine and some cookies. His parents joined them, too, Mona returned home from university, and all shared a light supper. With Dinu out of town and a bedroom available, Maria asked Emil if he wanted to spend the night. It was getting late and the streets were dark, with electricity being rationed. He gladly accepted and everyone retired around 10 o'clock.

At 4:00 A.M. the silent house was jarred by the prolonged shrill note of the doorbell. Constantin lifted the bedroom curtain and stared out; it was pitch dark. He turned to face Maria in dread and in silence. His wife jumped out of bed, grabbed a robe, and ran to the door. She cracked it open, leaving the safety latch on, and stared at four men in suits. Terrified, she ran back to the bedroom, her face ghostly white, body shaking.

"It's the Securitate (secret police)," she barely whispered to her husband.

Constantin held her close before slowly pulling away. "I'll go see what they want."

He was met by a tired and visibly uncomfortable man in a rumpled suit, who was maybe forty years old or so, his face pallid. "We're here for the professor."

"Constantin Giurescu?"

"Yes."

"That would be me," he told them.

"Are you sure?" The pallid man asked, incredulously shaking his head; he had expected someone older. Then he recovered. "We are here to take you to the Interior Ministry, and we have a search warrant for the house."

"You'll search first; you can't do it in my absence."

"Professor, a member of your family will be present. Now go and pack a bag so we can get moving."

He looked around and noticed three more members of the secret police's sinister entourage. Two guarded the front and back doors, fearing an escape. Another followed Constantin into the bedroom, possibly fearing a suicide attempt.

Maria's parents and her brother and Mona were sleeping upstairs. The commotion woke them up, and within minutes everyone had gathered downstairs. Desperation and fear were set on their faces at the sight of these men. The lead officer stepped forward and asked the family members to identify themselves. He stared down at his papers, probably verifying that no one else had to come along with them. After he satisfied himself, he barked an order, "You're all free; go back to your rooms."

Mona, Emil, and Maria's old parents nodded, and one by one they hugged Constantin.

In the meantime Maria packed some shirts, underwear, socks, soap, some shaving blades, whatever she could think of.

"Will he need these items?" she inquired.

"Yes, m'am."

She couldn't bring herself to ask anything else. The simple affirmative reply implied an extended stay. Unbearable pain was tugging at her heart, but she steeled herself against crying, thinking that "I can't give the beasts that much satisfaction."

The moment of departure had arrived. Constantin folded Maria in his arms and kissed her while she held on to him, whispering in his ear, "You shall return."

After minutes he gently pulled away, turned to face his arrestors, and nodded, "I'm ready."

They led him out into the yard and at the gate he turned around and saw Maria staring behind their bedroom window, a motionless shadow, already outside his reach.

A car awaited around the corner, its driver fast asleep. Had he had a long night? How many men had he delivered? He woke up fast when they opened the car door, rubbed his eyes and turned on the engine. They drove through empty streets, witnessing a glorious sunrise against the bright blue sky. Few people were out and about. "At least they're free," thought Constantin. They passed the former Royal Palace, now the seat of the government. Constantin's thoughts wandered to King Michael, did the king know what was happening in Romania? Or had the news become so filtered that nothing of this crackdown had reached him? Once past the palace his thoughts returned to the reality of his inexorable drive into the unknown.

The Ministry of the Interior flashed by them; they turned a corner and went to the back entrance. The car stopped in an inner courtyard and its passenger was escorted inside.

"Professor, please hand in your eyeglasses," the pallid man said.

"But I can't see anything."

"They'll be returned in a few moments."

He handed them in and glasses with dark, opaque lenses were given him in return.

He slipped them on and was led by hand, up and down flights of stairs and then up again until he felt dizzy. They finally stepped into a room and he heard the door closing.

"Okay, you can take them off now."

His eyeglasses were briefly handed back to him. He looked around: a tight compact room without a window, with a desk, a lamp with a dim bulb, a couple of chairs, and a thick rug.

The man standing beside him seemed sheepish. "He must be an underling," thought Constantin. He kept quiet.

"State name, position, wife, parents, and children's names for the record."

He complied.

Next there came the inspection. "I need your shoelaces and ties," the man told him.

The search of his bag yielded a pack of blades and a razor.

"They're looking for items I can use in a suicide attempt," he told himself.

"Now I need your glasses."

"Again?"

"Yes."

"But I can't see anything without them," he insisted.

"You won't need them where you're going. Hand in your wedding band."

"My wedding band?"

"Stop repeating my questions and just do as I say."

Constantin felt stabbing pains in his heart. His band inscribed with Maria's name was now taken away, barely an hour after their separation.

"Don't worry professor, it'll be returned to you later," said the man, perhaps guessing at his anguish.

Once these procedures were over, the dark glasses with the opaque lenses were handed back to him. Once more he was led by hand. They walked about a bit; then judging by the motion, they were in an elevator going up.

"So I'm not being taken down to a detention cell," he thought. Recalling how one of his friends had spent days in the basement of the ministry before being released, this reality did not bode well.

They stepped into another room. The glasses came off once again, and this time he was guarded by a large man with huge hands and a bovine face. They faced one another, him sitting and the man standing, for what seemed like a couple of hours. No questions were asked. Constantin's mind was racing: "Why am I here? What am I being charged with? Where am I headed?" The room didn't offer any clues. Heavy drapes covered a window; traffic was scant, so he couldn't guess the room's orientation—boulevards would have been a giveaway. On the wall was a large map of the country and the surrounding territory. His eyes lingered over the northern boundary and then jumped across the border, to the Soviet Union.

"God, please don't let them take me over there," he pleaded inwardly.

Then thoughts wandered back to Maria. Would she be going through a house search now? He hoped that Emil would have stayed there to be at his sister's side.

And then the wait was suddenly over. The beefy man motioned to him to stand up, grab his suitcase, and follow him. No dark glasses this time. The elevator went down, the door opened, and to his surprise he was met by six acquaintances: former ministers, a prominent attorney who had served in a governmental post, and a high-ranking general. But there was little time for greetings.

"You all follow me outside," yelled one of the guards.

Outside they were lined up alongside a long, dark van. A second, shorter van and two sedan cars were parked next to it.

"You're all numbers now," they told them; Constantin became number seven.

The guard opened the doors of the van and motioned to each man, shouting their numbers out loud. Each awaited their turn; once inside, they were handed a "food ration" of two loaves of bread, some cheese, and marmalade.

"They must be taking us far away," mumbled someone. Could they possibly be headed to the Soviet Union? There would later be time for speculations; as for now the guards were in a hurry to start the journey. Before closing the door, a bucket was brought in.

"What for?" asked one of them.

"For number one."

They were finally ready to depart and Constantin noted he had the best "viewing position." From his seat he could follow the road both through a half-opened door to the front of the van and a little window in the rear door as well. The people of Bucharest had awoken by now, and they were going about their business: buying milk, bread, and newspapers on this Saturday morning.

"They're free to walk around and don't realize the gift they have, nor did I," thought Constantin.

The drive out of town depressed him deeply. They passed Victory Street and the Boulevard Kisselef. How many times had he walked along those streets? Next was the Lake District where he and Maria had spent many happy times together.

They had barely left and depression already began to set in, becoming palpable. Before even leaving the city, the atmosphere in the van felt stifling and some of the "passengers" became agitated, others noxious. Some simply stared vacantly ahead, their faces a catatonic mask, while Constantin forced himself to stay alert trying to pick up clues of their journey.

When they passed the lakes north of the city, he suddenly remembered. He had been fishing there a year earlier or so, and a convoy of dark vans had stopped at the roadside. A couple of men had gotten out to stretch, and he had noticed them repeatedly peeking through the dark tinted windows, as if they were checking on something. They had looked odd to him, and he didn't quite know what to make of them. Now he understood; those cars had taken away men just like him, probably heading to wherever he was going. "Unlike the occupants of those vans, I have at least had an additional year of freedom," he thought sadly.

As the road continued north, some measure of relief was felt in the van:

"It means we're not headed to the Soviet Union."

"We won't be going to those death camps there."

"Are you sure the road isn't turning east?" someone asked. The Soviet Union was along Romania's eastern border.

"I'm sure," said another. "I saw a sign for Brasov" (a town to the north of Bucharest).

"They couldn't possibly take us to the Soviets," a fellow professor said.

"And why not?"

"There would be an international outcry. The United Nations wouldn't allow it."

"Of course it would," thought Constantin to himself. "It has done nothing so far." But he kept quiet, not wanting to further upset his friends and fellow prisoners.

After a brief stop to refuel, they marched on north as silence, fear, and fatigue set in. Constantin continued to monitor their passage and felt the need to follow their course, to remain present. He vowed to retrace the journey one day, but for now the more pressing thought was merely to survive. He was hungry, worried, and afraid like all the others. But he also began to realize that the wish to survive would have to override all other doubts and complaints.

The next stop was for lunch, but hardly anyone touched their food. Fear had knotted the chests and throats of the prisoners. They all stared at the bread then put it aside. The guards, however, appeared to be in great spirits, enjoying their meager meal. A lorry passed by, young people piled up and singing loudly, happily, in stark contrast to the somber spectacle at the side of the road. Then the music stopped suddenly. The future university professor of literature and well-known scholar Valeriu Rapeanu would recall, years later, being in that lorry:

"We didn't resume laughing or singing until we reached our destination an hour later," he told Dinu. "We saw the well-dressed men with their heads bowed and immediately knew those were no petty thieves."

At another stop, Constantin noticed a guard receiving and opening an envelope. He had heard rumors that in such cases no one knew the final destination at the outset. Directions were given and updated along the way, the mistrust that pervaded the entire society being evident even among their handlers and guards.

The road crossed into Transylvania and continued to the north. Dinner was at a roadside stop, and the night was spent in the van. Constantin nodded off and woke up with a jolt. In his dream he saw Maria the morning they returned from Istanbul in November 1945. She had stared at the porter with a red Soviet star and whispered, "Is that the thread pulling you to Siberia?"

In the dream she had tied a rope around him, and someone else, invisible to them, was pulling him away. Had her instinct been right? He woke up in a sweat and was unable to close his eyes. When the morning came, they were allowed to go outside and stretch their legs. Constantin spotted four dark vans passing them, seemingly in a hurry.

"There must have been a lot of arrests," he told himself.

Indeed 150 men or so had been arrested in the twenty-four hour span of May 5–6, 1950. They were former ministers who had served in the various royal governments from 1920 to1947, leaders of the Peasant and Liberal Parties, and heads of the former armed forces. A Who's Who of Romania's political life before World War II was thus rounded up. The notable exceptions were the few who had "jumped ship" and joined the Communist platform in 1944.

Subsequent arrest waves followed, and targeted other categories such as government representatives at the county level, activists of the now abolished traditional parties, and industrialists and merchants accused of sabotage.

The last large roundup would take place two years later in August 1952. It was then rumored that the number of those arrested exceeded the available prison space. The officials had scrambled and some men were kept at first in a stadium in Bucharest, not unlike the Jews of Paris in the famed Val d'Hiv hippodrome during WWII. From there the men were dispatched to jails around the country and forced labor camps like the Black Sea-Danube Channel project.

But for now Constantin's northward bound progress continued that morning. "What if we're going to cross the border into the Soviet Union to the north after all?" they started asking one another.

Discussion of their final destination was launched again. Several hours passed. The van finally stopped, having reached its destination before the sun set again and Constantin saw a high wall with a gate. They sat and waited forever until the heat inside the van became almost unbearable. When the gate finally opened, the van pulled into the courtyard of a prison surrounded by high stone walls, with windows rimmed in heavy nets of wire. A patch of blue sky above was the only reminder of the rest of the world.

With all the vans in, the gates were slammed shut.

The men were on one side—and the rest of their worlds on the other.

PART V
THE PRISON YEARS

Chapter Twenty-Six
THE PRISON THAT KILLS YOU SILENTLY

Constantin disembarked first, by virtue of his position at the back of the truck. The guards yelled, "Move, move it faster. Gather in the center of the yard and await your orders."

The men stepped down one by one and assembled slowly, despite the shouting. Constantin glanced around the courtyard and saw a dark building with rows of barbed wire windows and thick stone walls. A tall watchtower stood guard at one corner. Men in uniforms holding guns stood by the front gate and around the tower, and two soldiers were posted at the front door of the building. A man presumed to hold the highest rank, as judged by the stars on his shoulder boards, held a paper. This "welcoming committee" shoved the prisoners in a large room where names were called out and checked off a list.

When Constantin's turn came, he was asked, "Are you the author of *The History of the Romanian People?*"

"Yes."

"History is being written differently nowadays," the prison official spit out.

"It's possible, but the facts remain the same," Constantin replied.

The soldier stared back coldly but did not strike out at him. He might have been in a hurry, or perhaps he knew the prisoner's ultimate fate and that was punishment enough.

Trucks were heard coming up the road while the prisoners awaited their cell assignments. Gates opened once again, trucks pulled into the courtyard, and a new round of shouting commenced. More frenzied activity, and minutes later another larger group joined them. Constantin glanced around, and at once he recognized several former ministers, university professors, and army generals. They nodded at one another but otherwise obeyed the guards' instructions.

"No talking whatsoever," a soldier insisted after someone greeted an old friend.

Much later they would find out about the journey others had taken to travel here. Unlike Constantin's van, another one had no partitions inside so all the men sat huddled together. General Cihoski was inside it and he went mad on the first day of the journey, never to recover; he died soon after reaching his destination. Another van stopped for the night, and when the prisoners fell asleep, the guards came upon them with loaded guns, simulating an execution. Yet another group was detained at the Interior Ministry in Bucharest for over a month. Space was scarce there and the men slept in tight cells, packed like sardines. Almost nightly they were awoken by the agonizing screams coming from those tortured just doors away. Constantin's friend Nick Cornateanu was in that group and would recount the stay as "a month in hell."

As for now, men stared at the new arrivals, eyes questioning the faces and searching for silent clues. After names were shouted out loud, each man was then escorted to his assigned cell. Some were paired up, or even placed in small group cells. Others, like Constantin, would be held in solitary confinement. The cell assigned to him that first day was number 21 on the ground floor. The guard walked him down a grungy hallway, and turned left into another one with parallel rows of identical doors. There was a door at the opposite end, and judging by the layout, it might have led to the courtyard. Sentry guards stood at each end of the hallway. Constantin avoided looking at them, guessing that eye contact would be insolent. So instead he focused on his mental arithmetic game: 21 was 3 x 7, lucky seven— perhaps another sign he might survive.

The cell itself offered little optimism otherwise—a 15 x 6 x 11 feet cold stone box with a narrow bed, heavy metal door, and a high window that barely allowed a glimpse of the sky and tower. The floor was wooden plank, the ceiling was arched and several horizontal pipes for heating hung beneath the window. He took stock of the bed with its straw mattress and meager pillow, a pale blanket folded to the side. The sight of a bed suddenly made him ache with fatigue. It had barely registered just how tired he was until now, after two virtually sleepless nights and days, so he lay down as soon as the guard left. Minutes later someone opened the door. He would later vaguely recall being offered cold water from a pitcher, and then fell into a deep slumber. When he awoke, the sky's light spelled early morning; "I must have slept over twelve hours," he told himself.

That first morning he was handed his tin cup, a shallow bowl, and a spoon.

"I don't get a fork or knife?" he had asked.

The guard laughed sarcastically. "You're quite thick, mister! Don't you get it? You could use those to kill yourself or injure us."

Constantin inspected his "dishes": they were chipped and greasy. He decided not to say anything else, afraid of punishment. "I'll clean them whenever I get some water," he thought.

The first few days of imprisonment would later turn out to have been "atypical" for what would follow. The jailors had been caught unprepared for such a large number of "guests," and a daily routine hadn't yet been set in place. Formalities of new arrivals kept the guards busy and left little time for other "practices." So the days were a little more lax at first. Prisoners were allowed to sleep a little longer; the food was a little better, and physical torture hadn't yet started.

The location of the prison worried the inmates most at first. Since the guards spoke Romanian, they were still in their country and not Russia, and they thanked God today and every day for that. The road signs had pointed to the northern part of the Romania during the trip. The next clue was the ringing of church bells. Several tones could be differentiated once they learned how to listen closely. It meant there were a few churches and that, plus a large prison, indicated a sizable town. There weren't many large cities in northern Romania, and by process of elimination the best guess became Sighet, the capital of the Maramures County. This would later turn out to be correct.

These same church bells also punctuated their days, heralding wakeup and lights out, breakfast, lunch, and dinner as the routine was established. The first days, however, were in many ways also the hardest. Memories of their families, home, work, and "normal" life in general were fresh and overwhelming. Constantin paced around his cell, obsessively counting the steps to quiet his emotions.

"I must focus on the numbers, and can't let my memories take me over," he would tell himself.

But thinking of the loved ones keeps me going even if happy memories tear at my heart," he thought. "Quite a dichotomy."

Even the simplest of chores, such as washing a handkerchief, became a dilemma. You washed it and you ran out of the drinking water allotted for the afternoon. You didn't, and then you were stuck with a dirty garment in a tiny cell. Saving half of your meager lunch in its tin cup meant you couldn't get water in the same cup and went thirsty for hours. And the list went on. The mind wandered often to the small comforts of home, the ones previously taken for granted: "One never appreciates the mundane until it's gone," Constantin would mutter over and over.

His thoughts maddeningly kept returning to Maria: "What could she be doing now? Was she been harassed after I left? Did Dinu arrive the day after the arrest to comfort her? How are they going to survive?"

Then he would abruptly interrupt such a train of thought: "I can't drive myself crazy . . . I need to focus on my survival. I must come out of here alive, no matter what. If I don't make it, I can't be of help to them."

He'd resume the pacing and the counting. But moments later Maria's image would intrude again, "Is she preparing lunch? Or, perhaps she went to visit Emil and Wanda?"

"Stop it! Follow on with the arithmetic or all is lost."

Pivotal to survival was food, but on only the third day barley showed up on their "menu." Beans and a sliver of bacon had lasted less than forty-eight hours. Barley would become a fixture in their lives, being served for breakfast, lunch, and dinner. Its consistency varied between a pale "tea-like" liquid in the morning to a thicker puree of sorts mixed with oil, carrots, and occasionally other vegetables served later in the day. There would be weeks at a time when barley represented their only nourishment. As there was nothing to look forward to at meal times, Constantin had to look for other things to build his days around. After a few days, he figured out when to expect direct sunlight exposure in the cell. He remembered the sun's rays being good for you, and so he settled upon sitting on the bed and facing the sun for its few minutes of exposure. He also recalled exercise being beneficial so he instituted three daily walking and stretching sessions around the cell. One would take place in the morning, one after lunch, and the final one after dinner and before sleep. A thousand steps would be counted each time. And time would also need to be marked in this purgatory—a short scratch by the door for each passing weekday and a long one for Sundays. Special signs were reserved for the birthdays of his wife and children, which he marked with a swirl of sorts. The most ornate one would be for his wedding anniversary, April 15. Would he still be in jail by the time the next one rolled around?

His jailers warned that "destroying" property in the form of chipping, chiseling and the like carried a "serious penalty" unspecified to date. Well, Constantin had taken the time to assess his surroundings early in his stay. After careful observation he had concluded that the chipped and peeling wooden frame around the door could easily sustain new scribbles. Keeping track of time and events that kept him connected to loved ones were worth the risk.

Peering through the pinhole window, however, was a bigger challenge and carried grave consequences. The guards, either in the tower straight across or the one outside his door, could have easily seen him, and being caught would have brought severe punishment. Little by little by trial and error, he discovered the vantage point from which an outside guard couldn't spot him. As for the guard in the hallway, Constantin was served well by his hearing. Within days of solitary confinement, he felt a desperate yearn for any human contact, even if only visual. So he'd brave climbing on the bed, craving the sight of a familiar face, of those fortunate enough to be allowed a daily walk.

He was visited by the prison doctor during the first week, a mere formality, no longer than five minutes and supervised by a guard. "Do you have any ailments you are aware of?" he asked.

"No."

"Very well then," he said. "Anything you want to tell me?"

"My right shoulder blade is hurting. I sleep under a broken window pane and the cool air hits me every night"

"We'll see about that."

A brief examination followed; the doctor then checked the name off the list and went on to the next cell.

Uniforms were assigned during the same first week. One by one the prisoners were escorted to a large room on the second floor, where Constantin thought he saw shelves with clothing. His glasses had been confiscated in Bucharest and were never returned, so details were lost on him. An officer stepped in and asked him to strip naked. A moment of terror took hold: what could be in store? As he had no choice but to obey, off came the shirt and pants. He then hesitated until the officer pointed to the underwear. "Off, take it off, and we'll give you different ones."

He received pants in the customary prison pattern, black and off-white vertical stripes.

"Why do I have to wear this uniform?" protested Constantin. "I haven't even been tried, let alone sentenced."

"Look, I get my orders," he was told. "This is not my idea. Besides, you'll have all your clothing in good condition when you're released."

"Still. . . ."

"Listen, do you want to make trouble for yourself?"

"Trouble" had fast become a ubiquitous part of the guards' vocabulary.

"These pants are too small," Constantin told him. "Don't worry," replied the guard. "They'll fit just right in two weeks."

And indeed they did. As for the uniform, its sight depressed Constantin. As a child he had seen a convoy of prisoners marching in front of his house. Those men were wearing striped attire like his, and their feet had been chained together. But while they had murdered, robbed, and stolen, he stood here guilty of having served his country, without as much as a trial or sentence.

With his clothes gone, the last physical link to his former life was erased. Also, the prison attire hinted at a long stay. Dark thoughts took over, but again he was determined not to let the guards see him depressed.

"Do I get a receipt of my possessions?"

"Here, I'm writing it now."

He read the list carefully before signing it. Then holding a toothbrush, tube of toothpaste, and bar of soap, he was escorted back into the cell.

Days passed, and would have blended into one another had it not been for the scratches on the door. The work assignments hadn't yet been decided, so there was little to fill their days. A dreadful monotony awaited the inmates upon rising every morning to meals of barley three times a day. Hunger pangs took over after less than a week, and nothing abated it, obsessive famine dominating every hour of each day. Around the same time came his first shave, which was poorly executed by a large, brutal-looking, heavy-smelling barber. He received ten nicks that first time and soon learned to fear facial cuts more than worries about an unseemly beard.

A bout of depression overtook him on May 21, 1950—the day honoring Constantin's patron saint and Saint Elena. Those had been his parents' names, and thoughts wandered back to childhood celebrations and Maria's feasts of years past. Visions of the table laden with roast meats, salads, and a cake glazed in chocolate cream emerged from his memory. The empty stomach hurt so badly that the pain seared from the front to the back of the body. As these memories rushed out, tears rimmed the corners of his eyes and despair set in. What would have normally been a day of cheer and glad tidings became one of mourning and sadness. Drained and exhausted, he was soon overtaken by a deep slumber.

He woke up vowing to focus once again on his routine. The day turned out to be special: he was taken out for his first walk in the yard.

Orders were given before leaving the cell: "Head down at all times. You can't look at the windows under any circumstance. No talking, arms behind your back, steady pace . . . if not you'll get detention in the black cell."

He had no idea what the black cell was, nor did he wish to find out. So he resolved to follow the guard, trying to enjoy the fresh air and sunlight. He breathed deeply, inhaling the scents of spring flowers and young grass, his eyes closed for a brief moment trying to pretend the cold square walls weren't there. Despite keeping the head down as instructed, he couldn't help but see men like him, walking or digging something. The other thing he noticed on that first walk was the total silence, interrupted only by guards shouting or the chirp of a bird: the men strictly obeyed orders during those first few weeks. With passing months the men would start mumbling, and brief dialogues followed when they felt emboldened enough.

Nights were interrupted at times by a shrill alarm. There were shouts, gunshots, chaos, and guards running up and down the hall and slammed doors followed. The first time this occurred, Constantin vowed if he were ever part of what was happening to at least hit a guard over the head before being killed. To the end, the prisoners couldn't tell if an escape had been attempted or if the incidents were staged. However, the fear of God was instilled in their hearts, stifling any attempt to run away.

Without his glasses Constantin relied more and more upon his hearing. He learned to sit still on the bed with eyes closed, trying to decipher voices in the yard. One morning he thought he heard his friend Victor Papacostea's voice. They had attended university and then taught together there. After making sure there was no one at the door, he climbed on the bed and looked out the window. He squinted, and then again, forcing himself to distinguish facial features—something . . . anything. Eventually he was pretty sure that he had recognized Victor among the woodcutters in the yard. Minutes later the same voice was heard again, and this time he was certain. Risking severe punishment, he climbed on the bed once again and called out his friend's name. Had Victor turned his head slightly, as if confirming his identity? It had appeared that way. Constantin felt he now had a lifeline: a friend had been spotted.

Days later on a walk, he heard a whisper from the basement.

"Who is up there?" Was it bait? Should he answer? "I'm with the group of priests."

Then there was silence. He would later learn there were four bishops and twenty-one Greek Orthodox and Catholic priests from Transylvania at the prison. Their opposition to the new regime and its crackdown on religion had landed them there.

Other acquaintances were eventually spotted—in the yard during walks, in the food line, or in the bathroom. Despite his poor eyesight, he was jolted every time by how thin everyone appeared. "I must be thin, too," he told himself, as without a mirror he couldn't fathom how emaciated he was becoming. Exchanges were mostly mere nods. Names were sometimes passed along and added to a growing mental list. At night as he lay down, he recounted those suffering perhaps just on the other side of his cell walls. He remembered what positions they had held, party affiliations, and any memorable events that might have involved them, and the circle began to widen. He might have had a cell to himself but he was not alone.

Within weeks, and coinciding with the warm summer months, the level of noise mounted in the prison. The prison had been built in 1896. While the interior was now shabby, decayed after more than a century of neglect, the exterior and its thick walls stood proud testimony to the builder's skill. The paint was peeling, toilets did not flush, and pipes were rusty. The boiler/heater was broken and many windowpanes and light bulbs were missing. The prison, once again in high demand, was being renovated now. Despite this arduous activity, once construction was seemingly completed, the basement water pump still malfunctioned. When the floor flooded, prisoners were forced to carry water in small tins and use rags to wipe the floors. They complained, "The conditions are unsanitary, we'll all get sick. . . ."

No one listened. Hepatitis, diarrhea, and typhus became rampant. Some lingered ill for weeks while others lost the fight in days. Other repairs were equally unsuccessful. The toilets still didn't have drainage grates, and the draining pipes were still missing from the kitchen. Other work turned out better: windows were replaced, as were light bulbs, though the latter turned out to be more of a hindrance than a help. The bulbs were now left on throughout the night, and many found falling asleep nearly impossible. As for the repair of the central heating system, it took almost a year. Wood stoves were used the first winter, and the number of logs used depended on the mood of the guards.

After several months, Constantin was able to gauge the layout of the jail. It was "T" shaped, with a big central hall, and stairs leading to the second and third floors and to the basement. There were cells on all three floors and they varied in size and position. For instance, cell 17 became the most "desirable" one due to its position above the boiler room, with a steady stream of heat in winter. Cell number 12 had the distinction of being the worst, very damp and with the least natural light. Constantin "Dinu" Bratianu, the president of the National Liberal Party died there; he was eighty-seven years old.

Besides cells, each floor had primitive "bathrooms": a Turkish toilet and a separate room with a cold slab cement floor, a sink, and shower. The kitchen, food pantry, and administrative offices were on the ground floor. The barbershop and doctor's office were on the second. A chapel used to be on the same floor, but it had been converted into a storage shack once the Communists took over and religious worship was more or less outlawed. In the basement one found a boiler room, water pump, and two cellars (for potatoes, carrots, turnips, and the like).

Outside there were two yards. The larger of the two had an abandoned barn, and the watchtower. There had used to be an access door to the tower from the yard, but it had been covered with cement to prevent any potential escape or suicide attempt. The guards now entered the tower through the house next door, which had been taken over by the state police. This was also decided in order to limit contact with the prisoners and maintain the utmost secrecy.

The smaller yard was where they could see green grass and flowers: a lilac bush, two apple trees, a small vegetable garden, and a hedge growing on two sides and covered in light purple flowers in early fall. Two majestic firs on the street side of the fence were first trimmed so as not to obstruct the sentries' view, only to be chopped down later. Thick walls at least twenty feet tall surrounded the building and the yards, shielding it away from prying eyes.

It took Constantin and the others a while to understand who was guarding them, and what hierarchy was in place. The warden was a sickly man who had fought in Russia and had been taken prisoner there. He liked to reminisce about his early hardship, the lack of food in the Russian camp, and how he had missed his family. Perhaps in his way he tried to show the inmates how he "related" to their ordeal. He had acquired a habit of comforting them with hollow promises and words: "this too shall pass," or "you won't be here for long." One couldn't tell if he was indeed attempting to make them feel better, or if he was simply passing on empty statements. On occasion he was prone to a kind gesture; when Constantin was in solitary confinement, the warden brought him a sparrow. "Here, I brought you company, it'll make time pass more easily."

Constantin took the bird in his hand; he felt the shivers, opened his hand and released her. The poor sparrow flew around in desperate circles, knocking walls and flapping in every which direction. Constantin couldn't bear the sight and opened the window. The bird eventually found her way out.

The warden's demeanor was pretty even keel until he drank, which was frequently and heavily like most of the staff. Constantin later recalled one such instance in 1953 when he was going about doing his chores. He had seen the warden ranting and raving, and shouting slurred words. The inmates then found out from a friendly guard that the heavy American bombing in Korea had officials worried about the war spilling over into Europe. The warden had always been a good Communist lackey, even before the war when Communist Party ranks numbered less than one thousand members. He liked to preach its doctrine, and emphasized how the Communists didn't shoot you but killed you silently. And indeed it was disease, neglect, despair, and madness which robbed the lives of those in prison, hardly ever bullets.

The ones the prisoners spent the most time with were the guards. Some were beasts whose cruelty could hardly be forgotten. Others simply carried on their duties indifferently, having steeled themselves toward the suffering of the inmates. A few showed that they still had a heart, trying to ease the prisoners' pain by passing on news (internal politics, international affairs, fellow sufferers), or giving them extra food. Some of the inmates even ended up being favored by one guard or another, not unlike the "teacher's pet" in school.

Some of the guards lasted on the job for years, while others left after weeks. A lot of it probably had to do with their demeanor—the ability to look tough and control the inmates and deliver the party line. As for the latter, their weekly sessions of indoctrination were to remind them how evil the capitalist prisoners were. Attributes such as "vampires, exploiters, or beasts" were regularly used to describe their heinous "charges."

The guards were mostly known by their nicknames. Some had to do with their appearance or demeanor. Others simply fell into such categories as "Beasts," known as B-1, B-2, and so on, or "Ass"—A-1, A-2, etc.

Constantin was favored by Ciresica "Little Cherry," a short and stocky fellow with a round, ruddy face. Once in a while he brought around fresh carrots, at great personal risk. He knew prisoners craved fresh fruit and vegetables, and occasionally tried to supply them. Ciresica would walk into the cell and leave the door open. He had to have an unobstructed view of the corridor, as guards were as afraid of one another as they were of their superiors.

"Here, I have something for you," he would then say and quickly open up a fistful of grapes or cherries. Other times he would gently touch Constantin's shoulder and murmur a word of encouragement, "Don't give up, stay hopeful."

"Little Cherry" was also one of the few who didn't swear or use harsh words. He revered Iuliu Maniu, the leader of the Peasant Party, and often brought him extra food or an extra cup of tea. Maniu, a former prime minister, had guided the party to near-victory in the 1946 elections. Mr. Maniu was seventy-seven years old at the time of his arrest, and he survived three years in prison, until 1953.

Another guard nicknamed the "Aviator" (who had worked in aviation before the war) also had a soft spot for Constantin. When later on Constantin was again in solitary confinement and ill with hepatitis, the Aviator brought him extra milk at times. He had also warned him to beware of informers, though Constantin refused at first to believe that friends and suffering fellow inmates could be capable of selling out each other. But the Aviator proved to be right and his words prescient. Some of the informers hoped for a shorter sentence, while others wanted more food or an extra blanket, and decided to do anything in order to gain them.

Though favored by Little Cherry and the Aviator, Constantin was despised by the "Mongoloid," also known as B-1, who actually hated all the inmates. He was ugly beyond description, and his body odor was as awful as his temper and constant curses. The hatred toward his charges was palpable and perpetually manifest. None of the tasks he handed out were ever done to his satisfaction. The floors were never clean enough, the potatoes weren't cleaned properly, and the wood wasn't stacked just so. All these lapses made for endless opportunities to shout, hit, and make men repeat their chores.

B-2 was just as bad, an ex-convict who himself had spent five years in jail for murder. But being a good Communist, he was released and made a guard. It was also B-2 who came in one day accusing Constantin of having peeped out the window. "I saw you, you punk!"

"You must be mistaken; I was lying down on the bed."

"Are you telling me I'm a liar?"

"No, I'm just saying I couldn't have done it."

"You, you, rat, vampire. Get out. I'm taking you to the black cell."

He pushed him until they stopped by the door of the black cell.

"If you confess I'll let you go."

This happened early in his sentence, and Constantin was still quite naïve, not yet used to all the bestial tricks. He decided to confess, despite being innocent, in order to avoid the subhuman conditions of the black cell.

"Okay. I did it."

"Oh, here we go, I knew it! You liar; you get in immediately. Twenty-four hours in here should teach you a lesson," and opening the door, he pushed the prisoner inside.

Constantin did learn a lesson that day. Months later B-2 walked in front of the window and kept waving his hand. By now Constantin knew enough about their tricks not to respond. His silence infuriated the jailor whose gestures grew more agitated, only to be met by the same silence. Minutes passed, and then in a loud voice, he said, "The son of a bitch doesn't want to look out." "Or maybe he's dead?" he said before adding, "No such luck." Every time they crossed paths, Constantin stared at him with a hard, cold gaze, without words. Perhaps this silent treatment eventually affected B-2; or, perhaps a sliver of humanity rose within him. Late one summer he picked up two fresh tomatoes and offered them to Constantin. This gesture immediately drew his suspicion. Was he being baited? But being desperate for fresh vegetables, he grabbed the tomatoes and devoured them, thanking the guard.

The "Habsburg" was nicknamed for his Germanic look, blond and blue eyed, and his fine features. He presented an interesting dichotomy to the prisoners. The Habsburg was the one who subjected them to the ultimate humiliation—kneeling for hours at a time. He also took an almost manic pleasure in making the men repeat their chores. Constantin and cell 17 (Nick Cornateanu and others) were assigned to washing the floors one day. They had just finished their task when the Habsburg came by to inspect the outcome. He lifted up his eyes and exploded, "Did you look at the walls and ceiling? They are covered in dust! There, pick up your brooms and polish them off!"

The men dutifully did as they were told; when the guard returned, he started yelling, "What have you done! The floor is covered in dust now! Go wash it off!"

So the poor men wet the rags and started sweeping again. The floor and the walls gleamed now. But then the Habsburg suddenly noticed dust on some heating pipes on a far wall and demanded they be cleaned, too. That soiled the floor again so it had to be washed a third time before the guard declared himself satisfied.

Most guards were shallow and conceited, holding high opinions of their skill and position. A favorite quote of theirs was, "When I give an order, not even Christ himself can change it." In reality they were for the most part uneducated and devious dirty scoundrels. At times they would make up stories such as, "Those in cell 17 spoke too loud." They'd rush in, complaining of the noise, and then separate the inmates. The supervisors were then called and told, "The situation had been brought under control." It was nothing but a childish ruse to make the guards look good to their superiors. The "every man for himself" saying was elevated to new heights at the Sighet Penitentiary.

"Pithecanthropus Erectus" was the cruelest and most beastly of them all. His appearance was barely human, and his voice more like a growl, often clouded in smoke and alcohol. No deed was too low for him, even being caught stealing food from the meager scraps of the inmates. He would hit the prisoners with real gusto, often knocking them down, and stand there watching them wriggle in pain. He was the guard who had driven Gheorge Bratianu, president of the Liberal Party and a prominent historian, to suicide, after repeated beatings and verbal humiliations. After one such ugly, violent row, Bratianu was found dead in his cell having slashed his throat with a ragged stone.

In contradistinction, the Barber showed occasional signs of humanity. It was perhaps because he himself had been a prisoner in Russia, forced to work in the cold darkness of a mine. During Constantin's bouts of jaundice, he came by to check on him and offer words of encouragement. He had apparently known of inmates who had been yellow and ghastly sick and had survived. He was also the one they dared approach when something was desperately needed. There was little they dared ask for, but the Barber at least listened and didn't hit them.

Another guard by the name of Gavrila Pop also showed his heart. When Constantin spent his first Christmas at Sighet in solitary confinement, the guard softly sang carols outside his door. He also brought him carrots on occasion, much coveted by the men chronically deprived of fresh fruit and vegetables. Gavrila disappeared after one year; perhaps his good deeds had become known and he was terminated or transferred elsewhere.

As for the security officers and military guards, their interaction with the inmates was kept to a minimum. They were the ones entrusted to safeguard the prison and prevent escapes. In due time they, too would receive nicknames such as "The Gorilla" and "Tuberculosis" (also named The Fish by others), mostly based on appearance. But any exchange with these armed guards meant interrogation and often resulted in severe punishment; it was to be avoided at all costs.

These were the men, and this was their home.

Chapter Twenty-Seven
THE FAMILY'S TRAVAILS

After Constantin left with the security officers on the night of his arrest, two of the men left behind immediately started searching the house. They began in the main library, where they picked up each book; pages were turned and the volumes were shaken. The same procedure took place in Dinu's and Professor Mehedinti's studies. Then they moved on to the paintings, lifting them off the wall and inspecting each frame carefully. Cupboards and shelves followed, linen was unfolded, and jars of pickles and marmalade were carefully scrutinized. After hours of fruitless search and with their mission concluded, they left the house with a few of Constantin's papers. Among them was the brochure he had edited about Transylvania in 1942–1943, at the request of the Ministry of Propaganda. It had been published in six languages and the multitude of foreign languages might have aroused their curiosity.

When they were finally gone, Maria stood by the bedroom window and stared out. From there she could see the garden and the narrow alley lined with rose bushes all the way to the street. Her eyes had clung desperately to Constantin's silhouette in the moonlight until the gate had closed and he had vanished from sight. Then she had to maintain her composure and watch those dreadful men rumble through her house. It was only after their departure that the enormity of the morning's early-hour intrusion hit with brutal force. How long had it been since Constantin's last embrace? Barely a few hours had passed since the doorbell had awoken them. Peeking through the cracked-open front door and seeing the officers, she had known their mission right away. They had come to take her husband away, like they had done with Mihai Manoilescu and other dignitaries. The rumors had been true.

Packing a small suitcase had given her a measure of faint comfort. He wouldn't have been allowed one if they had planned to kill him right away. What followed was blurred in her mind, almost surreal. One moment she was there with her parents and Mona, speechless and staring in disbelief. The next the rest of the family was dismissed to the second floor bedrooms once their identities were established. Constantin was in each of her mental frames. She remembered his small, deliberate moves, as if conserving energy and emotion. The men in suits had barked orders throughout their stay. And finally, a dim, smudgy awareness lingered of their last embrace and her whispered entreaty, "You shall return."

Everyone had come down to the living room once the security officers had departed. They had stared silently at one another, too shocked to talk or even cry. Maria had held Mona closely, rocking her like a child. Her mother, Marioara, was the first to break the silence, launching in a tirade, "These beasts, these animals . . . how could they take him away like this, without interrogation, no trial, what an insult. . . ."

Marioara looked around at the others, and her voice choked out, "And what's going to happen to us now?"

Mona glanced at her mother but Maria's face remained stony, blank. Was she too wounded to even register her mother's bickering?

Maria's father had certainly heard. The man who hardly spoke up these days suddenly snapped, "It's not about us, Marioara, it's about Constantin." He ran his hand through his gray hair. "Could you focus on someone other than yourself for once?"

But the old lady still wasn't willing to let it drop. "I know, I know, but it's also about us now—how are we going to survive?"

"Like everyone else," her husband replied.

Unable to think of a suitable reply, she suddenly remembered her daughter. "Maria needs to lie down, maybe have a little brandy. . . ."

"Oh, Marioara, here you go babbling again, like that's going to bring her husband back."

Maria watched incredulously as her parents continued to quarrel over the shattered remains of her life. Too worn out to argue with them, she took advantage of her mother's opening. "Mother is right, I need to go to my room," and she practically ran out.

She lay down in the quiet of her bedroom. Her mind swirled and whirled, obsessively replaying the kaleidoscope of the warning signs, missed or ignored. Prominent politicians had been arrested the past year while they had hoped the lesser ones, like her husband, would be left alone. Even if they had decided to run, where could they have gone? Passports had been confiscated after the return from Istanbul in 1945, and one couldn't hide in a cave or a barn indefinitely.

She knew they had missed on their true chance for freedom: Istanbul. She remembered pleading with her husband and arguing against returning to Romania. She who normally didn't have premonitions had been overtaken by an unsettling feeling. Perhaps it had been fed by the chilling stories coming from Bessarabia, after that province was handed to the Soviets in 1940. The accounts of their occupation—death, rapes, cruelty, and destruction—were enough to instill terror in one's heart. She remembered having argued in Turkey about the pros and mostly the cons of a return home.

"Maria, dear, haven't we gone over this enough times? I love my country. I want to go on teaching her history. Who needs a Romanian historian in Switzerland or the United States?"

"And what if the country falls and the Soviets take over?"

"I told you already, our intelligence bureau thinks that by virtue of our switch to the Allied side, we'll be protected."

"Yeah, the same people who thought the Germans were bound to win at Stalingrad, isn't it? Mind my words: we are doomed if we go back."

It had been the first time in seventeen years of marriage that each had pulled in opposite directions over a critical issue. And then there had been her words in Constanta upon disembarking from the vessel Transylvania, and seeing the red star embroidered on workers' shirts:

"The thread is pulling you toward Siberia, isn't it?"

Now Maria blamed herself: why hadn't she fought harder? Why hadn't she trusted her instincts? What if . . . what if. . . .

She suddenly burst into tears and cried her heart out. She felt like screaming or breaking something but decided against it. It would only alarm the others, and they might start fussing again. After a while she felt drained of tears and energy and strangely calmer, and fell asleep. She got up an hour later, washed her face, and went down to the kitchen.

The house was so quiet. No one was arguing or slamming doors. The phone was silent, too. She stared at it and realized that something had to be done. Constantin's siblings must be told of their brother's fate, and his close friends and colleagues, too.

She went to the study where her father was hunched over the desk, scribbling an article that no one would publish. Her poor eighty-year-old father, who in less than five years had seen his professorship revoked, his Academy membership cancelled, his house confiscated, and now his son-in-law arrested.

"Father, we must let people know. And write to Dan."

She wondered if a letter to her son who was studying in France would even get there, since all outgoing and incoming mail was strictly censored.

"Maria, it might be better not to use the phone. People say 'they' listen in."

"All right, father. I'll wait for Dinu to return home and then go tell Lelia and Horia myself later today."

Dinu, her oldest, arrived later than day. He had looked forward to his first weekend home away from the new job at the road construction site. But what was meant to be a joyful occasion turned into one of grief. He unlocked the door and was met by deep silence. Then he stumbled on his uncle Emil sitting in the living room staring in space and humming absentmindedly.

He went to shake hands. "Is grandfather not well?"

"No, it's your father."

"He's ill?"

"No, he's gone."

"Gone? What are you talking about, Uncle?" shouted the young man. This outburst attracted his grandfather and brought Maria out of her room. Within minutes he learned of his father's fate, the brashness of youth making him unwilling or unable to comprehend this account. He kept asking questions and pressing for answers no one had. Then all fell silent. He glanced around the circle and took in his mother with her red, swollen face and his aged grandparents. Then it dawned on him: he had become the family's sole support.

The first days after Constantin's arrest passed in a whirlwind of activity. The news spread, and a quiet procession of relatives and friends came by the house. At times it felt rather like a wake. Then they slowly learned how many more politicians and top military leaders had been arrested at the same time. Jana, a distant cousin of Maria's, who lived close to the Central Police building, came to visit.

"The day after they took Constantin away, I was on the balcony. From there I can make out the inner courtyard of the police building, though it's quite far away. Midday or so, I saw at least two dozen men standing there. All were clutching a suitcase or bundle."

"Could you see their faces? Did you make out anyone you knew?" Maria asked.

"No, they were too far away."

"And what happened?"

"They were kept standing for quite a while, and must have been tired. I saw some leaning against the walls," Jana said. She hesitated, then added, "They were then loaded into dark vans and driven away."

Days later a friend came by with a second or third-hand account. A man, friend of a friend, had been fishing by the Snagov Lake just outside Bucharest. Dark vans had stopped along the roadside there.

"The men were closely guarded. Some were eating what looked like bread and cheese. The soldiers surrounding them seemed nervous, ill at ease. They kept glancing around." He paused, then added, "Eventually they rounded everyone up and took off, heading on the road to the north."

Anguish and dread overtook Maria, thinking where Constantin might have been taken. She was pretty certain he had been among those rounded up at the Central Police building and driven away in the dark vans, seemingly to the north. Beyond that lay the mountains, the Maramures, and, of course, the Soviet Union just to the northeast. There had to be someone who might have heard something, anything, about the fate of the men. So Maria ran from friend to relative to acquaintance, desperately looking for a clue. Her daughter Mona had a friend with connections in the Communist higher-up circles and in desperation reached out to him. The young man couldn't say much, as anything could have been considered an act of treason. But he was able to pass on that "The old dignitaries" were in prison.

"Where?"

"Don't know," he said.

He probably couldn't tell, and Mona didn't press him further.

"Pray that it's in Romania," mumbled Maria. "The Soviets would be brutal." She cringed at the thought. "Nothing could be worse than the Soviet camps, nothing."

Not knowing where her husband was imprisoned and how he was doing drove Maria to despair. Unable to sleep and hardly eating, she went to the local police precinct one day. The building was dark and depressing—the cold stone walls mirroring the demeanor of those working inside. The building was nearly deserted at midday; everyone was afraid of the police, and went in only if desperate or summoned.

She identified herself to a hostile sentry and was ushered inside, where she had to identify herself once again. This was followed by a physical search by a female employee. The woman was crude and nasty; Maria could almost smell the hatred on her breath.

"Sit and wait; we'll call you."

She sat all alone on a cold bench in a room which could easily hold fifty people or so. She waited for over an hour.

"Citizen Giurescu, you're next." She approached a window. "What is it that you want?"

"I want to find out about my husband. He was taken away less than a month ago."

"I know that; we signed for him."

"Is he alive?" she asked.

"I don't know."

"Where is he?"

"Again, I don't know."

Her heart sank and she lowered her eyes. The half-human behind the window must have sensed her weakening resolve. "Anything else?"

She responded with silence. Then turning and slowly walking away, she heard him spit out, "I wouldn't expect him back any time soon. Or at all." This was followed by a crackling, idiotic laughter, as if someone had just told the greatest of jokes.

Hopes for her husband's quick release withered away by the end of May. She incessantly recounted the little they knew—her new lifeline to Constantin. He had been taken from home and might have spent a night in Bucharest. He had probably been among the men loaded up and driven away in dark vans. People said the "old political guard" was taken to jail. No one knew or would say where to or for how long. And that concluded her knowledge of her husband's whereabouts since May 5.

Mona's contact heard through the grapevine that there would be no trials. The new Romanian Communist regime had the right to arrest its citizens and put them away without due legal process.

Besides agonizing about her husband's fate, survival became Maria's new focus. She felt fortunate to at least be in her own home. Some had been removed from their houses, and others had seen their estates confiscated. The "class oppressors" (as they were now labeled) had to share their wealth with those less fortunate, with the state feeling entitled to take possessions away from those who had worked hard. They were to be handed out to those who "had nothing," in order to erase the inequalities bred by the prior "imperialist" system. In doing so, general poverty was slowly ushered in as the great equalizer.

Among those who had lost their homes were their friends Gica Manescu, a surgeon, and his wife Sanda. With nowhere to go, they looked to friends for help, and Maria offered a room in her house. Suzanna and Titel, Maria's and Constantin's close friends, were also evacuated from their villa. They were allowed to load up their furniture, books and clothes, and along with their three children and Suzi's mother, they were crammed into a two-bedroom apartment. Suzanna was of the opinion that Maria should put away a few things in a "safe" place, with a cousin or trusted friend, or at least for a while.

As for Maria, she really didn't know what to do or what to expect. She believed the authorities had only been after her husband for his political past. After all, they weren't even wealthy, merely comfortable. She decided to consult with Dinu and her father.

"Should we put some paintings and jewelry away?"

"Maria, if they wanted the house, they would have taken it already," concluded her father. "Look at us. Ours was confiscated already."

She gave in to them. Her son and father made sense, though the world around them didn't. So they carried on. Maria went almost daily to the market with its dwindling goods looking for something to put on the table. Dinu gave his mother most of his small salary, and her father contributed his slight pension. Maria counted every penny to make sure there was enough left for gas, electricity, and water.

In late June they heard how the Korean offensive was heating up. This of course came to them through Western European broadcasts still captured on short-wave radios. Dinu had stayed up late listening to the radio, and was sound asleep on the morning of June 28 when the doorbell woke him up. Four men in police uniforms stared at him on the other side of the door. One looked like a gypsy, with a dark complexion and pitch-black eyes and the facial expression of a brute. The youngest seemed around 20 years old. He blushed and looked away. A man in his 40s, probably the leader, spoke up, "Does the Giurescu family lives here?"

"Yes, I'm Dinu Giurescu."

"I have an order stating you are to move out immediately," the older of them stated.

"Move? Where are we to go?"

"You've been assigned rooms on Moruzi Street."

Dinu glanced at a sheet of paper with the listing: "Giurescu-Moruzi"; it bore no official letterhead, no stamp or signature. He shook his head in disbelief, knowing that any argument would have been futile.

"You're allowed to take along some personal effects."

"What about the books, the furniture . . . ?"

"It all stays here. The state has taken ownership of the house and all its contents."

"Under what authority?" Dinu asked.

"That of the People's Republic of Romania."

He felt dizzy, his stomach churning; the library with its priceless manuscripts, the photographs and stamps, were among his father's treasured possessions. How could he abandon them? What choice did he have?

"What about my grandparents?" he asked.

"They're moving out, too. They've been assigned a room elsewhere, in a parochial house."

The noise had awakened Maria; she walked out of her room and at the sight of the men in the foyer, the world briefly blanked out. When she came around, Dinu was pressing a cold towel to her forehead. Her parents hugged each other in a corner, pale as ghosts. Her friend Sanda had also woken up and was standing next to Dinu.

One of the men took notice of her. "Who are you?"

"Sanda Manescu."

Glancing down at the papers, he asked, with a sneer, "And where's your husband, the doctor?"

"At the hospital, called in for an emergency," she said. "What am I to do?"

The man seemingly in charge stood quietly for a moment. He hadn't been given precise instructions on how to handle this couple.

"Is that your room?" he asked.

"Yes, it is."

He walked over and looked inside the room. "What about all these things?" he asked, motioning to the furniture and the paintings in her bedroom.

"Ours. We brought these things when we moved in."

"All right. We'll get a truck for you after we deal with the rest of the family. Go to your room and await instructions."

As shell-shocked as she was, Maria saw that thanks to her friends a few items were going to be saved, including three valuable Romanian Impressionist paintings.

The gypsy officer came to life. "Everybody else get going, one suitcase per person and a mattress. No photos, no jewelry, no books."

The old professor, white as a sheet, looked as if he would drop dead of a heart attack any minute. His wife sobbed and cursed at the same time, until her husband seemed to wake up to what was happening and gently led her to the room to start packing.

Dinu asked for a list of the house contents, but the gypsy elbowed him. "Get going, didn't you hear? List? What list? They're all ours now, you have nothing," he spat out.

In her shock, Maria barely remembered where anything was. Grabbing a large suitcase, she stuffed it with dresses, underwear, socks, and a coat; along with soap, sheets, and towels. When she grabbed some of

Constantin's shirts, the officer said, "He doesn't need them where he is, leave them behind." This sent chills down her spine.

The man in charge was getting restless. "Enough. Just take your mattresses and step outside."

Each family member gathered by the front door holding a bag in one arm and a mattress under the other.

"Now open up your suitcases for a final search," he told them all. After this last indignity, they were loaded onto a dark van waiting to take them to their new "home."

Maria pleaded once more, "Please save the books, take them to the university or academy. Some are priceless; people should have access to them."

"Don't worry about your precious books, just move on," yelled the gypsy.

She turned and took into the house one last time—the marriage, her children growing up, and their lives here, were just memories now. She had heard that before dying one saw a kaleidoscope of life's moments rushing by. Flashes of her own journey danced before her eyes. But death would have been infinitely preferable to this devastation: her husband taken from her, and now the house, too.

Maria would later have no recollection of the ride taking them to their assigned domicile. She couldn't tell which way they were going, nor did she care. Her parents were dropped off first, who knew where. She continued to stare vacantly ahead. When the car stopped again and the men barked the order to disembark, Dinu gently led her by the hand.

Later on, Sanda Manescu told them what had happened the day after their evacuation. A team of "comrades" first wrote down an inventory of the house: furniture, painting, china, even the jars of home-made preserves were all catalogued. Then the men had emptied the shelves, heaping papers into the courtyard, and setting them on fire. Manuscripts dating to back to the eighteenth century, rare first editions, and valuable photos were quickly reduced to a cup of ashes.

A few days later, Dinu and Mona went to visit professor Ralea, who had taught at the University with Constantin. After the war he had rapidly changed his political leaning and the reward had come in 1947 with the nomination of Romanian Envoy to the U.S. His tenure there had lasted three years, and by 1950 he was back in Bucharest. His reward for having switched "political gears" early was being able to maintain his residence and position. Dinu and his sister asked him for help in saving the books, but they were cut short and told nothing

A World Torn Asunder

could be done under the circumstances. The man was evidently unwilling to burn his newly found capital for a mere acquaintance.

Despite this setback, some of the books survived and were miraculously transferred to the Institute of History. Mona's "contact," the one with ties to the political hierarchy, had initiated the request at the urging of the family. Working through this channel was met with success, and some of the works thus escaped being turned into ashes.

After several months, Dinu heard from one of the neighbors. He described how for days people had gone to the house and walked out with vases, paintings, clothing, and chandeliers. Vans had driven up and were loaded with the furniture. Everything accumulated in twenty-four years of marriage, and by Constantin's parents before them, was scattered and gone forever.

Several families moved into the house after a while, a neighbor told them. A man wearing a police or security uniform occupied the first floor, which with its crystal-rimmed partition doors was the "prize" of the house. Maria and Dinu eventually said they didn't want to hear anything else concerning their house.

"I wish I had set it on fire myself," Maria spat out.

And she vowed to never walk down that street again.

Chapter Twenty-Eight
LIFE IN PRISON

As days became weeks, months, and then years, survival remained Constantin's primary focus, at almost any cost other than turning friends in. He continued to bet—with himself or the insects that kept him company—that if only one man was left standing at the end of this ordeal, he'd be the one. His desire to emerge alive and whole and to maintain an intact mind sustained him throughout the misery, incertitude, and isolation of Sighet.

This is not to say he wasn't plagued by doubts, because he was human, like the rest of them. There wasn't a day without moments of despair and self-doubt. Images of Maria and the children flickered across his mind, leaving searing pain. Thoughts of them were especially haunting in the evening, when they would have gathered at home around a meal. He tried to imagine their days, closing his eyes, and trying to guess the divergent tracks of their lives. His own suffering paled when he wondered what might have happened to them. The lack of news was the most maddening kind of torture, as all letters, calls, and visits were strictly prohibited. Guilt was overwhelming at times. He wouldn't have been in jail had it not been for his political activity. He wouldn't have landed in Sighet had they stayed in Istanbul. Hadn't Maria warned of the thread pulling him to Siberia? They could have all been living abroad in freedom, and could have escaped this horror. How could he—a learned man with deep knowledge of history and even politics—have been so blind? How could he have missed the signs? And why hadn't he trusted Maria's gut feeling, the one that had overwhelmed her since the war began? He had always relied on her common sense . . . until then.

When depression and guilt tried to take him over and tears welled up, he'd mutter: "What's done can't be undone," and he would try to jolt himself out of it. In order to stay sane, he recalled how others in similar situations had followed the same path. Some had become involved in politics, or built manufacturing or banking empires, forging a career and better life for themselves and their families. Like him, many had believed Romania's late-war switch to the Allies would protect their country from the Soviet Red menace, and they had returned home. The Allies would be coming to their rescue—why, they couldn't possibly sell them out cold. They were the same Allies who should have known the Romanian people's true feelings, despite the war course charted by their leaders up to 1944.

Well, that was then, and this was now. His lone hope was survival, so he could return to his loved ones and hopefully rebuild his career. The Communists' ultimate feat would have been the death or destruction of the "old guard," Constantin and his fellow sufferers. "That, they must be denied at all cost," he would mumble, boosting his morale. The old fear of having been forgotten by God, which had plagued him after his father's passing, had now returned. How he envied those in prison who fervently prayed, believing in God's deliverance. Faith had eluded him for years, and the current circumstances did little to incite a search for the Almighty.

In order to stay sane, he set about making up and keeping to a daily schedule. Wake up; eat meals; do chores; and lights out, were the linchpins of his routine. This focus helped him to control his mind and curb the despair worsened by the years of solitary confinement when he had only cursory interaction with the guards and inmates.

He tried to divide the day. A part was dedicated to rehearsing the chronology of Romanian history: dates and events were analyzed and enumerated. Time was set aside for future projects, when he'd continue to write the remaining volumes of the history of the Romanians. But he also thought of new books, such as the history of the city of Bucharest, the practice of fishing, and a collection of Romanian songs. In the more distant future, he also hoped to see his books translated into foreign languages. How he had loved the time in Paris and the latter trips with Maria: would he ever be able to again travel and present his ideas abroad?

Practicing languages occupied another part of the day. He'd pick a word, often randomly, and translate it in French, German, English and Latin. Once he felt confident, he moved up to using them in sentences, thoughts, and ideas in these languages. Other times he focused on categories: fruit, vegetables, furniture, clothing items and the like, and translated them in batches. And while at it, he attempted to analyze the similarities and differences between the various languages. Whenever he recounted English words, his thoughts wondered back to his friend Adrian, who had studied in London. How had he fared since 1950? "I see little reason for him to have been arrested," Constantin thought, "but I bet his engineering post must have been targeted."

Thoughts of family and friends were ever present. So he set about to repeat their addresses and phone numbers at night, hopefully building an invisible bridge to his real (other) life. By enumerating the facts of their lives, they were drawn into his current universe and the two mentally blended in one. And of course, he continued daily stretches and walks around the cell.

All in all, this program was his only hope to keep the mind intact and remain marginally fit until the day of his release, as one seemed to ensure the other.

He remained in solitary confinement for nearly two years, until January 1952. On January 25 of that year, one of the supervising officers came into his cell. It was an unusual sight, as the upper echelon stuck to their offices and rarely set foot in the prisoners' quarters. The presence of the sallow man in the stark uniform was definitely a reason for concern. Would there be another interrogation?

"Giurescu, stand up when I talk to you."

He got up from his bed. "Yes, Sir."

"Is there anything you want to complain about?"

Oh-ho, he thought, as he was baited. But he had learned his lesson with B-2, the beastly warden.

"No, sir."

"Nothing?"

"No."

There was complete silence—the officer must have been taken by surprise, since others must have fallen for this ploy.

After a few seconds, he said, "You're moving to cell 48."

"Very well, then," Constantin said without showing his relief.

"Gather your things and follow me."

He grabbed his tin, handkerchief, a little towel, and blanket, and followed the officer. When he entered cell 48, he immediately recognized his friend Nick Cornateanu, an engineer by training and minister of agriculture in Calinescu's short-lived government in 1939. Then he noticed two other men. He squinted hard and wished for the umpteenth time he had his glasses. As these two other occupants stood up, they were partially blocked by Nick, and it was hard to tell who they might have been. All he knew was that they were awfully thin, with bones jutting out and eyes sunken in. The inquisitive face of the officer was met by expressionless faces and silence, with no reaction from anyone. To acknowledge their acquaintance would have automatically meant being sent back to cell 21. After bland stares all around, the officer motioned toward an empty bed and warned, "I don't want to hear you making any trouble here. Otherwise you head back where you came from."

"No, Sir."

The officer looked at him sharply, "You answered no?"

"I mean there won't be any trouble here, Sir."

After the officer left, the men milled about for a while as if nothing had happened. They were most certainly watched through the peephole to gauge first reactions. Constantin looked around; for nearly two years, he had only been able to sneak furtive glances at those surrounding him. He now stared directly at his friends in suffering, and couldn't believe his eyes. They had aged a decade in less than two years. He almost didn't recognize them, and they in turn peered at him, wondering who was joining them.

"Constantin?" asked an incredulous weak voice. It was Aurelian Bentoiu, former minister of Justice in 1940, and Undersecretary of State at the same ministry prior to that.

"Yes, it's me, old friend."

"Who else is in here?" asked Constantin. "I can't tell without my glasses."

"George Strat."

Unbelievable! George, hero of the Oituz battle in the First World War, representative to the League of Nations and Undersecretary for Economy, had always been an imposing presence. The man he now faced had shrunk, and kept his head bowed down.

Nick got up and checked on the peephole; without anyone staring back on the other side, he extended his hand. Constantin shook it and held his grip for what seemed like minutes—it had been such a long time since he had felt any kind of human touch. But it still wasn't enough, and so he hugged Nick, letting his guard down. Poor George got up to and joined in the embrace with Aurelian tugging at their sleeves, too.

Nick was first to take stock, "Shhhh . . . I bet the beasts will return soon to check on us . . . go lie down for now . . . we have nothing but time ahead of us."

Belief in his eventual survival was truly renewed by being with others and communicating with them at all hours of the day and night. Just talking seemed extraordinary at first. A torrent of questions poured out of him on how they were arrested and traveled to Sighet. Before long the first two years of their imprisonment were fast pieced together. He also learned of the many others who had met the same fate, and of those who had already perished there.

Days and evenings passed easier now. Though conversations among inmates were strictly forbidden, the rule was rarely reinforced if you kept your voice low. Perhaps there were too few guards, or maybe they didn't really care.

To further keep themselves occupied, "lecture series" were held, mostly at night, and based on individual specialty—history, literature, geography, or personal recollections. Constantin presented a course in Romanian history and the history of several prominent cities. He also recounted the lives of various princes and rulers and seminal events. Biographies were reviewed and poems recited. Singing was forbidden, but Victor Papacostea, with whom he later shared a cell, hummed opera arias once in a while—one such occasion landed him in the black cell. Another favorite pastime was telling classic stories of Romanian literature. One inmate would take the lead, and then another would pick up from there, and before they knew it they had enacted the whole tale.

The other leading activity in the cells was language training. One member fluent in Hungarian taught the others bits and pieces. A few of them practiced their English on each other, Constantin among them. Most were fluent in French and German, but they had little chance in the last few years to speak these languages, and so the dialogues would toggle back and forth in spurts.

But most of their time was spent in far less literary pursuits. Occupants of a cell were assigned to work as a unit and a month after joining cell 48, Constantin and his friends were sent to kitchen duty, favored by most of the inmates. Peeling potatoes, chopping cabbage, and preparing their so-called soup was relatively easy and clean compared with sweeping and washing floors and cleaning the bathrooms. It also meant they could taste the food before serving it, adding a mouthful to their meager diets. Besides, this task gave them a preferential position on the food exchange market: jam, milk, bread, and even an occasional meat morsel were all traded for other items. The kitchen work became even more desirable starting in 1954, a year after Stalin's death, when their food allotment improved both in variety and size. This came as the terror which had gripped Romania was slightly relaxed, and its misery abated following the Soviet leader's death.

The guards knew kitchen duty was favored, so they rarely kept a crew on it for any length of time. It was almost as if they teased the prisoners with this relatively easy chore, and once accustomed to it, they were shuffled off to something more taxing. The alternative theory was that the inmates were "rotated" so they could equally benefit from it. But this would have implied that the guards still had a humane streak, which was not evident elsewhere.

Yard work, such as sweeping the pavement and chopping wood, was also favored by many. Besides the benefits of physical labor, they liked getting fresh air and a little sun, catching sight of others, and exchanging tidbits of gossip.

Constantin and three other inmates, Nick among them, were moved between cells 13, 17, and 18 several times. On September 24, 1954 they and six others, the so-called "liberal group" based on past party affiliation, were moved to the larger cell 18. It was through years of being cellmates that Constantin's and Nick's friendship grew stronger. While others shared their plight and cell, these two shared the same will to survive and were also closest in age. When one of them wavered, the other one reminded him of family and "life after" prison. When either was sick, they nursed one another to health the best they could, trading bread for soup and so on. The bond forged there would last the remainder of their lives.

Constantin remained with the "liberal group" for another ten months, with the exception of his isolation during one bout of hepatitis in October 1954. Together they were able to endure whatever torture their jailors doled out. It was never extreme physical abuse, but they soon learned how psychological torment was even worse. Its objective was to diminish or destroy the individual's spirit, by negating past achievements and instilling survival doubts in the prisoners' minds. To achieve this end, no task was deemed too menial.

Cleaning duty was the most dreaded task. The sewer system was antiquated, and water pumps didn't work despite the renovation. The inmates were forced to clean the sewer, often with their bare hands. Each time a man was "designated" to going down into the sewer, he would invariably emerge covered in filth. From down in the sewer, he handed out full buckets to his teammates. Despite their protests, they were instructed to empty the buckets in the garbage trench in the large yard, near the watchtower. Warnings of disease, as previously voiced, were disregarded by their jailors, and epidemics of typhoid fever and hepatitis A erupted and robbed many of their lives. Constantin himself had two bouts of hepatitis and nearly died. Bright yellow, nauseated, and unable to hold anything down, his body was shaken by deep chills while his mind reminded him how vital survival was. These waves of disease must have shaken those in charge, as the system of cleaning and disinfection improved somewhat in their aftermath.

Communication with the outside world was missed by all. Letters, phone calls, newspapers, books, and even listening to the radio were strictly forbidden. Therefore contact and communication between each other became of vital importance, as whispered tidbits were passed during walks and cleaning sessions. Scraps of paper with words cut out, as a kind of cipher, were hidden under bathroom tiles, among cabbage leaves, and in the boiler room. Wall tapping was popular but time consuming, so after a while abbreviations were used instead of full words, and those who knew Morse code practiced it. Communication between prisoners was particularly active when supervision was lax, such as after lunch and lights out at night. "News" was generally learned in the morning, mostly by the kitchen team listening to the guards.

Another kind of connection, with animals, birds, and insects, took place gradually. A spider with a cross on her back became Constantin's pet while in solitary confinement in cell 21. He was convinced she recognized him after a while. How else would you explain that she ran away only when a guard opened the door? He fed her crumbles and wished for her to stay. Her presence was registered as another "being" in the cell, an odd feeling given their obvious inability to communicate.

While he was part of cell 17, a baby eaglet fell in the yard one day and was taken in by them. They nursed him back to health, mending his broken leg with a wood splint and taking turns feeding him bits of food and giving him water. He was kept in the toilet until the guard B-2 figured it out and shot the bird, another senseless act of cruelty.

The prison dog was nicknamed "Lion," a big yellow animal with a threatening bark who was a "softie" at heart. Constantin had always loved dogs and mourned the loss of Gib, who, with an almost prescient sense, had passed away six months before his arrest. He gradually made friends with the "lion" during yard walks and, later on, during wood-chopping assignments. The dog had taken to Nick in particular; after a while he'd run wagging his tail, seeking him out among the throngs of scrawny and gray inmates in the yard. One day a more humane guard brought in a "prison puppy" and literally introduced him at roll call: a fluffy, defenseless little bundle. All delighted in his appearance and he was adopted on the spot.

The other not so silent companions were the birds. They served another purpose with fall and spring punctuated by flocks of geese flying in formation, heading either north or south for the season. Watching the graceful flocks Constantin envied their mobility and absolute freedom of movement. The sparrows were ubiquitous in the yard, on windowsills, or on the roof, and were mostly an annoyance with their non-stop chitchat. As for owls, they were heard from mostly in autumn. The cuckoo became an alarm clock and an unfortunately early one, and despite the nuisance of being woken up too early, Constantin still delighted in these sounds of nature. They reaffirmed their presence outside the cruel world of man, where age-old chimes, and rustles, still carried on. He was similarly comforted by the sight of spring blossoms and the rusting of the fall leaves heralding the arrival of a new season. Yes, nature carried on, as always, and one day, he too, would again be able to openly partake in the beauty of the sky, the forest, and the sea.

The chirping sounds of birds and the clap of thunder, the warmth of the sun and fragrant scent of the flowers sharply contrasted with the inhumane horrors inside the prison walls. Those he pledged he would later depict in a book for the generations to come. Among the most dreaded of these atrocities was the "black cell" mentioned earlier. Constantin had landed there several times, as had so many others, even if extremely ill. The nickname came from the lack of any light source: no window, light bulb, not even a candle. Other punishments included kneeling on stone floors, and assuming the "frog position," to be held for an extended time; skipping meals, and, of course, the beatings. His friends Nick, Victor, Vlad, and Dan were severely beaten and took days to recover. When Ion Lupas went on hunger strike, the guards beat him daily, even twice a day.

"Hit me over the head," he would scream "so you can finish me off."

The guard would reply, "I'm saving that for the end."

As for interrogations, they took place mostly at the onset of their imprisonment and included copious shouting, insults, and slapping. Once the prison officers established that not much was being extracted, the "dialogues" eased up. Inquests, however, returned in full force toward the end of Constantin's stay. A prosecutor visited the prison around that time. He was interested in caches of hard currency, jewelry, gold, or relations with foreign dignitaries before their arrests. He persisted and tried to pit prisoners against one another, divulging how "so and so had told me in confidence," only to come up empty-handed.

None of the men held at Sighet ever had a trial. Each had been arrested at home, driven to the jail, and left there to linger until dead or released. Early questions regarding the legality of the process were answered with threats of worse punishment to come. The prisoners learned to dread the beatings, black cell, diminished food rations, and soon stopped asking such questions. The stronger ones (mentally and physically) focused, like Constantin, on survival. The weaker, sicker, and older ones withered away and disappeared. Some pretended to be insane in order to be given a cellmate to watch over the madman. Others flared up at times, and took it out on one another, throwing punches and kicks.

They started dying even before reaching Sighet. Dr. Ciugureanu, for instance, died of a massive heart attack one day after leaving Bucharest. General Cihoski, as recounted, went mad during the journey, and died shortly after reaching his destination. Some committed suicide, hanging themselves or slashing their wrists or throats. Most others died of infections, heart attacks, or terminal diseases that went untreated. Medical supplies were either scarce or deemed too precious to waste on the prisoners. Even penicillin was withheld for infections and replaced with aspirin in some cases. As for those requiring special dietary foods (diabetics, colitis) they never received them.

The former governor of the Romanian National Bank was so ill at the end that he couldn't swallow anything. They thought he had stomach, or perhaps esophageal, cancer. Mihai Manoilescu, the former Foreign Minister who had been arrested a year earlier in 1949, perished early on, in December 1950. He was taken with the typhus, which was rampant among prisoners. Though he somehow survived the disease, his weakened heart gave out by the end of the year.

The leaders of Romania's main pre-WWII "traditional parties" both perished at Sighet. Gheorghe "Dinu" Bratianu, head of the National Liberals and former prime minister, committed suicide in 1953, as recounted; he was eighty-seven years old. The leader of the Peasant Party and former prime minister himself, Iuliu Maniu, also perished there in 1953; he was eighty years old.

The prisoners were never told when someone passed away. But the unmistakable signs were always there. A cart rolled through the yard in the dead of night. A thump heralded a body being thrown onto it. Screeches of a shovel cutting through gritty dirt sent shivers through the prison. And in the morning, one less helping of food was laid out by the kitchen "staff." Because communication was limited, one never quite knew who had left this world unless the victim had belonged to a group cell. Most of the men were buried in the "cemetery of the poor," a communal gravesite with no names and no crosses, and families found out about the passing of their loved ones only years later. Some heard through former inmates, after their releases, others through personal inquiries. Not once was a family notified of their loss.

Constantin tried to "steel" himself through the years. His heart bled for the departed ones and their families—who might never know. Being compassionate by nature, he wished he could alleviate the pain and misery around him. But he also learned that he needed to toughen himself in order to survive. Sorrowful emotions might have otherwise cascaded and brought him down, too.

Some gave up hope and stopped keeping track of time, but not Constantin. He never did, vowing to store it all in the memory bank if nothing else. Yes, he would be able to identify the precise day and date of his release when the time came. But even he was shaken by his fifth "anniversary" in May 1955. How many more years would this go on, and at what price to him and his family? But, even as he asked these questions, he kept hanging on to the piecemeal news, and reports of some releases, fueling the hope he might be next.

Chapter Twenty-Nine
"You are Free to Go"

On July 5, 1955, Constantin was called to the director's office. "What could this be about?" he wondered. The past days had been calm as he, Nick and the others in cell 18 had carried on with the assigned yard work. There had been no beatings, no one had been sent to the black cell, and no unusual threats had come from the guards. "No, it must be the usual," he thought, expecting a renewed interrogation. He braced himself to deliver the same replies given since his arrival.

He was escorted in and stopped in front of a desk, taking off his cap in sign of respect. He was left standing for a few minutes. He remained still and silent, afraid any slight gesture could irritate the director, who busied himself with a pile of papers while seemingly ignoring the man standing in front of him.

He finally looked up and spoke, "Constantin Giurescu, you are free to go."

He was so stunned that he nearly fainted, reaching for the table edge to steady himself, and he muttered incredulously, "You said free?"

"Are you deaf now? What part of it don't you understand?" The director shook his head and added, "But. . . ."

"Oh, here comes the "but," thought Constantin.

"But, you're not free to go home. You've been assigned to a domicile in the southeastern part of the country, in the village of Mazareni. You'll be escorted there."

Constantin kept silent, terrified of being tricked by another ruse. Would the wrong comment bring about a change of heart? He waited for whatever followed.

"You're not only deaf but mute, too," the director said impatiently. "I don't have the whole day. Here. You need to sign for receipt of your clothes, glasses, money, and wedding band. Then wait for the guard to take you to the train station. And remember: you aren't allowed to talk to anyone; otherwise you'll never see the light of day again. No winking, no muttering, no gesturing—nothing, you understand?"

"Yes, sir."

He wanted to run, but left slowly, walking in a measured pace so as not to annoy anyone. His clothes were brought out in a cardboard box, and a guard asked for a receipt signature. Constantin briefly looked them over: all the items were present, indeed, just as he remembered them. He first put on his wedding band, already feeling one step closer to Maria. The band felt dangerously loose on this ring finger: "I must make sure it doesn't slip off without my noticing it." Then he undressed and put on his pants, which floated around his much-thinner waist. The belt was so loose that he had to tie it like a ribbon in order to hold the pants up. The legs of the pants swam around his bony limbs; his feet seemed lost in the middle of his shoes. He stared at the socks: years of washing had reduced them to a tangle of threads. As they were his only pair, he had no choice but put them on. As for the jacket, it spread around him like angels' wings flapping in the wind.

Constantin stood up and said, "I'm ready." But the joy of his release was dampened by the knowledge of those he would be leaving behind. What hurt the most was his inability to say good-bye to Nick and his other cellmates, as any such request would have cancelled his release. Were the others going to be let go soon? Would they worry incessantly about what might have happened to him? With no answer in sight and a heavy heart, he was led out of the prison through the gate he had entered over five years earlier. He longed to turn around and take one last look, but he couldn't bear spotting his friends still languishing behind the walls. Straightening himself, he stepped out of the yard and into a waiting van.

They drove in silence, passing nearly empty streets and two churches. Once they reached the train station, the two men sat for hours in the stifling July heat until the sun started going down. Constantin cautiously looked around, trying to take stock of his new sort of freedom. The station was empty and remained so until their train arrived, and no cars or carts pulled up either. "They must restrict traffic around here on account of the prison," he thought. When he had to go to the bathroom, the man accompanied him and waited by the door. After he emerged he asked for a drink of water. The guard led him to a water fountain and stared as Constantin was finally able to drink to his heart's content. Cheese sandwiches on stale bread were brought out and some peaches—the best supper he'd had in years.

They finally boarded a train and traveled south through the darkness. The compartment could have easily held eight, but no one joined them. Was that done on purpose? Most likely, thought Constantin. He closed his eyes but sleep eluded him, the excitement of the release winning over the anguish and fatigue.

When dawn broke, he saw villages along the route, and fields of wheat and tree-covered mountains, for the first time in five years. Nature was even more beautiful than he remembered, and he drank it all in. As his eyes gazed at the sky in its infinite vastness, he saw proof that nature was always open and man's evil couldn't take that away.

The train stopped numerous times. He was surprised how quiet and under-populated the train stations were. Gone were the peasants with their loaded produce carts, and the ladies heading to the city in their Sunday best. Few people boarded or got off the train. When the guard opened the window to let in some fresh air and release the dreadful heat, he also noticed that people seemed quiet, too. His other first impression was how dull everybody looked: nondescript, with shapeless shades of beige and gray everywhere, a first view of Romania's new, drab Communist world.

The slow journey took almost twenty-four hours. The train finally pulled into Bucharest's North Station. Though more animated than the other stations, it too was but a pale, quiet shadow of its former self. A change of guard awaited him, and after reviewing the paperwork, the man said, "You're allowed to make one phone call to your family. Here, take this coin."

With his heart tied in a knot, he dialed the home number he had repeated over and over across the years. Instead of a ring a recording came through: "This number has been disconnected."

Panic set in, with cold sweat running down his back. He steadied himself, mustering as much calm as he could. Turning to the officer, he whispered, "Our phone is no longer connected. I need to call a relative."

"Go ahead, but we don't have the whole night."

He feared his siblings' numbers could be out of service, too. What if the whole family had been targeted after his arrest? Whom could he call? He decided on distant cousins and close friends Jean and Viorica. Their number had also been rehearsed and stored in the mental archive. "They'll probably be afraid to hear the phone ring this late," he thought. "But what alternative do I have?" After a few rings, she answered, the same cheerful voice he recalled.

"Viorica, it's me, Constantin."

She started shouting in joy, "Oh my God, oh my God." Sweet Viorica, who never raised her voice, was now screaming as loud as she could.

There wasn't much time. "Listen, Viorica, I need to know about Maria, is she all right?"

Viorica hesitated, to calm herself down; there would be time later for details. "Yes, she's healthy and so are Mona and Dinu. We don't know much about Dan."

"I can't talk much longer; you go see Maria and tell her I'm alive and being sent to Mazareni. I'll send details as soon as I'm allowed."

Viorica couldn't stop babbling, "We'd heard last year you were still alive in 1952. We never gave up hope."

"Neither did I. Kiss Maria for me. I have to go now."

After a bathroom break, the guard brought out some food: hard cheese, bread and jam, bologna, and some apples. Constantin had been given only a sandwich and a bottle of water on the long train journey. The sight of so much food made him realize now how starved he was. How long had it been since he had eaten such a variety at the same meal?

They sat at the station and spent the night sitting in silence; the guard smoked and read a paper while Constantin stared at the people coming and going. Just as in the villages passed earlier, the men were shabbily dressed in worn-out summer shirts, dusty berets, and old-looking shoes. The few women around were poorly attired, too, and looked tired. The night passed, and they boarded another train just before sunrise. It headed southeast through swirling wheat and cornfields under the blazing sun. The journey was considerably shorter than the prior one, but the heat was even more oppressive. The two passengers sat mostly in silence, lost in thoughts. Constantin received water at a rest stop, but no more food. Hungry again, he was scared to ask, afraid to irritate the guard. Despite being dirty, hungry, and exhausted, the feeling of semi-freedom kept him going. Obsessively he focused on the days just ahead, and being with his loved ones so very soon. The hours passed. The train slowed down and finally pulled into a station where the sign read Mazareni. "My home for the next sixty months," he thought. "Another five whole years."

Mazareni was a village literally in the middle of nowhere, a speck in the vast Romanian grain fields of the southeast. On a visit five years earlier, one wouldn't have even happened upon it simply because it didn't exist. This village could be thought of as a "Communist invention." Peasants and villagers from the southwest had been moved in 1951 to other parts of the country in yet another "diversion" created by the new leadership. By displacing the population, they had hoped to erase the region's historic and social character, while taking away land and possessions. Family roots put down centuries earlier were thus severed, and those displaced felt disoriented and like aliens in their new surroundings. But they were also terrified of further repercussions, and thus docility and humility became their new persona.

The Communists had begun molding their silly-putty socialist ciphers, indeed.

Hundreds had arrived in Mazareni at the same time with only a suitcase in hand. For the first two summer months, they had slept under the open sky, cooked on wood fires, and washed in a pond. They were then given wooden window and doorframes and allowed to build mostly one-room huts of mud and clay bricks, the structures left to dry in the sun. The room was bedroom, kitchen and bathroom, all in one. The "kitchen" consisted of a brick stove, while the "bath" was a basin and jug of water. The "facilities" were outside, a wooden shed with a hole in the middle. Several huts shared a well, and light was provided by the sun and candles.

Building the village from the ground up had also assured the authorities that there would be no church there. Faith was discouraged and frowned upon, though religion was not officially outlawed. But people had become fearful of attending a regular church service, as those reported doing so were later harassed under different pretexts.

The village may not have had a church or much else, but it certainly had a police station. That was where Constantin was first taken and "registered" upon his arrival. His escort introduced him to the local authorities and waited for the procedures to unfold. A man wearing a police uniform grunted, "Name and date of birth?"

Constantin obliged.

"Occupation?"

He was torn by this request. Whatever he chose was bound to irritate the man interviewing him. "He must know, anyway," he thought. "Former professor of history," he replied.

"Health issues?"

Constantin almost smiled at this one. Should he recount how all his teeth had fallen out? The seventy-pound weight loss? The insomnia and the nightmares? A liver which must have surely been damaged by the two bouts of hepatitis? "No serious ones, really," he recited."

Proper procedures were spelled out: he could not leave the village without written permission, and weekly reports were required. Visitors were allowed, but they couldn't live with him, and any medical attention had to be certified by a physician approved by police authorities. He waited patiently to be told where to live.

"You are to stay with the Piguleas."

"All right," he thought, "as if the names mean anything." He would soon discover that Vasile Pigulea and his wife Rada were honest, hardworking peasants, who had been stripped of everything but their honor. After all the formalities were carried out, the accompanying guard signed him off and left. Constantin now came under the direct supervision of the local police.

"Pick up your things and let's go." Small bundle in hand, he was escorted to his new "home," a five-minute walk away. The Pigulea's hut had one room where they slept, so Constantin was lodged in the entry hall where the stove was also located.

"It'll come handy in winter," he thought to himself.

Once the policeman left, he shyly introduced himself, "I'm Constantin Giurescu and I am grateful for your hospitality."

The couple stared at him incredulously. They had been told their "guest" was an ex-politician, ex-professor, and a capitalist vampire. Now they stared at a pale, rail-thin man who tried to smile and was incongruously thanking them.

"You can put your things by the bed," Vasile said. Constantin set down his small package. "That's all you brought?"

"This is all I have after five years in prison."

Rada stepped in and asked, "Are you hungry?"

Constantin sighed, "Very."

"Would you like to eat with us? We don't have much, but we'd like you to share it with you."

"Yes, please, I'd appreciate it very much."

She set water to boil on the stove, and then went outside, presumably to pick some vegetables. She came back and started chopping them. Constantin was staring at the potatoes, eyes ready to pop out of his sockets. She lifted her eyes and understood the sign.

"Would you like something to eat before the meal is ready?"

He lowered his eyes. "Yes, please."

From a rudimentary cupboard, she brought out some bread and a wedge of cheese. "Here, help yourself."

"How much may I have?"

She didn't understand the question at first, and then noted the hungry look in his eyes. "As much as you'd like; we don't have much, as I said, but you're welcome to share it with us."

Constantin stared at the food, and realized that this was the first time in years he could eat as much as he wanted. "Tonight will be the first time I won't go to bed hungry," he told himself and smiled. The woman stared at him silently. She had heard prison could make you mad, and she wondered about their guest.

They ate what seemed to him like the best soup-stew in the world, with bread dipped in sour cream. Once he was finished, Constantin felt dreadfully tired, every fiber of his being aching. The five-year ordeal was over, and tonight he would go to sleep without a guard peeking through a hole. There would be no roll call in the morning and no cleaning duty, and he would once again be able to eat to his heart's content.

The next day he wondered when he would be able to see Maria. He needed to send word to her right away, and there lay the problem. The Piguleas had no phone. He settled on writing a postcard. Should he send it to the home address? But the phone had been disconnected, a bad sign. What if Maria had had to move out? Perhaps they hadn't been able to afford keeping the house? Where would she have gone? Most likely somewhere nearby; the neighborhood had been the center of her life for over twenty years, with many friends around. He pondered and decided, "I'll send it to the church; the old priest is hopefully still alive. He'll know how to find her."

With the few coins returned to him on his release, he bought a card and stamp and mailed it later that day. He had written: "Father: please forward this to Maria. Maria: The village is Mazareni. I'm with the Pigulea family. Come as soon as you can. I love you—Constantin."

He reckoned it would take at least three or four days until it reached Bucharest. Maria should have it after another day or so. Could he hope for a visit in a week's time, or perhaps ten days? The true countdown had finally started.

His hosts continued to be kind and generous toward him. But they also appeared uneasy at times. Later he found out that they knew of his "story," the books, his politics, and the stay at Sighet. Were they afraid, or perhaps they felt in awe of his accomplishments? Or maybe they simply didn't know how to approach him. Should he be regarded as a brother in suffering? Constantin looked at them and saw another face of the tragedy that had befallen their country. In them he recognized once again the devastation brought on by the Soviets and their Romanian Communist allies. The sad fate of the country had become the great equalizer—all united in despair.

At first he couldn't get enough to eat. The incessant hunger of the last five years was slowly satisfied. He relished every meal, chasing away memories of barley derivatives eaten three times a day. He wondered if the woman found him obsessed with food, which he was. But then again she would understand by looking at him: physically he was a shadow of his former self. Now he could afford to eat as much as he could, with the new worry of putting on, rather than losing weight, as in his youth. But he also discovered how the body, starved for years, rebelled at first against large portions of richer foods. Craving protein, he had asked the Piguleas about the availability of meat. He was told it had almost completely disappeared from the market since 1950.

"Disappeared?" he asked incredulously. "You could find anything before: chicken, turkey, pork, veal, fish. . . ."

"It's all gone now," Rada said.

"How could it be gone? Don't people raise pigs and chickens any longer?"

"Not really. They can keep a few birds or a pig for themselves. The rest of the livestock is in cooperatives now."

"Cooperatives?"

"Yes, people's lands have been gathered up. Peasants are working together in these cooperatives, and the state sells what they grow or raise."

"So where are the chickens?"

"I guess this plan isn't going well; I wouldn't know, Professor. . . ." Pigulea's voice started trailing off. All of a sudden he feared repercussions, having been warned not to talk politics with his boarder.

As the first week moved along, Constantin imagined the progress of his letter. The old priest must have received it and rushed to Maria that very day or at the latest, on the morrow. She would have, of course, been waiting on pins and needles for a sign. What followed was less clear: did they have the money for the train tickets? Was she well enough to travel? Would Dinu and Mona come along, too? With each passing day he felt increasingly anxious and agitated, unable to sit still or stare at the sky any longer. This lasted until his first Friday night in Mazareni when he was summoned to the police station. Fear overtook him again, expecting the very worst and bracing for it.

The policeman said, "Your wife and family are coming to visit tomorrow." Constantin could barely hide his elation. "Remember the rules: they can't live here. We're watching you."

He nodded. "Do they need to register?"

"No. We don't get too many visitors around here; I know who gets on and off the train." For whatever reason, the policeman thought that was funny and he broke out into stupid laughter.

Constantin woke up early Saturday morning, bursting with anticipation, as the train was to pull in at around 8:00 A.M. He had asked Rada if he could boil some water and wash up before heading to the station. Then he shaved himself using soap. He had gone to the village store the previous day looking for shaving cream and soap. The former wasn't stocked: "I haven't carried it in a long time," he was told, so he bought two bars of "all purpose" soap. He had never heard of this item, as prior to 1950, one had shaving cream, body and laundry soap and so on. They had all been replaced now by a more proletarian "all-purpose" light-yellow greasy bar wrapped in thick white paper.

He then combed the little hair he had left on his otherwise bald pate. There was no mirror in the hut so he tried catching his reflection on a window. Would Maria be able to recognize him? He barely recognized himself: an old, bald, rail-thin man. Who would have thought he was only 54 years old?

The summer's morning air was still fresh, and he walked to the station almost mechanically, emotion choking him up. The long five-year wait was finally distilled into these few last minutes on the train platform. As he walked along, memories of their last moments together rushed through and overwhelmed him.

"Leave the past alone," he warned himself. "That was then, and this is now. We at least still have a life. We've survived and we'll be together again."

The air suddenly felt thick and still. Where was the train? Finally a crawling grey silhouette bellowing smoke sluggishly pulled into the station and came to a stop. And there was his Maria, thinner, grayer; but the same wide smile illuminated her face, and her dark eyes shone bright. He spotted Dinu at her side, a man now, also thinner and more rugged, bright blue eyes dancing in a smile. Looking at him, did they think they saw a ghost? A silent gasp and glimmer of disbelief fleetingly passed through Dinu's face, while Maria literally jumped into her husband's arms. Enough embraces and kisses followed to fill up the five long years of desperate loneliness.

Constantin was back, just as Maria had whispered to him when he was "escorted" from their house.

A torrent of questions was unleashed, followed by stories as they clung to one another, afraid to let go, all talking at once. Tears of joy and sadness flowed freely those first few hours, mingled with laughs and smiles.

They walked to a nearby field, wishing to revel in each other's presence away from other eyes. Holding both his wife's and son's hands, Constantin said his tales could wait. He first had to know what had happened to his family these last five years.

But once Maria's story began, it felt almost surreal to him, the absent observer whose presence at the center of the web had triggered it all. He listened to her tale, again reliving his arrest. She told of her worry and constant inquiries about his disposition, and fears that he may have perished. He heard of the hurtful response from the local police, and then rumors of the old guard being taken to prison. Then she recounted Dinu's new job working construction, and finally having their house and all their possessions taken away.

At this point the nausea began to build up until he whispered: "Excuse me," walked away, doubled over, and threw up. Maria and Dinu exchanged worried glances, unsure of what to do until Constantin returned by their side and shrugged his shoulders.

"Something I ate didn't sit right. . . ."

He didn't wish to tell Maria how sickened he was by the enormity of her ordeal, nor could he worry her further by falling apart at this junction. He breathed in deeply, then out and tried to relax, wishing the nausea away. Then he noticed Maria had brought a little picnic lunch.

She was fretting, "Dear, please, would you be able to eat something?" Constantin nodded his head, thinking of the sacrifices she must have made to bring these refreshments along. The three of them ate sandwiches and some fruit while sitting on the grass.

"Maybe the rest can wait, until our next visit?" she asked her husband.

"No, if you can stand the retelling, I want to hear about what happened next, after you lost the house. It helps fill in the years, as if I were there, and brings us closer together."

Maria reached over and touched her husband's hand. "Very well, dear," and carried on with her tale.

Chapter Thirty
SURVIVING COMMUNISM

Maria, Mona and Dinu were assigned two rooms in a decrepit-looking house located in one of Bucharest's slums. The surrounding streets were lined with tinsmiths, pretzel stands, and gypsies selling flowers and sunflower seeds. Matronly-looking women brought out stools; sitting in front of their dwellings they viewed the outdoor scene. Some wore rollers in their hair and others came out in slippers and a housecoat. A tramway passed through Maria's new street and shook the ground each time.

One of the policemen showed Maria to her room. It had soil for a floor, an anemic light bulb and no windows. "Where's the bathroom? The kitchen?" she wanted to know.

"The facilities (meaning the hole) are outside. You wash up in your room and share the stove with the other families."

With this brief explanation, they handed Dinu a piece of paper stating the new address, and took leave.

With the men gone, Maria sat down on the mattress and burst into tears. Hollowed, drained, and devastated, she cried and cried for what certainly seemed like hours. The last thing she remembered before falling asleep was Dinu, with his head on his knees, holding her hand, while Mona stared silently at the walls.

When she woke up, they looked around their surroundings and found them barely habitable. In the meantime Wanda, Emil's wife, had been alerted to the events of the morning and had rushed over immediately.

"You can't stay in this disgusting hole, it's a pigsty."

"The police said we have to, or they might come to arrest us otherwise."

"Nonsense, you're not officially moving anywhere; you'll be staying with family for a while, that's all."

"We can't burden you in that small apartment. It is better you take care of the grandparents if you wish."

"I am coming over from their new place. It's in a parochial home on the grounds of the Mavrogheni church. They're in a small but clean room. The apartment they share has a kitchen and bathroom with running water," Wanda said insistently. "Listen, you are the ones who need help. Please pick up your bags and come along with me."

Suitcase in hand, they followed Wanda out of the building. First a tram, and then a bus, were taken to her apartment across town. An hour later they arrived, hot, sweaty, tired, and dirty. Maria would later be unable to recall how long she had wandered the streets of Bucharest. It seemed so awfully long, though less than a day had passed since the evacuation.

That evening they were all able to enjoy a comfortable bed, a kitchen, and a bathroom with hot running water, the minimal comforts of a normal, civilized dwelling. But their housing situation was only temporary. On the one hand, Wanda and Emil's apartment was too small for its four occupants and three guests. On the other, new rules were issued forbidding citizens to live anywhere without official papers "assigning" them to a particular address. The offenders and those offering shelter were both subject to fines and other repercussions.

In desperation Dinu turned to an acquaintance working at the housing division of City Hall. A paper trail was begun, more like a charade. It started with the home having been vacated by the family's "departure." By doing so they had "generated" an empty house for the authorities. In exchange, the family was promised an authorization to live "somewhere else," location unspecified. The catch was that Dinu, his mother and sister had to find this other unnamed space themselves.

They were aided this time by Dinu's friend Bebe Ghitulescu, the one who had gone on to the construction school first. Bebe's father, an attorney, owned a three-bedroom apartment and was gracious enough to invite Maria and her children to move in as soon as the famous authorization came through.

Bebe and his brother shared a room, and his parents another. Maria, Mona and Dinu now moved into the third. Dinu and Bebe were away during the week at the construction site, so more space was then available to the other occupants. During their weekend visits, it felt awfully tight, but they were among friends and grateful to have a roof over their heads.

This arrangement unfortunately didn't last long. Dinu was away at work when one of the same men who had evacuated them from the house, Comrade Weber, showed up at the Ghitulescu apartment.

"Where's Dinu?" he had yelled. "I'll slap his face when I see him! How dare he move from the rooms I had assigned to his family!"

"He's away at work," said Maria. "Besides, here's the authorization stating we were allowed to find our own housing." She handed him the paper.

"It's no good. The police have to endorse the housing papers. We didn't stamp it."

"Dinu was told it was perfectly valid," Maria insisted.

"I just told you it isn't. As for Dinu, he'll get what he deserves when he returns on Saturday."

She shivered; was her son now targeted, too? "Will you need to see him?"

"That's none of your business." Handing her a paper, he said, "And this is your new address. Pack up and get going."

She glanced at the paper. The address was different from the original one, thank God. "Could it be any worse?' Maria thought to herself.

"As for you," Weber continued and turned to Mr. Ghitulescu. "You get something, too." He handed him a paper. "We are confiscating two of your bedrooms. The assigned families should arrive later today or tomorrow."

Ghitulescu shook his head in dismay. "This is what traitors who aid the capitalist beasts get," Weber spat out with a sneer, and then he stormed out. As for Comrade Weber, he never pursued his threats against Dinu. Once he established on a subsequent visit that the family did indeed live in the assigned space, he lost interest in carrying out a vendetta.

Maria was assigned two rooms in another shabby quarter. The relative improvement consisted of a wooden floor, a window, and a couple of light fixtures. Several rooms were lined up along a long hallway, and from there one went into an inner courtyard with a cold water pump. Opposite was a little gate that led to the "facilities."

On her first day there, Maria met a neighbor, a woman named Silva. She appeared to be in her fifties and wore a pale dress with sturdy, shapeless shoes. Maria introduced herself and used only her first name. Had the neighbors been informed of her identity? If so, would she be considered an "oppressor"? Would they relish her newfound misery? Or would they understand her plight and feel pity? Maria decided to keep their identity quiet for the time being.

Silva slowly sized up the other woman. "Come. I'll show you around."

"Yes, please, thank you," Maria said.

"Here's the yard; you see the door at the back?" She nodded her head. "That's where the facilities are." Silva walked her across the courtyard. "And here's the kitchen and the phone."

Maria took stock of an antiquated stove, some cupboards, and a table with chairs.

Silva continued, "Here's where we keep the food," and pointed to a pantry like closet. "We've labeled the shelves with our names."

"How many are here?"

"Four families."

Silva added, shaking her head. "Watch out for Gicu. He's married to Florica; they sleep in the room to the left of yours. I think he's not right in the head." She then pointed to the table and counter. "One more thing: we take turns cleaning."

Maria glanced around; judging by the look of the house, that hadn't happened in quite a while.

"I must go to work now," she heard Silva say. "I'll see you tonight and remember to keep the door locked at all times."

Maria didn't ask why; she didn't even want to guess.

Family and friends rallied to her side, though most had little to share. Some gave Maria a few furniture items; for instance, her other sister-in-law, Lelia, brought over a rug and some blankets. Her friend Suzana, Titel's wife, provided a table and a couple of chairs. Cousin Jana offered a floor lamp, and someone else added curtains and an armoire. For the sake of her son, Maria wished to give the place the semblance of a home, while making do with the little they had. Dinu came to this new "home" after a hard week away at work, and that first Saturday he was greeted with fresh flowers in a tin can.

They barely survived on his modest salary. He gave his mother more than half, keeping the rest for his housing and food needs on the road. Maria, together with another cousin named Geta, started making costume jewelry. Geta procured the stones, such as amethyst and amber, and the metallic links and silk thread from a nameless "source." They made necklaces, bracelets, and earrings, which were sold through trusted acquaintances and friends. Extreme care had to be taken, as any private business and craft was strictly prohibited. These generated a profit for the individual, and "personal gains" were a thing of the past, vivid reminders of the "capitalist oppressors." If caught, the women would have faced a jail sentence. But the money was desperately needed, so they carried on with their trade. Another source of sporadic income was the gloves, scarves, and sweaters knitted and crocheted by Maria.

Unlike Maria, many had been allowed to take furniture and varied household items from the confiscated houses. And so the central flea market of Bucharest gradually became a "social" destination in the early 1950s. Some joked, saying it was the new gathering place of "tout" (all) Bucharest, in the Francophile style that many still remembered. Shabbily dressed, sad-looking ladies selling expensive silver teapots or fine Rosenthal porcelain became a familiar sight on Saturdays. The market also provided rumors, gossip, and news, and some went there simply to "stay in touch."

Maria now focused only on the day at hand. She went about her chores, visited at times with the family and a handful of close friends, and cooked a special meal for Dinu on Sundays. She disciplined herself not to think of the future, as one couldn't guess what it had in store. She woke up and went to sleep every single day thinking of her husband, but when months and then years passed without news from Constantin, she feared the worse.

In mid-1952 his distant cousin Viorica, who had been most generous toward the family throughout their ordeal, called to say, "Could you come over today or tomorrow?"

"Are you all right? Did something happen?"

Maria immediately felt a panic seizing her body. Whenever something critical happened, one never wanted to share it over the phone, as conversations were monitored by the police. "It has to be awful," she immediately told herself. Her gut feeling was that it had to do with Constantin, and a wave of nausea overwhelmed her.

Viorica must have sensed her fear. "Maria, we're all healthy, the whole family, thank God. Just visit when you can."

Needless to say, Maria jumped on a tram and less than an hour later, she was sitting in Viorica's living room. She was greeted with sweet, strong Turkish coffee and a homemade butter pastry. Viorica's husband had been allowed to continue working as an engineer, a profession on the critical-job list, and his better income made for more plentiful food.

"My friend Sanda Anghel came by; you may recall her, the little red-haired busybody. Well, she had come across someone who had been in the Sighet jail. He was passing through Bucharest, en route to an undisclosed location."

The words Sighet jail made Maria freeze. She had heard of a maximum-security prison in the far north, and now she was able to put a name on that dreadful institution. She steadied herself holding on to the mantelpiece.

"Is he dead?"

"No, Maria, for Christ's sake, he was alive earlier this year."

"Did he send word? Did he say anything?"

"No, they can't talk among themselves. Constantin was seen walking in the courtyard, and that's all this fellow could tell me via Sanda."

For the first time in over two years, she had word that at least her husband was still alive. She breathed a little easier. "Any other details?"

Viorica face seemed suddenly grim; she wrapped her arm around Maria's waist, "Nothing you would want to know right now, please trust me. Let's just continue praying for his safe return."

Maria pondered. Viorica was right. Perhaps hearing about the sheer awfulness of Constantin's life might be too much to bear, and send her over the edge. So, she went back home and woke up the next day thinking about him and every day after that, too. But there were no further news. She kept telling herself, "any day now . . ." but months passed and they again became years.

Survival became the focus of their lives as the economic situation continued to deteriorate throughout the early 1950s. In less than a decade, Romania had gone from the breadbasket of Europe to a wasteland. Meat, margarine, marmalade, soap, sugar, flour, shoes were available only on "coupons." These were allocated based on income and profession, and only available to those living in cities. The markets and stores became virtually empty, guarded by sulking, rude saleswomen. One sometimes needed two or three visits to get enough cabbage, potatoes, and beans to feed one's family. For other available items, only a certain amount could be purchased at once.

Everyone on the streets and in the markets looked shabby, thin, and sad now. Smiles and laughs had completely disappeared. It was rumored police sometimes stopped people who were "looking funny" at posters praising the accomplishments of the Worker's State and the Communist Party. So it was best not to bring attention to yourself; walk just so, not too slowly and not too fast, and preferably look down. Someone had advised Maria, "Whatever you do, don't look different." She was in no danger of that, even if she tried. Her coat, sweaters, and skirts were worn out, her shoes almost falling apart, and the stockings mended.

Dinu continued to work on road construction sites. Projects took him around Bucharest, but more often than not also further away, into Moldova or the southeastern part of the country known as Dobrogea. When assigned to these distant sites he would take the train home on Saturday afternoon, spend Sunday morning with his mother, and then head back for another week of work. The crews varied from site to site, but some of the professional staff, such as engineers, accountants, and managers, was periodically assigned to the same project. During this time he became friends with a manager named Grigore Ioan, the two men working together several times during the early 1950s. The son of a pre-war diplomat and an editor in his youth, Grigore had become a pilot during the war and had fought in Bessarabia and Odessa. Now, like so many from "unhealthy" social backgrounds, he had reinvented himself, learning a trade. Dinu and Grigore's friendship would last for a lifetime.

Work on the road construction projects was monotonous. One woke up early, had a cup of tea and some bread, and worked all morning. Lunch was in a hall of sorts, where sour-looking women delivered food to the managers' table and the workers picked up theirs at a counter. The "menu" was set, with no choices; soup, potatoes, beans, cabbage, rice, and polenta were ubiquitous. The meat helpings were small, rare, and of dubious quality. After lunch the men worked again until the end of the day. The routine was broken up every two weeks on payday when the occasion called for cheap wine or beer. A celebration of sorts was held once in a while, usually honoring the National Day or the party leaders.

The fear and concerns of their daily lives continued to worsen, reaching a peak in 1952. As mistrust pervaded one's existence, people became fearful of neighbors, friends, and of course, the powerful secret police units named "Securitate." A new wave of arrests was launched once again along social lines—someone had to be blamed for the failed economic state. Constantin's friend Alex Rosetti, who had helped publish his books in the 1930s, was dismissed from the University in 1952. This happened despite his leaning left of center since 1947, and having shown a somewhat favorable attitude towards the new regime. By 1952 the political hierarchy found him "bourgeois minded" anyway and lacking a "Marxist orientation" and removed him from the teaching ranks. Alex still fared better than others though, because he was never arrested, nor was his house confiscated.

Many of those arrested were sent to a forced labor camp to build a canal connecting the Danube River to the Black Sea. It was meant to facilitate commercial transport to move much-needed imports. Years later, people would learn how many perished there in the blustery cold winter or the harsh summer heat, dying of extreme exhaustion and countless untreated illnesses.

To make matters worse, food and clothing shortages continued to parallel the growing political terror. And if this weren't bad enough,

Romania experienced possibly its harshest winter in a century in 1953–1954. It made the winter of 1941 seem mild in retrospect. It snowed and snowed until white piles mounted up to the second floor. Many stayed indoors for days on end. Those who lived on the ground floor, like Maria, dug out tunnels every day so they could go buy bread and milk. Firewood became scarce for cooking and heating, and the gas pressure was low. Dark days and nights blended into one another. Titel, the pediatric surgeon, told Maria of children dying in the bitter cold. His brother, an internist, said how many old people perished that winter as well.

The roads out of town were impassable, and trains didn't run for days. Once some of the tracks opened up, Dinu was able to visit for the weekend. He described the eerie feeling of watching the train advance on narrow tracks lined by snow reaching the roof of the carriages and threatening to collapse on them at every turn.

The cold eventually gave way, and the snow melting that spring seemed symbolically to herald a "softening" of the political atmosphere as well. This had actually begun a year earlier in 1953 after the death of Stalin, the tyrannical Soviet dictator and leader. Arrests abated, and various political initiatives were slowed down. But it still didn't mean that anxious families received news of their loved ones. This uncertainty continued unabated, and Constantin's fate remained unknown to his family, just like that of his brother, Horia, who was arrested in 1951.

Life somehow went on. Mona was married early on, in late 1950. Her husband, Ion Agirbiceanu, was the son of a priest and novelist. He was also Romania's premier nuclear physicist, who had been trained in Oxford, England before the war. The Communists needed their scientists, particularly ones with such unique skills. So Ion, despite his "unhealthy" social connections (via his father the priest), was allowed to carry on his work.

Maria moved once again in 1953 into a couple of rooms in a parochial house. The warmth of this new home and the support of the priest and his wife provided a sharp contrast to their previous cold, crowded house. A year later the authorities "approved" yet another move. This time Maria and Dinu joined her parents, who since 1950 had lived in a different parochial house. There they shared the residence with yet another couple. So three families now lived in a three-room apartment and shared a small kitchen and one bathroom. Maria again tried to make the best of it; though crowded, they were together and the small apartment started resembling a home. Its proximity to parks and one of the large lakes meant easy strolls and a quick escape from the dreariness of daily life.

Some said time stagnated, while others claimed days blended into one another and flew by. An unprecedented wave of rumors swept Bucharest in early 1955: political prisoners were going to be released. No one could say when and how, but reliable sources had quoted the information as "imminent." For five years Maria had steeled herself and refused to listen to the gossip, to avoid false hope. She dismissed this latest round as well, telling friends she didn't believe a word of it.

Then on July 7, just after dawn, the phone rang. Once again Maria stood frozen: early and late calls were mostly harbinger of bad news.

Dinu answered it. "Yes, good morning, Aunt Viorica."

Maria's curiosity piqued; why would Viorica call so early? She then heard her son's reply. "No, no one came."

Silence; she then saw her son turn white as a sheet, listening intently. "Oh, my God, that's extraordinary, thank you so much, I'll tell her right away."

Dinu hung up and almost swept his mother up in his arms, "Father is out, father is alive!" He released his grip. "He called Viorica this morning, on his way to an assigned domicile in a village named Mazareni."

"What else, what else?" Maria asked impatiently, her heart beating fast.

"He didn't say much else; it seems he was being escorted there. He would send word as soon as he had an address."

Fate had finally smiled upon them: she could believe and dream again of a future. Having waited five long years, Maria found herself glancing at the clock every hour. Would there be another phone call? Had something else happened?

Her prayers were answered when the priest from the church near their old house visited days later. Constantin had sent him a postcard addressed to Maria, saying he was in Mazareni awaiting his family's visit. The priest was asked to forward it to Maria. The man said that he had known of them being evacuated back in 1950, though he had lost touch afterwards. He inquired among his parishioners who had known the family and was given their new address. Without further ado, he said that he took a tram and came over to deliver Constantin's message.

Wasting no time themselves, Maria and Dinu took a local train to Mazareni on Saturday, but not before sending word to the official authorities. They had bought whatever food they could find—cheese, bread, salami—having heard awful tales of the starvation in jail. Soap and toothpaste and a couple of shirts and some socks were added.

The train ride was maddening, barely crawling along, stopping at nearly every village on the way. The heat was oppressive, and steam enveloped fields and floated around the scrawny trees like a shroud. They dozed off at times, only to wake up surrounded by the same parched, arid land. The trip seemed endless, almost symbolic of their five-year journey back to each other. Until all of a sudden, the train slowed down and came to a stop besides a dusty sign: "Mazareni."

A frail-looking man stood on the platform, his baggy pants flapping in the light breeze. The long wait was over.

Chapter Thirty-One
THE PRISON DIARY

Listening to his wife's tale, Constantin felt sick again. Her plight and that of his son and daughter was awful, and any self-pity he may have felt about his own misfortune paled when it came to that of his loved ones. Tears welled up in his eyes as she continued, while he clutched her hand tighter and tighter. Maria had survived, but the price had been steeper than he could have imagined. It was perhaps better he had not known any of this travail while in prison. The guilt he had experienced on many a day had ripped at him and tried to break his resolve. Had he known the truth, it might have been too much to bear.

"Father, I know you said your tale could wait, but I think it shouldn't. As you said, 'it fills in the years and brings us closer.'"

Constantin proceeded to give his wife and son a sanitized account of his years in jail. "There is so much time ahead for all the gruesome details," he thought. Instead, he highlighted the positive aspect of the inmates' camaraderie and the sporadic kindness of some of the guards. They wanted to know who had survived and who had perished, and as he recounted the names of those lost (as known at that time), it was Maria's turn to shed tears of sadness.

Constantin wanted to know if any of the families had been notified of their losses though he anticipated the answer before even asking the question.

"Why, we must get in touch with them . . . The Bratianu's . . . the family of Iuliu Maniu . . . Manoilescu's . . . Maria, next time you must bring me paper to jot down notes for them."

"Father, it might be better not to put anything in writing," said Dinu. "The mail is opened and read these days. God forbid they find out you're circulating stories about Sighet, and then you land back there again."

Maria, terrified at the prospect, reassured him, "We'll discreetly get in touch with whomever we can and gently break the news. Please let us handle this. As for now, the hour is advancing and I am hungry. How about we head to your house?"

"Dear, I must prepare you . . . it's not exactly a house. It's really more like a room."

"Well, whatever it is, let's go eat and meet your hosts."

From the field they walked back to the Pigulea's hut. Maria took out the remaining supplies she had brought along, and the women busied themselves preparing a meal.

"Here, we have a special surprise for you. We were lucky enough to get a bottle of white wine."

"Wine! My goodness, it has been more than five years since I've had a taste. What a treat. . . ." And his eyes shone happily.

Constantin had obtained written permission for his visitors to stay one night. Rada strung a curtain over the entry hall to give them some privacy, while Dinu slept in the barn. But when the time came for Maria to head home the following day, she hesitated. The fear of losing her husband again paralyzed her, while Constantin tried to assure her that he would be there on her next visit.

"How do you know?" she had asked, her voice wavering.

"I do because I believe in it. This is how I sustained myself these last years. You wish for something so strongly until you make it happen."

Her face lit up: her rock was back.

After that, the status of her visitation rights changed quickly. Within weeks officials dropped hints how exceptions could be made "under certain circumstances," which involved wine, cigarettes, and food items in exchange for "a blind eye." Bribes had become a ubiquitous part of daily life, and goods, services, and medical visits were bartered alike.

Maria's stays became longer—days at first, then weeks. From the second visit on, she brought much-needed items of clothing, some medicines, canned vegetables, and cookies, and "the great communicator"—cash. They also shared some of these items with their hosts, to whom both were so very grateful. The Piguleas, kind and generous with the little they had, had allowed Maria to share Constantin's bed by the front door. A new ritual developed, with a curtain hung at night and taken down in the morning. Maria helped with the cleaning and washing and folding of the laundry, as without electricity one couldn't consider an iron. She also cooked, seemingly all day long, as feeding Constantin became her focus that summer. It proved difficult at first, as his emaciated body struggled to accept rich foods in large portions. But little by little he became accustomed once again to a more normal diet and started getting stronger.

On his second visit a week later, Dinu asked his father about their mutual profession, "What are we going to do now?"

"We'll set down to work, that's what we'll do."

"Work? With whom? How?" he asked.

"Yes, work. Like before," Constantin insisted.

"In these times? With this regime?"

"Do you have an alternative?"

"No, but . . ."

"You still want to be an historian, or would you rather go on working construction sites?"

"Of course I'd love to teach and write, but. . . ."

"Dinu, no buts. We'll just have to figure out a way to function within these new parameters. They'll need classical historians sooner or later. But there will be no political compromise. We won't rewrite history," Constantin said, his cheeks flushed. "Listen, boy: the thought of working again kept me alive for five years. Next time bring some historical magazines and reviews published in the last five years. And pen, ink, and paper, so I can take notes."

His son nodded, amazed once again by his father's fortitude.

As the summer wound down, the scorching heat started losing its power, and by September the earth began smelling fresh again. Constantin still woke up early, unable to shake the routine of his prison years. Once light hit the walls of their hut, his eyes were wide-opened. Cherishing his newly found freedom, his thoughts often wandered back to the five long years of misery and despair in prison, and to those who had perished. Survival guilt took hold at times, threatening to break his resolve. He tried to remind himself that life went on, but his heart bled for all the tragic, senseless deaths, and for those who might still be in detention. An idea, vague at first, began to take hold: he would write his prison memoirs and start right away while the details were fresh. With pain, emotions, and memories still raw, they would shape the writing.

"Maria, I need more paper when you return next Saturday."

"It is hard to come by these days," she said. "I'll do my best. What do you need it for?"

"I'll try to write an account of the last five years."

"Oh, my God, do you realize what will happen if anybody finds out?" Maria asked in alarm.

"I'll be careful, work during the day when I'm alone . . ."

"Constantin, you could be sent back to jail . . . even if someone just claims to have heard of what you're writing, let alone if they get their hands on it."

"Maria, I need to do this," he said, holding her hands. "For the generations to come, so they can learn of our sacrifice. It will also be a tribute for the ones who died."

"You realize it will never be published. They'll kill you and all of us a thousand times first."

"This is for the future. One day it shall come to light," he insisted.

She stared hard at her husband. Pleading with him led nowhere when it came to his work. "Promise to tell no one else. You can't trust anybody these days. Promise you'll hide the papers from the Piguleas."

"I do."

He thought about the best hiding place as his writing progressed, but feared anywhere in the hut would attract undue attention. So he kept the pages in a neat stack, top sheets covered in innocuous historical factoids. One generally never thought of looking in the most obvious place. Besides, he wondered at his host's ability to read, having never seen a book or newspaper in the hut. The Piguleas in the meantime never asked what he was doing. They knew he was a man of letters and assumed he was carrying on with his craft.

Work restored a cadence to his days, the same structure he had struggled so hard to maintain even at Sighet. He started out with an account of the arrest, then the travel from Bucharest to Sighet. He wrote down notes about the layout of the jail, names of those who perished and of prison guards. He jotted down what they ate, how they filled their days, and the humiliation, abomination, and tragedy of it all. The account took shape, and soon a first draft was ready. He planned to add to it once he returned to Bucharest and heard tales from the others.

A couple of months later, he told Maria, "I have finished for now and need to figure out a safe hiding place." If the book were found, it would have meant mandatory life in prison for Constantin. It would have also brought long jail terms for the rest of the family and likely even those he lived with, the Piguleas.

"It can't stay in the family; we're all under the microscope," Maria said. "And besides, we can't have it at home in Bucharest where we share the apartment with the Chivus."

They reluctantly went over friends' names: anybody entrusted would be placed at risk. They eventually settled on Nick Caracaleanu, who had been Constantin's ministerial secretary. In 1950 Nick had seen his legal practice dismantled. But his political activity was deemed minor, so he avoided arrest and his house was never confiscated. After a few years as a clerk in a factory, he had recently been reinstated. Would he be willing to safeguard a manuscript that could potentially land him in jail?

Nick came to visit them in October, and as they walked through the field on an overcast day, he was told, "I have been writing down my prison memoirs."

Nick stared incredulously. "Weren't you afraid the peasants would peek at it?"

"No, not really. I don't bother them and they leave me alone. They seem like honest people. Besides, I'm not even sure they can read."

"You realize you'd never be able to publish it," added Nick.

"I know. Well, at least for now. If things ever change, there may be a chance. . . . Anyway, I wrote it for the future. They'll need to know what happened here."

"You're barely out of prison and you can relive the horror?" Nick asked incredulously. "It's all fresh in my head now; it is important to be accurate with the names and the details. . . . Nick, would you be willing to hide this manuscript somewhere safe?" Maria and Constantin held their breaths awaiting an answer.

Nick didn't even blink. "Of course."

Together they rolled the handwritten pages and placed them in a heavy glass bottle. Nick wrapped it in a towel, and never removed the bag off his shoulder until he reached his front door. After scrutinizing his house, attic, and cellar, he decided against them. The following morning he buried the bottle in the garden, at the foot of the cherry tree. "May you see once again the light of day," he whispered before smoothing the soil and crossing himself. (It was later published in America after the fall of the Soviet Union: Giurescu, Constantin C. *Five Years and Two Months in the Sighet Penitentiary.* English Trans. Mihai Farcas and Stephanie Barton-Farcas. Boulder, Colorado. East European Monographs, 1994.)

As for Constantin, he felt ready to move on once the manuscript was finished and handed over to Nick. The writing had been cathartic, but it had also made him live in the past. From tomorrow on, he would live in the present, while peeking into and planning the future.

A chapter in his life had been closed, in a manner of speaking. As for the sorrow, it would always remain deeply seated, with the remembrance of the lives stolen, a grand society and its way of life pulverized in a few brief years.

The fall season at Mazareni was unlike any Constantin could recall. He knew what to expect in Bucharest where old trees lining the boulevards went through the foliage dance of yellow, rust, brown, and dead. He remembered the same autumnal colors side by side with bright firs in the mountains. But Mazareni was a village in the midst of the vast low-lying grain belt. There were but a few scrawny trees, their vigor drained by the long, dry summer heat. So autumn was only heralded by the change in temperature and in the peasants' daily activities.

Cooler temperatures meant longer walks and also meant easier travel conditions, with people, pets, and bags of sausages no longer packed side by side in steaming cars. Suddenly, more friends came to visit. Perhaps some had waited to see if such visits would be frowned upon by the authorities. Word of mouth traveled fast in Bucharest, and people quickly knew if "so and so was interviewed by the police after visiting X at Mazareni."

Adrian came to visit in late September. Their friendship had gone from strength to strength since the fateful meeting aboard the *Transylvania* in the middle of the stormy Black Sea. He jumped out of a car as the train was coming to a stop and shouted, "I have brought with me a bunch of nobodies!"

Behind him climbed down the doctors Gica Manescu and the brothers Vereanu, all dear friends and fishing and hunting companions of years past. As none of them had been involved in politics, they had been allowed to continue practicing. Gica and Titel were surgeons, Titel's specialty being pediatrics, while Nelu Vereanu was an internist. They quickly filled their friend in on their lives. Nelu's private practice had been shut down, and he'd been assigned to a "municipal" hospital. Gica and Titel worked in state hospitals as well. Upon departing they reassured their friend they would all be fishing together before too long.

But the visits that continued to bring the greatest joy were those of his family, Maria and the children foremost. Maria spent increasingly more time with him as the local police granted approval for her stay with relative ease. Had they become accustomed to her presence and realized she wasn't a "troublemaker"? Perhaps they, too had hearts? Or maybe they simply didn't care after a while?

Maria and Constantin spent hours talking, as there wasn't much else to do in Mazareni. He heard how Bucharest had changed to the point of "you wouldn't recognize it." The city looked drab and dark, and its people were clad in nondescript coats and shoes purchased with "coupons." Maria told him who was dead, dying, or alive, and recounted the many funerals attended in the past five years. She also recalled the flea market where friends sold plates and vases in order to buy more bread. Everyone they'd known had been touched in some way, a whole society decimated by the new regime.

He heard his in-laws were living on a modest pension in a small flat with Maria. He also found out that his brother, Horia, now released from jail, was working as an office clerk. Constantin's sister, Lelia, and her family of four, whose house had been confiscated, were living in a tiny apartment and trying to pick up the pieces. After first hearing news of his siblings, he was finally overjoyed when both were able to visit him in September.

His brother-in-law Emil visited quite often. After his factory was confiscated and his law practice dismantled, he had been dispatched to do accounting work in a state-owned factory. The Communists could strip him of his factory, estate, and house, but couldn't take away his sense of humor. He impersonated party leaders, friends, his mother— no one was spared from his wit. Constantin also had the opportunity to reconnect with his daughter Mona, now a beautiful young woman, and met his son-in-law, Ion.

"How I wish I could have been at your wedding," he told Mona.

"But father, we didn't have one. You were arrested and we had just been thrown out of the house. We went to City Hall and signed a paper, that's what we did. Who do you think felt like having a celebration?"

But the issue of his return to Bucharest loomed large on his mind, particularly since the completion of the manuscript and without much to occupy him. One day he took Mona on a walk, just the two of them, and confided, "I survived at Sighet because I was determined to be with all of you again. But I don't know if I can make it through five more years in Mazareni."

"Father, we'll be with you every step of the way."

"I know you will. But everyone has a breaking point. I'm fifty-four years old. If I have to wait another five years, I'll be nearing retirement— a decade of my life wasted away."

Mona understood her father's unspoken plea. "I'll see what Ion and I can do."

Ion continued to hold a prominent research position at the National Physics Institute. Though not involved in politics through his work, he had access to some of the country's policymakers. Mona had her contacts, too, through trusted friend Adrian Brudariu, a well-connected lawyer.

Constantin spent days engrossed in books published since 1950, and filling in the news gaps from the past five years. He read and read and reached the conclusion: Romania was in for a long "occupation." People could continue to dream of the Americans coming to their rescue, but the historian in him saw the future. His country was to remain Communist for many years to come; the "Iron Curtain," so eloquently described by Winston Churchill, was there to stay.

And just as a bitter cold descended upon the dry lands in mid-November, stunning news was delivered by Mona. His release from Mazareni had been approved, with her lawyer friend's intervention with Prime Minister Groza having been successful.

He packed his few belongings and took leave from his hosts, grateful for their hospitality. They smiled shyly back, happy for him in their quiet way, and Rada handed him a sandwich for the journey.

After "checking out" at the police station, he headed to the train station. Skies were heavy and dark, and a cold wind sliced through his light coat. But nothing could dampen his happiness. The ordeal was over, his five-year forced domicile assignment miraculously commuted to five months.

He was homeward bound, to his beloved Bucharest.

PART VI
THE FINAL YEARS

Chapter Thirty-Two
BEGINNING THE CLIMB BACK

The journey back home was shrouded in rain, with steady drops falling on the train's windows while blustery, whistling wind sliced through the now empty cornfields. There was little to take in, and few passengers got on or disembarked. And there was also little to do, other than enjoy a cheese and salami sandwich he brought along for the ride. Constantin's thoughts wandered to the trip to Mazareni a few months earlier; it had been immediately after his release, escorted by a police guard. A feeling of elation suddenly overcame him:

"I am truly free now . . . why, I can even travel by myself again."

The simple things one took for granted had been stolen away from him during the past five years. Rediscovering them again brought the same delicious feeling a child had felt when being allowed to cross the street by himself, or when the young man had first sipped wine. He relished every moment of this newfound freedom.

It was late and dark when the train pulled into Bucharest's North Central Station. Unlike his arrival from Sighet a few months earlier, he could now roll down the window and lean out to scan the platform. They weren't crowded at that late hour, and he easily saw Maria hugging herself in what seemed like a light coat.

"Much too light for this cold weather," he told himself.

The next minute, with a small suitcase in hand, he was in her arms. Constantin had truly returned, just as Maria had predicted on the dark morning of his arrest in May 1950.

She guided him to a bus stop; the wait was brief, and once aboard they sat in silence. After so much anticipation, it was as if the adrenaline charging through him for so long had abruptly run out. For years he had reached deep down, focusing on survival and maintaining an intact mind—first at Sighet and then in Mazareni. Now very much alive and brimming with future projects, he was finally back home but completely drained of energy and eerily calm. He tried to think of the direction the bus was headed, but even that seemed too big of a challenge, so he closed his eyes. He could tell, however, that they were headed away from their old home. It was better this way; he wouldn't have to see the tattered remainders of their past life.

Maria was first to break the silence, her intuition surfacing once again. "You're so quiet. Have you perhaps noticed the bus is taking us away from our house?"

"How could she guess my thoughts?" he asked himself, while to Maria he uttered, "No, dear, I'm too tired to think. Besides, that's all in the past. We must begin to think about our tomorrows. As for right now, I am simply dreaming of something to eat."

She smiled, eyes brightening up. "You'll be pleased, dear."

She had saved food for days, and Mona and Viorica had also brought special treats, the family eager to make Constantin's first meal at home a memorable one. She couldn't wait to watch his face at the sight of the delicacies.

He suddenly looked around. It was nearly dark, and one could barely make out the outlines of the buildings and trees. Goodness how his vibrant, beautifully lit city had changed!

"Where are the streetlights, Maria?"

"There aren't many around. They've been missing for years," she replied.

Ever so methodical, he further inquired, "And they aren't being replaced?"

"No, as you see. They're probably too expensive. And no one seems to care if we twist our ankle on account of darkness."

For a while he tried to decipher some of the street signs; Maria had warned him that many streets had changed names in the last five years. But with the daylight now gone, he gave up, feeling too tired anyway.

"We're heading toward Kisselef," Maria said, knowing the name would elicit happy memories.

The name of the boulevard recalled to him their many walks to the park and the lakes, such a long time ago. Then the bus stopped, and they got off and walked a bit, and for a while he didn't recognize the neighborhood. After ten minutes or so, they turned onto a short, narrow street. His pace began to slow down, the many hours of travel and fatigue taking their toll.

"We're almost there," said Maria sensing her husband's exhaustion, and taking his arm she gently led the way.

She had told him that their apartment was in a house on the grounds of a church. So once he spotted the church spire, he knew they'd arrived. The two-story parochial house was surrounded by a large yard, and despite the darkness he noticed a couple of small dwellings.

Their flat was on the second floor. They shared it at the time with Maria's parents, Dinu, and another couple—Mr. Chivu and his blond, young, second wife. Each couple had a room while Dinu slept on a narrow sofa bed in the entry hall. The seven grownups shared the kitchen and a bathroom. Food supplies were kept on shelves, and the laundry was washed in a cauldron on the stove and hung to dry in the attic.

Maria's parents had been unable to travel to Mazareni and visit these past months. Despite being forewarned about the change in Constantin's appearance, Mrs. Mehedinti couldn't help but gasp at the sight of her son-in-law. Constantin thought she appeared unchanged, though the professor looked old and frail. After they hugged, Dinu lightened the mood by reminding everyone how hungry his father was. There was cheese on a platter, including feta, his favorite, together with bread and smoked bacon and salami. On a separate plate, he spotted cookies and fruit and a bottle of wine was in the middle of the table. His eyes opened wide. "What a feast!" He realized that they must have saved all this food for quite a while, and thanked everyone.

"You're right," replied Maria's mother who seemed to have lost none of her sharpness.

"And we did it gladly and from the bottom of our hearts," added Dinu, eager to intercede before his mother's reply started another argument.

"We all share the bathroom," Maria's mother continued to complain.

"That's what we did where I came from. Except we had no hot running water," replied her son-in-law. She didn't add anything else after that reminder.

They ate and talked and laughed, as he marveled at how good it felt to be surrounded by the family around the dinner table. Then Constantin's eyes began closing, sluggish after such a rich meal. "If you'll excuse me. . . ." He washed a bit and brushed his teeth, relishing the feeling of hot running water and clean scented soap. The last thing he remembered was how soft the pillow felt. It had been such a long time.

The next morning he was better able to take in his new surroundings. But more pressing business awaited him, first being the obligatory visit to the police precinct. There he needed to be registered and apply for a "Citizen ID," a socialist tool designed to track its citizens.

Maria had prepared him. "You don't speak without being spoken to, and you don't argue no matter what. Keep the dialogue at a minimum; anything can set them off."

With his discharge papers from Mazareni in hand, he walked up to one of the windows at the local precinct. The clerk looked them over and claimed to have never seen such documents.

"What's this, some new form?"

"It's my release from the forced domicile at Mazareni."

"And what I am supposed to do with it?" he asked.

"It's meant to confirm my identity, so you can understand why I am here. I am applying for an ID."

"It's no good. I need a birth certificate."

"I don't have one; it's gone. It was confiscated with everything else in my house five years ago," Constantin said.

"Can't do without it," the clerk insisted.

Constantin was losing his patience. But Maria gently tugged at his sleeve, having been through enough of these go-rounds in the past five years. She had thought of the official paper signed by the prime minister, which had allowed her husband to return to Bucharest ahead of schedule and had brought it along, too, just in case.

She removed it from her purse. "This release is signed by the prime minister. You think it might help you?"

The man turned pale and became quiet. Uneasy and confused, he added, "I'll need to see my supervisor."

"Why don't you do that, and we'll just sit here," Maria added.

Many minutes passed before he returned. "It's all right. Here are the forms you need to fill out. When you're ready, take them to window 7. They'll let you know when to come by and pick up the ID."

After filling out and turning in the forms, they returned home. In the pale sunlight, Constantin was now better able to make out his new surroundings. He took in the church, in the classic style of a late eighteenth-century Greek Orthodox house of faith. There were a few tombstones around it, some with monuments and statues. Just opposite the church was the statue of a prominent nineteenth-century historian. Was it mere coincidence or perhaps a good omen? The relative enclosure of the church and the thick trees behind the house gave one a sense of remoteness, despite its close proximity to the city center. He took it all in and thought, "I think I can work well here."

He took time rediscovering his city in the upcoming days. He could walk everywhere—to the city center, the academy, and the university, and of course to see his siblings. The buildings were the same, but the life had been extinguished from the city's soul. He saw sadness and hopelessness on people's faces and a tangible fear. The network of informers, which he had first encountered in prison, apparently pervaded the entire society. Even one's friends or relatives had taken to the practice in the hope of gaining a better position or an extra pound of meat. He was told that former politicians were especially monitored.

Maria had explained, "You need to be afraid at all times. You need to fear the secret police, and the uniformed police, and practically everyone else. There are clerks paid to monitor your whereabouts. As you have just been released from jail, you must certainly be targeted."

Maria's concerns were justified. Many years later some two hundred typed pages or so containing abundant details on Constantin's daily activities from 1956 to 1967 were returned to Dinu after he petitioned the new government for his father's police file.

As for now, the fear that had enveloped him in prison since 1950 was carried on outside its walls. Maria had added, "Be very cautious with the store clerks. Not only are they unpleasant, they're also dangerous. They've been known to report customers who complain about the lack of goods, or who come across as haughty."

He wanted to see this firsthand, so he visited several stores during his long walks. They were mostly empty, with few items on display. The saleswomen were invariably rude, chatting for minutes among themselves before tending to a customer. They also came across as condescending, almost delighting in telling people their item of choice wasn't available.

Staples such as flour, sugar, and butter were still sold on ration coupons in 1955. Meat was nowhere to be found. As for fish, people said they could hardly remember its taste. Some days you could buy eggs at the peasants' market, but not always. Clothing didn't fare any better. Affordable shoes were still on coupons and cost between 20–30 percent of Dinu's monthly wages. It wasn't easy, and they enlisted the help of friends, but little by little they managed to assemble a new wardrobe for Constantin. A suit, some shirts and socks, a couple of wool sweaters, and a pair of shoes—a bare minimum would have to do for now.

He also went to the peasants' market, finding it a sorry shadow of its former self, devoid of the bustle he remembered and enjoyed. He had already learned how most of the peasants' land had been confiscated by the state, and he could now see the results. The properties had been "glued" together to form jointly-owned so-called "cooperatives." It seemed like a noble idea, but as it often happens, it didn't translate well into practice. Six years after its inception, the results or lack thereof were obvious to all. People no longer felt an incentive to work hard, as the rewards and profits of their labor were no longer theirs. Though the bulk of the individual property had been confiscated, most were only allowed to keep a tiny plot to cover their family's needs. It was this land which generated the goods they now peddled to the market.

"Thank God many fruits and vegetables don't need much attention," thought Constantin, taking in the mountains of apples, potatoes, and cabbage lining up the market stalls.

But what struck him most was the eerie silence. He remembered people boisterously shouting and advertising their produce; instead, the peasants now quietly pointed things out. When you approached them, they'd whisper, "Sweet apples, sir, the best, freshly plucked from the garden," or "Try the rich creamy cheese." Shabbily dressed and gaunt-looking, they had fear etched on their faces, too.

Skies turned dark within days after his arrival, and sleet was followed by snow, restricting one's movement about town. Little by little Constantin realized they were all in a camp of sorts, albeit larger and with somewhat looser rules than where he had pined away for years.

The first month back went by fast without much really happening. He read voraciously, and going to the library gave purpose and structure to his days. He visited his siblings often and caught up on the family news. Horia had seen his military career terminated, and was working now as an office clerk. His sister Lelia's house had also been confiscated by the state. She and her family had moved into a rental, albeit of better quality than theirs, and in a pretty decent part of town. Lelia gathered the family for a special lunch one weekend, to celebrate the reunion of the family. Just like everyone else, she had saved for weeks, eager to make Constantin's first festive meal a memorable one.

Horia wanted to know, "What follows now?"

"What do you mean?"

"I mean, what will you do from now on?"

"I'll settle down to work."

"Work? What kind of work? You can't teach and you know they won't publish you either."

"It's bound to change sooner or later," was Constantin's reply.

Lelia and Horia exchanged knowing glances. Perhaps their brother was unwell after his ordeal, or perhaps he hadn't yet understood the new order. As for Constantin, he looked at them and glanced around the room. He saw faces resigned to the dull reality of their daily lives—drawn and tired and fearful. He had two options: either join them in their misery or carry on believing in his future.

"This can't last forever. Sooner or later they'll need true scientists again. Everything goes in cycles. My release, our release, is the first sign the ice is thawing."

"Whom do you want to work with?" asked Lelia's husband.

"I simply want to sit down to write again. I don't want to work with or for anyone in particular. But nor do I want to fold my arms and declare defeat. Is there an alternative?"

All kept silent, as they couldn't think of one.

Soon after his return Constantin received the phone call he had been waiting for: Nick had been released! Unlike Constantin, he had been allowed to come back home to Bucharest right away. Their reunion was joyous, though tinged by the deep sadness of the many who had not had a chance at this newly found freedom.

Though many delighted in seeing Constantin, some old acquaintances seemed less comfortable. Some were uneasy, perhaps even afraid of being seen with him. Others perhaps simply didn't know what to say: "Oh, and by the way, where were you these last five years?" would have hardly seemed appropriate. Gasps at his appearance and grimaces didn't help either.

"You can tell your true friends at times like this," he told Dinu. "Remember who helped you and who was kind to you. It's not the ones who only come to the parties."

And then all of a sudden Christmas 1955 was upon them. The holiday was no longer officially observed, as Communists were devout atheists and worship was frowned upon, but it was still celebrated in private. Churchgoers were tracked, and the information was sometimes used against them. But the ruling party had realized people still wanted a "winter holiday." So they had settled upon January 1 as the day to decorate trees and exchange meager gifts while you ushered in the New Year. Frosty the Snowman became the new symbol of winter cheer, having replaced Santa, who somehow had become a capitalist symbol.

"Even the fir trees look anemic now," Constantin had joked. "It's as if nature mirrors the general poverty of spirit."

There was no champagne to ring in 1956, but together again, at last, the family celebrated quietly. Glasses of wine in hand, they drank to the present and new beginnings, and expressed gratitude for the year that had brought closure to a long and painful chapter of their lives.

Constantin woke up the following day on January 1, and declared the time had come to look for work. "New year, new job," he told himself. Teaching remained out of reach for the time being, as his past political beliefs were considered as too dangerous to the new generation. However, research was not off limits, and he had asked Mona for help once again, remembering her instrumental role in his release through her friend Adrian Brudariu.

"Mona, I need to do something useful again. I can only read so many books and jot down so many notes. It's also about time I earned some money; your mother and brother are long overdue for a break."

"I'll see what we can do, father," was her reply.

After a couple of weeks, they received a call: the professor was invited to pay a visit to the President of the National Assembly, Dr. Petre Groza. Mona advised him, "It sounds like they're trying to extend you an olive branch. It's best to listen and not ask for anything right away. If you 'pass' this test, I'm sure something is going to give."

He dressed in his best and only suit and went early, anticipating security procedures. He was taken from floor to floor, repeatedly stating his name and showing his ID. His temporary residence permit—he'd only been back for less than three months—raised some frowns and puzzled others. In the end the presence of his name on the premier's daily list overrode the technicality of the pesky permit. He was finally taken to a large study, where he waited only for a few minutes. He glanced around: expensive gleaming furniture; crystal chandelier; a thick, rich rug; and fresh flowers on a table.

"Nice, so this is how our socialist leaders live and work," he told himself.

The president walked in, a well-dressed, tall man with a carnation in his lapel, and extended a hand. "Professor, so glad you could come."

"The pleasure is entirely mine."

"Well, Professor, I know what you went through. But see, it's all behind you now. Things will get better."

Constantin remained silent. What should he have said? Anything would have been hollow.

The president carried on, seemingly oblivious to his guest's silence. "Tough things happen when a revolution takes place, you must have understood that."

"As an historian, yes, I understood how some got caught in whatever the revolution entailed."

"I thought you did. Anyway, there's no need to be upset over spilled milk; it's over now."

Pleasantries of the same ilk followed for about a half hour, and though nothing was promised, a door was left ajar just as his daughter had predicted. Mona's friend Adrian had come through again.

Less than two weeks later, Constantin was hired at the research desk of the Institute of History. The assignment was at first temporary, with a renewal expected in three months pending "good behavior." Mona once again advised him, "Keeping your mouth shut will be more important than working hard."

It was with deep satisfaction—and yes, vindication—that he headed back to work nearly six years after his arrest. The first morning he walked in and presented his ID to the guard at the front desk, expecting the customary debate over the temporary permit. The gray-haired man read the name and lifted his eyes, "Are you the author of the *History of the Romanian People*?"

"Oh, here we go," thought Constantin. "Next comes the part where I'm informed that our history has changed." He nodded and awaited the man's comment.

But instead he heard, "I took some history during my philosophy degree and read parts of your books. You have a gift at writing, Professor." Then, he remembered and quickly glanced around making sure no one had overheard the conversation.

As luck would have it, the Institute was nearly across the street from their apartment, making it possible to come home for lunch every day.

"Who's working with you?" Maria asked, curious to know.

He rattled off a few names, former colleagues at the university, now also recycled to safer pastures. There were new faces, too: men and women of healthy proletarian origins who had rapidly climbed the professional ladder and were mostly full of contempt for the old guard.

Maria had said, "You don't care about their feelings, dear?"

"I most certainly don't; all I want is to be able to go to work again." And work he did, keeping to his projects and avoiding the gossip pits, and never complaining about anything.

And soon another olive branch arrived. Some 120 books (out of his initial extensive collection of over 1,000) were returned to him. They had been safeguarded, ironically enough, by his new employer, the Institute of History. He was overjoyed, and the volumes gave him renewed confidence in his ability to eventually rebuild his career.

Luck continued to run in the family that year. With the political situation slightly relaxing, Dinu embarked upon the search for a position closer to his specialty of history. A lenient new law had opened a door. He could resign from the construction site but rejoin within three months if his search proved unsuccessful.

He approached his father. "The National Art Museum is looking for a guide who can help with cataloging and archiving as well."

"Have you applied?"

"Yes, but I think they want someone with an art degree."

"You never know, go ahead and try, cataloging is cataloging. You had some formal training in that during the history course, who knows, it might help"

Constantin kept quiet, but he had reconnected with his friend Alex Rosetti, and the man knew the current museum director. Alex intervened and made it possible for Dinu to be interviewed. It must have gone well as Dinu was hired soon thereafter. And a few weeks into his new job, he literally "struck gold." Part of the Romanian treasury had been sent for safekeeping to Russia in 1917, toward the end of World War I. It was now being returned to Romania, presumably as a reward for her submissive behavior. Some of the objects were to be displayed in a major exhibit at the Art Museum, and Dinu was asked to participate in the selection process and to write historically accurate captions.

The big day finally arrived. As luck would have it, Dinu was selected to be personal guide to Dr. Groza, President of the National Assembly, the de facto Chief of State. After the father's earlier visit to the political leader, it was now time for the son to come within the president's peripheral orbit.

He later told of his disbelief in being so close, feet away, to the rank and file dignitaries, the very people who had turned his family's life upside down. The Secretary General of the Romanian Communist Party, Gheorghiu-Dej, also put in an appearance. He was observed glancing around the hall, seemingly more interested in the display spaces and layout of the building than in the exhibit. Dinu carried his assignment off with bravado, earning accolades from the museum director. It was this rare opportunity which helped him start a new career on the best possible footing.

A glimmer of hope began to take hold in the family again. With Dinu and his father both working in a professional capacity, they might just be able to crawl out of the desolation of the last few years and reclaim a little of their lost luster.

They were about to lower their guard slightly and try to relax. Then the Soviet tanks rolled into Budapest, Hungary.

Chapter Thirty-Three
A FAMILY IN PARTIAL RECOVERY

In 1956 the people of Hungary had felt a wave of change blowing through their country. Those close to them, like the Romanians, prayed and anxiously awaited the news. It had started with a fall student demonstration in Budapest, the Hungarian capital; a revolt was sparked, which then spread across the country. Pro-Soviet Communist leaders and members of the State Security police were arrested, former political prisoners were released, and Soviet troops were fought. By the end of October, the country had a new government that promised free elections and also threatened to pull out of the Warsaw Pact, the Eastern European states' alliance. People took to the streets in joyous demonstrations, embracing one another. The wind of freedom was blowing through and they dared dream again.

But a week later Soviet tanks rolled into Hungary, and the revolution was quashed. There were 2,500 dead, and over 200,000 fled the country. Others were deported by trains passing through Romania to Siberia or who knows where else, never to be seen again.

The Soviet Union had given notice to the world. This was how they punished those who broke ranks with them.

Constantin and Dinu listened tensely to the BBC updates as the Romanian official radio station remained mum on the topic. The unease grew with each piece of ominous news. Then by January 1957 the last remnants of Hungary's short-lived freedom were eradicated, and they heard how a new Soviet-backed government was safely ensconced in power.

The usual international condemnation followed with the customary speeches from Washington and London. But both sides ultimately stood by the lines drawn at the end of WWII. Eastern Europe had tacitly been allotted to the Soviets, and the Allies continued to abide by their end of the bargain. They were unwilling, and more than likely unable, to risk another global confrontation so shortly after the carnage and devastation of the last war.

Dinu felt defeated and deflated. For years in the early 1950s, he and many of his countrymen had kept up the hope that the U.S. would come to his country's rescue. This possibility had once again been raised by the events in Hungary and quashed by the subsequent defeat of the pro-democratic revolt.

"Father, we truly prayed for a miracle these past years. Didn't you?"

"Certainly, except mine was the release from jail. If you look at the big picture and all its moving blocks, you understand how the Allies had no alternative."

"You are right, and now I truly understand how the Americans won't help us after all," he thought with sadness. The idealist youth had become an adult realist. As for Maria, the events offered her an opportunity to remind them of her foreboding insistence in Istanbul just about a decade earlier not to return to Romania.

His husband took the news more philosophically, stating those were the cards they had been dealt. They had to live with them and do the best they could. The partition of Eastern Europe from the continent had once again been confirmed. To hope for a change anytime soon would have been a sign of folly, stupidity, or ignorance. So he chose to focus on rebuilding his career, while enjoying any good moments that life may offer. The country's fate was sealed for the foreseeable future. But his was still being written.

He worked long hours at the Institute and enjoyed them. He came across stacks of unpublished and valuable documents filed haphazardly. Constantin set down to organize them using a chronological system and subdivisions based on topics of interests—political, cultural and economic. Not only was he sorting them out, but they would also provide him with material for future writing. After months his presence in the work force was deemed "safe," and his temporary position was cemented into a permanent one. Another small measure of success came later that year when a couple of his articles were published in a low-profile history periodical.

These minor steps opened the door to a bigger one: writing a book and having it published. He chose the topic carefully, settling upon documents covering the Romanian Principalities in the eighteenth century. The content was innocuous enough and the volume was selected for publication in 1957. But his happiness was short-lived. Attacks from those teaching at the university history chair came fast and furious and were unrelenting. The facts stated in his book were based on documents and were in themselves indisputable. But the credibility of the author, his ability to be unbiased, and his credentials after a seven-year absence, were amply questioned. The witch-hunt was on again.

Constantin shrugged his shoulders and ploughed ahead. "A door has been opened," he told himself, "and that's what matters."

Others, such as writers, poets, and scientists, enjoyed a similar fate during 1956-1957. Many saw their works published for the first time since 1948, as some of the political pressure appeared to have eased off.

There were other encouraging signs, too. Several Soviet-oriented institutions were closed, such as the Romanian-Soviet Museum and Institute. Russian language, literature, and history were no longer mandated in Romanian schools. And the government returned a small number of real estate properties to their rightful owners. Maria's father, professor Mehedinti, widely considered the father of Romanian geographical science, was among them. Besides, he was considered a "safe" recipient, having played only a small political part many, many years earlier.

So part of his house was returned to the family, while the remainder would continue to house books from the collection of the academy. The Mehedinti house would have certainly been large enough to accommodate the entire family. But it didn't. Months earlier Constantin had returned home one evening to be told by Maria, "I'll never talk to my mother again."

"Don't worry dear; you'll get over it. It's not your first row."

"This time I really mean it. I've had it with her attitude and moods."

"Maria, be reasonable, she's still your mother," Constantin insisted.

"Her selfishness and ugliness of spirit takes precedence over that."

"Maria, what about your father?"

"She said she'd never let me see him again."

He tried to understand what might have happened. Details were sketchy: a fight over food supplies and who does what in the kitchen had provided the spark. The women had then apparently revisited all the ills one had brought upon the other over the years. Maria had never completely forgiven her mother for her early hostility toward Constantin, particularly during their courtship. Her mother had probably never quite forgiven Maria for having married a poor orphan. They had certainly had serious arguments before, but this one unfortunately lasted. And so divided they fell. When Maria's parents moved back into the family home, she and Constantin stayed behind. The family ties had been foolishly and irreparably severed.

Despite this dispute, life went on. The other couple sharing the flat, the Chivus, soon moved to an apartment of their own. Now Dinu could finally get a proper bedroom and Constantin a study again. With the little money saved they were able to buy a desk, some bookshelves, and a dining table and chairs. Curtains and a rug followed within months, the flat looking more and more like a true home. The prized paintings (saved by their friend Sanda when the house was confiscated) were displayed for the first time after years spent in crates.

One day Constantin paid a visit to Gheorge Tatarescu, the prime minister in whose cabinet Constantin had served in the late 1930s. Tatarescu was one of the very few high-ranking officials to have survived their jail sentence. He looked a shadow of his former self, but his mind was clear as ever. The two men talked for a long time about what had taken place and what the future might hold.

"Nothing will change for a long time," said the ex-prime minister.

Constantin tried to play devil's advocate, though in agreement with the former statesman: "Why? Why not hope?"

"Look at the Soviet Union. The revolution broke out there in 1917, and that bestial system has only strengthened since then. Look at the complete hold they have over people's lives," he said, making a fist. "And if that wasn't enough, it is impossible for the Western Powers to come to the rescue of Eastern Europe. The pie was carved in 1945, and no one wants to go to war to reclaim part of it."

Constantin nodded; his own thoughts had been echoed by the savvy politician, and his worst fears had been confirmed. Too many forces converged toward the same narrow course: a future that would indefinitely continue the country's present reality.

And just when they had gotten a taste of the somewhat more relaxed atmosphere, the screw was tightened again. A new wave of arrests took place during the spring of 1958, when remnants of the bourgeoisie were targeted as dangerous elements again. Some students and members of the faculty were accused of instigating discontent and were even dismissed. The accusations ranged from criticism of the regime to possession of outlawed books. Alleged connections with foreign dignitaries were also sanctioned, as any communication with foreign embassies' staff was strictly forbidden.

Some of those arrested were sent to jail again, two of Constantin's friends from Sighet among them. Aurelian Bentoiu and George Strat had been in cell 17 with him and Nick. Both were rearrested under fabricated claims and neither survived their second prison term. Others were sent to forced labor camps, with punishment sessions ranging between two to four years. The death penalty was also introduced for "major" economic crimes, and the prosecution eagerly manipulated some minor offenses into more serious ones. Darkness once more took hold of the country and her people, and the fear of neighbors, friends, and even family intensified.

Maria and Constantin lived from day to day. Memories of their long separation were still raw, and the prospect that it could happen again was tangible. Maria teetered on the edge, overtaken by worries, and smoked continuously.

If he had nerves of his own, he tried not to show them, and kept a low profile. The critics' wrath over the volume published in 1957 had triggered a new smear campaign against him, in the wake of which he wasn't allowed to publish for a while. Deep apprehension overtook him, and doubt crept up any time he heard a positive comment or compliment at work. Perhaps the encouraging words were meant to draw him out of the shell. Maybe they were trying to entice him to say things the instigators would later use against him. Then he'd snap out of it—the paranoia from prison had once again taken hold having him doubt a mere kind word.

And then a ray of unexpected hope: the summer of 1958 brought the departure of the Soviet troops from Romanian soil. Rumors of their retreat had circulated before and had not materialized. When foreign troops had departed from Vienna in 1955, people were hopeful in Romania, too, but their wait went on for another three years. The short-lived Hungarian revolution took place in the meantime and people's hopes were quashed again. In hindsight, the presence of the Soviet troops on the country's soil bolstered the Romanian authorities against similar turbulence taking place at home. Then in 1958 the Soviet troops left with no fanfare.

And so Romania and her people marched toward the end of the decade. Coupons and rations were eventually discontinued; one could now buy sugar or flour any day of the week, and food stores became better stocked. A wider range of clothing and shoes became available and more affordable. Foreign movies were shown once again, such as *The Magnificent Seven* and Laurence Olivier's *Hamlet*. All in all life began to feel more civilized.

And with daily life more or less tolerable, Maria began to fret about Dinu.

"He ought to get married; he's over thirty now," she would say.

"He'll get married when he wants to," replied her husband.

"You should talk to him and find out what his plans are."

"I'll do my best," he'd say to pacify her. But Constantin didn't want to press his son. Girlfriends had come and gone, and perhaps the next would be the one. Then one day a friend of Constantin passed away, dropping dead of a heart attack. The man wasn't even sixty years old, and his demise hit Constantin hard. While in jail, many had resigned themselves to a likely premature death. But since his release, Constantin felt life was on again. The suddenness of his friend's demise brought shivers and fear of what might lie ahead. He went to the cemetery to pay final respects and asked Dinu to accompany him. The summer air was balmy and heavy with the scent of the many flowers piled up on the fresh gravesite. He couldn't help but tell his son, "See, life is short. It can end unexpectedly, one could disappear overnight. You should think of starting your own family, boy. You don't want to be left alone."

They didn't have to wait long. Less than a year later, their oldest son broke the news, "I met this girl a month ago and asked her to marry me. She said yes. I'm bringing her tomorrow to meet you."

"You did what?"

Maria was stunned. Here was the news she had waited to hear, and which was supposed to thrill her. But it felt somehow diminished as she had not been consulted up to this point.

"Mother, I am engaged."

His parents stared at one another; Maria silently motioning to Constantin that it was his turn to reply. His father thought of the most logical question.

"Who is she?"

"Anca Dinu."

"Manoilescu's granddaughter?"

"Yes."

Maria knew the family quite well. Anca's maternal grandfather, Mihai Manoilescu, had been Foreign Affairs Minister during the 1940 ill-fated treaty that had relinquished part of Transylvania. The poor man had the misfortune of affixing his signature to the official surrender. After the Communist takeover, he was immediately portrayed as a dangerous enemy of the people and was among the first to be targeted. Arrested a year before Constantin, he was sent to the same Sighet Penitentiary, where he died on December 30 or 31, 1950. The exact date was never established due to lack of public records and eyewitnesses. The ultimate irony was that his official sentencing was issued only after his demise, while his wife and children had lived until the late 1950s with no knowledge of his fate. Later on, they weren't even able to pay final respects, since the body had been thrown into a communal grave.

And now his granddaughter was to become Maria's daughter-in-law. Dinu had met his fiancée at his cousin Mariuca's wedding in late July (Mariuca was one of Lelia's two daughters). Viorica, the distant relative Constantin had called upon the release from jail, was at the wedding, too. She had taken Dinu by the hand, "Come. Let me introduce you to a beautiful girl."

He resigned himself. "Okay." All he had to do, he figured, was to say hello, make a little polite conversation, and then take his leave.

"Here is Anca Dinu."

He was immediately taken aback. "At least this one is gorgeous," he told himself. "Tall, thin—just the way I like them," he thought.

They started talking, and he learned how Anca's best friend was none other than one of Viorica's granddaughters. Being more than ten years their senior, Dinu had not previously socialized with this "younger set." Conversation flowed so naturally that he accompanied her home and asked for permission to call. Several dates followed.

Maria and Constantin met the young woman the following day. All wore their best attire and Maria had prepared a cake. Dinu stepped through the door first, leading his fiancée. "Here is Anca."

She seemed awfully young, barely more than twenty, tall, thin, and extremely beautiful, with blue eyes, blond hair, and delicate features. They could see why their son had fallen hard and fast. The girl also appeared slightly nervous, probably overwhelmed by the suddenness of their engagement and the encounter with her future in-laws. Constantin also fidgeted around, not knowing quite what to say. Never one at a loss for words, Maria sized her up.

"Do you ever eat, my dear? You're so thin. "

The young woman smiled. "Of course," and then, looking over at the table with the cake and the tea service set out, she asked, "May I have a slice of that beautiful cake?"

Something about her looked vaguely familiar. Where could they have seen her before, she wondered? Then Maria suddenly remembered, "Are you the jumper?"

Another smile. "Yes."

She had seen photos and read accounts of Anca winning the junior high-jump competitions in years past.

"But I've since given it up. I needed to focus on my studies."

They soon learned that she was reading Italian language and literature at the university, and was about to start her senior year. She had wanted to be an architect, but hadn't been allowed to sit for admission exams, the young woman being penalized by virtue of her family's background. Prized spots such as at the architectural or medical schools were reserved for those of "healthy" origin, children of the proletariat.

"What do you do when you aren't studying?" Maria asked, as they sat down at the table and she poured tea for everyone, then cut the cake and handed Anca a piece.

"Read, hike, listen to music . . . and yes, dance. I love to dance," she said enthusiastically.

"What are your plans now?" Maria asked, now looking at both of them. "Have you thought of a date?"

Anca and Dinu glanced knowingly at each other. "We actually have. We're thinking early November."

"In less than three months!" Maria said in alarm, before she could catch herself.

Dinu chimed in. "Why not? We want to be together as soon as possible. We'd only need a couple of months to get organized. We don't want anything big, just family and close friends."

How times had changed thought Maria. She remembered her own long, secret engagement to Constantin. Then there was the official one, with the long preparations, numerous guests, a lavish reception, gifts that kept arriving. It seemed so long ago, and yet barely thirty years had passed. Then to her son, she said, "Sure, why not!"

The next two months went by in a blur of rushed and cursory preparations. The official ceremony took place on November 3 at the local district's city hall. Late fall's cold air had settled in the week before, but on the big day the sun shone brightly and it warmed up into the sixties. Family, colleagues, and friends gathered to celebrate together; happiness and optimism were tangible, as neither family had celebrated a joyous occasion in over two decades. Anca looked smart in a light beige color suit and kitten heels, while Dinu wore his only suit. All around smiles provided the best adornment for the brief ceremony followed by a small reception. It was given by Anca's parents at their apartment.

Church attendance continued to be frowned upon, and a religious marriage ceremony carried a potential penalty for a university student. But faith was very important to Anca and her family. So they settled upon an abbreviated ceremony headed by a priest in their home and attended only by the immediate family. It was to follow the larger reception and take place in the evening. The priest came dressed in civilian garb and changed into his robes at the apartment. This way no prying eyes would have seen him in his religious attire. And the bride was finally able to don a veil and a white dress—the smart, short kind with a wide skirt in the style of the 50s. A glimmer of hope for a brighter tomorrow wafted through the room, while the flicker of the wax candles flanked the bride and groom in the orthodox faith tradition. Anca's uncle and his wife acted as godparents while the rest of family uttered prayers for the newlyweds.

After the briefest of honeymoons—only three days—in the university town of Cluj in northern Transylvania, the young couple returned home to share the apartment with Maria and Constantin. For the couple to have their own place was out of the question. The two couples combined could barely afford the rent of the flat and other daily expenses—a sad testimony to the minimalism of their existence.

The apartment got more crowded, and fast. Within four years two girls joined the family. The two-bedroom flat became awfully busy and loud with three generations living, working, and playing side by side. Constantin thought it felt happy and lively, with the sight and sound of the children blotting away some of the awfulness of the past decade.

Maria's father passed away shortly after his first great-granddaughter was born. He was never to meet her. Maria and her parents never reconnected after the women's foolish argument in 1957. Her brother, Emil, periodically updated the two sides about the health and life of the others. Constantin would take him aside and ask questions about his in-laws, while Maria, for the most part, acted as if her parents were dead. It deeply saddened him. As one who had lost his parents so early, he felt she didn't appreciate the gift of their continued presence in her life.

Emil came by one day in October 1962. "Father is very weak; I think the end is near."

Maria's face tightened but she remained silent. Constantin struggled with his emotions, realizing it was too late to convince his wife to relent and see her father. The great man quietly passed away and was laid to rest by many of his former students and colleagues, but not by his daughter and her family. Though visibly shaken, Maria remained defiant. Constantin didn't say a word, but the day after the funeral he went to the cemetery by himself. It was his lonely goodbye to the man whose daughter he had married, and to the master educator he had long revered. Staring in silence at the tomb, the professor's salons came alive again, and so did the man at the podium—memories of years and a life long gone.

He also stopped at his parents' graves. Overgrown ivy had covered the stones. But someone must have been tending to them; it looked casual and orderly at the same time. He then remembered his sister telling of her occasional visits. Lelia had been a young child at the time of her parents' passing, but later had probably come here to dream of the parents she had hardly known and of a family life she never knew. Constantin sat down on the wrought iron bench and reminisced about his happy childhood days of so long ago. It was as if Professor Mehedinti's passing had also awakened dormant memories of his youth. He sat for a long while, with faces and stories dancing in front of his eyes—the cemetery always seemed to have that effect on him. With eyes closed he saw happiness and, oh, so much pain.

When he got up he was ready to once again look into the future.

Chapter Thirty-Four
REINSTATED AT THE UNIVERSITY

The winds of change blew through the country in the early 1960s, as the party leaders busied themselves designing a new direction for the country and its society. After fifteen years of clamping down on virtually every aspect of Romanian life, they had accomplished their initial goals. The new socialist state and its economy had been molded to their satisfaction. It was now time to redefine the individual's place, and to gloss over the image Communism had thus far projected to the world.

The changes coincided with an ever-so-slight nudge by their Soviet brother next door, with peaceful coexistence becoming the new political buzzword. The Eastern Bloc countries—known also as the Warsaw Pact—wished to show the world that they too were civilized. They were suddenly ready to learn from and interact with their peers abroad. Besides, a bilingual or multilingual professional with a PhD conversing with their American or French counterparts would be a great endorsement of their system's tolerance, or so thought the political higher-ups. Polished, highly skilled individuals would be a terrific advertisement for socialism as a whole. They would show the world how their capitalist enemy didn't hold a monopoly on education and expertise. More importantly, these same individuals would help position their country on a more competitive footing with the rest of the world. And better-trained professionals would also be able to gradually elevate the whole society under the "for the people, by the people" often-circulated slogan.

And so little by little, professionals were rounded up, particularly those classically trained prior to the war. Some of the men sent to prison to die ten years earlier were now in demand again, as being an intellectual became suddenly fashionable. Wealth and political affiliations prior to the war had cast a dark shadow over engineers, architects, and professors. This stigma had also been extended to their offspring, who had been considered of "unhealthy origin." Many, like Dinu, had been forced to forgo their training and to go to work in factories and on construction sites. Others like Anca had had to opt out of their first career choice and settle on whatever they could accomplish.

But all that would be forgotten as a new trend was ushered in.

Constantin was among those who benefited from this change. In early 1963 he was called in by the dean of the university.

"Professor, our own archives have been overlooked for quite a while. Would you be able to help straighten them out?"

"You mean, could I work here after hours? Or perhaps on Sundays?"

"Most certainly not. I am asking you to leave the institute and join our staff."

Without reflection or as much as a blink, he replied, "It would be my pleasure. When would you like me to start?"

"As soon as possible. I'll talk to the director over at the institute and get the paperwork in order."

Overjoyed at the prospect, Constantin practically ran home to share the news with Maria. But her reception was cool.

"They've asked me to join again, can you believe it?"

"You'll still being sorting out papers; it's not like you were offered a teaching post."

"Come on, it's a step in the right direction. Why can't you look at the glass as half full?"

"Because it's half empty. You are no longer the famous professor, and I no longer have my houses."

He didn't see the point in trying to convince her otherwise. But her refusal to muster any enthusiasm as their lives progressed in a positive direction left him with a sense of hopelessness. He had fought for survival and to reinvent himself, but nothing in his power could alter Maria's worsening melancholy.

And so the university rehired him in 1963, and once he set foot in the halls of the Faculty of History, he knew he had returned for good. Among the new hires—or, more correctly put, rehires—he held the unique distinction of having served jail time for his political activities. But of course, one never talked about that; it had all been part of the necessary fits and starts of the country's socialist revolution, as Premier Groza had pointed out in 1956.

With this new accreditation also came relative financial security, and the family could consider going on vacation. The last one Maria and Constantin had taken had been in 1946! Their great friends the doctors Vereanu had stumbled the previous year upon the hamlet of Cheia, a little over two hours northeast of Bucharest. They had fallen in love with the rustic dwellings and gorgeous scenery, and the following year they approached Maria and her husband.

"Why don't we all go this summer? The guys can fish for trout and the women can gossip, bake, and take long walks."

Constantin glanced at his wife and saw her face lit up at this prospect. "Good," he told himself, as he heard Maria replying, "Only God knows how much we need a break and some fresh air. Where would we stay?"

"We fell upon this couple, Marioara and Postolache Ciripoiu. They had a 'For Let' sign at the front gate. We inquired and they weren't charging much. They have three rooms so we could all fit."

It was Maria's turn to glance at Constantin; she wondered if the statement would bring back painful memories of Mazareni. She was reassured by his smile; perhaps he was already imaging himself fishing rod in hand.

"How would we travel?"

"That's a little tricky. We go by train and connect in Valeni."

Constantin couldn't help but interrupt, "Like in my childhood when we went to Grandpa's in Chiojd and changed horses and had refreshments at the Valeni Inn!"

"Then from Valeni we take this miniature train for another hour or so."

By evening's end the three couples had a plan. Suzanna Vereanu, known as Suzi to her friends, would write to the hosts and wire some money as a deposit. Mid-July was chosen as a departure date.

The spring flew by and the big day arrived. The journey to Valeni was smooth and uneventful. After disembarking they glanced across the tracks. There awaited an old-fashioned train with a steam engine that blew smoke, hissed, and cranked. Nearly an hour later, and after countless turns and twists not for the faint of heart, they had arrived at their destination.

"But where is it?" Maria had asked.

"Why, you're staring at it." On the last downslope before pulling into the station, she could see a handful of houses nestled in a "bucket" amidst the mountains. Cows and an explosion of bright wild flowers dotted the pastures and the river water was crystal clear.

Their hostess, Marioara Ciripoiu, was on hand to help with the luggage, having brought a cousin's horse-drawn cart. Her husband was working, she had explained—he painted houses and did repairs. A cheerful woman, she laughed her way back to the cottage, while her guests drank in the scenery. Yes, this was an auspicious start to a long-awaited vacation.

After a few days of gazing at the mountains and breathing in fresh air, Maria and Constantin realized how much they had missed the majestic beauty of the forests. He was able to reconnect with his old love of fishing—the rapids teamed with trout in Cheia. They had virtually no gear in those days and simple rods, worms for bait, and a tin box to store the fish had to suffice. But the happiness of being on the stream and waiting for the fish to bite made up for the lack of supplies.

At night friends gathered around the wooden plank table. They drank cheap wine or plum brandy, ate polenta and cheese, and recounted the exploits of their days. The joy of life had somehow been restored, and Constantin felt grateful for every free day.

A year later, in 1964, they decided to venture back to the seaside. Constantin's back had been bothering him of late and Nelu, the doctor, had advised to try some gentle swimming and exposure to the sun. The choice of a vacationing spot was a thorny one. Mangalia was bound to bring back painful memories and Constantin worried for Maria. She had been the one who worked with an architect to design their house there, had overseen its construction, and had run it for years. The cottage there (just like the properties in Bucharest, Predeal, and the vineyard) had been confiscated and nationalized as part of the wealth-redistribution plan in 1949–1950. Returning to the place they loved, but unable to stay in their own house, would tear at Maria's heart. So her husband consulted her.

"Dear, we need to pick a place and make some inquiries before summer is upon us."

"I assumed we were going back to Mangalia."

He certainly hadn't expected this reply. "Why would you assume such a thing?"

"Because we love it and already know the lay of the land. And for the same reason we chose it twenty years ago. It's a city but not a large one, though I'm sure it's grown since."

"I never dreamt you'd want to go back there."

"What difference does it make where we go? The houses are gone regardless of where we vacation. Besides, I'll be busy with Marina," she added, referring to her two-and-a-half-year-old granddaughter.

"Why, aren't Anca and Dinu joining us?"

"No, Anca says the baby is too young to travel so they'll stay behind in Bucharest. I think they just want some time alone." The other granddaughter was barely four months old.

"What sort of vacation will it be for you to run after a two-year-old all day?"

"It'll be just fine and keep me busy, less time to think about the obvious. Besides the girl's feet are rather flat and walking on sand will help her strengthen the sole arch."

"Where on earth did she learn all these medical tidbits?" he wondered. One day she was lecturing them on the benefit of healthy foods and emphasizing the importance of fresh fruits and vegetables. The other, she was fighting with the pediatrician over using "my own syringe" for the children's shots, "because I sterilize it myself." Maria never ceased to amaze him.

"One more thing: Suzi and Titel are also thinking of going."

"Even better."

Together they made inquiries and found what sounded like a perfect rental. It offered rooms and lunch, with the hosts also willing to supply items for breakfast and supper. The charming cottage was near the boardwalk, and from its backyard one could see the sea, while the front garden was full of dahlias, roses, and grape vines.

Despite new hotels on the boardwalk and blocks of apartments at its center, it was still the city they had fallen in love with three decades earlier. They rediscovered its abundance of flowers, small vines, and the smell of fresh bread and salty pretzels. There were still Turks peddling ice cream, but pastries and corn on the cob were gone—the latter taken in "monopoly" by gypsy women. Also gone was the abundance of seafood they remembered well. Unaware at first of fishing restrictions, Maria had asked if they could have grilled sardines for supper.

Their hostess had replied, "I wish, m'am, but there aren't any around."

"Don't your men go fishing any longer?"

"Yes, they do, but we can't sell them."

"I see. God forbid you might make a bit of money. This way we're all hungry and poor."

"M'am hush, talk like this could be dangerous."

"Well, I see you are an enterprising woman. You must have friends. Go spread the word; I will pay one-and-a-half times the going rate so we can have grilled sardines tonight."

And indeed, some individuals had found a way around this prohibition. Sooner or later they had realized it wasn't easy to police the entire town. One merely had to be cautious, and watch out how much one was selling and to whom. A black market where one bartered goods had eventually grown up here and elsewhere, with policemen or city officials often "in the loop" in exchange for sums of money or produce.

Once in Mangalia, Maria couldn't bear to go see their house, just as she had warned. But Constantin went was anxious to record the changes which must have surely taken place. Titel accompanied him. It wasn't far from their rental, a mere fifteen minutes or so. One walked through a small park, past the Greek ruins of the old colony of Callatis, and then along the beach and veered north. He was immediately set aback once the destination was reached.

"Goodness how the foliage has grown; you can barely see the house. What do you think that large building is?"

Titel, a pediatric surgeon, was familiar with the dwelling. "It's a children's hospital. They had a smaller tuberculosis unit not far from here, but the space was getting tight. Besides, they wanted an all-purpose hospital, not just focused on one disease."

"I wonder who lives here." Later on they would find out it was the director of the facility. It certainly made perfect sense as his "commute" likely took less than a minute from home to the office.

"Look how worn-out the house seems." The exterior paint was pale, watered down by the sun, wind, and rain. He glanced up to his old study, where thick ivy wrapped around the walls. For a moment he saw himself standing by the window and waving to the children on the beach, and a deep sadness took hold. Then he noticed that his friends' houses hadn't fared any better. All had been nationalized and assigned to "more deserving" citizens, sound members of the working class, "the proletariat."

"Why, some villas are gone. Manoilescu's house used to be right behind us."

"They must have been torn down to make way for the hospital and other buildings."

The surrounding silence struck him, too. One used to always keep the windows open and never locked the doors. Teenagers played volleyball and tennis, and listened to jazz music at night. No one was running around now, and there was no music to be heard.

"A whole world is gone," he uttered softly. "But I am among the lucky ones, who're alive and can still afford to return to the seaside."

Titel gently squeezed his friend's arm, "The sun is going down fast; shouldn't we head back home? I don't want Suzi and Maria to worry."

Then Constantin glanced at the home one more time before turning around. The gatekeeper of family memories had again dipped into the past. But by now he knew there was no benefit in dwelling on it when the future beckoned.

Fresh salty air, gentle walks on the beach, and rest worked their magic again, just as in years past. When they returned to Bucharest, Constantin was energized and ready to sit down to work. And a pivotal political moment of the year enabled him to significantly expand his scientific activity.

In the spirit of the openness breezing through the Romanian society, the Romanian Communist Party had passed the "April Declaration" in 1964. It decreed that each nation's party was entitled to its own position, tacitly blessed by the Soviet Union. The purpose of the declaration was to show to the world how Eastern European countries were becoming increasingly independent, no longer mere puppets in the hands of the Moscow regime.

A whiff of this newly found freedom had been felt the previous year. The Romanian leader had publicly expressed condolences when the U.S. President John Kennedy was assassinated in 1963. Such a gesture toward the West would have been unheard of a few years earlier.

Later that year the Romanian secretary general, Gheorghiu-Dej, visited the Warsaw Pact headquarters. Shortly after returning home, he fell gravely ill. Some rumored that it was cancer, while others thought poisoning or irradiation. The state-controlled media kept mum, and the secretary passed away a few months later in the spring of '65, being laid to rest with all due honors. Had the Soviets wished to eliminate an old timer emblematic of the '50s and start anew with a fresh face? Or had it all been a coincidence?

No one would know. But soon all became familiar with the new Party secretary: Nicolae Ceausescu. The rising star of the party and a staunch believer in its doctrine, he had joined when the party counted less than one thousand individuals in its ranks. Ceausescu came from a dirt-poor family—his father a notorious drunk. As for Ceausescu's wife, Elena, it was rumored she was a gypsy who craved academic honors and wished to amass great personal wealth. Only time would tell what this new leadership would bring. For now the country enjoyed a new freedom dictated by the strong rhetoric pleading for independence and noninterference in internal affairs.

Many, like Constantin, were now able to return to their previous positions. In 1965 his career finally came around full circle, deemed "safe enough" to return to the teaching podium at the Faculty of History and to be reinstated. And so, quietly, without fanfare, he was welcomed back to the offices he had been evicted from in 1948.

The university term started on October 1, which was a mild, sunny day. Constantin chose to walk along the Kisselef Boulevard where old oak trees were already tinged in gold. He moved about leisurely, savoring every minute of a day that would never be forgotten. And though not one to reach for metaphors, he suddenly thought of the Phoenix, which had risen from the ashes to resurrect itself. Then slowly his articles began to be published regularly, and the ban on his books was eventually lifted.

The younger generation of the family was fortunate as well. Dinu was hired as a researcher at the Ministry of Foreign Affairs. Those in charge wished to understand world events between the two World Wars, as many documents had been banned in the aftermath of the Communist takeover. Materials needed to be studied and presented in a concise manner to Romania's new breed of diplomats. Dinu's wife, Anca, did equally well. She was hired as a teaching assistant at the university, with an emphasis on Italian and Romance Linguistics.

Cultural life suddenly blossomed everywhere. Books were published again; theater thrived, and particularly in Bucharest; and classical music became fashionable once more. Foreign movies were introduced gradually, providing their script didn't have a political slant and the stars maintained a sense of decorum.

Some were even allowed to travel abroad for work at conferences, meetings, and the like. But personal travel was still greatly restricted. In this respect the country's citizens were truly equal: no one owned a passport. If you desired one, a lengthy application had to be filled out. You stood in line for hours to submit the papers, and then waited for weeks or months. When the response finally came, the request was almost always denied. If you were fortunate enough to travel for work purposes, you had to hand in the passport to the proper authorities within twenty-four hours of your return home.

All in all, life was progressing once again in a more normal direction. With the added perspective of his mounting years, Constantin felt that the pain and suffering had not been in vain. He hadn't merely survived: a decade after the release from jail, he was teaching again at the university and his works were being published. Amidst this renewed good fortune, one cloud lingered on his horizon: Maria, whose bitterness ironically deepened just as their lives improved. She had rallied throughout his prison term and had survived incredible poverty and hardship. But now it was as if her resolve had been extinguished.

She talked increasingly of their past lives, before all of it had been taken away, and on many a day she appeared unwilling and unable to enjoy their newly found relative comfort. Constantin began to see how Communism could break one's soul and how some wounds were too deep to heal. While cold and hungry, one fought for survival. But after surviving, some took a step back and understood the magnitude of what had been lost. Constantin was a fighter who didn't forget the past but charged ahead, aiming for a win at the end of the day. But others, like Maria, had been irreparably broken, the emotional toll too deep to be reversed.

The day he understood the depth of her wounds was when he was allowed to travel to Vienna, Austria, to do some research at the Historical Archives. He was overjoyed, even more so as the authorities informed them that Maria could join him on this trip.

"Maria, I would have never dreamt this possible. To be chosen over others, to be sent in an official capacity, all expenses covered ... let's start packing."

"I'll put together whatever you need, but I'm staying home."

"You can't be serious."

"Yes, I am. I don't wish to go."

"Please, Maria. You can rest while I work; we can visit museums and churches together. You've never seen the city. I hardly remember anything myself but always dreamt of returning."

"No and no," she had said, weary and tired. "It's too late. You can't turn the clock back. They took everything away from us and are baiting you with morsels now."

"But, Maria isn't it better to focus on all we've accomplished since 1955? Why always dwell on the past?"

"It's easy for you to talk like this. You got your professorship back; you're writing your books and now you'll travel again. But *my* land, *my* houses are gone, and nothing will bring them back. Go, just go."

He headed to Vienna alone on what should have been a joyous celebration of their fortieth anniversary, and sadness tinged his wonder at going abroad again. The train journey from Bucharest to Vienna took one day and a night. Passport checks at the Romanian-Hungarian border were lengthy. Stern-looking soldiers in military uniforms asked many questions and wanted to see all the official papers. Once they reached the Austrian border, the formalities took considerably less time. At the crossing-over point, Constantin looked out the window: thick barbed and electrical wire fences were lined up along the Hungarian side.

"So no one can get out," thought Constantin. "You die the moment you attempt to flee."

By contrast, no reinforcements were present on the Austrian side.

Vienna struck him as austere. He wasn't surprised—the city had been free for only a little over a decade. The country had been annexed by Nazi Germany in 1938 and had remained in Germany's grip until the end of the war. The German retreat had been fast, and the city never saw significant street fighting, nor did it suffer the Allied bombing which razed so many German cities. A provisional government was then quickly established with Soviet approval, and secession from the Third Reich was immediately declared.

The country itself was initially divided into American, British, French, and Soviet zones, and so was Vienna, its capital. In 1955 Austria's independence was recognized by the four powers, and permanent neutrality was declared. But the Viennese were still weary in 1966, and often appeared distant, though courteous and correct. Constantin kept glancing around and couldn't believe how well-dressed people appeared. He had almost forgotten what old-world elegance looked like. Ladies in suits, hats, and matching shoes and gloves, and gentlemen in suits and overcoats, reminded him of the streets of Bucharest before the war.

He worked hard but also had time to visit museums, churches, and historic locales. He marveled at the majesty of the city, its imperial splendor still apparent. The emperor might have been gone since 1919, but the city was still cloaked in the aura of his reign. The imperial palace, the Hofburg, was now a museum, including the treasury of the crown jewels. Its crypt, where past emperors were buried, had become both a tourist attraction, and a site of pilgrimage for the Austrians still mourning their lost past. As for the summer palace outside the city at Schonbrunn, it had just been magnificently restored, another testimony to a glorious age.

Constantin tried to retrace his childhood steps hoping to awaken dormant memories. The house they had first lived in at number 2, Alserstrasse, had been torn down to make way for an apartment building. He was more successful finding their subsequent address in the suburb of Neuwaldegg, where time appeared to have stood still. Little houses with gardens seemed oblivious to the ravages of two world wars and over sixty years of turmoil. The walnut tree he remembered was still there; the hunchback owner would of course have long been gone. Sadness overcame him when thinking of a child's harsh words for the poor woman when he wasn't allowed to gather walnuts fallen to the ground. "Hey, Mommy, here comes the old hunchback woman."

He could almost hear his mother's voice, admonishing him in a melodious, measured manner, yet loud enough for all to hear, and the child's apology.

He also spotted the park and its pond, the one he thought of as a lake. In his memory he could still see the old gentleman dressed in morning coat and top hat. He kept throwing a stick in the water, and his fox terrier would pick it up deftly and return it to him.

And of course, up came vivid images of his mother. He could almost see her inspecting cheese and fruit at the market, or hear the sound of her piano playing. The old, elegant city had released a rush of deeply buried memories in a rather Proustian way.

Strong emotions would be stirred once again on Austrian soil nearly a year later. As a sign of his rising academic prominence, Constantin was selected to participate in a history congress in Linz, Austria. Maria didn't need convincing this time; their son Dan, still living in Paris, was to travel there to meet with them. His father hadn't seen him in over twenty years. Dan had graduated from the School of Architecture in Paris and was now practicing his trade. Because he had left Romania to study and had never returned, he was technically still a Romanian citizen. If he decided to visit home, the authorities could have prevented him from going back to France and his family. Hence he had been unable to visit his parents and siblings for all these years. In the late 1950s he had married Odette, a beautiful redhead from Normandy, and Maria and Constantin were to now meet their first grandson, Paul, nearly nine years old.

This second trip to Austria was once again by train. What should have been the preamble to a joyous reunion was once again tinged by Maria's sadness, anger, and her inability to enjoy the good fortune in their lives.

"Do you realize how much we have missed of Dan's life?" she asked her husband on the train.

"Yes, but we can't do anything about it now, can we?"

"You always say that," she said in a huff. There was a moment of silence. "We couldn't go to their wedding. We've never met his wife. Paul is almost nine and we don't know a thing about him."

"So we'll start learning now. I'm sure we'll meet Odette soon."

"It won't make up for the rest."

"But it's better than nothing," Constantin countered.

Maria put her hands to her face. "These Communist beasts have taken everything from me. They robbed me of my possessions and my grandson's childhood."

"Maria, please let the past rest. You should be thrilled we are traveling together again. You should remember I am alive and teaching again."

"Stop preaching to me."

After that she kept quiet, but sulked most of the journey. But it was all seemingly forgotten the moment they laid eyes on Paul and Dan. The boy was awfully shy and awkward at first. They were used to their granddaughters jumping about and their peals of laughter. Here stood quietly this thin, tall boy with blue-green eyes. But by the second day he must have figured the granddad taking him to the pastry shop, the "konditorei," was all right after all, and the icy reserve thawed quickly between them.

The week flew by much too fast, with scientific meetings blending in with family walks and meals. On the last evening Dan shared the surprise he had saved all week. Odette was pregnant with their second child. They had tried since Paul's birth and had suffered much heartache in the intervening years, he went on saying. All the heartache was behind now and in three months or so, they would celebrate the arrival of a new baby.

"Life is good again, luck is smiling upon us," thought Constantin. The family was growing and he was back on top of his profession. Not only was he teaching again, but he was also increasingly allowed to publish. The latest book, *The History of the City of Bucharest*, had just come out, and had enjoyed a warm welcome. The content appealed to the specialists, while the public enjoyed the many photographs. This same public appeared increasingly interested in whatever he had to say. Invitations to speak on the radio and even television began to multiply; PhD students sought him out as an advisor, and colleagues asked him to review their new books. All these activities brought in additional income, and he was able to buy a better radio, a television set, and eventually even a car. A small Fiat was followed by a medium-sized Renault.

He was back, healthy, and successful again, and looking forward to a busy future. With his faith restored, it seemed possible to reach up to the stars once more. So much so that the seed of an impossible dream was sowed and began to take hold. If his dream were successful, Maria might smile again, too.

Chapter Thirty-Five
TRAVELING THE WORLD, HOME AT LAST

The year 1968 would later be remembered as the year which could have been. Late January brought news, via BBC radio, of Alexander Dubcek being elected to power in Czechoslovakia. A reformist in the true sense of the word, Dubcek started off with loosening restrictions on travel and press censorship. Small private enterprises were encouraged. The country was to be divided into two federal republics: Czech and Slovak, each granted relative autonomy. This would have finally settled the issue of the two ethnicities, each wishing for a state reflecting their identity. But you would have never known of such momentous events if you listened only to Romanian radio or television. The change of leadership in Czechoslovakia, one of the country's allies in the Warsaw pact, was flatly reported—business as usual.

Hope grew in Romania and the other Warsaw countries; perhaps the changes in Prague meant that the Soviet grip was truly relaxing. Perhaps Romania's new young leader would be emboldened too and follow in the Czechs' footsteps. Maybe there really was a breath of fresh air sweeping through Eastern Europe.

But, like other progressive movements, this too was short-lived. Via the BBC and Radio Free Europe, one heard the rumbles of the Soviet bear waking up. The Czech reforms had crossed a threshold and had begun to threaten the Soviets' domination of the region. Then, during the summer of 1968, came news of high-level talks between the two sides.

On August 21, Constantin, Maria, Anca, and the girls were in Cheia, while Dinu was at work in Bucharest. Without television in the mountains and with newspapers arriving only once a day, they had to rely upon the radio to find out the daily news. Constantin woke up early that day and set down to write, as with every morning. Maria stayed in bed for a while longer to listen to her small portable radio. He was deep in thought when the door opened. He turned and stared at Maria, tears running down her face, hands wringing nervously.

"Russian tanks have rolled into Prague with foreign troops from other Warsaw Pact countries."

They stared at each other in silence; a sense of déjà vu had stopped them cold. They remembered the other Russian tanks, those which had poured into Romania in 1944 and recalled the plunder and destruction that followed.

"We must call Dinu right away."

There was no telephone in the cottage they rented, but the post office held several phone booths. Constantin began dressing right away. He couldn't reach his son that morning, so he returned to the cottage; and glued to the radio they waited for events to unfold. Constantin listened intently and said little, waiting to hear the facts. By midday the Romanian president held a rally and announced his position. To everyone's surprise, he strongly condemned the invasion of Czechoslovakia, advocating each country's right to national sovereignty in clear and concise language. To many this came across as a clear provocation; was Romania going to be next?

Maria's fear ran so deep that she began shaking: the nightmare was returning. Why, the Soviet tanks were probably already poised across their border.

"Those beasts are returning, and this time they'll kill us all. And maybe that's better than being thrown in jail and having everything taken away again."

"Dear, please calm down," her husband tried to mollify her, but to no avail.

In the meantime, Dinu had called the post office and had sent word of being on his way. The women packed quickly and got the children ready, the girls blissfully unaware of the potential disaster coming their way.

They left early the following day, having agreed they needed to be together and await further developments in Bucharest. Would Romania, too, be punished for her defiant stand? They also discussed their options in the car ride back to Bucharest, with Maria still haunted by their return from Istanbul in 1945.

"Do you remember how we had been warned against coming back? How I begged you to stay in Turkey?"

He recalled hers and some of his friends' advice and how many times he wished he had heeded it. But it wasn't only the two of them; the rest of the family needed to be consulted. He asked his son, "Would you, Anca, and the girls be prepared to leave if we need to?"

"We'll go where and when you go," Dinu replied.

Constantin reflected and analyzed and made up his mind. "This time there is no turning back. If the Soviets invade, we must flee the country."

They packed the car trunk in the dark of the night. Neighbors could have seen them in broad daylight and might have reported them to the police. They threw in clothes, dry foods, official papers, and items of hygiene—all the while praying they would never have to resort to fleeing their country.

They slept little that first week, with the adults taking turns at staying awake, just in case. Rumors were rampant. The Romanian leader had met with his counterpart from Yugoslavia, who was also critical of the Soviet invasion of the Czechoslovakia. Were the two of them plotting something? Someone else had heard of Soviet tanks advancing along the northern border, but it seemed that they had been ordered to retreat. A friend told them how in Mangalia the lights had been dimmed at night; Soviet ships were seen close to the Romanian coastline. With no official confirmation or retraction forthcoming, the rumors only added to the uncertainty.

Yet, with each passing day, people breathed easier. By mid-September they concluded the Soviets were not coming, after all. The trunk of the car was unpacked, and life resumed its normal course. School was back in session on September 15, and the university followed suit two week later.

Another upheaval in their lives had been averted.

As for Constantin, he could now truly look forward to what promised to be a monumental trip: a first visit to the United States. His ties with U.S. historians actually predated World War Two. His editor had sent the first volume of the Romanian History in 1935 to several American universities. A professor named Upton Clark had written a very favorable commentary in the *American Review*. Professor Clark had visited Romania in the early 1920s and taken an interest in the country. He returned in 1940, and Constantin, then Minister of Propaganda, had organized a series of conferences on his guest's behalf. A deep collegial bond was forged, and their correspondence was maintained until the Communists stopped all foreign contact.

The dialogue had been terminated by the Warsaw Pact alliance and its Iron Curtain, and many years of silence followed. As the Romanian society opened up in the mid-1960s, American scholars started making forays to Romania once again. Constantin had the opportunity to meet colleagues from Boston, Boulder, Indiana University in Bloomington, and the University of Washington in Seattle. He offered his expertise when consulted, and they toured old churches and museums together. The Americans reciprocated his hospitality: five invitations were received to lecture in the U.S. in 1968. The historian was invited to choose topics that might be of interest to an U.S. audience. One was the controversy surrounding Transylvania: was it Romanian, or was it Hungarian? Much information had been unearthed during the research undertaken prior to writing his *Transylvania in the History of the Romanian People*. He also chose to lecture about Count Dracula, not the legend, but rather the prince and ruler.

So Constantin had spent the better part of 1968 preparing his presentations and stepping up English lessons. He recalled the dark days in jail with Nick and how their cell group had periodically practiced their English vocabulary. It was as if he had known it would come in handy one day. He now met twice a week with his friend Adrian, who had studied in Britain years ago. He was so convinced the whole world was going "English" that he insisted his little granddaughters start learning the language, too.

As the authorities were preparing his passport and coordinating his itinerary with the Romanian embassy in Washington, a phone call came from the cultural attaché in Washington.

"Professor, five more lecture invitations have come forth."

"Are they asking for different topics?"

"No, they are happy to choose from the list you have already offered to other colleges."

"How will all this travel be paid for?"

"The International Research and Exchanges group based in New York, headed by Mr. Alan Kassoff, has graciously agreed to sponsor your travel."

"My visa will need to be extended. And my return flight has to be changed."

"We'll take care of all that."

What had started as a series of five talks would become a five-week tour spanning from winter in Detroit to the balmy weather of Tucson, Arizona.

And so in late September 1968, at age sixty-seven, he embarked on his first airplane ride and trip across the Atlantic Ocean. About to be airborne for the first time, unease took hold:

"Here I am sitting in this aluminum box of sorts . . . with no control whatsoever." Glancing around he noticed how many passengers didn't even pay attention to the flight attendants demonstrating safety procedures. Then he was gripped by the shrinking landscape below and the beauty of the clouds, and gradually relaxed.

As for the tour, it was a huge professional and personal success. The U.S. universities extended him a warm welcome; student audiences were interested in his topics and had many questions. He was mesmerized by the country's prosperity and by the comfort of so many working Americans. The busy streets were full of cars, the lights shone brightly at night, and the stores were packed with goods. People were brightly dressed and the airports were open day and night with countless flights landing and taking off—all in sharp contrast to the drab universe back home. Americans were easygoing, open, and friendly, and some appeared quite naïve, more like grown-up children that still marveled at the world around.

The conferences were so successful, that four years later came an invitation to teach in New York. Columbia University had inaugurated a Romanian History course, and Constantin was asked to be the first lecturer in residence. An invitation extended to Maria was once again turned down.

"My health is failing, I can't travel that far."

"Let's go to the doctor and run some checks. Perhaps it's not as bad as you think."

"Nelu says I have a heart condition," she said, referring to their friend and family doctor, "and has put me on medication."

"I trust Nelu's judgment. When did you start the medication?"

"About a month ago."

"Are you feeling better?"

"Yes."

"Then you're well-treated, and you should be able to travel. Please think about it; we could explore New York together; it is a fascinating town."

"Please don't insist; I am just not up to it. Besides, the girls need me at home."

Heart tinged with sadness, he gave up and traveled alone at the beginning of January 1972. He spent the spring semester living and teaching on the campus of Columbia University in New York City, arguably the most cosmopolitan city in the world.

His love affair with the United States continued with an attendance at the International Congress of History held in San Francisco in the summer of 1975. Constantin was among those chosen to represent his country in a worldwide forum, a far cry from the humiliation and suffering endured in prison two decades earlier. Two more tours of the United States followed in 1976 and 1977, and his early trip to the U.S. was prominently featured in his *Travel Diaries* published in 1971.

Back home his career went from strength to strength. Each year saw his books and countless articles in print. Full professorship at the University of Bucharest was followed by the highest scientific recognition of the country when elected as a full member of the Romanian Academy in 1974. The customary first step would have been a corresponding membership, which was extended to him, but he turned it down.

"I'm seventy-three years old, and I have published countless books and have an international reputation. I don't have the luxury of time on my side. Either you elect me full member, or I turn you down," he said.

Elect him they did, to the same body which had counted his father and father-in-law among its members. It was with deep emotion that he took to the podium to deliver his acceptance speech. Always a meticulous dresser, he had chosen his grey suit and red striped tie carefully, and had shined his shoes brightly. Family and friends sat in the audience next to colleagues and students present and past. Once all the seats were occupied, people started leaning against the walls, two and three deep in some areas.

He was introduced warmly by a senior member of the body. Then he stood up and took in the room before launching into the lecture. His brother and sister, Dinu, Anca and her parents, the girls, Titel, Nelu, Nick, Adrian, and so many others were there. Seemingly everyone had come but Maria, who was at home and unwell. Maria, whose health was failing without a real medical diagnosis, had never recovered her zest for life or for her husband's new academic life.

Constantin was indeed back, but the price to him, Maria, and the family, had been steep. His career had been rebuilt and its pinnacle reached once again. But the joy had been extinguished from his bond with Maria. She had remained loyal and supportive, but there was nothing but sadness etched on her face. The teaching, books, and tours—all these had been about him, he realized. The vacations, television, better clothes, and car had done virtually nothing for his wife. It was time to attempt his one impossible dream, the one that would make it right for Maria, too.

He had understood how she would feel vindicated only by regaining possession of a home. After all, it was her heart, money, and efforts that had made their homes possible. Professorships and volumes were not within her reach, but living once again in Constantin's family house she had rebuild would validate their good fortunes for her, too.

Could he possibly ask the authorities for the restitution of his Bucharest home? Would his newly found prominence be enough to back this unprecedented request? After the spattering of homes returned in the late 1950s, such as Maria's parents', none of the other estates and houses confiscated in the late 1940s had been returned to their rightful owners.

"There's nothing to be lost, only to gain," he convinced himself. "I must at least try for her sake."

He presented a thick file of documents one day to the Central Party Committee building and filed petition number 14856. The clerk took the stack of papers, signed receipt of it and set it down. Months passed before Constantin was called for a first audience.

"Professor, I have read your unusual request. Why would we possibly heed it?"

He pondered. His resumé had been detailed in the application; by drawing attention to himself he might come across as self-conceited. He had to turn it around and somehow make it look good for the regime. "Because our leadership may wish to exercise their spirit of generosity by rewarding me for my efforts in promoting Romania's history."

"We'll give it serious consideration, Professor. You shall hear from us soon."

More interviews followed. And no one was more stunned than Constantin, when, during the early fall of 1973, the family was awarded back half of their house. The other half was to be rented (from the state) by Dinu and his young family. The news was delivered to him in a thick envelope. He saw the sender's address: "Central Political Committee" and his hands shook slightly. He opened it uneasily, nervous about the outcome, until he read the first words. He practically ran to the sofa where Maria sat knitting.

"Dear, you won't believe it, the best of news."

She barely lifted up her eyes, "Have you been invited to another conference?"

"No, much better than that."

"Well, what is it, I'm listening."

"We got the house back!"

She didn't even ask which one, as she *knew*. Her dark eyes shone, and when her face lit up he saw his Maria of ages ago; she was finally back, too.

It took weeks to assign the renters of the house to their new quarters. When the house was finally empty, Constantin, Maria and Dinu stepped inside, overwhelmed with emotion, ghosts of a life past hugging the walls.

Dinu's wife stayed behind that first time. "This is your day; yours and the parents'."

Maria walked around slowly, as if in a daze, touching the walls and caressing the heavy crystal doors as if they were a child. Then she took stock of her surroundings and saw how numerous repairs were needed.

"These walls look awful, the paint is peeling off everywhere; I swear they haven't been painted since we left. And look at these tiles, what color are they supposed to be?"

Dinu inspected the hot water heater and found it rusty, while the refrigerator was broken. Even Constantin, who was normally absent-minded, couldn't help notice the state of disrepair. "Why, I swear these must be the same sinks and tubs we left in 1950."

"Yes, indeed, and chipped and filthy. These people must have lived like pigs! Let's go check the attic and cellar," added Maria. They found them full of junk and dust. They looked at one another. How and where would they begin?

Maria sprang immediately into her old command mode. "I'm going to call Marioara from Cheia. Her husband can paint and do repairs while she'll clean," she said, referring to the couple from whom they rented the mountain cottage. He was a skilled painter, and there was nothing Marioara couldn't polish to a shine.

A plumber recommended by friends also took over that end of the project. New tiles, fixtures, and appliances were soon installed. The interior and exterior were scrubbed and repainted. The hardwood floors and crystal-rimmed glass doors were bright again. The roof was repaired and the attic and basement cleared. While this was taking place, books and other small items were periodically brought over in the car.

"What are we going to furnish the house with?" the women pondered. They were, after all, going to move from a two bedroom apartment to a two story (plus basement) home.

"We'll just bring in what we have and spread it around," they decided.

"Then little by little we'll buy what else we need," Maria added.

Maria and Constantin would be occupying the first floor; Dinu and his family the second one. The two men would each have their own study and there would once again be a formal dining room. The washing machine wouldn't be in the kitchen anymore; there was now a laundry/ironing room in the basement. And the family of six would enjoy two and a half bathrooms, instead of sharing a single one.

They had planned to move into the house early in December. But the repairs and refurbishing took quite a bit longer and were finally ready only on December 23.

"Does it really make sense to move in on Christmas Eve?" asked Dinu. "Let's just stay put, celebrate here, and move the day after."

But his mother would have none of it. "The house is ready. I've been waiting for this to happen for twenty-four years. I'm moving in today."

"All right mother, please don't get agitated. We must go together; it is too complicated otherwise. But tell the girls they can't have a tree this year. There is too much to do."

That brought a chorus of protests from the children, now nine and eleven. "It's not Christmas without a tree," they insisted.

"You'll have a tree tomorrow, when you go to your other grand-parents on Christmas Day; you'll enjoy it there," said their father.

"No, we want ours."

Their mother had had enough of the argument. "Okay, you'll have it, but neither your father nor I have time to decorate. Dinu, go to the market and buy a tree and take it over to the house. After that it's your problem, girls."

"Yes, Mommy!"

And so on the afternoon of December 24, a fir tree showed up amidst crates, suitcases, boxes, and books. Anca had had the foresight to keep apart the boxes of ornaments and lights so the girls could start decorating it.

She had told her mother-in-law, "It's actually working out better than I thought; this is keeping them occupied. I can unpack and sort things out in peace."

Dinu went to the basement and turned up the gas heat. It was quite chilly already, and the temperatures would further drop after the sun went down. Being able to adjust your temperature setting struck him as extremely luxurious. Yes, it felt good being home again.

It was only fitting that they were back in the family house to celebrate two milestones a couple of years later. In 1976 Maria and Constantin celebrated both their fiftieth wedding anniversary and his seventy-fifth birthday. The anniversary celebration drew together family and old friends: Nick, Adrian, Titel, Nelu, and Gicu all gathered around the festive table. Horia, Emil, and Lelia were even able to reminisce how the house had looked when the young couple had moved in, in the late 1920s. Those walls had seen so much hope, happiness, and pain in nearly a half century. And on that anniversary day, the house once again opened up its beautifully crafted crystal doors upon an evening of cheer and fond recollections. Constantin stood up and raised a glass of champagne:

"Being able to stand here today, together, has exceeded my hopes. There was a time when I only wished to survive and not lose my mind," he said hesitantly. "I then hoped to be able to work and make myself useful again." He paused and looked around at his family and friends. "But none of it would have been possible without Maria's support and love. She dared believe otherwise when we seemed to have no future left. Here's to Maria!"

She was caught by surprise and her face lit up. A wide smile made her beautiful dark eyes dance, too. And for a moment he caught a glimpse of his bride of fifty years past. She raised her glass and bowed slightly. "And to all of you, too. We have been very fortunate, indeed."

Constantin's thoughts fleeted back briefly to the dark days in Sighet and to those who perished there. So many gone before their time, so many had come back broken, while he had been allowed to survive, return, and thrive once again.

He took in once again the smiling faces of the family and friends gathered to help celebrate their golden anniversary. And so it was on the eve of April 15, 1976, and in the home built by his parents, that Maria and Constantin's lives came full circle.

Chapter Thirty-Six
FIFTY-ONE YEARS TOGETHER

Constantin returned from Heidelberg, Germany, on November 6, 1977. He had been expected a day earlier, but a change in the conference program had led to a 24-hour delay. Dinu had gone to the airport to pick up his father as previously arranged, and waited at the gate watching scores of passengers file past him. It became obvious his father wasn't among them. Dinu called the Romanian Academy, which had coordinated the arrangements, he was told of the mix-up. Several hours later he arrived home to find a telegram hastily dispatched by his father: "Arriving tomorrow instead of today."

Twenty-four hours later Dinu was once again at the airport greeting his visibly tired father. "But it was well worth it," his father reassured him, deeming the trip a great success. The lectures had been well received, and their delivery in German greatly appreciated. It was good to be home, but there was a pressing matter and he asked, "Do you have news of Nick?"

"I do," replied Dinu in a barely audible voice.

"Well, get on with it."

"Nick passed away two days ago."

Constantin's face bore its pain stoically, and as one not given to emotional displays, a few moments passed silently. When he spoke his voice was shaky, "I wasn't there at the end." And then he had an afterthought and asked, "Has there been a funeral yet?"

"No, his wife wants you to attend."

They had spent nearly three years together in captivity, each day a stark reminder of their frail mortality. They had seen friends die and had heard the clunk of the wooden carts removing dead bodies from the building in the middle of the night. They had lived to celebrate their own survival and good fortune and had shared many a story over a bottle of wine. And now one had passed on without the other at his side.

Once home Constantin hugged Maria a bit more tightly than usual. "It's good to be home, I've missed you, dear."

If she noticed anything different, she certainly didn't let on. "It's good to see you, too. Come, I have a light snack for you." She knew the eggplant salad and apple strudel was bound to please him.

Later that evening, he called Nick's wife Claire. He heard how his friend had slipped into a coma with Claire by his side. She told Constantin, "He didn't recognize anyone . . . and then at the very end, he smiled with his eyes wide open; a small nod toward me, and then silence."

"I wished I hadn't traveled to Heidelberg," he said.

"You know he wanted you to attend the conference. He was so proud of you, we all are. But I have a request: could you please deliver the eulogy tomorrow?"

"Do you even have to ask?"

Constantin slept in fits and starts, and awoke to a slow drizzle. The rain had tapered off by the time they reached the cemetery, though the skies remained dark and heavy. He glanced around and took in the wet tombs, barren trees, and rust-colored leaves lying around in haphazard piles. It all suddenly reminded him of another dreary fall day, when his father had been laid to rest some sixty years earlier.

Standing by the casket and surrounded by a crowd of mourners, he delivered a short but moving eulogy. Overt references to time spent in Communist jails were still barred from public address. But how could he leave out that defining time of their lives?

"Nick forced me to believe in survival when doubts overwhelmed our dark days together. He was always there . . . his kindness matched only by his intelligence and zest for life. Nick was the one friend everyone should have."

When it was all over, and with a heavy heart, Constantin returned home where pressing business awaited him. His latest volume, *Controversial Topics in Romanian History,* was due to come out on November 11, and he had an appointment with the publisher. Here he was just days away from meeting his latest "child," after years of research and writing and long months of proofreading. Excitement mounted as the delivery approached. The content and the cover were known to him, but how would the sum of the parts be greeted by the public?

On November 11 at 11:00 A.M., Constantin walked into the publisher's office. A stack of brand new books were gleaming on the desk while the man offered his hand and a smile:

"Congratulations, Professor! Well done—once again! I hope we'll soon head to a second printing."

"That's up to the readers."

"Nonsense, your books always sell well."

"You are too kind."

They exchanged a few more pleasantries before he left the office with several copies for the family and a few close colleagues and friends. A promise was also extracted from the publisher to have several others sent to his house.

He was heartened by the sight of the book, and composed enough to call a pesky television reporter who had been requesting an interview for weeks and who had been leaving repeated messages for him. "Are you free tomorrow night?"

"I am, Sir."

"I am available at 6:00 P.M. Why don't you come to my house, at number 47 Berzei Street and bring along a list of questions."

"Fantastic, see you then, Sir."

November 12 began as a perfectly ordinary day. Dinu and Anca worked; the girls went to school, and Constantin spent the morning writing. Maria prepared lunch, and the three generations took it together around 2:00 P.M. or so. Constantin then retired for his customary mid-afternoon nap. He must have had a headache upon awakening, with the acetaminophen wrap on his nightstand as testimony. And he must have been thirsty: a glass of freshly squeezed lemonade sat on the desk. The television reporter arrived at 6:00 P.M. as promised, and was greeted by Marina, the elder granddaughter.

"I'm here to see the Professor, he expects me."

"Very well, have a seat, I'll let him know."

She opened the door of the study, but her grandfather was not at his desk. She checked the kitchen, living room, and knocked at the bathroom door without luck. Then she checked his bedroom: the bed was tidied up and the room empty. He couldn't have left while expecting the reporter's visit, could he? She stepped into the study again, and suddenly heard a noisy gasp. Her grandfather lay collapsed between the desk and the bookshelves, hidden from sight.

Nelu, his friend and doctor, lived around the corner, and when called he arrived within minutes. He took Constantin's blood pressure and found it extremely high. After a brief examination, he sadly shook his head. An ambulance arrived in the meantime, and as the van sped out of the courtyard, Anca returned home from work.

"My goodness, what happened, did Mica have a heart attack?" she shouted, using her nickname for Maria.

"No, it's Grandpa," answered the girls. "He fell down. Now he can't talk or move."

"Oh dear God, please God spare him. Where's your father?"

"He went with the ambulance and said you should stay home with us."

Dinu returned home close to midnight. The lights were out on the first floor where Maria slept, so he decided to first go upstairs to his wife. "There is no hope. The doctors did a CT scan and saw massive blood on the brain. They think it was brought about by a blood pressure spike. I asked them to keep him comfortable; I said please, no pain. The doctor put him on morphine: it's calming and takes care of pain, too. Then I was asked to leave, as families can't stay overnight in the intensive care unit."

"How long?" asked his wife.

"No one knows, but the amount of blood leaked is significant."

"Now you need to go downstairs to talk to your mother. She closed the bedroom door hours ago, but I'm sure she's awake."

He descended quietly and knocked at Maria's door.

"Come in. How is he?"

Dinu sat on her bed and took her hands: "The doctors have no hope. There was a large brain hemorrhage."

"Your father never wanted to be a burden to anyone. When are you going back to the hospital?"

"At the crack of dawn. Can I get you anything, Mother?"

"You can't bring your father back, that's what I want. Go, try to get some rest."

Barely hours later, at 5:00 A.M., the hospital called to announce that the professor had peacefully passed away. Dinu suddenly remembered his father's seventy-fifth birthday a year earlier. A reporter had asked Constantin to share his future wishes. He had replied, "First I wish for more time, and then a sudden end. Living like a vegetable brings suffering for both the individual and the caregivers." God had granted him another healthy year and his second wish.

Dinu stepped back into his mother's room, noticing the swollen eyes and the red face.

"He's gone, isn't he?" she immediately said. He nodded quietly and hugged her tightly. She softly added, "Fifty-one years together, and now he left me. Dinu, I need some time alone, tell the others not to disturb me."

Later she emerged from her room wearing a dark housecoat, the hair carefully pulled up and a bit of powder on her swollen face. "She's rallying," thought Anca. Maria's way to deal with the heartbreak was to take command and stay busy:

"You must immediately send telegrams to Dan and Mona." Dan had lived in France since 1946, while his sister Mona had emigrated from Romania to the United States in 1970. "Have you called Lelia, Horia, Emil?" she then asked, referring to Constantin's siblings and her brother.

"Yes. Emil wants to come over if you wish to see him."

"Call him back; he can join us later. Have you called the university and academy?"

"Yes. They're stunned."

"They'll probably want to be involved in everything."

"Possibly."

"You must go to the cemetery where your grandparents are buried. There will be business to tend to."

"Mother, would you like to come along?"

"No."

The following days passed in a blur. Dan arrived from Paris, the first time he had set foot on Romanian soil since 1946. The phone rang off the hook, all day and through the evening, and telegrams of sympathy poured in. The family opted for a public remembrance to be held in the Great Hall of the Faculty of History at the university, followed by a private burial. As for Maria, she remained steadfast in her desire to stay home, "This way my memories will remain intact."

Thursday, November 18 was cold but sunny and bright. Hundreds filed past the casket surrounded by a mountain of floral arrangements in the Great Hall of the Faculty of History. Tributes followed on a background of mournful music. When it was all over, family and close friends headed to the cemetery, hoping for some privacy. It wasn't to be: many students and colleagues had followed, so a large crowd amassed once again. People pushed to get closer and gawkers joined in the spectacle until Nelu and Titel took charge, asking that the family be allowed to mourn. After the last prayer was said, and the priest had sprinkled holy water over the casket, the time had come to say good-bye. Constantin was laid to rest alongside his parents, and a granite monument was later placed there, bearing an effigy of his profile and signature cast in bronze.

Two days later Dan said goodbye to the family. There was a chilling moment at the airport where police officers "noticed" that he was "still a Romanian citizen." It would have been well "within their rights" to prevent his return to Paris. Mustering as much calmness as he could, and dripping in cold sweat, Dan replied that he had also been a French citizen for over two decades. Panic set in deep down, knowing he was at the whim of the officers. The men consulted a supervisor wishing to prolong the mental games. It was eventually decided that he "could go this once."

"I'd be careful next time," they warned him.

"There will be no next time," he told himself, while to the men he said, "Thank you."

Maria's zest for life had been extinguished long ago, quashed by Constantin's arrest, the confiscation of their properties, and the years of financial and emotional hardship. The last connecting thread to the life of the family was cut with her husband's passing.

She withdrew gradually after the funeral, and the following summer she declined to travel to the seashore for the family vacation. She gave up cooking meals, and increasingly took to her bed. Maria was greatly weakened by a series of health problems, some of them incompletely diagnosed given her unwillingness to be hospitalized. Under difficult circumstances and with limited resources, she was competently treated at home by Dr. Stefanescu, her niece's husband. She suffered more heartache when her brother, Emil, passed away in 1981. By then she was entirely bedridden and had withered away, and all agreed she must have had some sort of cancer. The end of July 1982 brought her the joy of her oldest granddaughter's marriage. The following day Maria lost her ability to speak and passed away on August 17, 1982, and was buried next to her husband.

For the family it was the end of an era.

As for their beloved country, she was in the midst of yet another transition.

EPILOGUE
THE COLLAPSE OF TYRANNY

Six months before Constantin's death, on March 4, 1977, an earthquake of magnitude 7.2 on the Richter scale struck Bucharest. There were 1,500 lives lost, most in large buildings that collapsed in the center of Bucharest. Countless other structures—blocks of flats, houses, monuments—were damaged. Rumors were heard of how beloved churches such as Enei, in the very center of the capital, stood to be demolished. The historic eighteenth century Vacaresti Monastery (and former prison) could meet the same fate, said others. The gossip was to be soon confirmed with declarations coming from the top leadership. It was said that architectural and historical gems were "in an advanced state of deterioration" and "under danger of imminent collapse." So in order to protect the city's citizens, bulldozers and cranes were brought in and the buildings were razed down, church, monastery, and all. The Communists' appetite for the remolding of the country's past had been whetted. It would only usher in the grander plan to implement urban redesign across the country.

This hit Dinu very hard as an historian. So, with a camera hidden under a bulky trench coat, he walked the streets of Bucharest on Sundays when demolitions came to a halt. Each week he chose a new neighborhood and walked about, the scenes reminiscent of German cities bombed during WWII. He photographed hungrily, roll after roll of film completed and safely tucked away. If discovered he would have faced arrest, and the material would have been confiscated. But he carried on, wishing to capture the images of devastation and the city's architectural persona being erased. It was now the turn of the buildings, much like his parents' generation had been decimated by the Communist onslaught after 1945. There would be a time and place for the world to witness this visual testimony, just as his father's memoirs would one day see the light of day.

Dinu didn't only take photographs of this demolition. From 1979 to 1985 he made thirty-one interventions—in the form of filed protests and press articles—on behalf of his country's patrimony. He answered the call as an historian and Romanian citizen, but each of the attempts fell on deaf ears.

The destruction continued unabated, rolling into a much larger wave of demolitions in big cities across the country. Romania's traditional urban architecture was being swept away and the country's history effaced. A new urban habitat was built to house the newly molded socialist being. Dinu would not conform to that effacement as well, and his days in Romania were numbered.

After Maria's passing, Dinu inherited her half of the house, and his family moved into the first floor quarters. The second floor apartment, which they had previously occupied, belonged to the state and was going to be rented out. New neighbors arrived, a kind family with a little girl and an older son.

Dinu and Anca carried on with their teaching assignments at the Institute of Fine Arts and Faculty of Romance Languages, respectively. In 1984 their oldest daughter, Marina, defected to the U.S., a decision strongly supported by her parents, who wished a better life for their children. After their daughter's departure, Dinu was allowed to continue teaching and writing, but he was under careful watch and scrutiny.

It all came to a halt during the fall of 1986 when he found out his home—his grandparents and parents' house—was slotted for demolition. A large part of the neighborhood was to be razed in order to build a wide boulevard leading to a monumental new "Museum of Romanian History." This news, still unofficial at the time, was delivered by a former student with access to the construction drafts. Subsequent inquiries confirmed the unthinkable. The home purchased by Dinu's grandfather in 1910, the house of his youth and where his parents had died, would become the latest casualty of the urban redesign frenzy. The house's return to the family a decade earlier had symbolized Constantin's recognition and his return to scientific preeminence. That symbol would now be forever gone.

For Dinu and Anca, it meant reaching the point of no return. Until then they had carried on hoping that times would right themselves again. But this last act of useless destruction showed how utterly hopeless their future had become. On February 16, 1987, the day after he turned sixty years old, Dinu and Anca applied to leave Romania and emigrate to the U.S. together with their youngest daughter. Having worked for a combined total of thirty-seven years, Dinu retired before being dismissed from the Fine Arts Institute. By virtue of his application to emigrate, he had overnight become an unreliable citizen who could no longer be trusted to teach Romania's students.

It took months to sort through their belongings. The most painful part was allocating the family's books. Some were donated to the central library of the university and others were gifted to family, students, and friends, while many were sold. A few were shipped to the U.S., where they would await their owners' arrival. A lifetime of furniture, objects, photographs, and the like had to be dealt with, and pain and sadness enveloped the family during this time.

And then—a ray of hope came in mid-July 1987. A phone call from the U.S. embassy in Bucharest informed Dinu that he and the family had been awarded political refugee status by the U.S. It wouldn't have been possible without the help and support of Roger Kirk, the U.S. ambassador to Romania at the time, who would become a lifelong friend. This situation placed Dinu and Anca in an awkward position, with a new country and future to go to, but no means to get there. To date they had not yet received a response to the emigration petition filed with the Romanian authorities.

Finally, at the end of July, they had to vacate their house. Anca and Dinu were taken in by a couple of friends in their two-bedroom flat, while their daughter went to live with a friend while awaiting their passports.

The day cranes and bulldozers came to raze the house, Dinu stood across the street stone-faced and camera in hand. The police drove up and warned him against the use of the photos for public display. He had replied, "It's the house of my childhood and my youth . . . I feel sick, deeply sickened. The government promised to let us go, but we haven't seen our passports yet. Let us go; my family and I can't hold back for much longer. . . ."

Then the one-year anniversary of their application arrived and went. In a phone call to her daughter in the U.S., which was monitored by the police, Anca threatened to commence a hunger strike in sign of protest. A couple of days later, the family was informed that their departure had been formally approved.

Anca, Dinu, and Ena, their youngest daughter, left for America on March 27, 1988. The day before, a prayer was said for them at the Schitu Magureanu church, which they had attended in recent years. They were sent off by family and friends, hearts heavy, faces stained with tears; Dinu's Uncle Horia—eighty-five years old—was disconsolate.

"When God closes a door, he opens a window elsewhere," they told themselves. Now they were about to find out the truth of this saying.

After a brief required stay in Rome—a U.S. immigration formality—they departed for New York on April 12. At the Rome Fiumicino Airport came a moment of panic: Pan Am officials asked for their passports at the gate. Would they be prevented from leaving, after all? The passports were quickly returned, and upon boarding they were stunned to discover all three had been upgraded to business class! No explanation was offered, and they weren't about to ask for one. But it did seem a wonderful omen as they embarked upon their new life.

In America Dinu benefited from the steady help and support of friends and colleagues such as Professor Stephen Fishcher-Galati, Professor Istvan Deak, Mr. Allen Kassof, and Dr. Claude Nicolau. Professor Deak was instrumental in securing Dinu a one-semester teaching assignment at William Patterson College in New Jersey in 1988–1989. With Dr. Nicolau's help a similar one-year assignment was secured at Texas A & M in College City, Texas between 1989–1990. Professor Fishcher-Galati repeatedly provided research, writing, and traveling grants.

The Giurescus and IREX (International Research and Exchange Board), headed by Mr. Allen Kassof, went back a long time. The Board had sponsored Constantin's first lecture tour in the U.S. in 1968. Twenty years later, it introduced the son Dinu to representatives of the World Monument Fund and The Samuel Kress Foundation. The task at hand was to write, illustrate and publish a volume, *The Razing of Romania's Past*. The majority of its photographs were those taken by Dinu in Bucharest on Sunday strolls when he made the rounds of the demolition sites. The book was officially launched in April 1989, in New York and Washington, DC, as the author celebrated his first-year anniversary in the U.S.

While Dinu taught and wrote, Anca studied for a degree in library science at Columbia University, and worked first at New York University Law Library and then for a year in College Station, Texas. Their younger daughter, Ena, was able to enroll in a master's degree program in art history at New York University, while their eldest daughter Marina began medical school at Mount Sinai in New York City in 1988. Lives were being rebuilt with hope for the future. But fate was to beckon one more time.

DECEMBER 1989—BUCHAREST, ROMANIA

The fall of 1989 rolled in delivering the unthinkable: the collapse of Communism in Eastern Europe. True, a different breeze had blown through the region since Gorbachev had launched his Glasnost (openness) in the Soviet Union, and had told the world of the need for "Perestroika"—economic reform.

But the real wave of reform started in earnest when the Polish labor movement, "Solidarity," was legalized and allowed to participate in parliamentary elections. Their candidature met with decisive success, and the first Polish noncommunist senate in forty years was sworn in, in September 1989. The floodgates that would wash away Communism had been opened.

Hungary's revolt was next, in October. Then November 9 delivered the seminal moment of that autumn of hope: the fall of the Berlin Wall—the very symbol of the divide between East and West. The world watched as euphoric German crowds dismantled the barrier that had kept brothers apart for nearly thirty years. President Reagan's famous, prescient words: "Mr. Gorbachev, bring down this wall!" had become reality. Anything seemed possible now.

Czechoslovakia followed later that November, unfolding its own "Velvet Revolution." By the end of December, the country had a new president, the writer Waclav Havel, while Alexander Dubcek, who had led the short-lived Prague revolution in 1968, became speaker of the Parliament.

Bulgaria's long-term Communist leader Teodor Jivkov was also ousted late that fall and was replaced by a moderate; the days of the socialist reign were numbered there as well.

All eyes were now on Romania.

Dinu watched history unfold from College Station, Texas, wondering if his native country could be next, despite the lack of encouraging signs coming from Bucharest that fall. The Romanian leader Ceausescu appeared as defiant as ever and in total control. Invited to attend a round-table discussion at the university in early December 1989, Dinu was asked if his country would follow suit. The answer was brief: "Theoretically yes, but no one knows when." And indeed no one could have predicted the events that soon followed.

People started rioting in the Romanian western town of Timisoara as early as December 16. The crowds had first amassed in sign of dissent for the government's attempt to evict a Hungarian Reform church pastor. Thousands gathered, and when they returned the following day, a general protest against the government and the country's leadership began to emerge. The party's buildings were stormed, and symbols of Communist authority were thrown out, including the president's books; retaliation by officials and the police was violent. In the meantime, the remainder of the country was unaware of the unrest, since it was not broadcast by the state-controlled media. Eventually, with the news streaming in via Radio Free Europe and The Voice of America, Romanians heard of the protests taking place in the western part of their country. Even their "glorious leader" Ceausescu saw that the situation was serious enough to cut short a trip to Iran.

He returned to the capital of Bucharest, and on December 21 called a large rally in Palace Square in order to condemn the recent events in Timisoara. He addressed the crowd in his customary rant, praising the accomplishments of the regime and offering token pay raises. All of a sudden, the booing started and swelled up, drowning him out. A bewildered president admonished the crowd, fumbled and then faltered, searching for words. The roar of the masses grew. Within minutes Ceausescu, his wife, and high-ranking officials had taken refuge inside the building of the Party's Central Committee. In the meantime a riot broke out in the square and spilled into the surrounding blocks. The police and its secret branch, "Securitatea," anti-terrorist units, and the army were deployed as demonstrations swelled overnight and carried into the following day.

Bucharest woke up on December 22 to mounting chaos. Having inexplicably decided not to flee the country overnight, Ceausescu attempted to make one more plea to his citizens and took to the same central balcony. He couldn't even get the words out of his mouth before the protests began and he had to run for cover. Within minutes a helicopter was whisking him and his wife away from the city.

Their flight was brief and their freedom short-lived. By mid-afternoon the fleeing party was arrested. An "Extraordinary Military Tribunal" was hastily formed, the constitutionality of which remains a topic of debate. A brief trial was held on Christmas day, and death sentences were handed out to the presidential couple. Nicolae and Elena Ceausescu were executed by a firing squad as they frantically ran around the building's inner courtyard.

In the meantime, shooting—sometimes fierce—took place in the capital for several days. Unlike Czechoslovakia, Romania was not to have a "velvet" revolution but a rather bloody one, with over one thousand lives lost in the overthrow of the Communist regime.

Over six thousand miles away, Dinu watched on TV the December 22 events unfolding in his native country. The rollercoaster of emotions reminded him of the other seminal historical moment he had witnessed: the king's abdication in 1947. Despair had then overtaken the nation, whereas now hope and joy enveloped all those watching, from near and afar.

His reverie was cut short by a phone call from Radio Canada. A specialist fluent in both English and French was needed to spell out the events of the day for their audience. A live radio interview was followed by another one later the same day, and a Canada TV interview on December 22. One continent and one ocean away, Dinu was thus able to participate indirectly in the momentous change of Romania's fortunes.

A couple of months later, in February 1990, Dinu's friend Allen Kassoff, director of the IREX organization, asked him to travel to Romania as part of a group. Their mission was to assess the opportunity to reopen a cultural dialogue and exchange with Romania.

While in Bucharest, Dinu met with the new dean of the Faculty of History at the University of Bucharest. He was asked, "You're returning to Bucharest, aren't you?"

"Only if appointed to the university and allowed to teach a course of Romanian contemporary history," he replied. His interest in the country's recent past had been awakened during the summer of 1989, spent studying Romanian documents at the National Archives in Washington, DC. The events that had taken place after 1940 were cast in a very different light through the prism of U.S. diplomatic documents. Up to that point his knowledge of the era had been based on his life experiences and the distorted historical version manufactured by the Communist regime. The "treasure trove" of documents uncovered in Washington convinced him of the need to teach the real course of events that had unfolded almost a half-century earlier.

On a personal note, and forty-one years after his graduation, Dinu was able to finally take to the podium once held by his father and grandfather. The family circle was complete.

With the curtain lifted on the reign of Communist terror and brutality over the last forty-two years, it was time for Constantin's prison memoirs to come to light. The manuscript had been buried in the backyard of his friend Nick Caracaleanu and kept there for many years. Then, during the early 1980s, Professor Paul E. Michelson (Huntington University)—a great friend of the family—smuggled the manuscript to the U.S. It was now ready to travel back home.

The monograph, *Five Years and Two Months in the Sighet Penitentiary*, was published in 1994, both in Bucharest and in the U.S. and distributed there by Columbia University Press in New York City.

The future of a free Romania for which Constantin had written his prison tome had now come to pass.

His voice was heard one more time—his last testimony to a country and its rich heritage that he so loved.

ABOUT THE AUTHOR

Marina Giurescu, MD was attending medical school in Bucharest, Romania when she defected to the United States in 1984. She re-did her medical education at the Mount Sinai School of Medicine 1988-1992, did her internship in pathology at Mount Sinai Hospital in New York, and her residency in radiology at the Yale-New Haven Hospital, followed by a one year fellowship at Memorial Sloan Kettering in New York.

She has been working as a radiologist for the Mayo Clinic in Scottsdale, AZ since 2000 and as an asisstant professor in their College of Medicine. She has given many presentations at medical gatherings in Scottsdale and around the country, and has coauthored a half-dozen peer-reviewed articles for medical journals.

In regards to her authorship of *A World Torn Asunder*, she was born in the early 1960s and lived with her grandparents for the last fifteen years of her grandfather's life. Growing up as a child, she heard the inside and outside of all the family stories and had a particularly close relationship with her beloved grandfather, Constantin. While having a scientific bent and attracted early on to mathematics and the medical sciences, both her grandfather and her father, the historian Dinu Giurescu, were historical giants in their home country of Romania and the authors of countless books. She can be reached at: www.MarinaGiurescu.com.

Other Books by
Bettie Youngs Book Publishers

On Toby's Terms

Charmaine Hammond

On Toby's Terms is an endearing story of a beguiling creature who teaches his owners that, despite their trying to teach him how to be the dog they want, he is the one to lay out the terms of being the dog he needs to be. This insight would change their lives forever.

Simply a beautiful book about life, love, and purpose. —**Jack Canfield, compiler,** *Chicken Soup for the Soul* **series**

In a perfect world, every dog would have a home and every home would have a dog like Toby! —**Nina Siemaszko, actress,** *The West Wing*

This is a captivating, heartwarming story and we are very excited about bringing it to film. —**Steve Hudis, Producer**

Soon to be a major motion picture!

ISBN: 978-0-9843081-4-9 • ePub: 978-1-936332-15-1 • $15.95

The Maybelline Story

And the Spirited Family Dynasty Behind It

Sharrie Williams

Throughout the twentieth century, Maybelline inflated, collapsed, endured, and thrived in tandem with the nation's upheavals. Williams, to avoid unwanted scrutiny of his private life, cloistered himself behind the gates of his Rudolph Valentino Villa and ran his empire from a distance. This never before told story celebrates the life of a man whose vision rocketed him to success along with the woman held in his orbit: his brother's wife, Evelyn Boecher—who became his lifelong fascination and muse. A fascinating and inspiring story, a tale both epic and intimate, alive with the clash, the hustle, the music, and dance of American enterprise.

A richly told story of a forty-year, white-hot love triangle that fans the flames of a major worldwide conglomerate. —**Neil Shulman, Associate Producer,** *Doc Hollywood*

Salacious! Engrossing! There are certain stories, so dramatic, so sordid, that they seem positively destined for film; this is one of them. —*New York Post*

ISBN: 978-0-9843081-1-8 • ePub: 978-1-936332-17-15 • $18.95

It Started with Dracula

The Count, My Mother, and Me

Jane Congdon

The terrifying legend of Count Dracula silently skulking through the Transylvania night may have terrified generations of filmgoers, but the tall, elegant vampire captivated and electrified a young Jane Congdon, igniting a dream to one day see his mysterious land of ancient castles and misty hollows. Four decades later she finally takes her long-awaited trip—never dreaming that it would unearth decades-buried memories, and trigger a life-changing inner journey. A memoir full of surprises, Jane's story is one of hope, love—and second chances.

Unfinished business can surface when we least expect it. *It Started with Dracula* is the inspiring story of two parallel journeys: one a carefully planned vacation and the other an astonishing and unexpected detour in healing a wounded heart. —**Charles Whitfield, MD, bestselling author of *Healing the Child Within***

An elegantly written and cleverly told story. An electrifying read. —**Diane Bruno, CISION Media**

ISBN: 978-1-936332-10-6 • ePub: 978-1-936332-20-5 • $15.95

The Rebirth of Suzzan Blac

Suzzan Blac

A horrific upbringing and then abduction into the sex slave industry would all but kill Suzzan's spirit to live. But a happy marriage and two children brought love—and forty-two stunning paintings, art so raw that it initially frightened even the artist. "I hid the pieces for 15 years," says Suzzan, "but just as with the secrets in this book, I am slowing sneaking them out, one by one by one." Now a renowned artist, her work is exhibited world-wide.

A story of inspiration, truth and victory.

A solid memoir about a life reconstructed. Chilling, thrilling, and thought provoking. —**Pearry Teo, Producer, *The Gene Generation***

ISBN: 978-1-936332-22-9 • ePub: 978-1-936332-23-6 • $16.95

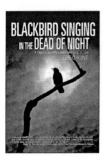

Blackbird Singing in the Dead of Night

What to Do When God Won't Answer

Gregory L. Hunt

Pastor Greg Hunt had devoted nearly thirty years to congregational ministry, helping people experience God and find their way in life. Then came his own crisis of faith and calling. While turning to God for guidance, he finds nothing. Neither his education nor his religious involvements could prepare him for the disorienting impact of the experience.

Alarmed, he tries an experiment. The result is startling—and changes his life entirely.

In this most beautiful memoir, Greg Hunt invites us into an unsettling time in his life, exposes the fault lines of his faith, and describes the path he walked into and out of the dark. Thanks to the trail markers he leaves along the way, he makes it easier for us to find our way, too. —**Susan M. Heim, co-author,** *Chicken Soup for the Soul, Devotional Stories for Women*

Compelling. If you have ever longed to hear God whispering a love song into your life, read this book. —**Gary Chapman,** *NY Times* **bestselling author,** *The Love Languages of God*

ISBN: 978-1-936332-07-6 • ePub: 978-1-936332-18-2 • $15.95

DON CARINA

WWII Mafia Heroine

Ron Russell

A father's death in Southern Italy in the 1930s—a place where women who can read are considered unfit for marriage—thrusts seventeen-year-old Carina into servitude as a "black widow," a legal head of the household who cares for her twelve siblings. A scandal forces her into a marriage to Russo, the "Prince of Naples."

By cunning force, Carina seizes control of Russo's organization and disguising herself as a man, controls the most powerful of Mafia groups for nearly a decade. Discovery is inevitable: Interpol has been watching. Nevertheless, Carina survives to tell her children her stunning story of strength and survival.

ISBN: 978-0-9843081-9-4 • ePub: 978-0-9843081-9-4 • $15.95

Living with Multiple Personalities

The Christine Ducommun Story

Christine Ducommun

Christine Ducommun was a happily married wife and mother of two, when—after moving back into her childhood home—she began to experience panic attacks and a series of bizarre flashbacks. Eventually diagnosed with Dissociative Identity Disorder (DID), Christine's story details an extraordinary twelve-year ordeal unraveling the buried trauma of her past and the daunting path she must take to heal from it. Therapy helps to identify Christine's personalities and understand how each helped her cope with her childhood, but she'll need to understand their influence on her adult life.

Fully reawakened and present, the personalities compete for control of Christine's mind as she bravely struggles to maintain a stable home for her growing children. In the shadows, her life tailspins into unimaginable chaos—bouts of drinking and drug abuse, sexual escapades, theft and fraud—leaving her to believe she may very well be losing the battle for her sanity. Nearing the point of surrender, a breakthrough brings integration.

A brave story of identity, hope, healing and love.

Reminiscent of the Academy Award-winning *A Beautiful Mind,* this true story will have you on the edge of your seat. Spellbinding! —**Josh Miller, Producer**

ISBN: 978-0-9843081-5-6 • ePub: 978-1-936332-06-9 • $16.95

Truth Never Dies

William C. Chasey

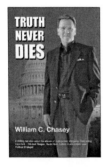

A lobbyist for some 40 years, William C. Chasey represented some of the world's most prestigious business clients and twenty-three foreign governments before the US Congress. His integrity never questioned.

All that changed when Chasey was hired to forge communications between Libya and the US Congress. A trip he took with a US Congressman for discussions with then Libyan leader Muammar Qadhafi forever changed Chasey's life. Upon his return, his bank accounts were frozen, clients and friends had been advised not to take his calls.

Things got worse: the CIA, FBI, IRS, and the Federal Judiciary attempted to coerce him into using his unique Libyan access to participate in a CIA-sponsored assassination plot of the two Libyans indicted for the bombing of Pan Am flight 103. Chasey's refusal to cooperate resulted in the destruction of his reputation, a six-year FBI investigation and sting operation, financial ruin, criminal charges, and incarceration in federal prison.

A somber tale, a thrilling read. —**Gary Chafetz, author,** *The Perfect Villain: John McCain and the Demonization of Lobbyist Jack Abramoff*

ISBN: 978-1-936332-46-5 • ePub: 978-1-936332-47-2 • $24.95

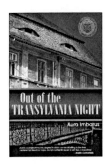

Out of the Transylvania Night

Aura Imbarus

A Pulitzer-Prize entry

"I'd grown up in the land of Transylvania, homeland to Dracula, Vlad the Impaler, and worse, dictator Nicolae Ceausescu," writes the author. "Under his rule, like vampires, we came to life after sundown, hiding our heirloom jewels and documents deep in the earth." Fleeing to the US to rebuild her life, she discovers a startling truth about straddling two cultures and striking a balance between one's dreams and the sacrifices that allow a sense of "home."

Aura's courage shows the degree to which we are all willing to live lives centered on freedom, hope, and an authentic sense of self. Truly a love story! —**Nadia Comaneci, Olympic Champion**

A stunning account of erasing a past, but not an identity. —**Todd Greenfield, 20th Century Fox**

ISBN: 978-0-9843081-2-5 • ePub:978-1-936332-20-5 • $14.95

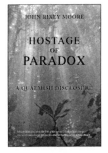

Hostage of Paradox: A Memoir

John Rixey Moore

Few people then or now know about the clandestine war that the CIA ran in Vietnam, using the Green Berets for secret operations throughout Southeast Asia. This was not the Vietnam War of the newsreels, the body counts, rice paddy footage, and men smoking cigarettes on the sandbag bunkers. This was a shadow directive of deep-penetration interdiction, reconnaissance, and assassination missions conducted by a selected few Special Forces teams, usually consisting of only two Americans and a handful of Chinese mercenaries, called Nungs. These specialized units deployed quietly from forward operations bases to prowl through agendas that, for security reasons, were seldom completely understood by the men themselves.

Hostage of Paradox is the first-hand account by one of these elite team leaders.

A compelling story told with extraordinary insight, disconcerting reality, and engaging humor. —**David Hadley, actor, *China Beach***

ISBN: 978-1-936332-37-3 • ePub: 978-1-936332-33-5 • $24.95

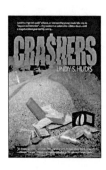

Crashers

A Tale of "Cappers" and "Hammers"

Lindy S. Hudis

The illegal business of fraudulent car accidents is a multi-million dollar racket, involving unscrupulous medical providers, personal injury attorneys, and the cooperating passengers involved in the accidents. Innocent people are often swept into it.

Newly engaged Nathan and Shari, who are swimming in mounting debt, were easy prey: seduced by an offer from a stranger to move from hard times to good times in no time, Shari finds herself the "victim" in a staged auto accident. Shari gets her payday, but breaking free of this dark underworld will take nothing short of a miracle.

A riveting story of love, life—and limits. A non-stop thrill ride. —**Dennis "Danger" Madalone, stunt coordinator for the television series,** *Castle*

ISBN: 978-1-936332-27-4 • ePub: 978-1-936332-28-1 • $16.95

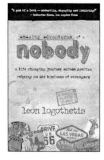

Amazing Adventures of a Nobody

Leon Logothetis

From the Hit Television Series Aired in 100 Countries!

Tired of his disconnected life and uninspiring job, Leon Logothetis leaves it all behind—job, money, home, even his cell phone—and hits the road with nothing but the clothes on his back and five dollars in his pocket, relying on the kindness of strangers and the serendipity of the open road for his daily keep. Masterful storytelling!

"Leon Logothetis takes budget travel to another level…in his wry and hopeful new book." —**New York Post**

"A gem of a book; endearing, engaging and inspiring." —**Catharine Hamm, Los Angeles Times Travel Editor**

"Warm, funny, and entertaining. If you're looking to find meaning in this disconnected world of ours, this book contains many clues." —**Psychology Today**

ISBN: 978-0-9843081-3-2 • ePub: 978-1-936332-51-9 • $14.95

Trafficking the Good Life

Jennifer Myers

Jennifer Myers had worked long and hard toward a successful career as a dancer in Chicago, but just as her star was rising, she fell in love with the kingpin of a drug trafficking operation. Drawn to his life of luxury, she soon became a vital partner in driving marijuana across the country, making unbelievable sums of easy money that she stacked in shoeboxes and spent like an heiress.

Steeped in moral ambiguity, she sought to cleanse her soul with the guidance of spiritual gurus and New Age prophets—to no avail. Only time in a federal prison made her face up to and understand her choices. It was there, at rock bottom, that she discovered that her real prison was the one she had unwittingly made inside herself and where she could start rebuilding a life of purpose and ethical pursuit.

"A gripping memoir. When the DEA finally knocks on Myers's door, she and the reader both see the moment for what it truly is—not so much an arrest as a rescue." —**Tony D'Souza, author of** *Whiteman and Mule*

"A stunningly honest exploration of a woman finding her way through a very masculine world . . . and finding her voice by facing the choices she has made." —**Dr. Linda Savage, author of** *Reclaiming Goddess Sexuality*

ISBN: 978-1-936332-67-0 • ePub: 978-1-936332-68-7 • $18.95

Voodoo in My Blood

A Healer's Journey from Surgeon to Shaman

Carolle Jean-Murat, M.D.

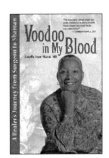

Born and raised in Haiti to a family of healers, US trained physician Carolle Jean-Murat came to be regarded as a world-class surgeon. But her success harbored a secret: in the operating room, she could quickly intuit the root cause of her patient's illness, often times knowing she could help the patient without surgery. Carolle knew that to fellow surgeons, her intuition was best left unmentioned. But when the devastating earthquake hit Haiti and Carolle returned to help, she had to acknowledge the shaman she had become.

"This fascinating memoir sheds light on the importance of asking yourself, 'Have I created for myself the life I've meant to live?'" —**Christiane Northrup, M.D., author of the New York Times bestsellers:** *Women's Bodies, Women's Wisdom* **and** *The Wisdom of Menopause*

ISBN: 978-1-936332-05-2 • ePub: 978-1-936332-04-5 • $24.95

MR. JOE

Tales from a Haunted Life

Joseph Barnett and Jane Congdon

Do you believe in ghosts? Nor did Joseph Barnett until the winter he was fired from his career job and became a school custodian to make ends meet. The fact that the eighty-five-year-old school where he now worked was built near a cemetery had barely registered with Joe when he was assigned the graveyard shift. But soon, walking the dim halls alone at night, listening to the wind howl outside, Joe was confronted with a series of bizarre and terrifying occurrences.

It wasn't just the ghosts of the graveyard shift that haunted him. Once the child of a distant father and an alcoholic mother, now a man devastated by a failed marriage, fearful of succeeding as a single dad, and challenged by an overwhelming illness, Joe is haunted by his own personal ghosts.

The story of Joseph's challenges and triumphs emerges as an eloquent metaphor of ghosts, past and present, real and emotional, and how a man puts his beliefs about self—and ghosts—to the test.

"Thrilling, thoughtful, elegantly told. So much more than a ghost story." **—Cyrus Webb, CEO, Conversation Book Club**

"This is truly inspirational work, a very special book—a gift to any reader."
—Diane Bruno, CISION Media

ISBN: 978-1-936332-78-6 • ePub: 978-1-936332-79-3 • $18.95

The Law of Attraction for Teens

How to Get More of the Good Stuff, and Get Rid of the Bad Stuff!

Christopher Combates

Whether it's getting better grades, creating better relationships with your friends, parents, or teachers, or getting a date for the prom, the Law of Attraction just might help you bring it about. It works like this: Like attracts like. When we align our goals with our best intentions and highest purpose, when we focus on what we want, we are more likely to bring it about. This book will help teens learn how to think, act, and communicate in the positive way.

ISBN: 978-1-936332-29-8 • ePub: 978-1-936332-30-4 • $14.95

Fastest Man in the World

The Tony Volpentest Story

Tony Volpentest

Foreword by Ross Perot

Tony Volpentest, a four-time Paralympic gold medalist and five-time world champion sprinter, is a 2012 nominee for the Olympic Hall of Fame

"This inspiring story is about the thrill of victory to be sure—winning gold—but it is also a reminder about human potential: the willingness to push ourselves beyond the ledge of our own imagination. A powerfully inspirational story." —Charlie Huebner, United States Olympic Committee

"This is a moving, motivating and inspiring book." —**Dan O'Brien, world and Olympic champion decathlete**

"Tony's story shows us that no matter where we start the race, no matter what the obstacles, we all have it within us to reach powerful goals." —**Oscar Pistorius, "Blade Runner," double amputee, world record holder in the 100, 200 and 400 meters**

ISBN: 978-1-936332-00-7 • ePub: 978-1-936332-01-4 • $16.95

The Lost Army

Gary S. Chafetz

In one of history's greatest ancient disasters, a Persian army of 50,000 soldiers was suffocated by a hurricane-force sandstorm in 525 BC in Egypt's Western Desert. No trace of this conquering army, hauling huge quantities of looted gold and silver, has ever surfaced.

Nearly 25 centuries later on October 6, 1981, Egyptian Military Intelligence, the CIA, and Israel's Mossad secretly orchestrated the assassination of President Anwar Sadat, hoping to prevent Egypt's descent—as had befallen Iran two years before—into the hands of Islamic zealots. Because he had made peace with Israel and therefore had become a marked man in Egypt and the Middle East, Sadat had to be sacrificed to preserve the status quo.

These two distant events become intimately interwoven in the story of Alex Goodman, who defeats impossible obstacles as he leads a Harvard University/ National Geographic Society archaeological expedition into Egypt's Great Sand Sea in search of the Lost Army of Cambyses, the demons that haunt him, and the woman he loves. Based on a true story.

Gary Chafetz, referred to as "one of the ten best journalists of the past twenty-five years," is a former Boston Globe correspondent and was twice nominated for a Pulitzer Prize by the Globe.

ISBN: 978-1-936332-98-4 • ePub: 978-1-936332-99-1 • $19.95

Bettie Youngs Books

We specialize in MEMOIRS

. . . books that celebrate

fascinating people and

remarkable journeys

In bookstores everywhere, online, Espresso,
or from the publisher, Bettie Youngs Books
VISIT OUR WEBSITE AT
www.BettieYoungsBooks.com
To contact:
info@BettieYoungsBooks.com

CPSIA information can be obtained at www.ICGtesting.com
Printed in the USA
BVOW080032240113

311445BV00002B/10/P